C++ WITH OBJECT-ORIENTED PROGRAMMING

RECENT COMPUTER SCIENCE TITLES FROM PWS PUBLISHING COMPANY

ABERNETHY AND ALLEN, *Experiments in Computing: Laboratories for Introductory Computer Science in Think Pascal*

ABERNETHY AND ALLEN, *Experiments in Computing: Laboratories for Introductory Computer Science in Turbo Pascal*

ABERNETHY AND ALLEN, *Exploring the Science of Computing*

AGELOFF AND MOJENA, *Essentials of Structured BASIC*

BAILEY AND LUNDGAARD, *Program Design with Pseudocode*, Third Edition

BELCHER, *The COBOL Handbook*

BENT AND SETHARES, *BASIC: An Introduction to Computer Programming*, Fourth Edition

BENT AND SETHARES, *BASIC: An Introduction to Computer Programming with the Apple*, Third Edition

BENT AND SETHARES, *Microsoft BASIC: Programming the IBM PC*, Third Edition

BENT AND SETHARES, *QuickBASIC: An Introduction to Computer Science Programming with the IBM PC*

BORSE, *FORTRAN 77 and Numerical Methods for Engineers*, Second Edition

BOYLE, *FORTRAN 77 PDQ*, Second Edition

BURKHARD, *C for Programmers*

CAVERLY AND GOLDSTEIN, *Introduction to Ada*

DECKER AND HIRSHFIELD, *Pascal's Triangle: Reading, Writing, and Reasoning About Programs*

DECKER AND HIRSHFIELD, *The Analytical Engine: An Introduction to Computer Science Using HyperCard 2.1*, Second Edition

DECKER AND HIRSHFIELD, *The Analytical Engine: An Introduction to Computer Science Using ToolBook*

DECKER AND HIRSHFIELD, *The Object Concept*

DERSHEM AND JIPPING, *Programming Languages: Structures and Models*

EGGEN AND EGGEN, *An Introduction to Computer Science Using C*

FIREBAUGH, *Artificial Intelligence: A Knowledge-Based Approach*

FLYNN AND McHOES, *Understanding Operating Systems*

GIARRATANO AND RILEY, *Expert Systems: Principles and Programming*, Second Edition

HENNEFELD, *Using Microsoft and IBM BASIC: An Introduction to Computer Programming*

HENNEFELD, *Using Turbo Pascal 4.0–6.0*, Second Edition

HOFFMAN, *Computer Graphics Applications*

HOLOIEN AND BEHFOROOZ, *FORTRAN 77 for Engineers and Scientists*, Second Edition

JAMISON, RUSSELL, AND SNOVER, *Laboratories for a Second Course in Computer Science: ANSI Pascal*

JAMISON, RUSSELL, AND SNOVER, *Laboratories for a Second Course in Computer Science: Turbo Pascal*

KAPPS AND STAFFORD, *Assembly Language for the PDP-II, RT-RSX-UNIX*, Second Edition

KORSH AND GARRETT, *Data Structures, Algorithms, and Program Style Using C*

LANE AND MOONEY, *A Practical Approach to Operating Systems*

LI SANTI, MANN, AND ZLOTNICK, *Algorithms, Programming, Pascal*

LOUDEN, *Programming Languages: Principles and Practice*

MARTINS, *Introduction to Computer Science Using Pascal*

McKELVEY, JR., *The Debugger's Handbook: Turbo Pascal*

MEARS, *BASIC Programming with the IBM PC*, Second Edition

MOJENA, *Turbo Pascal*

MOJENA AND AGELOFF, *FORTRAN 77*

PAYNE, *Advanced Structured BASIC: File Processing with the IBM PC*

PAYNE, *Structured BASIC for the IBM PC with Business Applications*

PAYNE, *Structured Programming with QuickBASIC*

POLLACK, *Effective Programming in Turbo Pascal*

POPKIN, *Comprehensive Structured COBOL*, Fourth Edition

RILEY, *Advanced Programming and Data Structures Using Pascal*

RILEY, *Data Abstraction and Structure, an Introduction to Computer Science II*

RILEY, *Programming Using Turbo Pascal*

RILEY, *Using MODULA-2*

RILEY, *Using Pascal: An Introduction to Computer Science I*

ROB, *Big Blue BASIC: Programming the IBM PC and Compatibles*, Second Edition

ROJIANI, *Programming in BASIC for Engineers*

ROOD, *Logic and Structured Design for Computer Programmers*, Second Edition

RUNNION, *Structured Programming in Assembly Language for the IBM PC*

SMITH, *Design and Analysis of Algorithms*

STUBBS AND WEBRE, *Data Structures with Abstract Data Types and Ada*

STUBBS AND WEBRE, *Data Structures with Abstract Data Types and MODULA-2*

STUBBS AND WEBRE, *Data Structures with Abstract Data Types and Pascal*, Second Edition

SUHY, *CICS using COBOL: A Structured Approach*

WANG, *An Introduction to ANSI C on UNIX*

WANG, *An Introduction to Berkeley UNIX*

WANG, *C++ with Object-Oriented Programming*

WEINMAN, *FORTRAN for Scientists and Engineers*

WEINMAN, *VAX FORTRAN*, Second Edition

C++ WITH OBJECT-ORIENTED PROGRAMMING

PAUL S. WANG
Kent State University

PWS PUBLISHING COMPANY
Boston

PWS PUBLISHING COMPANY
20 Park Plaza, Boston, MA 02116-4324

PWS Publishing Company is a division of Wadsworth, Inc.

I(T)P™

International Thomson Publishing
The trademark ITP is used under license.

Library of Congress Cataloging-in-Publication Data
Wang, Paul S.
  C++ with object-oriented programming / Paul S. Wang
    p. cm.
  Includes index.
  ISBN 0-534-19644-6
  1. Object-oriented programming (Computer science) 2. C++ (Computer program language)
I. Title.
QA76.64.W36 1994   93-37110
005.13'3 — dc20   CIP

Sponsoring Editor: Michael J. Sugarman
Associate Developmental Editor: Susan M. Gay
Production Editor: Abigail M. Heim
Marketing Manager: Nathan Wilbur
Manufacturing Coordinator: Lisa M. Flanagan
Editorial Assistant: Ken Morton
Interior and Cover Designer: Abigail M. Heim
Cover Photo: Michael de Camp, ⓒ The IMAGEBank, Inc.
Typesetter and Interior Illustrator: Pure Imaging
Cover Printer: New England Book Components
Text Printer and Binder: Maple Vail Book Manufacturing Group

Printed and bound in the United States of America

95 96 97 98 — 9 8 7 6 5 4 3

CONTENTS

CHAPTER 2 \ C++ PRIMER PART II: OVERVIEW   49

CHAPTER 3 \ C++ FEATURES AND CONSTRUCTS   74

CHAPTER 4 \ ARRAYS, POINTERS, AND REUSABLE CODE   115

CHAPTER 9 \ OOP TECHNIQUES   300

CHAPTER 10 \ TEMPLATES   340

CHAPTER 11 \ **OBJECT-ORIENTED DESIGN**   **367**

PREFACE

C++ is widely accepted as the language of choice for object-oriented programming (OOP), a technology that is revolutionizing the software industry across the country and around the world. OOP creates programs that are well organized, easy to understand and modify, flexible, and reusable in many different situations. It reduces complexity and makes software production and maintenance more economical. No wonder industry has subscribed to the concept and moved into OOP rapidly and in such large scale. Among OOP languages, C++ is by far the most popular. The language is being standardized jointly by the International Standards Organization (ISO) and the American National Standards Institute (ANSI). C++ is available on most computer systems, including PCs.

As the C++/OOP trend grows, the need for training in this area has increased significantly. At Kent State University, an OOP course was first offered in 1986 to a dozen students. Today, the "C++ with OOP" course enrolls more than 40 individuals. The interest from computer science majors and business students as well as from industrial people is tremendous.

This book introduces C++ and its effective use for OOP. C++ is popular for several reasons: It supports OOP well; it is compatible with ANSI standard C; and it combines OOP with traditional procedural-oriented programming. The power of C++ makes the language more complicated and a challenge to learn and teach well. The C++ constructs must be matched with clear and precise OOP concepts. Then, the C++ language mechanisms must be understood not only individually but also in combination to achieve OOP objectives. The techniques should be demonstrated in realistic programs to show their applications in practice. The benefits of OOP can then be fully appreciated. These are the goals of this book.

Complete C++ Coverage

This textbook anticipates the needs of students and covers C++ as an integral, self-contained language. This approach has proven better in the classroom than teaching C++ as an extension of ANSI C. In addition to the basics, arrays, pointers, functional arguments, header files, and other important subjects not directly connected with OOP are included so that C++ is presented completely. OOP is introduced and illustrated throughout the text with well-constructed and interesting examples. The examples evolve as new material is covered, providing many chances to revisit familiar code and to focus on the new features being introduced.

Clear Introduction to OOP

What makes C++ so important is the fact that it supports object-oriented programming well. Thus, OOP concepts and techniques are taught as an integral part of C++ programming. The approach brings OOP concepts down to earth so that they are easily grasped. Object orientation is introduced early and demonstrated with many complete examples. How these techniques are applied to solve problems and how they make programs more flexible and reusable are clearly shown.

Key OOP concepts such as data abstraction, encapsulation, information hiding, genericness, inheritance, and polymorphism are presented clearly and comprehensively. Basics on object-oriented design are also included. Again, these are illustrated by many C++ examples, including a bank account example that is carried through many chapters.

Hands-on Approach

The best way to learn programming is to write programs. With clear concepts and good examples, the text encourages the writing of interesting programs early. Training in both procedural- and object-oriented programming is provided. Chapters 1 and 2 form a primer introducing essential components of C++ and OOP to get things started quickly. Sections on object-oriented thinking and C++ programming tips are provided to help beginning programmers.

A pocket calculator simulation program is introduced in Chapter 5. This program evolves with each new chapter through programming exercises. Finally, in Chapter 11, a substantial pocket calculator program emerges that connects many key OOP concepts and C++ constructs.

Comprehensive Coverage

It is possible to use the book as the sole text for a course. Besides the basic topics, library functions, the I/O stream classes, program organization, use of header files, error and exception handling, preprocessing, and compilation are covered. UNIX- and PC-specific information for C++ is given in several appendices.

Object orientation is emphasized with topics on building software objects, comparing external behavior versus internal workings, reducing complexity with encapsulation, deriving new objects based on existing ones, writing generic codes reusable in many situations, creating software black boxes that are plug-compatible in usage, and establishing polymorphic procedures that work for multiple types of objects.

The C++ template facility is also covered. Examples show how to write a set of functions or classes with a single template definition. A template hash table class illustrates the practical use of templates. Object-oriented design techniques, methods, applications, and error/exception handling are also included.

OOP Made Easy

C++ is a large and complex language. It is easy to get lost in the maze of new OOP concepts and the supporting C++ constructs. No effort is spared to make this complicated subject easy to grasp and understand. The approach is to begin with simple topics and key concepts as a foundation. Then, advanced topics are added in a logical sequence that is easy to follow. The materials are organized to anticipate questions and provide answers. Clear, interesting, and realistic examples show how to write object-oriented programs and how to apply the concepts and techniques introduced.

Inheritance, a key OOP feature, tends to be difficult for beginning programmers. A clear mental picture is painted of a derived class and its relation with a base class upon which it is built. Furthermore, specific principles on class derivation and its proper usage are supplied. Multiple inheritance is also covered with clarity and good examples.

Polymorphism and plug compatibility are central OOP techniques that require sophistication to use well. An entire chapter is devoted to this subject and provides enough material to challenge even the most advanced students.

Flexible Usage

The book contains more than enough material for a three-credit programming course at the junior or senior or the beginning graduate level. No C background is assumed, but appropriate programming experience, to appreciate software complexity, is highly recommended. Knowledge of C or ANSI C will reduce the amount of work involved. At a lower level, the material in the beginning chapters should be covered carefully. Advanced topics such as user-defined free storage management (Section 8.9), templates (Chapter 10), and object-oriented design (Chapter 11) can be omitted. At a higher level, Chapter 1 can be assigned to students for advance reading to allow more class time for later topics.

For a class with substantial programming experience, object-oriented programming projects, as suggested by the end-of-chapter exercises, can be emphasized. In this case, the design considerations covered in Chapter 11 may be discussed much earlier.

The preprocessing and compilation material in Chapter 12 can be introduced (or assigned for reading by students) whenever the instructor feels it is appropriate in a course. Chapters 3 through 10 are central to this text and should prove challenging and rewarding to any reader.

The book can also be used as a valuable supplement to a general course on OOP or a course on object-oriented design with C++ implementation.

Right for Your System

C++ is presented in a system-independent manner. The examples will run on any reasonable C++ implementation including workstations, PCs, and multi-user servers. Chapter 12 gives general information on preprocessing, compiling, and executing programs. Appendices 1 and 2 give specifics for compilation and execution with UNIX-based systems such as Unix System Laboratories (USL) C++ and GNU g++ as well as PC-based systems like Borland C++ and Microsoft C/C++. Other systems are similar.

The Free Software Foundation offers g++, a good implementation of C++ that can be obtained free of charge from

The Free Software Foundation
675 Massachusetts Avenue
Cambridge, MA 02139
(617) 876-3296

Easy Reference

As an instructional guide, this text follows an incremental approach, whereby new concepts are built on old ones to make understanding easy. However, the book is also a valuable reference tool. Information has been organized for easy reference with tables, figures, displayed syntax explanations, examples, and summaries. All key C++ constructs are collected in an appendix for quick review. Another appendix summarizes usage of special member functions. Other appendices cover debugging, library functions, and the mixed use of C++ and C. Accurate cross referencing and a comprehensive index help locate information contained in the book.

Code Disk Included

Throughout the text, concepts and programming constructs are amply illustrated with examples of practical importance. There are more than 270 files containing complete source codes that are ready to compile. The machine-readable examples are available on disk in the back of this book, which contains both UNIX and DOS files. Disk installation directions appear on the page facing the disk.

Acknowledgments

The 1993 C++ classes at Kent State University used the draft version of *C++ with Object-Oriented Programming* and deserve many thanks for providing valuable classroom feedback leading to numerous improvements. Simon Gray, a computer science graduate student and a good teacher, read early drafts and made corrections and suggestions. He also suggested the idea of a homework project that evolves with the material. I am grateful to him. The book also benefited from industrial contacts who are proponents of the object-oriented technology. In particular, I wish to thank Martin Griss of Hewlett-Packard Laboratories (Palo Alto, California), W. B. Adams of Goodyear Tire and Rubber Company, Technical Computer Operations (Akron, Ohio), and Arun Jain of BP Research (Warrensville, Ohio) for involving me in their object-oriented projects. The book has gone through several rounds of reviews, and I would like to thank the following reviewers for their suggestions and corrections:

Kulbir S. Arora
SUNY, Buffalo

Charles H. Burris, Jr.
Seattle Pacific University

Douglas Campbell
Brigham Young University

H. E. Dunsmore
Purdue University

Linda J. Elliot
LaSalle University

Frank Kelbe

Paul W. Ross
Millersville University

Marvin Solomon
University of Wisconsin, Madison

I would like to thank both editors, Mike Sugarman at PWS Publishing Company and Frank Ruggirello at Wadsworth Publishing Company, for their expert handling of this publication. Sincere appreciation goes to Susan Gay and Abigail Heim at PWS Publishing as well. Also important to the writing of the book and to testing the extensive set of examples is the excellent computing equipment provided by the Institute for Computational Mathematics of the Department of Mathematics and Computer Science at Kent State University.

My daughter Laura, an economics major, suggested the term *appendant* (used in connection with class derivation). She deserves all the credit if the term works, and I deserve all the blame if it does not. Finally, I would like to thank my wife, Jennifer, for her understanding, support, and encouragement.

Paul S. Wang
Kent State University

C++ WITH OBJECT-
ORIENTED PROGRAMMING

INTRODUCTION

Object-oriented programming (OOP) has become a major trend in computing and is increasingly accepted as the paradigm of choice for software development in industry as well as academia. OOP offers certain advantages over traditional programming approaches that make software easier to build, maintain, modify, and reuse. Knowledge of object-oriented (OO) techniques will make you a better programmer.

There are many programming languages that support OOP. Some, like SMALLTALK, are pure and thorough in their object orientation. Others, like C++ and CLOS (Common Lisp Object System), support a combination of object-oriented and traditional procedure-oriented programming. Among these, C++ stands out as the predominant OOP language. The widespread acceptance of C++ can be attributed to two major factors. First, C++ provides a well-designed set of mechanisms to fully support OOP needs. Second, C++ is an extension of the already popular and standardized ANSI C. Therefore, C++ is the top choice for introducing OOP concepts and techniques to new and experienced programmers.

What Is OOP?

The central idea of OOP is to build programs using software *objects*. An object can be considered as a self-contained computing entity with its own data and programming. On modern workstations, for example, windows, menus, and file folders are usually represented by software objects. But objects can be applied to many kinds of programs. An object can be an airline reservation record, a bank account, or even an automobile engine. An engine object would include data describing its physical attributes and programming governing how it works internally and how it interacts with other related parts (also software objects) in an automobile.

A system for a personnel department would have engineers, secretaries, and managers as software objects. An air traffic control system would have runways, airliners, and passenger gates as software objects. Thus, in OOP, the software objects correspond closely to real objects involved in the application area. This correspondence makes the computer program easy to understand and manipulate. In contrast, traditional programming deals with bytes, variables, arrays, indices, and other programming artifacts that are difficult to relate to the problem at hand. Also, traditional programming focuses mainly on the step-by-step procedures, called *algorithms*, to achieve the desired tasks. For this reason, it is also known as *procedure-oriented* programming.

OOP Advantages

A large computer program is among the most complex mechanisms ever built. The cost of design, implementation, testing, maintenance, and revision of large software systems is very high. Thus, it is important to find ways to make these tasks easier and less frequent. In this direction, OOP has enormous potential.

For reasons that will become clear, OOP offers these main advantages:

- *Simplicity:* Because software objects model real objects in the application domain, the complexity of the program is reduced and the program structure becomes clear and simple.
- *Modularity:* Each object forms a separate entity whose internal workings are decoupled from other parts of the system.
- *Modifiability:* It is easy to make minor changes in the data representation or the procedures used in an OO program. Changes within an object do not affect any other part of the program provided that the *external behavior* of the object is preserved.
- *Extensibility:* Adding new features or responding to changing operating environments can be a matter of introducing a few new objects and modifying some existing ones.
- *Flexibility:* An OO program can be very flexible in accommodating different situations because the interaction patterns among the objects can be changed without modifying the objects.
- *Maintainability:* Objects can be maintained separately, making locating and fixing problems and adding "bells and whistles" easy.

- *Reusability:* Objects can be reused in different programs. A table-building object, for instance, can be used in any program that requires a table of some sort. Thus, programs can be built from prefabricated and pretested components in a fraction of the time required to build new programs from scratch.

OOP Concepts

The breakthrough concept of OOP technology is the attachment of program procedures to data items. This concept changes the traditional segregation between data and programs. The wrapping together of procedures and data is called *encapsulation*, and the result is a software object. For example, a window object (Figure 0.1) in a graphical user interface system contains the window's physical dimensions, location on the screen, foreground and background colors, border styles, and other relevant data. Encapsulated with these data are routines (procedures) to move and resize the window itself, to change its colors, to display text, to shrink into an icon, and so on. Other parts of the user interface program simply call upon a window object to perform these tasks by sending well-defined *messages* to the object. It is the job of a window object to perform appropriate actions and to keep its internal data updated. The exact manner in which these tasks are achieved and the structures of the internal data are of no concern to programs outside the object. The *public interface* formed by the collection of messages understood by an object completely defines how to use that object. The hiding of internal details makes an object *abstract*, and the technique is sometimes referred to as *data abstraction*.

The separation of *public interface* from *internal workings* is not difficult to understand. In fact, it is common practice in our daily lives. Consider a bank teller for example. Customers go to any bank and talk to any teller using the same set of messages: account number, deposit, withdrawal, balance, and so on. The way each bank or teller actually keeps records or performs tasks internally is of no concern to a customer. These tried-and-true principles simplify business at all levels and can bring the same benefit to organizing programs. As an OO program executes, objects are created, sent messages, and destroyed. These are the only allowable operations on objects. The internal (*private*) data or procedures in an object are off limits to the *public*. The decoupling of the private mechanisms in objects from routines outside the objects significantly reduces the complexity of a program.

It is often the case that more than one object of the same type is needed. For example, multiple windows often appear on workstation screens. Normally, objects of a given type are *instances* of a *class* whose definition specifies the private (internal) workings of these objects as well as their public interface.

FIGURE 0.1   A WINDOW OBJECT

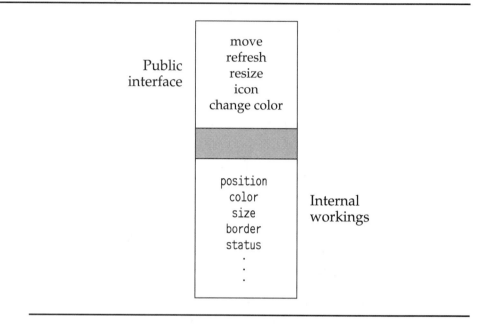

Thus, in OOP, a class would be defined for each different type of object required. A class becomes a blueprint for making a particular kind of object. A class definition and appropriate *initial values* are used to create an instance (object) of the class. This operation is known as *instantiation*. The term *object* can sometimes refer to either a class or an instance of a class.

The OOP technology also calls for easy ways to construct objects on top of other objects. There are two principal methods: *composition* and *inheritance*. Composition allows existing objects to be used as components to build other objects. For instance, a calculator object may be composed of an arithmetic unit object and a user interface object. Inheritance is a major OOP feature that allows the derivation of a similar or related object (the *derived object*) from another object (the *base object*). In C++, this is done through class derivation. A *derived class* can *inherit* the properties of its *base class* and also add its own data and routines. For example, a graphics window, a text window, and a terminal emulator window can all be derived from a basic window class. Also, a check, an invoice, and an application form can all be derived from a basic business form class. Inheritance allows the extraction of commonalities among similar or related objects. It also allows classes in OO software libraries to be used for many different or unforeseen purposes. In these examples, derivation is from one base class, so it is called *single inheritance*. It is also possible to derive a class from several base classes (like inheriting characteristics from both parents) to achieve *multiple inheritance*.

Another hallmark of OOP is *overloading*, the assignment of multiple meanings to operators and function names. Such operators and functions are *overloaded* with different duties. For example, the operator +, primarily associated with addition of numbers, can be overloaded to add one list (a user-defined object) to another by combining the two lists. Overloading can simplify programs and make the same operation work for many different types of operands.

Furthermore, OOP allows *polymorphism*, the ability for the same procedure to work with different objects as interchangeable *black boxes*. Polymorphism allows the creation of different (but related) objects that are interchangeable under a set of operations. If a problem-solving procedure is set forth using only these operations, then it works for all such objects. For example, a procedure for driving a car can then be made under polymorphism to work for all types of vehicles that can be driven. Such procedures are *polymorphic*.

Obviously, OOP has many powerful concepts. C++ provides a set of well-designed language mechanisms to help achieve these goals. Only through actual programming can the many implications of these concepts be fully understood.

Evolution of C++

C++ is a general programming language that is compatible with ANSI C. In 1980, Bjarne Stroustrup of AT&T added classes and a few other features to C resulting in a language known as "C with Classes." Later, in 1983 and 1984, several extensions were made, notably operator overloading and virtual functions, resulting in a language called "C++." With a few further revisions and refinements, C++ became generally available in 1985.

As object orientation grew into a major trend, so did the use of C++ as a language. C++ supports both traditional procedural programming and OOP well. This is important because most real programs need a mixture of object and procedure orientations. Today, C++ is the most popular OOP language. All major computer vendors offer C++ on their machines. Implementations of C++ include the standard-setting USL C++ (from AT&T), Hewlett-Packard C++, GNU g++ (C++ from The Free Software Foundation), Borland C++, and Microsoft C++. Due to its popularity, C++ is now being standardized jointly by ANSI and ISO. Currently, the definition of C++ is provided in the *Annotated C++ Reference Manual* by Ellis and Stroustrup. It is expected that C++ will become a major language for the 1990s and beyond.

Features of C++

C++ provides all the usual facilities necessary for writing procedures. Major OOP features of C++ include classes, operator and function overloading, references, inline functions, single and multiple inheritance, virtual functions, and templates. There are also free storage management operators and default function arguments.

The C++ class defines software objects by enclosing data members as well as function members. Members can be designated *private*, *protected*, or *public*, providing a convenient way to define the public interface and the private domain of an object.

Class derivation is the C++ mechanism for inheritance supporting both type relations and code reuse. Both single and multiple inheritance are possible. The virtual function mechanism supports polymorphism and allows the definition of interchangeable objects under a uniform external interface. The C++ abstract base class mechanism allows for extraction of commonalities among related classes as well as planning their interfaces.

The *template* facility supports *type parameterization*, allowing a function or a class to be defined with yet-unspecified types that only become known when it is referenced (actually invoked) in a program.

C++ also provides an object-based I/O library. I/O operators (>> and <<) make receiving and displaying data simple and straightforward. These operators can also be overloaded to perform input and output of user-defined objects.

You will learn all about these and other features of C++ and how to use them effectively to write object-oriented programs.

Organization of Materials

This book introduces C++ and its effective use for OOP. C++ is covered completely — from the basics to advanced topics and from procedural programming to OOP. Knowledge of another programming language and some programming experience are required. Prior knowledge of C will reduce the amount of work involved. Access to a C++ compiler is necessary. The material is suitable for a three-credit programming course or a course on C++/OOP, at the undergraduate or beginning graduate level.

The material is organized and presented so that it is simple, concise, and easy to follow. The best way to learn programming is to write programs. Thus, you will begin writing whole programs early. Interesting examples and challenging exercises encourage this hands-on approach. The early chapters are quite basic and form a primer of information on many elementary aspects of C++, including objects, to get you started quickly. There are many simple examples, a guide on effective object-oriented thinking, programming tips, and style guides. The pace, however, does pick up. When you are through, you will have gained a level of unusual proficiency in C++ and its use for OOP. The book contains enough advanced material to keep even experienced programmers happy.

As a language that supports OOP, C++ contains many more features than a regular procedure-oriented language like C or Pascal. It is important that each construct is covered well. This requires not only explaining the syntax and semantics of each construct but also illustrating how it can be applied to advantage. Furthermore, effective ways to combine different constructs in solving real problems are emphasized. OOP is introduced and integrated into the presentation so that it is not some artificially added-on subject, but rather a natural way of writing programs. Throughout the book, examples show how a problem is broken into logical chunks that are easy to tackle and how programs are modular, object-oriented, separately tested, and reusable. Many objects and whole programs are of such a nature that they can be reused frequently in the future.

C++ Primer
Part I: Basics

Chapters 1 and 2 form a primer presenting essential information for beginning C++ programmers. The material is carefully organized to give you a good start. The overall program structure and a well-selected set of introductory topics are presented so that you can write interesting and complete programs quickly.

Part I of the C++ primer focuses on basic information: program structure, constants, variables, expressions, arrays, functions, and simple input/output. The control-flow constructs if, while, for, and do-while are introduced. The necessary basic details are presented quickly and completely in preparation for more interesting and central topics to follow. The examples and their variations should be tested on your system.

If you have some background in C, you can read through this chapter very quickly. However, since there are many differences between C and C++ programming even at the basic level, it is a good idea to look at the examples. If a detail is required later, you can always find it here easily.

1.1 Object-Oriented Program Structure

A program is a set of instructions, written in a programming language, to solve a given type of problem or to perform specific kinds of tasks. A C++ program consists of *functions* and *classes*. Functions codify the solution procedures required. Classes describe *objects* that represent interacting entities that play a role in the solution process. Objects are used to closely model actual or logical entities in the problem domain. One important aspect of OOP is identifying these entities and their interactions in the solution process.

A function receives *arguments*, performs predefined computations on the arguments, and returns results. A *function call* activates (or *invokes*) a function, passes arguments to the function, and produces the values it returns.

A class is a blueprint for objects. It describes an object's data structures and their associated operations. Once a class is defined, objects belonging to the class can be declared and used in a program. A class provides a name under which data and function *members* are collected into one unit. This computing unit can be made to operate independently of other parts of the program. By using objects, a large program can be built with many small, independent, mutually interacting units. Object orientation can significantly reduce program complexity, increase flexibility, and enhance reusability.

Thus, in C++, procedures are coded by functions, which will be explained here, and objects are defined by classes, which will be introduced in Chapter 2.

1.2 \ FUNCTIONS

A function contains *statements* that specify a sequence of computing actions to be carried out and *variables* that are used to store values needed and produced during the computations. Some of the variables may be objects, and the problem solution usually involves interactions among objects.

For any program, one function must be named main. The function main is the *entry point*, the place where execution of the program begins. Aside from this basic structure, C++ is flexible. Functions and classes can be defined in any order and can be contained in one or several source code files.

A function can be viewed as a self-contained computation procedure. The arguments are its input, and the computation result, or *return value*, is its output (Figure 1.1).

A well-organized procedure contains many small functions that perform well-defined duties. A function can call other functions and make use of objects in the course of its computations. In this way, a complex procedure is broken down into a series of steps that are individually straightforward but combine to achieve the given goal.

FIGURE 1.1   A FUNCTION AS A COMPUTATION UNIT

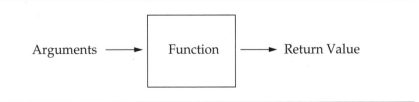

A function definition consists of a *header* and a *body*. The function header states the function name and the type of the return value. The header also specifies variables, known as *formal parameters*, which receive the incoming arguments. These formal parameters are used in the function body to perform computations.

The function body consists of a sequence of *declarations* and *statements* enclosed in braces, {}. A declaration supplies information to the C++ compiler, and a statement specifies actions for execution. The many different declarations and statements and their meanings will be described as we proceed.

The general form of a function is

```
valuetype name ( type arg1, type arg2, ... )    (function header)
{                                               (body begin)
        declarations and statements
}                                               (body end)
```

The *valuetype* specifies the type of the value returned by the function. If it is omitted, the function is presumed to return a value of type integer (int). If the function does not return a value, then its *valuetype* is given as void.

Depending on the number of arguments needed, the header may specify zero or more formal parameters. If there are no formal parameters, the parameter list is given as an empty list, (). Furthermore, the function body may contain zero or more declarations and statements. (Section 1.3 gives more basic information on statements.)

To begin, let's consider a very simple program that consists of just one function main.

```
#include  <iostream.h>

int main()
{     int i = 10, j = 20;
      int k = (i + j)/2;
      cout << "i is " << i << "\n"
           << "and j is " << j << "\n";
      cout << "average is " << k << "\n";
      return(0);
}
```

For this function, the header is simply the function name main and an empty list of formal parameters. An empty argument list cannot be omitted and indicates that the function takes no arguments.

The function body just given begins with the declarations

```
int i = 10, j = 20;
int k = (i + j)/2;
```

establishing the three variables i, j, and k, each of type int (single-precision integer). A variable must be declared before it is used. A simple declaration consists of a *type name* followed by a list of variable names separated by commas and terminated by a semicolon. Each variable may also be given an optional *initializer* after an equal sign (=). The expression

```
(i + j)/2;
```

is evaluated, and the resultant value is used to initialize the variable k. There are different kinds of expressions. An *arithmetic expression* involves arithmetic operators such as +, -, *, and /. Generally, an *expression* is a constant, a variable, a function call, or an expression connected by operators.

Here are a few more variable declarations:

```
int age = 8;
float rate, speed;
char c, d;
```

These declare the variable age of type int, rate and speed of type float (single-precision floating-point), and c and d of type char (a single character).

Variables, such as i, j, and k, declared in a function body are used within the function and will not conflict with any variable with the same name used elsewhere. Therefore, such variables are said to be *local* to the function.

After the declarations in main, there are two output statements using the built-in output object cout. C++ provides *I/O stream classes* that are used to establish objects to perform input and output. The built-in stream object cout sends output to the terminal. Data for output are passed to cout with the *output operator* <<, as in

```
cout << "average is " << k << "\n";
```

In C++, a sequence of characters enclosed in double quotes is a *character string constant*. The notation \n stands for a NEWLINE character, which causes the output to start another line. (More will be said about character strings later.) As you can see in the example, the operator << can be used consecutively to output a sequence of different quantities.

To use the C++ I/O stream facility, a program must specify the line

```
#include <iostream.h>
```

near the beginning. It includes the standard C++ *header file* iostream.h. A header file supplies the necessary codes for using programs written in another file. This line must be present for any program to use the C++ I/O stream. You should get in the habit of always putting this line at the beginning of your program.

By following a popular naming convention for C++ source code files, this example program can be put into the file average.C and then compiled. For example, on a UNIX system, a command such as

```
CC  average.C
```

compiles with the C++ compiler CC. Your computer may have the C++ compiler under another name (for example, g++) or may even provide a convenient program development environment. (Chapter 12 provides more general information on compilation. Appendices 1 and 2 show how to compile and run C++ programs on several widely used computer systems.)

After compilation, the executable program should be in a file under a standard name — for instance, a.out on UNIX systems. Your system may use another standard name.

Now run the compiled program. These lines should appear:

```
i is 10
and j is 20
average is 15
```

As mentioned, the active parts of a function are its statements, the subject of Section 1.3.

1.3 \ STATEMENTS

A statement specifies program actions at run time. The computational steps in a function are expressed by a sequence of statements that perform in ways predefined by the language. The statements are *executed* one by one in the given order when the program runs.

C++ provides a full complement of statements that will be described shortly. Generally, statements fall into two categories:

1. *Simple statement:* One single statement terminated by a semicolon (;).
2. *Compound statement:* Zero or more statements grouped together by { and }. A compound statement has the same structure as a function body. In fact, the function body is itself a compound statement. A compound statement can be used anywhere a simple statement can.

For example, each statement in the main function of average.C is a simple statement. Together they form the compound body of main. A compound statement is sometimes also referred to as a *block*.

A common programming mistake is to forget the semicolon terminator. When this happens in a program, because the C++ compiler cannot easily determine that a semicolon is missing, it will almost always complain about some other alleged syntax problem. These erroneous complaints can be very confusing. So be sure to use the semicolon where it is needed:

1. A declaration always ends with a ;.
2. A simple statement is terminated by a ;.
3. There is no ; after a compound statement — in other words, after the closing } of a block.

For an example of item 3, see the while statement used by the factorial function in Section 1.4.

1.4 \ THE while STATEMENT

Let's consider another simple function — in this case, one that computes n factorial for a nonnegative integer n. Recall n factorial is $n! = n * (n-1) * \cdots * 3 * 2 * 1$. Hence, $1! = 1, 2! = 2, 3! = 6$, and so on.

```
// factorial function computes n! for nonnegative n
/* version 1 */

int factorial(int n)
{     int ans = 1;
      while (n > 1)
      {   ans = ans * n;
          n = n - 1;
      }
      return(ans);
}
```

Note that the first two lines in this example do nothing but are nonetheless very important. The C++ compiler ignores all characters starting from the two-character sequence // to the end of the line. Also ignored are all characters or lines enclosed in /* and */. These markers allow comments, auxiliary information, or *documentation* to be supplied to make a program easy to understand.

The function factorial is defined with one formal parameter n of type int. The return value is of type int also. If control flows off the end of a function or returns through a return with no argument, the return value is undefined and the function *valuetype* must be void.

In this factorial function, the while statement

```
while (n > 1)
{   ans = ans * n;
    n = n - 1;
}
```

specifies repeated execution of two statements forming a *loop*. The *condition* n > 1 (enclosed in parentheses) controls how many times the body of the while loop (enclosed in braces) is executed.

Here is the way while works (Figure 1.2):

1. Test the condition. If n is greater than 1 (the condition is true), then the body of while is executed once. If the condition is false, then the body is not executed, the while statement is finished, and control goes to the next statement.

2. Go back and execute the previous step.

Because the continuation of the loop depends on the condition being true, such a condition is known as a *continuation condition*. The variable n in this example is called a *loop-control variable* because its value changes for each repetition of the loop and it determines when the loop stops.

Take a particular value for n — say, 4 — and follow the actions of this while loop to see how the variable ans actually becomes *n*! (24 in this case).

FIGURE 1.2   THE while LOOP

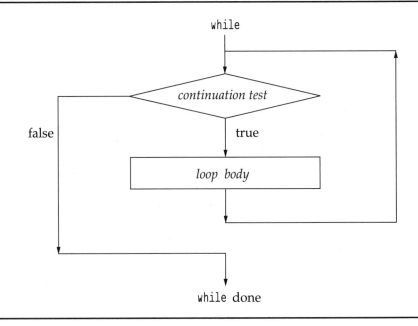

A Main Program for factorial

To test factorial, we can write a main program to call the function:

```cpp
#include <iostream.h>

int main()
{  cout << "Please enter n :";
   int n;                          // declaration of n
   cin >> n;                       // input from keyboard
   if ( n >= 0 )
      cout << "factorial("         // display answer
           << n << ")="
           << factorial(n) << "\n";
   else
      cerr << "factorial("         // display error message
           << n << ") undefined\n";
   return(0);
}
```

The first statement in the main function displays a request for the user to enter the value of n. The second statement is a *declaration statement*, one that introduces a new variable into the program. After n is declared, an integer value is read into n using the built-in input object cin and the *input operator* >>. If n is nonnegative, then the return value of the call factorial(n) is displayed through cout. Otherwise (n is negative), a message is displayed through the built-in error output object cerr.

Put the functions factorial and main (in that order) into a file; then compile and run the program. It should produce the message

```
Please enter n :
```

Now type in a small integer—say, 5—then press RETURN. If it works correctly, the display

```
factorial(5)=120
```

should appear on your screen.

1.5 \ SIMPLE CONDITIONAL STATEMENTS

Let's now look at the if statement in the factorial example. The if ... else statement provides *conditional branching* and can be used in the simple form

```
if ( condition )
    statement one
```

```
else
        statement two
```

The parentheses around the *condition* are mandatory. The condition is first tested to decide which one of the two given statements is executed. If the condition is true, then only *statement one* is executed; otherwise, only *statement two* is executed. Because a statement, by definition, can be either simple or compound, then statement one or two here can be compound in the form { st_1; ... st_n;}.

The else part can also be omitted, resulting in the form

```
if ( condition )
        statement
```

The effect is to execute the given *statement* only if the *condition* is true. Failing this, the statement is skipped over, and control flows to the next statement after the if statement.

The following statement

```
if ( n > 0 )
        m = m + n;
else
        m = m - n;
```

assigns to m the absolute value of n plus m. The condition

```
n > 0
```

is a *relational expression*. Its value is *true* only if the current value of n is greater than zero; otherwise, its value is *false*. The > is a relational operator. Table 1.1 lists the relational operators for numeric comparisons.

Do not confuse the relational operator == with the assignment operator =. If you use one less equal sign, the test condition becomes an assignment, which is perfectly legal in C++. The value of the assignment now, mistakenly, becomes

TABLE 1.1   RELATIONAL OPERATORS

OPERATOR	MEANING
>	Greater than
<	Less than
==	Equal to
!=	Not equal to
>=	Greater than or equal to
<=	Less than or equal to

the test result. This mistake will not cause compilation or execution errors; however, the answer produced will be wrong.

The logical constants *true* and *false*, also known as *Boolean values*, are represented by integers: *false* by zero and *true* by nonzero. Because of this, the condition

```
if ( n != 0 )    // n not equal to 0
```

is the same as the simplified condition

```
if ( n )
```

1.6 \ CHARACTERS AND CHARACTER INPUT AND OUTPUT

For every C++ program, there are three standard I/O channels:

1. *Standard input:* The standard input channel reads from the keyboard and is represented by the built-in I/O stream object cin.
2. *Standard output:* The standard output channel outputs to the terminal screen and is represented by the built-in I/O stream object cout. Standard output is used for normal display to the terminal screen.
3. *Standard error:* The error output channel outputs to the terminal screen immediately without any intermediate character buffering or delay. It is represented by the I/O stream object cerr. Standard error is used for displaying error or diagnostic messages.

To illustrate character input and output, two of the most basic operations, we can write a program that does the following:

1. Reads characters from standard input.
2. Converts any uppercase characters into lowercase characters.
3. Writes all characters out to standard output.

We first write a function that converts uppercase characters to lowercase characters. The lower function is called with a character and returns the lower case of this character:

```
#include <ctype.h>

char lower(char c)
{    if ( isupper(c) )         // if c is upper case
        return( tolower(c) );  // turn c into lower case
     else return(c);          // else c is unchanged
}
```

The library functions isupper and tolower (supplied by the header file <ctype.h>) make writing this function simple. The test isupper(c) returns nonzero (logical true) if c is an uppercase character. Otherwise, it returns zero (logical false).

So, again, we use the if construct:

```
if (character is upper case )
    compute and return lowercase value
else
    return character unchanged
```

Now all the main program has to do is to call the function lower on each input character and output what lower returns:

```
#include <iostream.h>

int main()
{       char c;
        char lower(char);              // function prototype
        while ( cin.get(c) != 0 )      // input character
            cout.put( lower(c) );
        cout.flush();
        return(0);
}
```

Note that the function lower is declared before it is used in the body of main. A function must be declared before it is used. The declaration

```
char lower(char c);
```

tells the C++ compiler that lower is a function that takes one argument of type char and returns a value of type char. In general, such a declaration takes the form of a function header terminated by a semicolon and is called a *function prototype*. Parameter names in a function prototype are optional but can provide valuable indications of the nature of the parameters. Thus, the preceding function prototype can also be given as

```
char lower(char);
```

The I/O stream objects cin and cout have internal routines or *member functions* that can be invoked to perform well-defined duties. For instance, the get member function of the object cin, when given a character variable c, will read from standard input a single character and assign that character to c. A member function is accessed through an object by the notation

object. member

where the dot (.) is the *member-of* operator. The function call cin.get(c) returns zero only when end of file is reached. The *not equal to* sign != is a relational operator. (See Table 1.1 for all available relational operators.) Thus, the while loop in our example will repeat until end of file is reached. When input is from the keyboard, a system-dependent convention is used to signify the end of input. For example, under UNIX systems, you type a ^D (control-D) at the beginning of a line. (See Appendix 2 for some other conventions.)

After the character c is read from standard input, the character lower(c) is written to standard output by

```
cout.put( lower(c) )
```

where put is a member function of cout.

After the while loop is finished, cout.flush() is called to make sure that any buffered output is sent before the program terminates. Other useful facilities provided by the built-in I/O stream of C++ will be covered as needed.

Put this program into a file — say, lowercase.C — then compile and run it. Now type a mixture of uppercase and lowercase characters on the keyboard and press RETURN. You should see the same line displayed with all uppercase characters turned into lowercase characters. Type as many input lines as you like; then terminate the input properly.

1.7 \ MORE BASIC CONSTRUCTS

Having considered a few selected examples and having an idea of the overall structure of a C++ program, we are ready to examine some more frequently used expressions and statements.

The for Statement

C++ has the usual arithmetic operators +, -, *, and /. In addition, there is also the integer remainder operator % (for example, 15 % 6 is 3). But there is no power, or exponentiation, operator. The for statement can be used in a power function to raise integers to integer powers:

```
int power(int a, int n)
{     int i, ans = 1;
      for (i = 1 ; i <= n ; i = i+1)
            ans = ans * a;
      return(ans);
}
```

In this function, the for specifies a loop and takes the following general form:

```
for ( init statement
      cont condition ; incr expr )   (loop control)
      statement                      (loop body)
```

The loop body can be a simple or a compound statement. The loop control consists of an initialization statement (with its own terminating semicolon) and followed by two expressions (a continuation condition and an increment expression) separated by another semicolon.

In the function power, the *init statement*

```
i = 1;
```

is executed before the for loop starts. The *cont condition*

```
i <= n
```

is then tested. If true, the *statement,* or body, of the for loop is executed once. The *incr expr*

```
i = i + 1;
```

is then executed, followed by a reexamination of the test condition. If it is true, the body is executed once again. If it is false, the for statement is finished. Figure 1.3 further illustrates the control flow of for.

The for is a specialized while, and the iteration keeps going only while the test condition remains true. Thus, it is possible for the body of the for to be *skipped without ever being executed* if the test condition is false to start with. It is

FIGURE 1.3   THE for LOOP

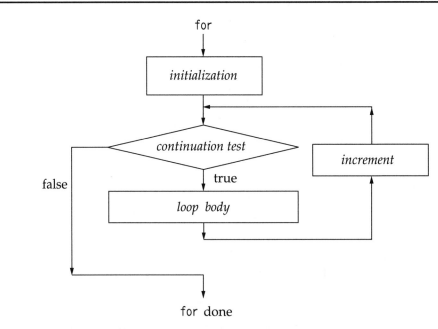

also worth noting that only two semicolons are used in the loop control part of the `for`. (Details on the forms of expressions themselves are discussed in Section 1.9.)

The initialization statement can be a *null statement*, one that consists of just the ending semicolon and specifies a no-op, an operation that does nothing. It is possible to omit one or more parts in the `for` loop control. The absence of a part indicates a no-op. Thus, an infinite loop can be written as

```
for(;;) { /* loop body */ }    // infinite loop
```

It is also possible to write a `for` with a body that is empty or a null statement:

```
for ( /* control */ ) { }    // empty loop body
for ( /* control */ ) ;      // null loop body
```

In this case, the loop body is a no-op, and the effective computations would be contained in the loop control.

Instead of declaring the loop control variable i outside the `for` construct, it is common C++ practice to move the declaration statement for i inside the `for` if possible:

```
for (int i = 1 ; i <= n ; i = i+1)
    ans = ans * a;
```

Because the declaration statement is a statement, it can appear anywhere a statement can. The control variable i retains its last value after the `for` loop whether it is declared before or in the loop control.

The function `power` assumes that the exponent n is nonnegative. It does not work for a negative n. Strictly speaking, there should be a check for the sign of n before the `for` loop is entered. Another concern is the size of the answer. If the answer exceeds the maximum size for the type `int`, `power` will fail. The handling of arithmetic overflow and underflow is implementation-dependent. It could happen that the variable `ans` suddenly becomes zero when overflow occurs. These problems can be solved as you become more familiar with the language (Section 11.6).

Increment and Decrement Operators

The unary operators ++ (increment) and -- (decrement) are used to increase or decrease the value of an integer variable by 1 (which is especially useful in loops). Applied to a variable i, these special operators perform four separate functions in a single step:

1. Access the current value of i.
2. Add or subtract 1 from this value.

3. Assign the new value to i.

4. Produce the old or new i as the value of the expression.

Specifically, we can use

```
i++      (increment after — gives value of i, then adds 1 to i)
++i      (increment before — adds 1 to i, then gives value of i)
i--      (decrement after — gives value of i, then subtracts 1 from i)
--i      (decrement before — subtracts 1 from i, then gives value of i)
```

The idea is to combine referencing the value of a variable with assigning a new value to the variable to get shorter, more efficient code. For example,

```
j = 2 * i++;
```

means use the current value of i in the multiplication with 2, then change the value of i by adding 1 to it. Thus, it is shorthand for

```
j = 2 * i;
i = i + 1;
```

but more efficient. Similarly, the increment-before usage in

```
j = 2 * ++i;
```

is short for

```
i = i + 1;
j = 2 * i;
```

which is very different from the increment-after operation.

Here is the power function with the increment operator:

```
int power(int a, int n)
{    int ans = 1;
     for (int i = 1 ; i <= n ; i++)
         ans = ans * a;
     return(ans);
}
```

Note that we could have written ++i instead of i++ in the loop control of the for because the value of this increment expression is not used.

A yet more efficient implementation of power combines n-- with while, a construct explained in Section 1.4:

```
int power(int a, int n)
{    int ans = 1;
     while (n-- > 0)
         ans = ans * a;
```

```
        return(ans);
}
```

Note that the n-- in the while condition here cannot be replaced by --n. However, assuming n is nonnegative, the relational expression n-- > 0 can be replaced by the simple n-- without changing the meaning of the while loop.

Use of the increment and decrement operators sometimes can make code more difficult to read and can contribute to errors in a program. You should strive for readability over terseness in your programming.

The do-while Statement

The while and the for loops test the continuation condition at the beginning of the loop. If the condition is false to begin with, the while or for loop body can be skipped without being executed. The do-while loop is the same as while, except it tests the continuation condition at the end of the loop (Figure 1.4). Therefore, a do-while loop body is executed *at least once*.

The general form of the do statement is

do *statement* while (*condition*) ;

where the loop body is again a simple or compound statement.

The Multiway if Statement

We have seen the simple if-else statement and how to use it. Here is the general form of the if statement:

FIGURE 1.4   THE do-while LOOP

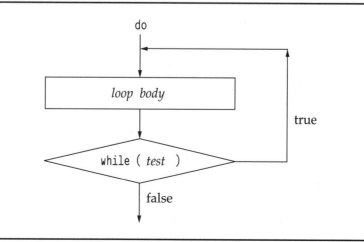

```
if ( expr1 )
      statement-1
else if ( expr2 )
      statement-2
...
      . . .
else
      statement-i
```

There can be zero or more else if parts. As stated before, the final else part is optional.

This pattern specifies a multiway branching: If *expr1* is true, *statement-1* is executed; otherwise, if *expr2* is true, *statement-2* is executed; ...; otherwise, if nothing is true, *statement-i* is executed. In other words, the logical expressions are examined in order, and the first true expression triggers the execution of the corresponding statement. At most, one of the statements is executed. Control then goes to the next statement beyond the entire if statement.

To apply the if statement, we can write a function, compare, that takes two int quantities, a and b, and returns 1, 0, or −1, depending on whether a is greater than, equal to, or less than b, respectively:

```
int compare(int a, int b)
{    if ( a > b )
         return(1);
     else if (a < b )
         return(-1);
     else
         return(0);
}
```

Actually, it is not necessary to insist on getting 1, 0, and −1 from compare. Following the convention established by the C++ library function strcmp (string compare, Section 6.1), the return value should be positive, zero, or negative, depending on the relative size of the two quantities being compared. Hence, the function compare becomes simply

```
int compare(int a, int b)
{    return(a-b);
}
```

A statement within an if can be another if to form a *nested* if statement. The function even_or_odd returns 2, 1, or 0 for a positive even, positive odd, or neither, respectively:

```
int even_or_odd(int a)
{   if ( a > 0 )                    // outer if begin
```

```
        if ( a % 2 == 0 )    // inner if begin
              return(2);
        else
              return(1);      // inner if end
                              // outer if end
    return(0);
}
```

The arithmetic operator % computes the remainder (Section 1.9.1). With nested if statements, a good question to ask is, To which if does the else belong? There are two logical possibilities: (1) Associate the else with the inner if, making the statement part of the outer if another if-else statement; (2) associate the else with the outer if. This potential ambiguity is known as the *dangling else* problem. In C++, an else or if else clause automatically goes with the immediately preceding open if. An if without an else can be closed by enclosing the if statement in {}, making it a compound statement.

1.8 \ DATA TYPES AND DECLARATIONS

There are only four *basic data types* in C++: char, int, float, and double. The effects of all C++ operators on the basic types are defined by the language.

Data Type char

We have used characters in a limited way without details of the character type. A char type is a single byte (typically, 8 bits), enough to hold one character in the character set. A common standard is ASCII (American Standard Code for Information Interchange). A char byte represents a character with an integer encoding defined in the character set. In ASCII, each character has a nonnegative integer code. For instance, the characters Z and z are represented by 90 and 122, respectively.

Like 'A' and 'Z', a character constant is specified within single quotes. The value of a character constant is merely its integer code. For example, in ASCII, '9' has numeric value 57. A character constant and its equivalent integer value are interchangeable in usage. However, by using the character constant notation, you can make your program *character-set-independent* and easier to read.

A few special characters are specified by two-character *escape sequences* such as '\n', the NEWLINE character discussed earlier. Table 1.2 contains a list of all such escape sequences.

TABLE 1.2   CHARACTER ESCAPE SEQUENCES

\n	NEWLINE	\r	RETURN
\t	TAB	\v	VERTICAL TAB
\'	SINGLE QUOTE	\"	DOUBLE QUOTE
\\	BACKSLASH	\b	BACKSPACE
\f	FORMFEED	\a	BELL
\?	QUESTION MARK	\0	Null character
\ooo	Octal byte	\xhh	Hexadecimal byte

Any constant, byte-size, bit pattern can also be specified using a notation with one to three octal (base 8) digits (0–7) or with one to two hexadecimal (base 16) digits (0...9, a...f, A...F). Some byte-size patterns (anything over 127) do not correspond to any character code in ASCII. Table 1.3 shows a sample of characters in various notations.

Data Type int

The type int holds an integer quantity. The size (number of bits) of the int type is machine-dependent and normally reflects the machine word size. In addition to int, there are short int and long int types. Again, their sizes are machine-dependent. Typically, on a 32-bit computer, C++ offers a 16-bit short int, a 32-bit int, and a 32-bit or 64-bit long int. By omitting the int, these types may be specified simply as short or long.

TABLE 1.3   CHARACTER REPRESENTATIONS

CHARACTER	CONSTANT	INTEGER VALUE	BIT PATTERN	OCTAL NOTATION	HEX NOTATION
Zero	'0'	48	00111001	060	0x30
NEWLINE	'\n'	10	00001010	012	0xa
Plus sign	'+'	43	00101011	053	0x2b
A	'A'	65	01000001	0101	0x41
a	'a'	97	01100001	0141	0x61
^D	'\04'	4	00000100	04	0x4

The signed and unsigned Integers

Integer types such as int and char normally are interpreted with a leading *sign bit*. This means that if the leading bit is 0, the quantity is positive; otherwise, it is negative. Thus, if a char uses 8 bits, then the value ranges from -128 to 127. Hence, about half of the available representations are taken up by negative values.

In cases where the negative values are not needed, a representation with a leading sign bit will waste 50% of the possible values. However, this can be avoided. The qualifiers signed and unsigned can be used on int, char, and other integer types to enable (the default) and disable the use of the sign bit. An unsigned number obeys integer arithmetic modulo 2^n, where n is the number of bits in the type. Therefore, for $n = 32$, unsigned int values range between 0 and $2^{32} - 1$. The signed and unsigned representations of a positive integer are the same.

The maximum and minimum values of various data types are implementation-dependent and are kept in the standard header files limits.h and float.h. Symbolic constants such as INT_MAX and INT_MIN (typically, $2^{31} - 1$ and -2^{31} on a 32-bit computer) are defined in limits.h.

The short test program

```
#include <iostream.h>
#include <limits.h>

main()
{   unsigned int a = INT_MAX + 1;
    cout << a << "\n";
    int b = INT_MAX + 1;
    cout << b << "\n";
}
```

will show you the value of INT_MAX and the meaning of unsigned versus signed quantities.

Forms of Constants

An integer constant is composed of an optional sign (+ or -) followed by a sequence of digits. An integer given in octal or hex begins with a 0 (zero) or a 0x prefix, respectively. If an integer constant given in your program is large and does not fit into an int, the compiler will take it as a long. You can also use trailing characters to explicitly indicate long, unsigned, and so on, as shown in Table 1.4.

A single-precision floating-point type, float, has a size suggested by the machine architecture. A double-precision floating-point type, double, typically

TABLE 1.4   INTEGER AND FLOATING-POINT CONSTANTS

-9876	int	-9876L or -9876l	long
1234U or 1234u	unsigned	1234UL or 1234ul	unsigned long
025	Octal number	0xFFF	Hex number
025L	long octal	0xFFFul	unsigned long hex
3.14159	double	314e-2 or 314E-2	(3.14) double
3.1416f or 3.1416F	float	314e-2l or 314e-2L	long double

uses twice as many bits as float. There is also long double, which usually supplies yet more precision.

A floating-point constant contains a decimal point (3.1416), an exponent (31416e-4), or both. The type is assumed to be double unless the constant has a trailing f or F (float) or l or L (long double). (See Table 1.4.)

Variables and Identifiers

A variable is an *identifier* referring to a memory location holding a value. There is more to an identifier than just variable names. It can be a function name, a class name, a symbolic constant, and so on. An identifier consists of a sequence of letters, digits, and underscores (_) whose first character must not be a digit. Note that uppercase and lowercase letters are different. An identifier can be of any length. Identifiers containing a double underscore (__) or a leading underscore may conflict with implementation-generated identifiers or those used in libraries and should be avoided by most users.

As mentioned before, the data type of a variable must be declared before it is used in a program. When a variable is declared, it can also be initialized. For example,

```
char shift = 'a' - 'A';
int i = 7;
float x = 1.2f;
long double pi = 3.141592653589793L;
```

In general, a variable can be initialized with arbitrary expressions involving constants, other variables, and function calls. The different types of expressions are described next.

1.9 \ OPERATORS AND EXPRESSIONS

Constants, variables, and function calls are the simplest sorts of expressions. When combined with operators, they form more involved expressions. Whether an expression is simple or complicated, it always gives a value.

An operator acts on operands. A *binary* operator takes two operands, and a *unary* operator takes only one operand. In an expression involving multiple operators, the order in which the operations are carried out is very important. In the expression

```
a + b / c
```

the division is carried out before the addition. Thus, the operator / takes *precedence* over +. Generally, arithmetic operators take precedence over logical operators, which take precedence over assignment operators. Consider an expression involving operators with the same precedence:

```
a / b * c    // equivalent to (a / b) * c
```

Its value can depend on the *associativity* of these operators. Most operators associate left to right, causing the expression to be evaluated from left to right. A few groups of operators associate right to left. (The relative precedence and associativity of all operators are shown in Appendix 6.) Parentheses can be used to override the precedence and associativity rules, as in

```
(a + b) / c
a / (b * c)
```

The available operators and expressions are presented in the following subsections. For easy reference, the operators and expressions are summarized in Tables 1.5, 1.7, 1.8, and 1.9.

1.9.1   Arithmetic Expressions

Table 1.5 shows the variety of arithmetic expressions. When the divide operator / is used on two integers, an integer quotient is produced. Any fractional part is discarded. The increment and decrement operators can be used only on actual variables. Therefore, an expression like (a+b)++ is incorrect.

The arithmetic operator % provides the remainder, or modulo operation, for integer operands. To compute i modulo j means to divide i by j and take the remainder. If both i and j are nonnegative, then the result is nonnegative and smaller than j. Otherwise, the only guarantee is that the absolute value of the result will be smaller than the absolute value of j. Furthermore, % does not work for floating-point numbers. The modulo operation (mod for short) is useful in many situations.

TABLE 1.5   ARITHMETIC EXPRESSIONS

EXPRESSION	DESCRIPTION
a/(3.4+b)-3*c	Usual precedence and type conversions
i/4	Integer division truncates any fractional part
i % j	Integer remainder; denominator j should be positive
x*x*x	No built-in power operator
++i, j++	Pre/postincrement (integer only)
--i, j--	Pre/postdecrement (integer only)

Consider computing the next tab position, given any current column position. On a typical CRT terminal, tab stops are set eight columns apart. So, the next tab stop is given by

```
c - (c % 8) + 8
```

for any current column position c.

1.9.2 Relational and Logical Expressions

We have already used some relational and logical expressions. The set of all *relational* operators is listed in Table 1.1. The *logical* operators are given in Table 1.6. All forms of relational and logical expressions are shown in Table 1.7.

The relational operators have higher precedence than the operator && (logical and), which takes precedence over || (logical or). *Evaluation of a logical expression stops as soon as the logical value of the whole expression is determined.* This may leave some operands unevaluated. For example, the expression

expr1 && expr2

is true only if both *expr1* and *expr2* are true. If *expr1* turns out to be false, the value of the whole expression must be false; therefore, *expr2* is not evaluated. Similarly, in evaluating

TABLE 1.6   LOGICAL OPERATORS

OPERATOR	MEANING
&&	Logical operator *and*
||	Logical operator *or*
!	Logical operator *not* (unary)

TABLE 1.7   RELATIONAL AND LOGICAL EXPRESSIONS

EXPRESSION	DESCRIPTION
0	Logical false
1 or nonzero	Logical true
a > b, a < b, a >= b, a <= b	Relational expressions have logical values
a == b, a != b	Equal, not equal
a > 0 && a < 1	True if first *and* second relations are true
a > 1 || a < -1	True if first *or* second relation is true
a || ! b && c	Logical expression: a *or* [(*not* b) *and* c]
a > b ? a : b	Conditional expression: if (a > b), then value is a; else b

expr1 || *expr2*

if *expr1* is true, the value of the whole expression is true, and *expr2* will not be evaluated.

The unary operator ! (logical not) *negates* the logical value of its operand. The negation turns true into false, and vice versa. The operator ! has precedence over all relational and other logical operators. For an example of a rather complicated logical expression, see the readline function in Section 1.13.

C++ also features the *conditional expression* formed with the *ternary* operator ?:, which takes three operands:

expr0 ? *expr1* : *expr2*

The expression has value *expr1* if *expr0* is true, and *expr2* otherwise. Thus, the expression

c = a > b ? a : b

sets c to max(a,b).

1.9.3   Assignment Expressions

An *assignment* is a statement as well as an expression because it produces a value—that of the left-hand side after the assignment is made. Hence, an assignment can be used anywhere an expression can. Furthermore, in the same spirit of the increment and decrement operators, the assignment operator = can combine with other operators to form efficient shorthand expressions. The allowable combinations are shown in Table 1.8.

TABLE 1.8   ASSIGNMENT EXPRESSIONS

EXPRESSION	COMMENT
a = b = 1	a = (b = 1)
(c = cin.get()) != EOF	Assignment expression used in a relational expression
a += b	Shorthand for a = a + b
a *op*= b	Shorthand for a = a *op* b Allowable *ops*: +, -, *, /, %, <<, >>, &, ^, |

To see assignment expressions in action, let's consider a function that computes the sum of the squares of the first n odd integers:

```
int sum_squares(int n)        // n is assumed positive
{   int sum = 1, i = 1;
    n *= 2;                    // n = n * 2
    while ( (i += 2) < n )
        sum += (i * i);
    return(sum);
}
```

In sum_squares, the assumption is made that the argument n is positive. The while loop is completely bypassed for the case $n = 1$. The parentheses around i += 2 in the while condition are necessary because assignment operators have lower precedence than almost all other operators. For the same reason, the parentheses around i * i are unnecessary but included for readability.

1.9.4   Bitwise Operations

There is also a group of operators for dealing with data at the bit level. These include << (left-shift) and >> (right-shift) as well as the bitwise logical operators & (and), | (or), ~ (not), and ^ (exclusive or). The bitwise operators take only operands of integer types. Table 1.9 shows the available bitwise operations where the *ones complement* is obtained by flipping each and every bit of an integer.

Unlike increment and decrement operators, bitwise operations do not alter their operands. Thus, j = i << 4 produces an integer value equal to left-shifting i by 4 bits without damaging the contents of i. If modifying i is what you actually desire, use

```
i <<= 4;
```

TABLE 1.9   **INTEGER BITWISE EXPRESSIONS**

EXPRESSION	COMMENT
n & 017	Bitwise *and*; value is n with all but lower 4 bits masked away
i | j	Bitwise i *or* j
i ^ j	Bitwise i *exclusive or* j
i << 4	Value is left-shift i by 4 bits
j >> 5	Value is right-shift j by 5 bits
~n	Ones complement of n

A 1-bit left-shift on an integer is normally equivalent to multiplying by 2. Thus, the preceding operation results in a value 16 times that of i.

Bitwise operations provide an alternative way to compute the next tab stop. By zeroing out the last 3 bits of the current column position c, you can use the expression

```
(c & ~07) + 8
```

to produce the position of the next tab stop. The bit pattern ~07 (bitwise not that is applied to octal 7) is all ones except the lowest 3 bits. It is used as a *mask* by the bitwise & operation to produce the same value as c but with the last 3 bits zeroed out.

Bitwise operations not only allow manipulations at the bit level. They also provide an efficient way to perform certain arithmetic operations involving positive or unsigned integers. For example, left-shifting the number 3 by 1 bit gives 6. Conversely, right-shifting 6 by 1 bit gives 3.

1.9.5   Functions and Operators in C++

Note that the operators >> and << perform bitwise shifting as well as input/ouput. C++ supports *function overloading* and *operator overloading*, assigning multiple duties to functions and operators. Thus, a function/operator under the same name can perform different duties, depending on what arguments it receives. Take the left-shift operator << for example. It can perform the added duty of sending data to an output stream object such as cout. The C++ compiler knows which one of the multiple duties an overloaded operator should perform by examining the declared types of the operator's operands.

For an operator to be overloaded, at least one of its operands must be an object (of user-defined type). Hence, the meaning of an operator in relation to

C++ built-in types cannot be changed by overloading, which is a reasonable policy. How to define classes and how to create objects are topics yet to be covered — not to mention overloading operators. But all of this will be explained as we proceed.

Just as an operator is overloaded, so also can the same function name be overloaded to perform different duties (Section 3.5). The ability to overload can significantly reduce the number of functions, with different and often difficult-to-remember names, in a software system. Overloading also makes it easier to write *generic code*, routines that work for many different data types. These points will become clearer as your experience with OOP increases.

1.10 ENUMERATIONS

The *enumeration type* is a user-defined integer type consisting of a number of symbolic names, known as *enumerators*, representing constant integer values. Enumeration provides a convenient way to associate symbolic names to integer constants.

The declaration enum is used to establish a new enumeration type:

```
enum name { symbol₁[ = val₁],
            symbol₂[ = val₂],
            ...
          };
```

The declaration establishes *name* as a new enum *tag*. The constant integer values val_1, val_2, and so on are optional. For example,

```
enum Days { MON=1, TUE=2, WED=3, THU=4, FRI=5, SAT=6, SUN=7};
```

declares the enum tag Days and defines the constant enumerators MON, TUE, and so on. The integer values of the enumerators are explicitly specified here. If unspecified, the enumerators are given consecutive integer values following the last specified entry or from zero. Thus,

```
enum Days { MON=1, TUE, WED, THU, FRI, SAT, SUN };
```

is an equivalent declaration of Days. The values of the enumerators do not have to be distinct, allowing declarations such as

```
enum Days { MON=1, TUE, WED, THU, FRI, SAT, SUN,
            mon=1, tue, wed, thu, fri, sat, sun};
```

Enumerators must be declared before they are used. Also, the names of the enumerators must be distinct from other identifiers in the same scope (Section 3.1). This means that having used MON in Days, you cannot, in the same scope, use MON again in another enumeration type—say, WeekDays—or use MON as a variable.

Once an enumeration tag is established, *enumeration variables* of that type can be declared and used. An enumeration variable should take on only the values defined in the enumeration type:

```
Days j = MON;
```

Thus, the enumeration variable j is an integer variable intended to take on only the values MON through SUN inclusive.

Here are a few more examples of enumeration types:

```
enum Boolean { NO, YES, FALSE=0, TRUE };    // NO = 0, YES = 1
enum white_space
{    SPACE = ´ ´,
     NEWLINE = ´\n´,
     TAB = ´\t´,
     RETURN = ´\r´};
```

Boolean values 1 and 0 are used in mathematical logic to represent true and false, respectively. Thus, the function string_match (Section 1.14), which returns 0 or 1, can be declared as

```
Boolean string_match(char str[], char line[])
{  ...
   ...
        return(YES);     // match
   ...
   return(NO);           // no match
}
```

Anonymous enumerations are declared by leaving out the name part. An anonymous enumeration is sometimes an alternative to #define constants (Section 12.4):

```
enum { TABLE_SIZE = 256,  TERMINATOR = -1 };
```

There are, however, significant differences between an enumeration constant and a symbolic constant established by #define. The latter is not restricted to representing integers and is effective in one file only, whereas the former must be an integer and obeys scope rules.

Without explicit type-casting (Section 3.12), an enumeration variable can be assigned only an enumerator. Thus,

```
Days j = 2;     // error; cannot convert int to Days
```

does not work. C++ does not automatically convert an integer to an enumerator, but converting an enumerator to an integer is automatic. In particular, arithmetic operations involving enumeration variables and/or constants are performed by first converting to integers. Thus,

```
int k = MON + WED;     // o.k.
```

works just fine.

1.11 \ ARRAYS

Basic Concepts

An array is composed of consecutive memory locations, *array cells*, each of which holds data of the same type. For example,

```
int b[10];
```

declares b an array and defines for it 10 cells, b[0] through b[9], each just large enough to hold a quantity of type int. Unlike some other languages, in C++, *array indexing goes from 0 to the dimension* −1. This is important to keep in mind. Here are some typical usages:

```
b[0] = 17;
n = b[i+1] - 13;
for (i = 0 ; i < 10 ; i++) b[i] = 0;
```

The array b can be declared and initialized to hold the first 10 prime numbers as follows:

```
int b[]={2,3,5,7,11,13,17,19,23,29};
```

When the array size is left unspecified, the C++ compiler figures out the dimension of b from the number of data items supplied. Figure 1.5 provides a graphical representation of the array b.

Once an array is created, its cells can be used to store and retrieve data of a given type. Cells are accessed using the index notation b[i], where each array cell can be thought of and treated as a separate variable. Thus, an array can be viewed as a set of subscripted variables.

FIGURE 1.5   THE INTEGER ARRAY b

b[0]	b[1]	b[2]	b[3]	b[4]	b[5]	b[6]	b[7]	b[8]	b[9]
2	3	5	7	11	13	17	19	23	29

Character Arrays

In C++, a character string, or simply *string*, is represented by a character array. The notation

```
"Happy Birthday"
```

specifies a string constant. Figure 1.6 shows the structure of an array containing this string. The special *null character* '\0' (BACKSLASH zero) is used to mark the end of a character string. The null character has an integer value of zero.

The array can be created using a sequence of assignments:

```
char str[15];       // declare str character array length 15
str[0] = 'H';
str[1] = 'a';
    .               // and so on
    .
    .
str[12] = 'a';
str[13] = 'y';
str[14] = '\0';     // string terminator
```

An easier way to perform such initialization uses the notation

```
char str[15] = {'H', 'a', ... , 'a', 'y', '\0'};
```

A much easier, but entirely equivalent, way is to initialize using the following shorthand notation:

```
char str[] = "Happy Birthday";    // convenient char array initialization
```

As before, the compiler figures out how large to make str in order to accommodate the character string and the extra terminator at the end.

To illustrate the usage of character strings, let's consider the function strequal(x,y), which returns 1 (for true) or 0 (for false), depending on whether the character strings x and y are equal or not:

```
int strequal(char x[], char y[])            // formal array parameters
{   int i = 0;
    if ( x == y ) return(1);                // same memory locations
    while (x[i] == y[i])
    {   if (x[i] == '\0') return (1);   // strings equal
```

FIGURE 1.6   A STRING AS A CHARACTER ARRAY

```
        i++;
    }
    return(0);                              // strings unequal
}
```

The header of strequal declares two formal array parameters, x and y. In general, the notation

type var[]

as part of the formal parameter list declares *var* an array of the given *type*.

Follow the code to see how strequal works. If the condition (x == y) is true, then x and y refer to the same memory location. This means that a string is being compared to itself and 1 can be returned immediately. If x and y point to different memory locations, they can still contain the same characters and be equal. So, we use a while loop to compare the individual characters to determine whether they are equal or not.

Now test strequal with the main program:

```
#include <iostream.h>

// put strequal here

int main()
{   char a[]= "abcde";
    char b[]= "abcde";
    char c[]= "abcd";
    if ( strequal(a,b) )
        cout << "a is equal to b\n";
    if ( ! strequal(b,c))                   // strings unequal
        cout << "b is not equal to c\n";
}
```

A handy-to-use set of string-manipulation library functions, including one that compares two strings, is available. These functions will be discussed in Section 6.1. You might want to check them out before you needlessly reinvent a string function that already exists.

1.12 POINTERS

Basic Concepts

A *pointer* is the address of the memory location where an object or a piece of data is stored. A pointer variable can be declared by preceding the variable name with *. Here are some examples:

```
int *i, *j;    // values of i and j are pointers to int
char *c;       // value of c is a pointer to char
long *k;       // value of k is a pointer to long int
float *x;      // value of x is a pointer to float
double *y;     // value of y is a pointer to double
```

The memory location where a variable stores its value is obtained by the *unary address-of operator* &. Thus,

```
int i = 512;
int *j;        // declare j to be an int pointer variable
j = &i;        // j is assigned the address of i
```

results in j being a pointer to where 512 is stored. To be specific, let's assume the value of i is stored at memory location 49132. The variable j then has the value 49132. To obtain the value 512 through j, we use the *unary value-of operator* *. For instance, *j + 2 gives 514. The notation *j is equivalent to a variable of type int. To illustrate this, consider

```
*j = 0;
```

This puts 0 where the value 512 was formerly, so i is now 0 also. The pointer concept is illustrated graphically in Figure 1.7.

Memory locations in a program are referenced relative to a starting location, and an address is usually, but not guaranteed to be, a value that can be stored in a single machine word.

Array Assignments

For an assignment u = v, normally the variable u gets a copy of the value of v. In C++, this is correct except for arrays. In fact, an array name — take b for instance — is actually a *constant pointer* to the first cell of the array. Therefore, the array name cannot be used as a variable on the left-hand side of an assignment. Hence, the following is incorrect:

```
int foo[10], b[10];
foo = b;               // incorrect; array name foo is not a variable
```

FIGURE 1.7   THE MEANING OF A POINTER

Pointer variable j   Variable i

| *address* | | *value* |

To make an array assignment, we need a pointer variable of the correct type on the left-hand side of the assignment. To assign b to a variable x, we use the code

```
int *x;
x = b;     // array assignment is by pointer
```

Now the elements of b can also be accessed via x. Keep in mind that the cells of the array b are still where they were, only now x can also access them. Thus,

```
x[3] = 96;
```

will result in b[3] containing 96 as well.

Similarly, when an array name is used in a function call, a pointer to the first cell is passed to the called function.

1.13 \ AN EXAMPLE

The readline function reads a line from standard input, stores the line in a character array, and returns the length of the line. This function will be useful in other programs to obtain user input.

```
int readline(char s[], int len)     // len is length of array s
{      char c = '\0';
       int i = 0;
       len--;                         // leaving room at the end
       while ( i < len && cin.get(c) && c != '\n' )
              s[i++] = c;
       if (c == '\n') s[i++] = c;
       s[i] = '\0';                   // string terminator
       return(i);
}
```

The while condition in readline is the most complicated expression we have encountered so far. It consists of three conditions connected by two logical operators. The effect is to read characters into the array s until either the array is full, the end of file is reached, or a '\n' is read. After the while, the '\n', if any, is deposited into the array, and then the string terminator '\0' is added at the end. The number i of actual characters read is then returned.

Normally, a text file, including that supplied through the keyboard, consists of complete lines, each terminated by a '\n' character. The last line in the file is no exception. The readline function makes this assumption. Therefore, the returned value is always the number of characters read even when end of file is reached.

The file readline.C can be established as follows:

```
#include <iostream.h>
const int SIZE = 100;

// put definition of readline here

int main()
{       char line[SIZE];
        int n;
        while ((n = readline(line, SIZE)) > 0)
            cout << "n=" << n << "\t line=" << line;
        return(0);
}
```

Here the C++ const declaration (Section 3.8) is used to establish a constant identifier SIZE for the quantity 100. A const identifier is used in place of the actual constant in the source code. Assignment to a const identifier is not allowed. Do not use numeric constants in programs; use constant identifiers with meaningful names instead. This approach not only makes programs easier to understand but also allows you to modify every occurrence of a constant by simply changing the const definition.

Compile and run the program to get an output looking something like this:

```
n=8     line=ABC DEF
n=12    line=123 456 789
```

1.14 \ ITERATION CONTROL

Iteration is the repeated execution of a set of statements in a program. Such repetitions make it possible for a short program to perform a very large number of operations. The constructs while, for, and do-while are used to perform iterations.

An iteration is normally specified by the following components:

1. *Control variables:* One or more variables that take on new values for each successive repetition.

2. *Successor statements:* One or more statements that assign new values to the control variables in preparation for the next repetition.

3. *Loop body:* A sequence of zero or more statements that is executed once for each repetition.

4. *Continuation condition:* A logical or relational expression tested before or after each repetition. If the condition is true, then the next repetition is performed; otherwise, control flows to the program statement just after the iteration construct.

In addition to normal termination via item 4, the loop body may contain statements that cause *early termination* of the iteration. An example is the function in_string, which determines whether a string contains a particular character:

```
int in_string(char c, char *str)
{     int i = 0;
      while (str[i] != '\0')
      {   if (str[i] == c) return(1);      // return true
          i++;
      }
      return(0);                           // return false
}
```

The control variable i, initially 0, is incremented by 1 for each repetition. Normal termination comes when the string str has been completely examined and no match for c has been found. Early termination via the return statement occurs as soon as a match for c is found in str. Here are a couple of calls to this function:

```
in_string('g', "abcdefgh");
in_string('/', filename);
```

A shorter implementation of in_string uses the for construct:

```
int in_string(char c, char *str)
{     for (int i = 0 ; str[i] != '\0' ; i++)
          if (str[i] == c) return(1);
      return(0);
}
```

The break and continue Statements

In the in_string example, we used the return to terminate an iteration early. This technique is restrictive and cannot be used to break out of an iteration without causing the entire function to return. The break statement is used in such situations. When break is executed, control transfers immediately to the first statement after the current iteration. An application of break is found in the function monotonic, which examines an integer array and returns 1 or 0, depending on whether the sequence of integers is *monotonic* or not. A sequence of values is monotonically increasing if each value is no smaller than the previous one. Similarly, a sequence is monotonically decreasing if each value is no larger than the preceding one.

```
int monotonic(int a[], int n)              // n is dimension of a
{     for (int i = 0 ; i < n - 1 ; i++)
```

```
            if (a[i+1] < a[i]) break;
        if (i == n - 1) return(1);              // increasing
        for (i = 0 ; i < n - 1 ; i++)
            if (a[i+1] > a[i]) return(0);
        return(1);                              // decreasing
}
```

Try this program with various increasing, decreasing, repeating, length-one, and other sequences of integers.

The continue statement is similar to break. But, instead of breaking out of a loop, continue *goes to the end of the loop body*. Within while or do-while, this means that control transfers immediately to the test-condition part. Inside for, it transfers to the increment step. In other words, continue skips the rest of the loop body to reach the loop control of the next repetition. To demonstrate how this can be convenient, let's consider string_match, a function that determines whether a given character string, str, is contained in another character string, line. The function returns 1, 0, or −1 for true, false, or error, respectively.

```
int string_match(char str[], char line[])
{   if ( str[0] == '\0')              // str is empty
    {   cerr << "string_match: empty match string\n";
        return(-1);
    }
    for (int i = 0 ; line[i] != '\0' ; i++)
    {   if ( line[i] != str[0] )     // first char is different
            continue;                // skip rest of loop body

        // compare remaining characters
        // until first mismatch or end of string
        for ( int j = i + 1, k = 1;
                line[j]==str[k] && str[k] != '\0';
                j++, k++
            ) { }

        if ( str[k] == '\0')         // end of str is reached
            return(1);               // successful match
        else if (line[j] == '\0')    // end of line is reached
            return(0);               // no match possible anymore
    }
    return(0);                       // failed to match
}
```

The function string_match uses a straightforward strategy. The string str is matched, in turn, with a series of substrings starting at line[0], line[1], and so on. A successful match returns the value 1. Otherwise, the next substring is used. The value 0 is returned when there are no more substrings to match with str.

In string_match, a nested for loop is employed. The outer for iterates over the substrings line[0], line[1], and so on. If the first character of the substring does not match str[0], the program skips the rest of the loop body and continues with the next substring.

The inner for is interesting because it has an empty body and two loop-control variables, j and k. Also, the *comma operator* (,) is used in the increment expression. Two expressions connected by a comma become one expression whose value and type are those of the second expression. Expressions connected by commas are evaluated sequentially from left to right. Such a sequence of expressions can be used anywhere a single expression can.

The algorithm used in string_match is unsophisticated and inefficient. One immediate improvement is to stop matching and return 0 as soon as the substring becomes shorter than str because no further match is possible. Try to implement this modification.

The goto Statement and Labels

Structured programming advocates avoiding the arbitrary transfer of control provided by the goto statement. In fact, it is possible to write code without ever using goto. Experts generally agree that goto should be used rarely if at all. However, sometimes goto can be used to advantage. Mainly, it is useful in breaking out of a deeply nested loop because break gets you out of only the immediately enclosing loop.

```
while ( ... )
   while ( ... )
   {
       . . .
       for ( ... )
       {
           ...
           if ( /* something wrong */ ) goto error;
           ...
       }
   }

   . . .

return( ... );
error:    // take care of errors here
```

The general form of the command is as follows:

goto *label*;   (label must be in the same function)

A *label*, such as error followed by a colon (:), is placed in front of the target statement for control transfer. A goto label has the same form as a variable and can be attached to any statement in the same function as the goto. A label must be unique, appearing in only one place, although it can have several jumps to it.

1.15 \ Multiple Choice

While the if ... else if ... else construct remains the general-purpose decision-making mechanism, the switch statement provides a very handy way to select among a set of predefined choices. The syntax is as follows:

```
switch ( expression )
{
      case constant-expr1 :
          statements
      case constant-expr2 :
          statements

      default:
          statements
}
```

The switch construct is like a structured multiple goto. The switching *expression* is evaluated first. The resulting value is matched against each integer-valued constant case label. In a switch, all case labels must be distinct. Control is transferred to the matching case or to the default if nothing matches. There is no sequential, case-by-case matching at run time; control is transferred directly. If the optional default case label is not given and if nothing matches, the execution of switch is successfully completed.

Following control transfer to a case label, the statements at the selected label *and all statements under other case labels after it* will be executed in sequence. This behavior is called *fall through*, and it makes switch very different from a multiple if. The break statement can also be used to break out of the switch statement. It is often the last statement for each case in order to prevent fall through. With fall through completely prevented, the order in which the case labels are given becomes unimportant. At each case label, there can be zero, one, or more statements. This allows several case labels to precede one group of statements, making it convenient for certain situations.

Experiment with the following test program to familiarize yourself with these concepts about switch:

```cpp
int main()
{    int j = 4;
     cout << "1: switch(" << j << ")\n";
     switch(j)
     {   case 1:
         case 3:   cout << "A: case 1 or 3\n";
         case 5:   cout << "B: case 5\n";
         default:  cout << "C: case default\n";    // deliberate
         case 2:   cout << "D: case 2\n";
     }
     j = 2;
     cout << "2: switch(" << j << ")\n";
     switch(j)
     {   case 5:   cout << "E: case 5\n";
         default:  cout << "F: case default\n";
         case 2:   cout << "G: case 2\n";
     }
     return(0);
}
```

The output produced is as follows:

```
1: switch(4)
C: case default
D: case 2
2: switch(2)
G: case 2
```

1.16 \ SUMMARY

Functions and objects are the basic building blocks of a C++ program. Functions codify procedures, while classes define independent computing agents called *objects* (introduced in Chapter 2). The source code of a program may involve many functions and classes contained in one or more files. Every program contains the special function main, which is the entry point of the program. Any program that uses the standard I/O objects cin, cout, and cerr should include the header <iostream.h>.

All items such as functions and variables must be declared before use. C++ is a language with strong typing: Every quantity has a type and the compiler checks for type correctness in a program. There are only four basic data types:

int, char, float, and double. Type qualifiers like short, long, and unsigned are used to obtain size and sign variations of these basic types.

An array is a sequence of memory locations to store data of a given type. A character string is an array of characters terminated by ´\0´. Array elements are indexed starting from zero. Memory locations where data of a particular type is stored are represented by pointers. There is a close relationship between pointers and arrays.

Constants (regular or enum) and variables are combined by operators to form expressions. There are arithmetic, relational, logical, increment and decrement, assignment, and bitwise operators. There is no power operator for exponentiation. Additionally, there is the ternary conditional operator (?:). Frequently used control-flow statements include if, while, for and do-while, break, continue, and switch.

C++ supports function and operator overloading, assigning multiple meanings to the same function or operator. Built-in operators can be overloaded to work with objects in ways specified by the programmer. Use of the operators >> and << for I/O is an example of operator overloading.

EXERCISES

1. Write a simple main program to display some single characters, strings, integers, and floating-point numbers using the cout object.

2. Certain identifiers are reserved by C++ and cannot be used for other purposes. Name 10 reserved words in C++.

3. Take the factorial function and add a check to detect any negative input. If the argument is negative, an error message is displayed using cerr and the value zero is returned.

4. Explain why calling factorial(j) repeatedly with j being 0, 1, 2, . . . is very inefficient. Write a more efficient function to produce a list of factorial values.

5. Write a program expand.C that replaces all TAB characters in its standard input (cin) by an equivalent number of spaces and sends the result to standard output (cout). (*Hint:* Follow the example lowercase.C.) You may assume that tab stops are eight characters apart.

6. Consider the function readline. What would happen if the line read is longer than the size of the array s? Add a check for this condition and insert the appropriate error-handling code for readline.

7. Consider the bitwise shift operations of integer quantities. In what exact situations do the left- and right-shift operations actually correspond to multiplication and division by 2?

8. Write a function `octal_display(int n)` that displays the integer n in octal notation.

9. Consider the `octal_display` function in Exercise 8. Rewrite the function to use bitwise operations to achieve the modulo-8 and the divide-by-8 operations.

10. Examine the following function definition and spot any syntax problems. Try to compile it and see what your compiler says. Explain in detail the source of any error.

```
int myabs(int a)
{   if (a >= 0)
      {   return(a); };
    else
      {   return(-a); };
}
```

11. Write a function `string_cmp` that compares two strings x and y. The returned value is 1, 0, or −1, depending on whether x is greater than, equal to, or less than y, respectively, using lexicographic (dictionary) ordering.

12. Write a function `is_leap_year` that takes an integer year and returns zero if false and nonzero if true. (*Hint:* Use the % operator.)

13. Write a program to count the number of decimal digits in any integer given to the program through `cin`.

14. When reading from `cin`, end of file is normally reached when the user types a control-D (or a control-Z or some other system-dependent character) at the beginning of a line. Find out what the convention is on your system.

15. A *bitonic* sequence of integers consists of one monotonic sequence of zero or more elements followed by another. For example, both 2,2,3,4,3,2 and 4,3,1,2,7 are bitonic. Using the `monotonic` function in Section 1.14 as a model, write a `bitonic` function.

16. Using `switch`, write a program to count the number of SPACE, TAB, NEWLINE, and FORMFEED characters in a file.

C++ Primer
Part II: Overview

This chapter completes the two-part C++ primer. By building on the basics in Chapter 1, an overview of C++ is presented and enough aspects of the language are covered so that you can write interesting and complete programs. Still, many details are left for later chapters.

Classes and objects are key C++ constructs that support data abstraction and encapsulation, two of the most central techniques of OOP. These concepts are introduced here. A bank account example is used to illustrate the ideas in a clear and intuitive manner and to show how classes and objects are defined and used.

Argument passing in function calls is described, covering passing by value and passing by reference in detail. The inline function feature used to avoid function call overhead is also introduced. The way a C++ program receives arguments from its invoking environment is also described. This information helps you in writing programs that receive arguments and options given to the program when it is first invoked.

Object-oriented problem solving involves modeling interacting objects in a given problem. The methodology is demonstrated by solving a simple problem in plane geometry. The C++ class and objects are put to use in the solution. A complete C++ program is given.

Input and output operations are critical for programming. Enough C++ input and output to the terminal and to files are introduced to give you a good start. Also included are error-handling techniques, source code formatting suggestions, and effective object-oriented thinking in C++.

2.1 \ DATA ABSTRACTION AND ENCAPSULATION

One of the most central features of OOP is the division of the whole program into smaller autonomous entities, called *objects*, with well-defined interactions. This feature significantly reduces overall complexity and helps the quality of the program in many different ways. An object organizes data and related operations into a *black box*, which hides the internal data structures, representations, and procedures from outside view. A data structure is *concrete* when its exact details are known. Traditional programming approaches depend heavily on concrete data. OOP, on the other hand, emphasizes *data abstraction* and encourages hiding the details of data by presenting only the data's *behavior*. For example, if you do not know the details of the construction of a car, you can still drive it effectively if you know behavior such as "steering clockwise makes the car turn right." This leaves the implementation of steering to the black box, which can use one of several alternatives: regular, power-assisted, rack-and-pinion, and so on. In addition to structures, the object also contains mechanisms, or procedures, that are necessary to operate the structures. These procedures are *attached* to the structures to form one inseparable unit. This technique is called *encapsulation*.

2.1.1   Classes and Objects

The C++ *class* construct supports data abstraction and encapsulation. A class describes the construction of an object and serves as a blueprint to build objects. It specifies the internal workings as well as the external interface of an object. A class has a name, or *tag*, and specifies *members* belonging to the class that may be data, functions, or objects. Once a class is defined, the class name becomes a new data type and is used to declare variables of that type. A class-type variable is an *instance* of a class and is called an *object* of that class.

To begin, let's consider a simplified class representing bank accounts:

```
////////    File Account.h    ////////

class Account                      // class name
{ public:
      Account(unsigned n, double b); // constructor
      void   deposit(double amt);   // deposit amt into this account
      int    withdraw(double amt);  // withdraw amt from this account
      double balance();             // balance inquiry
      /* other public members */
    private:
      unsigned  acct_no;            // account number
```

```
    double    acct_bal;              // current balance
    /* other private members */
};
```

Class names should appear as *capitalized nouns*, which is the style recommended and followed in this book. Here the class Account is declared and takes the following general form:

```
class Name
{
      class body
};
```

If you are new to C++, you may sometimes forget the final semicolon in a class declaration. This can cause many unpleasant errors. One way to remember the semicolon is to type in the form class *Name* {   }; before you insert the *class body*, which in itself can be very involved.

The class body consists of declarations for data members, function members, or both. Member declarations are supplied in the usual way — namely, with declarations and function prototypes. However, *no initializers are allowed for data member declarations*. Except for overloading, all members must have distinct names. The class Account contains the data members

```
unsigned  acct_no;          // account number
double    acct_bal;         // current balance
```

which are the identification number and current balance of a bank account. Function prototypes in a class definition specify member functions of the class. For example,

```
void deposit(double amt);
```

declares deposit to be a member function. The actual code for member functions is usually defined in a separate implementation file.

2.1.2   Information Hiding and Member Access Control

An object can be thought of as an independent computing agent (a tiny computer) with its own storage and instruction set. The data members define the storage, and the function members provide the instruction set.

The C++ class construct also specifies access control to its members. In the class definition, members are sectioned into groups to achieve information hiding:

- *Public members* of an object can be accessed by all functions in a
  program.

• *Private members* of an object can be accessed only by member functions of the same class.

All a user, or *client*, of a class needs to know is the public interface (Figure 2.1). As long as the public members are well documented, there is no need to know any implementation details. In the case of deposit, all that matters is putting a given amount, amt, into the account. Thus, knowledge of internal details is confined to member functions. The class now provides Account as an *abstract data type*.

An object embodies the abstract data item. Values stored in an object constitute its internal *state*, and public members of an object form its interface to the outside (other functions and objects). Thereby, an object *encapsulates* (envelops) a set of data and function members. The encapsulating object is called the *host object* of its members.

Although all members, function or data, are thought of as being contained within each individual object, C++ achieves this effect without having to replicate the member functions. The memory required for each object is essentially for storing the data members.

The Account data members acct_no and acct_bal are put in the private section, so their access is limited to member functions. No operations other than those specifically provided by the Account class can be performed on these private quantities. In designing a class, you, the OO programmer, must design the public/private grouping to support effective use and to maximize information hiding.

FIGURE 2.1   AN OBJECT

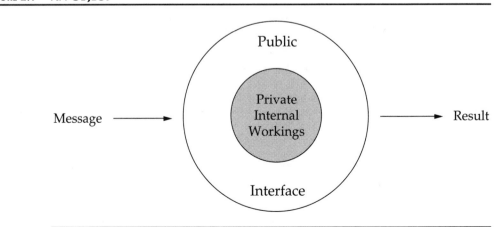

2.1.3   Member Reference Notations

Once a class is declared, the class name can be used to declare objects. For example, variables of type Account can be declared as follows:

```
Account sally(5551234, 600.0);    // object sally
Account bob(5556789, 540.0);      // object bob
```

The variables sally and bob are Account objects, each with a given account number and a beginning balance (Section 2.1.5).

We already know that not every member of an object is accessible from the outside. When permitted, the members of an object are accessed with the *dot* (.), or *member-of*, operator. For example,

```
bob.acct_bal -= 30.50;           // decrease bob's balance            (1)
sally.acct_bal += 10.75;         // increase sally's balance          (2)
sally.deposit(25.60);            // deposit into Account object sally
double bal = sally.balance();    // retrieve balance of Account object sally
sally.withdraw(25.0);            // take 25 out of Account object sally
```

Because acct_bal is a private member, the assignments on lines 1 and 2 can be used only by member functions of Account.

Clearly, the general syntax to reference a member is

object.member

Pointers to Class Objects

Pointers to class objects are also very useful. For example, the pointer variable acnt_ptr

```
Account* acnt_ptr = &bob;        // pointer to object bob
```

is initialized to point to the Account object bob. But it can also be assigned another value:

```
acnt_ptr = &sally;               // now *acnt_ptr is sally
```

When you are dealing with a pointer to an object, the members can be referenced directly through the pointer with the -> operator:

objptr -> member

This notation is equivalent to *(*objptr).member*. An example is

```
acnt_ptr->deposit(11.79);        // deposit into Account sally
```

2.1.4   Class Member Functions

Generally, a class declaration is kept in a header file, which can be included by any file that wishes to use objects of the class. For example, the declaration for Account can be put in the header file Account.h. Member functions of a given class are usually defined in a separate .C file. For instance, the Account.C file begins with

```
///////    File: Account.C    ///////
#include  "Account.h"

void Account::deposit(double amt)
{   if ( amt > 0 )
        acct_bal += amt;
}
```

While the file-inclusion notation

```
#include <iostream.h>
```

specifies a system-supplied header file, the notation

```
#include  "Account.h"
```

is used for a header file written by a user (Section 12.3).

The notation Account::deposit puts the name deposit within the scope (Section 3.1) of the class Account, making it a member function. The double colon (::) is the *scope operator*. If Account:: is not placed in front of the function name, then it is just a regular function, not a member of class Account.

Note that deposit() takes only one argument, the amt to be deposited. There is no mention of the target account to make the deposit. As a member function, deposit is always attached to a specific account when it is called. In OOP, member functions are not pure procedures, but procedures attached to an object, such as an accelerator to a car. There is never a need to worry about which car you are driving when you depress the accelerator. To emphasize the point, some OOP literature refers to attached procedures as *methods* and to invoking such procedures as *passing a message* to an object. You should be aware of such widely understood OOP terms, even though these particular phrases will be used only occasionally in the C++ context.

Because deposit is a member function, it can access other members in the host object (acct_bal for example) directly, without using the *object.member* notation. All members in a class are accessible by member functions.

2.1.5   Constructors

In the class Account, the member function named Account is a special member. In general, a member function with the same name as the class itself is called a *constructor* and is treated differently from other member functions. The purpose of a constructor is to provide user-defined initialization when an object of the class is first established. For example, the declaration

```
Account bob(5556789, 540.0);      // object bob
```

allocates space for an Account object bob and passes the values in parentheses to the constructor Account(unsigned, double), defined in the file Account.C as

```
Account::Account(unsigned id, double amt)
{   acct_no = id;
    if ( amt > 0 ) acct_bal = amt;
}
```

to provide the desired initialization of the data members acct_no and acct_bal. No return type of any kind is allowed in declaring a constructor, which should never return a value.

At this point, you should have enough information to write the member functions withdraw and balance yourself.

2.2 \ FUNCTION CALLS AND ARGUMENT PASSING

A function is either unattached or encapsulated in a class. The function header specifies the number and type of *formal parameters* required. In C++, a function is identified not only by its name but also by its formal parameter list. Thus, the same function name may be *defined more than once* with different formal parameters. This is known as *function overloading* (Section 3.5).

When a function is called, the correct number and type of arguments must be supplied. The arguments in the function call are known as the *actual arguments*, or simply *arguments*. The definition of factorial has a formal parameter n. In the function call factorial(j), the variable j becomes the actual argument. When a function call is executed, the data or objects referenced by the actual arguments are bound to the formal parameters and can be used in the body of the function. This binding is called *argument passing*.

When a function with more than one argument is called, *there is no guarantee of the order in which arguments are evaluated*. Therefore, no code should depend on any specific order of argument evaluation. Thus, the function call

```
power(i++, i);             // incorrect usage
```

is wrong because the result depends on which of the two arguments is evaluated first. You should use instead something like this:

```
i++;
power(i-1, i);
```

Parameters in a function header are formal in the sense that any name can be used for them without changing the meaning of the function. The same situation is found in mathematics where the notations $f(x) = x^2$ and $f(y) = y^2$ define the same function.

Formal parameters are local to a function. When a function call is made, a copy of the value of the actual argument is passed to the corresponding formal parameter. In other words, arguments are *passed by value*. With pass by value, a function can work only on copies of the actual arguments, not on the actual arguments themselves. Therefore, the actual arguments will have the same values before and after the function call.

When necessary, it is possible to modify data in the calling function. One way to achieve this is by passing *pointers* as actual arguments. Recall that a pointer is the memory location, or address, of an object or a piece of data. Once the called function gets the address, it can proceed to modify information stored at that address. As a result, data in the calling function is altered indirectly.

Unlike basic data types and objects, there is no automatic copying of the elements in an array when it is passed as an argument. Instead, the address of its first element is passed. (This is the value of the array name.) Therefore, the formal array parameter becomes another name by which the same array elements can be accessed.

Reference Parameters

Pass by value can be expensive if the arguments represent large data objects. It is possible to pass function arguments without copying with *pass by reference*. C++ supports *reference* formal parameters for functions. A reference parameter is an alias for the actual argument passed (without copying) in a function call. An assignment to a reference parameter actually assigns a value to the corresponding actual argument. A reference parameter is used most often for the following purposes:

1. To pass an argument without making a copy of it (which is more efficient than pass by value).
2. To allow the called function to modify the actual argument.
3. To collect data produced by the called function.

To declare a reference parameter in a function header, you put the character & after the type name and in front the parameter name. For example, the function

```
void swap(int& a, int& b)
{   int tmp = b;
    b = a;
    a = tmp;
}
```

uses two int reference parameters, a and b, to interchange the values of its actual arguments. In general, the & before a parameter declares a reference and is not to be confused with the address-of operator used in expressions. The line

```
int tmp = b;
```

may look a little suspicious at first because tmp is of type int but b is of type int&. It simply means that tmp gets the value of the actual argument represented by the int reference b. Thus, the following code works:

```
int r = 7, s = 11;
swap(r, s);        // now r is 11 and s is 7
```

The values are switched because a and b are reference parameters that become aliases for r and s, respectively, when swap is called. In other words, the effect of the call swap(r,s) is

```
int tmp = s;
s = r;
r = tmp;
```

Also, recall the cin.get(c) usage. It works because cin.get takes a reference parameter (char& c). A reference parameter is one form of the C++ *reference*, a feature explained in Section 3.7.

2.2.1   Inline Functions

The C++ coding style sometimes calls for defining many small functions that are very simple. For such small functions, function call *overhead*, the argument passing and the value-returning activities associated with a function call, becomes significant compared to the amount of time spent in the called function. To reduce this overhead and to increase code efficiency, C++ allows you to declare functions inline. For example,

```
inline int MAX(int a, int b)
        { return (a > b ? a : b); }

inline double ABS(double a)
        { return (a > 0 ? a : -a); }
```

A call to an inline function is *expanded* by the compiler so that the effective code is substituted at the place of call and run-time function call overhead is avoided. An inline specifier advises the compiler to make an inline expansion if possible. An implementation may expand only inline functions containing straight-line code with only a few statements. Usually, no conditionals (if), loops (while, for), or other branching statements are allowed. In most situations, these limitations coincide with good programming practices.

2.3 \ COMMAND-LINE ARGUMENTS

The main function is special in C++ because it marks the starting point for program execution and is not called by other functions in the program. However, it is possible to supply arguments to a C++ program when it is invoked. The *command-line arguments* are passed as character strings to the function main.

A main function expecting arguments is normally declared as follows:

```
int main(int argc, char *argv[])
```

The parameter argc is an integer. The notation

```
char *argv[]
```

declares the formal array parameter argv as having elements of type char * (character pointer). In other words, each of the arguments argv[0], argv[1], . . . , argv[argc-1] is a character pointer. The meanings of the formal arguments argc and argv are as follows:

argc   The number of command-line arguments, including command name
argv[n]   A pointer to the *n*th command-line argument as a character string

If the command name is cmd and it is invoked as

```
cmd    arg1 arg2
```

then

argc   Is 3
argv[0]   Points to the command name cmd
argv[1]   Points to the string *arg1*
argv[2]   Points to the string *arg2*
argv[3]   Is 0 (NULL)

The parameters for the function main can be omitted if they are not needed.

Now let's consider a program that receives command-line arguments. To keep it simple, all the program does is echo the command-line arguments to standard output:

```
///////   the echo command   ///////
#include <iostream.h>

int main(int argc, char *argv[])
{     int i = 1;                  // begin with 1
      while (i < argc)
          cout << argv[i++]       // output string
              << " ";             // output SPACE
      cout << "\n";               // terminate output line
      return(0);
}
```

The program displays each entry of argv except argv[0]. To separate the strings, the program displays a SPACE after each argv[i], and the last argument is followed by a NEWLINE.

Note that main is declared to return an int and the last statement of main is

```
return(0);
```

The return value of main indicates, to the invoker of the program, whether the program executed successfully and terminated normally. This value is referred to as the *exit status*. For example, on UNIX systems, a zero exit status indicates successful or normal execution of the program, while a nonzero (usually positive) exit status indicates abnormal termination. Thus, it is advisable to always use a return statement in the main program, even though it would work without one.

2.4 \ PROBLEM SOLVING WITH OBJECTS

The purpose of OOP is to solve problems better with object orientation. To illustrate what this means in a simple way, let's consider a problem from plane geometry: Given four vertices A, B, C, and D in the x–y plane, determine whether $ABCD$ is a rectangle.

Clearly, one direct way to make the determination is to decide whether the neighboring sides of $ABCD$ are all mutually perpendicular. An ad hoc procedure could be written for this purpose, and the problem would be solved. But this approach is the traditional procedure-oriented one.

The OO approach first identifies the interacting objects in the problem domain. Here the objects are the vertices and the sides. The sides are determined by the vertices, and the orthogonal properties of neighboring sides lead to the solution. Further analysis leads us to the identification of a vector as the object needed because it can represent a vertex or a side. Thus, for the OO solution of the given problem, a Vector class is first established.

2.4.1 A Simple Vector Class

Vectors in two-dimensional space are familiar geometric objects. A vector **v** has an *x* component and a *y* component:

$$\mathbf{v} = (x, y)$$

Vectors also have well-defined arithmetic and other kinds of operations.

Next, a class Vector is defined to model two-dimensional vectors:

```
///////   File: Vector.h   ///////

class Vector                    // class name
{ public:
    Vector() {}                 // default constructor
    Vector(float a, float b);   // constructor overloaded
    Vector operator-(Vector a); // operator overloading
    float  inner(Vector a);     // vector inner product
    int    nonzero();           // host vector nonzero
    void   display();           // displays host vector
    /* other members not shown */
  private:
    float x, y;                 // data members
};
```

For the class Vector, there are two private data members:

```
float  x, y;
```

They represent the *x*- and *y*-direction components of a vector. In addition, there are several public member functions. The member function inner

```
float inner(Vector a);
```

receives a Vector object argument and returns a float value. The actual code for inner is defined in the file Vector.C:

```
///////   File: Vector.C   ///////
#include   "Vector.h"
#include   <iostream.h>

float Vector::inner(Vector a)
{  return(x * a.x + y * a.y);   }

int Vector::nonzero()
{  return ( x != 0.0 || y != 0.0 ); }
```

Again, because inner is a member function, it is allowed to access the private members x, y (in the host object) and a.x, a.y (in object a). Usually, data and function members can be accessed only through an established object of the class. For example,

```
Vector u(2.0, 3.0), v(4.0, 5.0);
u.inner(v);
```

computes the inner product of the vectors u (host object of inner) and v (argument to inner). Here the Vector v is passed to the member function inner of the object u. Because the data in the host object (u in this case) are already available, inner requires only one argument. The member function nonzero is simple. It tests whether the host vector is a zero vector.

An object should normally know how to display itself. This can usually be done by defining a member function display. For Vector, it can be a function

```
void Vector::display()
{     cout << "(" << x << ",    "
          << y << ")";
}
```

in the file Vector.C. Thus, the code

```
v.display();
```

produces the display

```
(4.0,  5.0)
```

2.4.2 The Default Constructor

The Vector constructor is overloaded as constructors usually are:

```
Vector::Vector(float a, float b)
{   x = a;
    y = b;
}
```

This version provides the desired initialization of the data members x and y.

The second constructor of Vector takes no arguments and does nothing. A constructor that takes no arguments must be present to allow the usage

```
Vector u;
```

where no initialization is intended. The no-args constructor is referred to as the *default constructor*. Two points can be made about supplying default constructors:

1. If a class defines no constructor at all, then a default constructor that does nothing is supplied automatically.

2. If a class defines any constructor, then no default constructor is automatically supplied. This is fine if the default constructor is not needed. However, if it is needed, an appropriate one must be given explicitly.

One trap that a C++ beginner may fall into is the use of

```
Vector u();    // warning
```

to declare u as an object. This code instead declares u as a function returning a Vector value.

Note that the Vector default constructor is completely defined in the class declaration rather than merely being declared with a function prototype. Functions included in this way are automatically inline (Section 2.2.1) for added efficiency.

Overloading the '–' Operator

The Vector member function operator– supplies a procedure for subtracting any given Vector from the host object and returns a difference Vector. Specifically, you are overloading the subtraction operator –. Here is its definition:

```
Vector Vector::operator-(Vector a)
{    Vector tmp;
     tmp.x = x - a.x;
     tmp.y = y - a.y;
     return(tmp);
}
```

To subtract vector w from v, either the long notation

```
u = v.operator-(w);    // long
```

or the short notation

```
u = v - w;             // short
```

can be used. The shorter code is transformed into the long form by the C++ compiler. The short notation gives the appearance that the built-in – operator now works for Vector objects. This is the intended effect of operator overloading.

The OO Solution

Now that we have the Vector.h and Vector.C files in place, we can construct a solution for the given problem that makes use of the Vector class. The approach is simple:

1. Represent the given vertices *A*, *B*, *C*, and *D* as four Vector objects.
2. Subtract neighboring vertices (vectors) to get the sides that are again vectors.
3. Determine perpendicularity from the inner product of neighboring sides.

We first need a function to test orthogonality:

```
/////// File: rect.C ///////
#include <iostream.h>
#include "Vector.h"

inline float ABS(float x)
     { return (x > 0 ? x : -x); }

int perpendicular(Vector& a, Vector& b)
{   return ( a.nonzero() && b.nonzero()
           && ABS(a.inner(b)) < 0.00000001 );
}
```

The function takes two Vector reference arguments and tests whether they are perpendicular: Each is nonzero, and their inner product is zero. The inline function ABS computes the absolute value.

With the perpendicular test, our task is now reduced to reading the four vertices from the user and testing whether the neighboring sides (as vectors) are all perpendicular. Each point is read from user input into a vector by the following:

```
Vector get_vec(int i)  // input a point as vector
{   float x,y;
    cout << "x" << i << "= ";
    cin >> x;
    cout << "y" << i << "= ";
    cin >> y;
    return(Vector(x,y));
}
```

The main program looks like this:

```
int main()
{   cout << "Enter vertices 0,1,2,3 \n";
    Vector p[4];                              // vector array      (1)
    for ( int i = 0; i < 4; i++)             // input all four points
       p[i] = get_vec(i);
    Vector u = p[0] - p[3];                  // vector difference  (2)
    Vector v;
```

```
for ( i = 0; i < 3; i++)            // process all sides
{  v = p[i+1] - p[i];               // vector difference  (3)
   if ( ! perpendicular(u, v) )     // check perpendicularity
   {   cout << "No, not a rectangle.\n";
       return(1);
   }
   u = v;
}
cout << "Yes, a rectangle.\n";
return(0);
}
```

```
//////// 	End of file rect.C 	////////
```

After the coordinates for the four vertices are read (in sequence), four vectors are in the array p[4] whose declaration (line 1) invokes the Vector default constructor four times. A vector u (line 2) representing one side of the quadrilateral is then calculated. Vector subtraction is performed by the overloaded - operator (line 2). A second Vector object v is made for an adjacent side (line 3). The perpendicularity of u and v is checked. After all sides are checked, the right conclusion can be made.

Assuming the file Vector.o has already been produced, compile rect.C with Vector.o and run the program.

The ability to work with vectors that correspond to real geometric objects allows the solution to be stated simply and elegantly with geometric concepts and also makes it much easier to explain and understand. More importantly, the Vector class can help in many other situations in plane geometry. Hence, the class has potential for reuse.

Furthermore, the OO solution is easily adaptable to changes in the problem specification. For instance, determining whether $ABCD$ is a parallelogram involves almost no change to the program. You just add a member is_parallel(Vector b) to Vector if it is not already there.

2.5 \ C++ I/O Streams

Section 1.6 mentioned cin, cout, and cerr — three ready-made objects for I/O in each program. These objects are *instances* of the I/O stream class, which is part of the C++ library. Character I/O offered by cin.get and cout.put are part of this facility.

While these standard objects take care of terminal I/O, there are occasions when you want direct I/O from/to a specific file. This can be done by setting up new I/O objects connected to the desired files. The declaration

```
fstream myobj(filename, mode);
```

establishes the object *myobj* as an instance of the built-in file I/O class fstream and connects *myobj* to the file specified by *filename*, a character string. The modes are specified by class-defined constants. If *mode* is ios::in (ios::out), then the file is opened for input (output). (See Section 6.6 for other possible modes.) For example,

```
fstream myin("mydata", ios::in);
fstream myout("myresult", ios::out);
```

establishes the object myin to read the file mydata and the object myout to write the file myresult.

From your knowledge of C++ classes, you can deduce that the fstream class has a constructor supporting the declarations of myin and myout. If myresult is a new file, it will be created. Otherwise, its contents will be replaced. Once established, these file I/O objects are used in much the same way as cin and cout. Open files are automatically closed when your program terminates. An open file can also be specifically closed by calling the member function close():

```
myin.close();
myout.close();
```

To use file I/O objects, you need to include the header files as follows:

```
#include <iostream.h>
#include <fstream.h>
```

For an example involving file I/O, see Section 2.6. Other input/output functions provided by the C++ stream library are discussed in Section 6.6.

2.6 ERROR HANDLING

A very important aspect of programming concerns the handling of possible errors during the execution of a program. Many kinds of errors can occur at run time. The main program may be invoked with incorrect arguments. A function expecting a positive argument may be passed a negative value. Arithmetic operations can overflow or underflow. A well-written program should detect errors and take appropriate actions.

Displaying Error Messages

The main program should first check the arguments supplied on the command line for correctness. If the arguments are unacceptable, then a clear message should be displayed stating the nature of the error and its cause (if known).

Use the object `cerr` for sending error messages to ensure that they appear on the terminal immediately without buffering. A conditional statement such as

```
if (argc != 3)
{   cerr << argv[0] << ": expects 2 arguments but was given "
        << argc-1 << "\n";
    cerr << "Usage " << argv[0] << " input-file output-file\n";
    exit(1);
}
```

checks the number of command-line arguments supplied. Note that the value of `argc` is, by definition, the number of command-line arguments *plus 1*. Always identify the program unit or subunit displaying the error message. The command name identifies which program is announcing the error. When appropriate, a function name further narrows down the error location. In this example, the program refers to its own name as `argv[0]`, which is better than assuming a specific file name.

After displaying an error message, a program may continue to execute, return a particular value not produced normally, or elect to abort. The standard library function `exit` is called to terminate the execution of a program:

```
void exit(int status);
```

When `exit` is called anywhere in a program, the entire program is terminated. For normal termination, *status* should usually be 0. For abnormal termination such as an error, a positive *status*, usually 1, is used. To use `exit`, you should include the header file `<stdlib.h>`:

```
#include <stdlib.h>
```

File I/O objects maintain internal error states that can be checked for any failure. For example, after the code

```
fstream myin(file, ios::in);
```

you should use a test like this:

```
if ( myin.fail() )
{   cerr << "Can't open " << file << "\n";
    exit(1);
}
```

The `fstream` class (Section 6.6) member function `fail()` returns 1 if the file failed to open.

An Error-Handling Example

The lowercase.C program (Section 1.6) can be rewritten with appropriate I/O and error handling. The intention is to define a **lowercase** command that works with standard I/O when given no arguments or that works with specific files when given an input file and an output file. Of course, the principal function is still to map all uppercase letters into lowercase letters.

```
///////   Program lowercase.C   ///////
#include <iostream.h>
#include <fstream.h>
#include <stdlib.h>
#include <ctype.h>

// put function lower here

void doio(istream& in, ostream& out)        // reference parameters
{   char c;
    while ( in.get(c) )
        out.put( lower(c) );
    out.flush();
}

int main (int argc,  char* argv[])
{   if ( argc == 1 )                          // use standard I/O
        doio(cin, cout);
    else if ( argc == 3 )                     // use files given
    {   fstream infile(argv[1], ios::in);
        if ( infile.fail() )                  // (1)
        {   cerr << argv[0] << ":can't open input file "
                << argv[1] << "\n";
            exit(1);
        }
        fstream ofile(argv[2], ios::out);
        if ( ofile.fail() )                   // (2)
        {   cerr << argv[0] << ":can't open output file "
                << argv[2] << "\n";
            exit(1);
        }
        doio(infile, ofile);
    }
    else                                      // (3)
    {   cerr << "Usage: " << argv[0]
            << " infile outfile\n";
        exit(1);
```

```
    }
    return(0);
}
///////   End of lowercase.C  ///////
```

The main program of lowercase.C anticipates common errors: failure to open the input file (line 1), inability to open the output file (line 2), and wrong number of arguments (line 3). In the last case, a brief guide of how to use the command is displayed.

2.7 \ OBJECT-ORIENTED THINKING

The traditional approach to program design involves breaking down a given problem into a number of steps. Each step is either simple and straightforward or may have to be broken down further. The sequence of steps forms a procedure that solves the given problem. This approach is known as *procedure-oriented decomposition*.

Object orientation involves a whole new way of thinking. Program design begins with identifying the interacting entities, or objects, in a given problem. In a banking application, for example, objects can be accounts, customers, credit records, monthly statements, and so on. The key is thinking in terms of quantities present in the problem domain rather than programming artifacts in the computer language domain. An object may represent a physical item such as a monthly statement or a logical item such as a transaction. The objects must be self-contained and must correspond to well-understood concepts in the problem domain. Thinking with the *language of the problem*, not the language of the computer, is essential. Some objects may have to be further broken down into smaller constituent objects. This approach is known as *object-oriented decomposition*. Objects thus identified lead to software objects, defined by classes, that simulate real ones in the problem domain.

The interactions among the problem-domain objects must then be considered carefully to define the external behavior of the objects and their interdependence. Class definitions of the different objects can then be coded. The set of all public data and function members forms the *public interface* of objects in a class. The public interface must support the intended external behavior precisely. The public interface determines how objects are used by other parts of the program. Hiding behind the public interface are internal implementation details kept from outside access. Thus, object orientation decouples the internal workings of objects from the rest of the program and significantly reduces program complexity. Internal data and procedures can be modified without affecting other parts of the program as long as the public interface is preserved.

A good OO design takes into account features such as generalizations of the given problem, possible future extensions, reuse of existing code, ease of modification, and so on. These ideas will become more concrete as you become more familiar with OOP mechanisms and their proper use under C++.

2.8 \ C++ PROGRAMMING TIPS

Here are some basic programming tips and things to remember to improve your C++ programs:

- Include <iostream.h> to use standard I/O streams.
- Include <stdlib.h> to use standard library functions such as exit.
- Declare functions, variables, and classes before using them.
- Always terminate a declaration or a class definition with a semicolon.
- Terminate a simple statement, but not a compound statement, with a semicolon.
- Remember that a character string is an array of characters terminated by '\0'.
- Use zero-based indexing for arrays. So, int arr[100] has its index running from 0 to 99.
- A character is represented by an integer and can be used as such.
- There is no exponentiation operator.
- The address-of operator & produces a pointer.
- The value-of operator * produces a value through a pointer.
- Except for reference parameters, arguments of functions are always passed by value.
- Loops in C++ use continuation conditions. The iteration ends when the condition becomes false.
- Logical false is zero, and logical true is anything else.
- Learn useful idioms such as for(;;) (infinite loop), for(int i=0 ; i < j ; i++), while(i--), and while(cin.get(c)). (Idioms will be pointed out throughout the book.)
- Apply the ternary operator ?: to form conditional expressions; use the % operator to compute the remainder.
- Avoid hard-coded constants and use const identifiers instead.

2.8.1 Function Style

If you develop a consistent formatting style in which to render your programs, you will avoid syntax errors and make the programs readable. The function style used in this book is explained here with an example:

```
// logical function equal compares strings x and y
// returns 1 if x is equal to y, 0 otherwise

int equal(char x[], char y[])              // (1)
{    if ( x == y ) return(1);              // (2)
     int i=0;                              // (3)
     while (x[i] == y[i])                  // (4)
     {   if (x[i] == '\0') return(1);      // (5)
         i++;                              // (6)
     }   /* end of while */                // (7)
     return(0);                            // (8)
} // end of function equal                 // (9)
```

Use comments to document the purpose and the effects of the function, the meaning of the arguments, and the value returned. Format the function body as follows:

1. Start the function header flush with the left margin.

2. Format the function body as a compound statement. Line up the opening brace with the function name. Indent all statements one level.

3. Keep statements on separate lines for readability.

4. For the body of a statement such as if, while, for, and so on, some programmers prefer to always use a block, even if it contains only one statement.

5. Keep a simple statement on one line. Some programmers may prefer using another line for the body of the if statement. That is all right as well.

6. Indent statements inside a block another level.

7. Line up the closing brace for while vertically with the opening brace. A comment can be added to clearly indicate the end of a multiline construct.

8. Always put a return at the end of a function if it returns a value.

9. Line up the closing brace of a function vertically with the opening brace. If the function is lengthy, a comment at the end will help as well.

10. Include comments alongside key statements to explain their purposes.

Use names in all caps for symbolic constants (#define or const, Sections 12.4 and 3.8). Give functions and variables meaningful names (in all lower case), using the underscore (_) to connect multiple words when appropriate.

2.8.2 Class Style

A consistent set of conventions for defining classes is also recommended:

1. Use capitalized nouns for class names. Account and Vector are examples. Join multiple words, and abbreviate if necessary, while capitalizing each word, as in BankAcct and GroupLeader.
2. Put each class definition in a separate header file. Put member function definitions in a corresponding .C file, which uses #include to include its own header file.
3. In a class definition, put public members first and carefully document public member functions with comments. Specify the meaning of arguments.
4. Give only extremely simple member functions inside the class definition.
5. If a class has any constructor, provide a default constructor.

Program examples in this book follow the formatting conventions closely. However, because explanations are usually included in the text, the examples tend not to be extensively commented.

2.9 \ SUMMARY

Objects encapsulate functions and data to form an independent computing unit. An object hides internal workings and is used only through its public interface, achieving data abstraction. The isolation of object internals from the rest of the program greatly simplifies the program. A class describes the structure of an object and controls outside access to class members, which can be data, functions, or other objects. Once defined, a class name becomes a user-defined type and is used to establish objects or instances of the class. An object is the host of its members and the members are accessed via the host object with the operators . and ->.

Using objects to solve problems is natural and effective. An object-oriented solution involves identifying the interacting objects in the problem domain and building classes to model their behavior. A sequence of interactions among the objects can represent the solution to the given problem. Changes in the problem specification can be handled with modifications in the interactions. The Vector example makes these points clear.

Both freestanding and member functions in C++ can be overloaded. When a function call is made, the actual arguments are evaluated in an unspecified order. Normally, arguments are passed by value, that is, the called function receives a copy of the arguments being passed. Pass by reference is accomplished using reference parameters. Inline functions can avoid run-time function call overhead. The function main can receive arguments supplied on the command line.

Important topics to consider in order to write interesting programs include establishing I/O stream objects for reading and writing files, handling of errors, object-oriented thinking, programming tips, and formatting recommendations. This overview gives you a cross-sectional view of C++ and sets the stage for learning the elaborate constructs of later chapters.

EXERCISES

1. Consider the Account class in Section 2.1. Add a member function void display() to this class.

2. Add a member function transfer() for the Account class that transfers a given amount from another account to the host account. Also implement the same function as a nonmember.

3. Consider class member function definition and invocation. If the function deposit can be defined as

   ```
   void Account::deposit(double amt)
   {    acct_bal += amt;    }
   ```

   why can it not be used with the notation Account::deposit(400.0); to deposit 400.0?

4. Consider the Account class in Section 2.1. Are the following declarations correct? Possible? Explain why.

   ```
   Account paul;
   Account mary;
   ```

5. Consider the default constructor definition inside the class Vector definition. Is a semicolon missing at the end? Explain.

   ```
   Vector() { }
   ```

6. Suppose sally is already declared as an Account object with an account identification and initial balance. Is the call sally.Account(new_id, new_balance) possible? Why?

7. Write a reverse-echo program that takes all words on the command line and displays them backward, character by character.

8. Let words in a file be character strings separated by one or more white-space characters (SPACE, TAB, NEWLINE). Write a program to count the number of words in the input file (cin).

9. Modify the word-count program in Exercise 8 to take an optional argument, which is the name of the input file.

10. Add the '==' operator to the Vector class. Add the member function is_parallel(Vector) to test whether a vector is parallel to the host vector object. Given any four points A, B, C, and D, use Vector objects to determine if ABCD is a parallelogram.

11. Define Vector_3d to be a three-dimensional vector class.

12. NIM is a game in which two players alternate in drawing counters, pennies, or the like, from a set of 12 arranged in three rows of 3, 4, and 5 counters, respectively. With each move, a player is allowed to draw either 1, 2, or 3 counters. The player who draws the last counter loses. Write a program to play NIM with one person or with two. (*Hint:* Consider a NIM board object.)

C++ Features and Constructs

Information provided in Chapters 1 and 2 represents an overview of C++ programming. This introductory material allows you to write complete programs containing functions and classes. We now begin to cover many subjects in depth and to show the usage of important features provided by C++.

Identifiers in C++ occupy a single *name space* in which each identifier is uniquely distinguished by the spelling of its name. Identifiers also obey scope rules that limit the extent to which each identifier is known in a program. There are four different scopes for identifiers, and familiarity with them is critical for program writing.

Functions that call themselves directly or indirectly are *recursive*. Two examples of recursion are given that will be reused later in the book.

Following OOP principles, a Fraction class is defined whose objects represent rational numbers. Fraction represents a typical abstract data type. It also motivates many other topics: canonical data representation, arithmetic operator overloading, object assignment, and the host-object pointer.

Effective use of function overloading is an important aspect of OOP, and the C++ overloading mechanism is described in detail. Usage, limitations, and invocation rules for overloaded functions are explained. Also, how a function can take optional, variable-length, and read-only arguments is shown.

Proper use of declarations is critical to programming. Rules for declaring and using local and global variables are given. Protecting per-file variables and sharing global variables across multiple files are explained. Additional declarations establish reference variables as well as alternative names for existing types.

Because not all data sizes are known at compile time, there is a need to allocate storage at run time. The free storage operators new and delete are described. A circular buffer object brings dynamic storage allocation and many other constructs together in an interesting application.

Operands of operators and arguments of functions sometimes are converted from one data type to another in order to perform the operation. Rules for implicit and explicit type-casting are explained. Suggestions are given on how to use header files and organize programs into independently compilable modules.

Many subjects are introduced here and provide a good foundation for topics discussed in later chapters.

3.1 \ IDENTIFIER SCOPING

Identifiers are names used in a program for various purposes such as for functions, parameters, variables, constants, classes, and types. Identifiers are regulated by *scoping rules*, governing the extent (the parts of the program) to which the names are known. In C++, all identifiers are contained in the same *name space*. This means that each identifier can be used for only one purpose within the same scope. In different scopes, identifiers with the same spelling are actually *distinct*. There are four different scopes in C++:

1. *Local scope:* Within a function or a block.
2. *Function scope:* The entire extent of a function.
3. *Class scope:* The entire extent of a class.
4. *File scope:* Within the same source code file.

A goto label is the only identifier with function scope. A label is known to all parts of a function within which it is declared. This must be the case if a goto statement is to transfer control to a label positioned later in the function. A discussion of each of the other three scopes follows.

Local Variables

A variable must first be introduced into a program before it can be used. The scope of a local variable extends from where it is defined to the end of its immediately enclosing block (compound statement). Formal parameters are local to the function. A variable declared inside a function/block is said to be *local* to the function/block. Local variables are private to the block in which they are declared and cannot be accessed from the outside. For example, the variables in, out, and c in the function doio (Section 2.6) are local. A local variable normally only comes into existence every time its declaration statement is executed and is destroyed automatically after its enclosing function/block is exited. Such variables are known as *automatic variables*.

Local variables are normally automatic. However, if a local variable is declared static, then it is not an automatic variable. Instead, it is created and initialized at compile time and retains its most recent value even after the function/block is exited. This same value is available when the function/block is entered again. Consider a function that keeps track of how many times it is called. The two lines

```
static int my_count = 0;
my_count++;
```

can be put in the function to do the job.

External Variables

Not all variables are local. It is also possible to use *external variables*, which are not local to any function or block. Since an external variable can be shared by many functions, it is sometimes referred to as being *global*. Because its value can be set and used by any function, an external variable provides a way, in addition to argument passing, for functions to communicate data. Unlike automatic variables, external variables always exist and retain their values until the entire program is terminated.

An external variable must be *defined* by a type declaration outside of all functions in a source code file. When placed outside of functions, the declarations

```
int overall_maximum;
int global_count = 0;
char name[]= "John Smith";
Vector v_i(1.0, 0.0);
Vector v_j(0.0, 1.0);
```

define the external variables overall_maximum, global_count, the character array name, and the Vector objects v_i and v_j. When an external variable is defined, it is allocated storage and is initialized with either zero or a supplied value. A variable can be defined only once. If the compiler detects an attempt to define a variable more than once, it will complain and fail.

To use an external variable in a function, at least one of the following conditions must be met:

1. The variable has been defined earlier in the file.
2. The variable has been declared extern earlier in the file.
3. The variable has been declared extern in the function.

To use v_i, you can put the declaration

```
extern Vector v_i;
```

in the function. When many functions share an external variable, this coding can be tedious. It is easier simply to put the necessary extern declarations outside the functions at the beginning of a file — once and for all.

Consider obtaining the total number of function calls made during a run of your program. Define an external global_count and initialize it to zero as shown earlier. Then just do global_count++ once in each function.

File Scope

A global variable is an example of a *file scope* identifier, a name known from its point of declaration to the end of the source code file. Other identifiers that usually have file scope include function names, enumeration symbols, class tags, and typedef names (Section 3.9).

The scoping rules can be illustrated further with an example:

```
long x;
float y;
int z;

fn(char c, int x)       // parameter x hides global x
{     extern int z;     // refer to global z
    double y = 3.14159; // local y hides global y
    { char y;           // hides first local y
        y = c;          // assign to second local y
      ::y = 0.3;        // assign to global y
    }
    y = y / 3.0;        // assign to first local y
    z++;                // increment global z
}
```

The global variable float y; is hidden by the local double y; in the function fn. This local y is in turn hidden by the local variable char y; inside the block. As control exits the block, the variable y of type double resurfaces. This further illustrates the scope rules. (More will be said about variables and their declarations in Section 3.6.1.)

Note how the *file scope operator* :: is used to refer to the global variable y from within a local scope.

Class Scope

In C++, each class has its own scope. Enclosed in class scope are names for data, function, typedef, and enum members. Even another class can be put inside a class scope. The name of a data or function member has *full class scope* and is global to the entire class independent of where it is declared in the class. For example, the names acct_no and acct_bal are used like global variables in the member functions of class Account (Section 2.1). Also, a member function can refer to another data or function member declared later in the class definition *without requiring forward declarations.*

Unless qualified, a class member name is generally not recognized outside its class. For example, neither the function name deposit nor the data name acct_bal is recognized outside Account directly. Remember that Account::deposit had to be used to define this member outside of Account. In general, a *class scope operator ClassName::* in front of an identifier explicitly specifies the class scope within which the identifier is interpreted. Vector::inner and ios::out are two more examples.

The class scope operator can be illustrated further with the Vector constructor:

```
Vector::Vector(float x, float y)
{   Vector::x = x;
    Vector::y = y;
}
```

Because the formal parameters shield the class scope data members x and y, the Vector:: notation is required. In general, the file and class scope operators are used only in name-conflict situations.

Another way to qualify a name and to put it in a specific class scope is to use the object member-of notation, as in the following examples:

```
sally.balance()
u.inner(v)
bob_ptr->deposit(11.79)
```

Similarly, a class scope identifier hides a file scope identifier with the same name. Suppose there is also a file scope function inner(). In this case, a member function of Vector must use ::inner to access the file scope function.

3.2 \ RECURSION

Many problems are solvable by a type of algorithm that reduces the original problem into one or several smaller problems of exactly the same nature. The solutions of the smaller problems then combine to form the solution of the original problem. These subproblems can be further reduced by applying the same algorithm *recursively* until they become simple enough to solve. A recursive algorithm can be implemented most naturally by a recursive function.

Greatest Common Divisor

Consider computing the *greatest common divisor* (gcd) of two integers. The gcd of integers a and b is defined as the largest integer that evenly divides both a and b. The gcd is not defined if both a and b are zero. A negative a or b can be replaced by its absolute value without affecting the gcd. Hence, we can assume that a and b are nonnegative and not both zero. The recursive algorithm to compute $gcd(a, b)$ can be described by the pseudocode:

1. If b is zero, the answer is a.

2. If b is not zero, the answer is $gcd(b, a \bmod b)$.

It is interesting to note that the idea for this simple but effective integer gcd algorithm is credited to Euclid, a Greek mathematician (ca. 300 B.C.).

The recursive function for Euclid's algorithm is straightforward:

```
int gcd(int a, int b)    // integer greatest common divisor
{   if ( b == 0 )
        return(a);
    else
        return ( gcd(b, a % b) );
}
```

Note that the function gcd calls itself and that the value of the arguments for each successive call to gcd gets smaller. (See Table 3.1 for an example.) Eventually, the second argument becomes zero and the recursion unwinds: The deepest recursive call returns, then the next level call returns, and so on until the first call to gcd returns.

TABLE 3.1   RECURSION OF gcd(2970,1265) = 55

CALL LEVEL	a	b
1	2970	1265
2	1265	440
3	440	385
4	385	55
5	55	0

When a function is called recursively, each new invocation gets its own set of formal parameters and automatic variables, independent of the previous set. This is consistent with how automatic variables and formal parameters are normally treated.

Another good example of recursive programming is the *quicksort* algorithm.

Quicksort

Sorting means arranging data items into a specified order. Items are sorted to make retrieval easier. Imagine trying to look up (retrieve) a phone number from an unsorted phone book! Among many competing sorting algorithms, the quicksort algorithm remains one of the fastest.

Let's consider arranging an array of integers in increasing order with quicksort. The idea is to pick any element of the array as the *partition element*, pe. By exchanging the elements, the array can be arranged so that all elements to the right of pe are greater than or equal to pe and all elements to the left of pe are less than or equal to pe. Now the same method is applied to sort each of the smaller arrays on either side of pe. The recursion is terminated when the length of the array becomes less than 2:

```
void quicksort(int a[], int i, int j)
{    // sort a[i] to a[j] inclusive
     int partition(int a[], int, int);
     if ( i >= j || i < 0)
         return;
     int k = partition (a, i, j);   // k is position of pe
     quicksort(a, i, k-1);          // sort left subarray
     quicksort(a, k+1, j);          // sort right subarray
}
```

The function quicksort is called with the lower index i and the higher index j of the array. If j is greater than i, the function partition is called to select a partition element and to split the array into two parts. The returned value of partition is the index of the partition point. The smaller arrays to either side of pe are then sorted by calling quicksort recursively.

The function partition is not recursive, and a simple implementation is easy. Let's consider an efficient partition and see how it works.

The arguments to partition are the array a and the two indices low and high. The range of the array from a[low] to a[high] inclusive is to be partitioned. Basically, the middle element is chosen to be the pe. By searching simultaneously from both ends of the range toward the middle, elements belonging to the other side are located. Out-of-place entries are interchanged in pairs. Finally, the searches in opposite directions end when they meet somewhere in the range, pinpointing the location for the partition element.

The partition function begins by exchanging the rightmost element with pe. Starting from both ends, the left-to-right search locates an element greater than pe and the right-to-left search finds an element less than pe. The two elements located are exchanged (with the inline function). Thereafter, the searches in opposite directions continue. Eventually, no more exchanges are needed, and the searches meet somewhere between low and high inclusive. This is the partition spot that contains an element greater than or equal to pe. The pe at the rightmost position is now interchanged with the element at the partition position. Finally, the index of the partition element is returned:

```
inline void exchange(int b[], int i, int j)
{     // array b is modified
      int t = b[j];
      b[j] = b[i]; b[i] = t;
}


int partition(int a[], int low, int high)
{     // partition a[low] through a[high]
      register int pe;
      int i = low;
      int j = high;
      // choose middle element as partition element
      exchange(a, (i+j)/2, j);     // move pe to right end
      pe = a[j];
      while (i < j)
      {     while (i < j && a[i] <= pe) i++;
            while (i < j && a[j] >= pe) j--;
            if (i < j) exchange(a, i++, j);
      }
      if (i != high)
            exchange(a, i, high);  // move pe to partition location
      return(i);                   // return index of pe
}
```

Another feature of quicksort is that the reordering is performed *in place*. No auxiliary array is used, as is required by some other sorting algorithms. The best way to understand how quicksort works is to try, by hand, an example with less than 10 entries.

3.3 \ A CLASS OF FRACTIONS

Now let's consider dealing with ordinary fractions like $\frac{1}{2}$ and $-\frac{1}{3}$. A fraction is, of course, the ratio of two integers: a numerator and a denominator. A user-defined type can be built for fractions by creating a class Fraction. The class supplies a set of necessary operations on fractions and hides implementation details of data representation and internal manipulations.

The Fraction.h file contains the class declaration:

```
///////   file Fraction.h   ///////
#include <iostream.h>

class Fraction
{  public:
       Fraction() { }                     // default constructor
       Fraction(int n, int d,             // constructor, d != 0
              int reduce = 1);            // optional argument
       void display();
       Fraction operator -(Fraction& y);  // binary difference
       Fraction operator -();             // unary negation
       int       operator >(Fraction& y); // relational operators
       int       operator==(Fraction& y);
       int is_zero() { return(denom == 1 && num == 0); }
       int is_one()  { return(denom == 1 && num == 1); }
       int is_int()  { return(denom == 1); }
       int floor();

       /*  other members not shown */

    private:
       int num;                           // numerator
       unsigned int denom;                // denominator
};
```

There are quite a few members in the Fraction class: the private data members num and denom, constructors, arithmetic and relational operators, logical tests, and so on. Only a few typical members are shown here so that the class definition remains uncluttered and thus easy to read. In practice, a full complement of member functions would be included to support the intended use of the objects.

A class usually encapsulates a data structure with its manipulation procedures. In designing a class, an important task is to decide on the internal data representation, which is isolated from outside view. In this way, internal routines keep the data representation consistent in any way that is appropriate;

outside routines are not affected. Here are some internal representation items to consider:

1. A fraction is kept internally as a pair of integers, num and denom.
2. The numerator num is an int that can be positive, negative, or zero.
3. The numerator carries the sign of the fraction and the denominator can be kept positive — hence, the type unsigned int. The denominator can never be zero.
4. Another design decision is whether to allow equal but different-looking fractions (for example, $\frac{1}{2}, \frac{2}{4}, \frac{3}{6}$) to exist. If not, and equal fractions must have the same numerator and denominator, then all fractions must be reduced to the lowest terms. A data representation in which all equal quantities are represented uniquely is known as a *canonical* representation. Keeping fractions canonical is desirable, and this convention should be enforced when appropriate.
5. A fraction can be zero, and it is represented by num = 0 and denom = 1.

It is possible to design the Fraction class to help enforce such conventions and not to have them just as principles that you can choose to follow or ignore. This is one major advantage over traditional programming environments.

The canonical representation conventions are enforced by the Fraction constructor as follows:

```
///////   File Fraction.C   ///////
Fraction::Fraction(int n, int d, int reduce)
{    if ( d == 0 )
     {   cerr << " Fraction: denominator is 0\n";
         exit(1);
     }
     if (n == 0)
     {    num = 0; denom = 1; return; }
     if (d < 0)
     {    n = -n; d = -d; }
     int g;
     if ( reduce && (g = gcd(n,d)) != 1 )  // remove gcd
     {    num = n/g;
          denom = d/g;
     }
     else {  num = n; denom = d; }
}
```

This constructor takes the given arguments n and d and constructs a fraction $\frac{n}{d}$. The denominator d should not be zero. The third argument, reduce, is designated as *optional* and takes on the default value 1 if not supplied in a call (Section 3.4).

If the flag reduce is zero, then n and d do not need reduction. Otherwise, the fraction is reduced by removing the gcd (Section 3.2) between n and d.

Let's now examine a representative set of member functions in the class Fraction. First of all, the functions is_zero, is_one, and is_int have their entire definition contained within the class declaration. Class member functions so specified are *inline* and may be compiled without run-time function call overhead.

Functions can also be explicitly designated inline in a header file. For example,

```
inline void Fraction::display()
     {  cout << num << "/" << denom;    }

inline int Fraction::operator ==(Fraction& y)
     {  return( num == y.num
              && denom == y.denom );
     }
```

As always, the class scope operator (Fraction::) puts the function names in the intended class scope. Only very simple functions should be inline; other functions should be defined in an implementation file (Fraction.C in this case).

The operator '-' has been overloaded here to handle the unary negation:

```
Fraction Fraction::operator -()  // unary negation
{  return(Fraction(-num, denom, 0));
}
```

Given a fraction

```
Fraction r(3, 4);
```

the unary negation -r is shorthand for the function call

```
r.operator-()
```

The answer is computed simply by constructing a fraction with a negated numerator.

3.3.1 Object Assignment

The object assignment

```
Fraction s;
s = -r;
```

copies the return value of operator-() into s.

Without user-supplied definitions, very few built-in operations work on class objects. However, the assignment operation is so basic that it does have a default meaning on objects. Unless otherwise defined by the user, *object assignment* involves assigning each corresponding data member on the right-hand side to that on the left-hand side.

3.3.2   Arithmetic Operations

An example of fraction subtraction, as a typical binary arithmetic operation on fractions, follows:

```
// fraction subtraction
Fraction Fraction::operator -(Fraction& y)
{  if ( num == 0 )                        // trivial cases  (1)
      return(Fraction(-y.num, y.denom, 0));
   else if ( y.num == 0 )
      return(*this);                      // host pointer   (2)
   else                                   // subtract fractions
      return( Fraction(num * y.denom
                       - y.num * denom,
                       denom * y.denom ) );
}
```

Here the infix notation

```
r - s              // r and s are Fraction objects
```

becomes shorthand for the function call

```
r.operator-(s)
```

Namely, the object s is passed to the member function

```
operator-(Fraction&)
```

of the object r. The reference parameter causes the argument s to be passed without copying.

Here is a simple main program that puts fractions to use:

```
///////    File:  tstFract.C    ///////

#include "Fraction.h"

int main()
{   Fraction x(1,30), u(-1,60), v(-1,60);
    Fraction y;
    y = x + u + v;   y.display();    // gives 0/1
    y = x - u + v;   y.display();    // gives 1/30
    return(0);
}
```

3.3.3   The Host-Object Pointer

The fraction subtraction function uses the pointer this (line 2), which deserves careful explanation. Recall that a host object for a member function is the object containing that function. In C++, a member function is called with an extra pointer argument, this, supplied by the compiler, which is a pointer to the host object and is known as the *self-pointer* or *host pointer*. This host pointer is crucial to the operation of a member function. For example, the code (line 1)

```
if ( num == 0 )
```

is simply shorthand for the actual code executed:

```
if ( this->num == 0 )
```

Thus, when referring directly to another data or function member in the host object, a member function really relies on the self-pointer (this) to do the job.

The self-pointer can also be used explicitly by member functions when there is such a need. In fraction subtraction, *this, the host object itself, is the answer if zero is to be subtracted (line 2). The pointer this is not a fixed quantity; it depends on the host object in question. For host object r, it points to r; for host s, it points to s.

Fraction is another example of using class to build new data types from existing ones. Fraction is now an abstract data type because it is characterized only by its external behavior. Specific implementation details are hidden and immaterial to users of fractions. By attaching all related routines to the data, encapsulation is achieved. A fraction object is therefore self-sufficient, and it even knows how to display itself. By operator overloading, Fraction objects can be treated almost as built-in types (for example, r - s).

3.4 \ OPTIONAL AND VARIABLE-LENGTH ARGUMENTS

A function usually takes a fixed number of arguments. But there are situations when it is convenient or even necessary to relax this rule. The Fraction constructor already took an optional argument (reduce). Let's take a look at defining functions with optional arguments. Furthermore, note that it is possible to define functions with an *arbitrary* number of arguments.

Functions with Optional Arguments

An argument of a function becomes *optional* (may or may not be supplied in a function call) if it has been given a *default value*. Optional arguments must be grouped at the end of the formal parameter list. The = *value* syntax is used to supply a default value. For example, the class

```
class Time
{  public:
      Time() {}
      Time(int hr, int min, int sec = 0, char ap = 'A');  // (1)

      /*  other member functions  */

   private:
      int second, minute, hour;
      char a_or_p;    // 'A' or 'P'
};
```

can be defined to supply Time objects. Here an overloaded constructor takes zero, two, three, or four arguments. The default value for the fourth argument is 'A' (for A.M.). Thus, Time objects can be established as follows:

```
Time t1(2, 30, 0, 'P');   // 2:30 PM
Time t2(9, 15);           // 9:15 AM
Time t3(6, 15, 30);       // 6:15:30 AM
Time t4;                  // uninitialized
```

The default value can be supplied in a prototype declaration or the definition of a function. And, it can be supplied anywhere in the source code as long as it is specified only once. The C++ compiler will complain if a default value is supplied more than once. A default value cannot be supplied to an argument unless all arguments to its right have been made optional already. Therefore, the additional declaration

```
Time::Time(int, int = 0, int, char);
```

anywhere (after line 1) makes the min argument also optional. This is possible but not advisable. Rather, always supply all the default values in one prototype declaration at a place where any potential caller can see how to supply arguments. The usual place for such a prototype is in a header file, where the meaning of the arguments as well as other possible values for the optional arguments are clearly documented with comments.

   To further ensure code clarity and consistency, it is good practice to use the same header for a function in all its declarations and prototypes. The default values can be commented out in all places but one. Thus, the implementation of Time::Time should look like this:

```
Time::Time(int hr, int min,
           int sec /* = 0 */, char ap /* = 'A' */)
{  hour = hr;
   minute = min;
   second = sec;
```

```
    a_or_p = ap;
}
```

If all arguments are optional, then the function can be called with no arguments. When such a function is a constructor, then it is not necessary to supply another default constructor. In fact, it would be an error to supply one because a call with no arguments becomes ambiguous.

The initial value for an optional argument can be a constant expression or any expression involving no local variables. Specifically, global variables, static members (Section 5.10), and enum members (Section 1.10) can be used.

Functions with Variable Number of Arguments

In addition to optional arguments, C++ supports functions taking an indefinite number of arguments. The concept is natural for functions such as sum, product, max, and min.

The notation

```
int sum(int argcnt, ...)            // variable args notation
```

is used to declare sum as a function of one or more arguments. The first parameter is argcnt, and it is of type int. The ellipses (...) indicate that the number and type of the remaining (undeclared) arguments may vary. An indefinite parameter declaration must begin with at least one named parameter, such as argcnt in this example. A function declared in this way may each time be passed a different number of arguments of arbitrary types.

At run time, when a function with an indefinite number of parameters is actually invoked, the number and type of the arguments being passed in the particular call must somehow be made known to the called function. There are several ways to do this. If the types of the undeclared arguments are fixed, this information can be hard-coded in the called function. Alternatively, the count and types of the unnamed arguments may be supplied in the leading named arguments. Instead of the argument count, a terminator marking the end of the unnamed arguments may be appropriate in certain applications. Again, the terminator used may be fixed or supplied in a leading named argument.

The principal problem for a function taking a variable number of arguments lies in *referencing the unnamed arguments*. Macros (Section 12.4) defined in the standard header <stdarg.h> provide the solution. These macros are as follows:

va_list   (argument pointer type — declares argument pointer)
va_start (variable argument start — initializes access to unnamed arguments)
va_arg   (next variable argument — accesses individual unnamed arguments)
va_end   (variable argument end — cleans up before returning from function)

These concepts can be made clearer with an example. Let's define the function sum:

```
#include    <stdarg.h>        // header for variable argument list

int sum(int argcnt, ...)     // argcnt gives number of other args
{     va_list ap;             // argument pointer
      int ans = 0;
      va_start(ap, argcnt); // initialize ap
      while ( argcnt-- > 0 )// process all args
           ans += va_arg(ap, int);
      va_end(ap);            // clean up before function returns
      return(ans);
}
```

The type va_list is a macro to declare a variable ap (argument pointer), which is used to refer to each unnamed argument in turn. The macro va_start initializes ap to point to the first unnamed argument (Figure 3.1). To locate the first unnamed argument, va_start also needs the last named argument, argcnt in this example. Once ap is properly initialized, the macro va_arg is used to return the next unnamed argument on the argument list. The va_arg macro also advances ap to point to the next argument. To do this, va_arg needs the type, thereby the size, of the unnamed argument. In sum, the type int has been given. After all such arguments have been retrieved, the pointer ap is then given to the macro va_end to perform the required cleanup actions. We can use a simple main program to test sum with a different number of arguments:

```
int main()
{     int total;
      total = sum(5, 1,2,3,4,5);
      cout <<"sum= " << total << "\n";
      total = sum(8, 1,2,3,4,5,6,7,8);
      cout << "sum= " << total << "\n";
      return(0);
}
```

FIGURE 3.1   VARIABLE-LENGTH ARGUMENTS

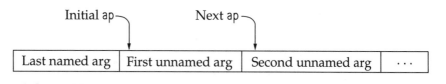

Notice that the second argument of va_arg is a type name and not a variable. Therefore, if a function wishes to obtain unnamed arguments of mixed types, several different va_arg statements, controlled perhaps by a switch or an if, should be used. For example, in an arrangement where the type of an unnamed argument is given by a string contained in the previous unnamed argument, you can use a code like this:

```
double x;  int i; char* t;
/* ... */
t = va_arg(ap, char*);
if ( strcmp(t,"double") == 0 )
    x = va_arg(ap, double);
else if ( strcmp(t, "int") == 0 )
    i = va_arg(ap, int);
/* ... */
```

Because the number and type of arguments are unknown at compile time, the space to receive incoming arguments must be allocated at run time, a principal job of va_start. The duty of va_end is to return dynamic storage used. (More on dynamic storage management can be found in Section 3.10.1.)

At this point, all possible specifications for arguments of functions have been covered, paving the way for a thorough look at the C++ function overloading mechanism, which plays such an important role in object-oriented programming.

3.5 \ OVERLOADING FUNCTIONS

Traditionally, a function performs a specific duty that is programmed for it. C++ supports *function overloading*, adding extra duties to existing functions. This is done simply by defining multiple versions of a function with the same name, but the versions must have different *signatures*. The function name and the number, order, and types of its formal parameters constitute a function's signature. We have already used some overloaded constructors. As another simple example, let's consider the power function (Section 1.7) with the prototype

```
int power(int a, int n);            // integer power
```

You can overload power to compute powers of double quantities:

```
double power(double a, int n)
{     double ans = 1.0;
      for (int i = 0 ; i < n ; i++)
          ans *= a;                 // no overflow check
```

```
        return ans;
}
```

Now the same power can compute powers of int and double — how convenient! Furthermore, you can add the duty of computing powers of fractions:

```
Fraction power(Fraction a, int n)
{     Fraction ans(1, 1, 0);        // ans is 1
      for (int i = 0 ; i < n ; i++)
          ans = ans * a;            // * of Fraction
      return ans;
}
```

Note that power, not Fraction::power, is used in the preceding definition. Thus, you are not dealing with a member function of the class Fraction. Had you used Fraction::power, you would be adding a function in the scope of Fraction and not overloading the file scope function power. Thus, overloading occurs only if additional meanings are assigned to a function name in the same scope. When a function definition involves default arguments, it results essentially in several versions of an overloaded function taking different numbers of arguments.

There is no practical limit on how many different duties can be piled on the same function name. The added definitions can also be in different places or files in a program.

Distinguishable Signatures

To overload a function, the new definition must carry a signature *distinct* from all existing ones (in the same scope). For example, all of the following function prototypes have distinct signatures:

```
int power(int a, int n);
int power(int a, unsigned n);
int power(int a, short n);
double power(float a, int n);
double power(double a, int n);
double power(int a, float n);
double power(float a, float n);
Fraction power(Fraction a, int n);
double power(Fraction a, float n);
Fraction power(Fraction a, int* n);
```

Remember that the return value type is not part of the function signature. The C++ compiler produces an error message and the compilation fails if the overloading signature conflicts with an existing signature. For example, each of the following signatures conflicts with either of the other two:

```
double power(double a, int n);       // three mutually
double power(double a, const int n); // conflicting
double power(double a, int& n);      // signatures
```

For any type *TP* that is not a pointer or reference, the types *TP*, const *TP*, and *TP&* cannot be distinguished when function signatures are compared. However, the types const *TP&* and *TP&* can be distinguished. For similar reasons, so can const *TP** and *TP**. Thus, the signatures

```
double power(double a, int& n);
double power(double a, const int& n);
```

do not conflict as long as the signature

```
double power(double a, int n);
```

is not included.

Since arrays are always passed as pointers in function calls, the types *TP** and *TP[]* (with or without array dimension) are not distinguishable as far as the signature is concerned.

Function Call Resolution

When a function call is made to an overloaded function, the C++ compiler automatically deduces, from the actual arguments, the correct version of the function, in the indicated scope, to invoke. This activity is termed *call resolution* and is performed by matching the number and type of the actual arguments with the different signatures of an overloaded function:

1. If there is an exact match, then call that version.
2. Otherwise, match through standard type promotions (Section 3.12).
3. Otherwise, match through standard conversions (Section 3.12).
4. Otherwise, match through user-supplied conversions (Section 8.7).
5. No match or an ambiguous match (more than one) is an error.

In C++, operators can also be given extra duties. Operator overloading is similar to function overloading but becomes more involved for certain operators (Section 8.1).

3.6 \ MORE ON DECLARATIONS

Knowing how declarations work and how to use them properly and effectively is just as crucial to programming as familiarity with classes, functions, statements, and expressions.

The C++ compiler takes expressions and statements in a source code file and produces corresponding machine codes to run on a particular computer. Unlike an expression or an executable statement, a declaration does not specify run-time code. Instead, declarations provide necessary or supplementary information so that the compiler can generate the required codes. In other words, declarations instruct the compiler, whereas executable statements specify program actions.

Some declarations, such as int and float, provide necessary information without which compilation of a C++ program cannot succeed. For example, to produce code for x + y, the compiler must know the types and sizes of x and y. This information is given by declarations like int x; and double y;. Other declarations, such as the register and inline modifiers, give auxiliary information to help the compiler produce more efficient code.

3.6.1   Declarations and Definitions

When a declaration also causes storage allocation for a variable or constant or specifies a function/class body, then it is called a *definition*. In a program, one definition, at most, is allowed for each variable, constant, function, and class. No repeated definition is allowed even if it is entirely the same.

Declarations of automatic variables and declarations with initialization are common examples of definitions. However, declarations such as

```
extern int x;                // external variable declaration
float cube_root(float);      // function prototype declaration
class Vector;                // forward class declaration
float Vector::inner(Vector a); // member function prototype
```

are not definitions because they do not allocate storage. The storage for x should be provided by a unique definition somewhere else in the program. In a C++ program, multiple declarations of the same quantity, usually in different files, are allowed provided that all declarations are consistent.

File Scope Declarations

We already know that a declaration placed inside a function or block is local and that a member of a class has class scope. A local declaration defines an automatic variable, unless the declaration is preceded with the extern modifier and not followed by an initializer—in which case, the variable refers to the same variable in file scope.

If a declaration is not placed inside any function, block, or class, it is called a *file scope declaration*. Function and class definitions are usually given at file scope.

For variables, if a file scope declaration is a definition, then it creates a file scope (global) variable. Since C++ disallows duplicated definitions, it is important to know when a file scope variable declaration becomes a definition:

1. A file scope declaration with an initializer is a definition. For example,

```
int counter = 0;
extern int max = 0;
int a[] = {1,2,3,4,5};
char name[] = "Wang";
```

2. A file scope declaration with extern but without an initializer is not a definition.

3. A file scope declaration without extern or an initializer is taken as a definition. For basic types, an initial value of zero is assumed; for class objects, the default constructor will be called for initialization.

Internal and External Linkage

The C++ compiler compiles each source code file as a separate *compilation unit* and generates a corresponding .o file. When multiple .o files are put together into an executable program, global names of variables, objects, functions, and classes used across multiple files must be *linked together*. A global identifier in a file to be linked with like identifiers in other files has *external linkage*. Otherwise, the global identifier has *internal linkage* and is not linked with identifiers in other files with the same name. For example, a global variable int population shared by two source code files has *external linkage*.

Let's examine how linkage is determined. First of all, a file scope identifier automatically has external linkage, unless specifically declared otherwise. To make external linkage explicit, you can add the extern specifier in front of any global identifier declaration:

```
extern int population;
extern class Account;
```

External linkage allows use of the same global variables across files but brings with it the danger of global-variable-name conflicts between those files, especially if the files are written at different times or by different programmers.

A per-file global variable can be protected by giving it *internal linkage*. To attain internal linkage, you simply add the static specifier to its file scope declaration. Variables with *internal linkage* are not accessible from other files. For example,

```
static const int TABLE_SIZE = 64;
static int max;
```

3.6.2   Using Local and Global Identifiers

The following practical rules summarize concepts regarding declarations covered so far:

1. Declare a local variable inside a function or a block. Such variables can be initialized. A local variable is automatic unless specified static.

2. Define a global variable with external linkage exactly once in a file using a file scope definition with initialization.

3. Define a file scope variable with internal linkage exactly once in the file using a file scope definition with the static specifier and initialization.

4. Place file scope extern declarations at the beginning of a file for all global variables defined or used in other files. This is usually done by including the appropriate header files (see Section 3.13).

5. A function or file scope variable declared static is local to a file.

6. A function must be declared with a prototype before called. For functions returning int, such declarations can, but should not, be omitted. To use a function defined in another file, place the function prototype, with or without extern, at the beginning of the file.

7. A class must be declared before objects of that class can be established. This is usually done by including the header file supplied by the class.

In the next few sections, coverage of C++ declarations continues with *type&* (reference), const, and typedef.

3.7 \ REFERENCES

Reference parameters (described earlier in Section 2.2) are just one form of *references* in C++. A variable declared *type&* is a *reference* of the given *type* and must be initialized when declared. For example,

```
int a;
Account sally(55123, 450.0);
int& ra = a;              // ra is reference to a
Account& rsally = sally;  // rsally is reference to sally
```

The reference variables ra and rsally become aliases of the actual variables a and sally. The initializer of a reference must be an *lvalue*, an expression that can be used on the left-hand side of an assignment. Common lvalues include variables (x), array cells (a[i]), and dereferenced pointers (*ptr). Constants and results of expressions such as (2 * a + 3) are not lvalues. Thus, for example, the codes

```
int& wrong = 256;                // reference initializer
Fraction& bad = Fraction(2,3);   // must be an lvalue
```

are not possible. The general syntax for declaring a reference variable is

type& refname = lvalue;

where the & signifies a reference declaration and is not to be confused with the address-of operator. It cannot be because it is used after a type name. The initializer *lvalue* must be of the same or a compatible type. Several reference variables can be declared on one line, as in

```
int& ra = a, & rb = b;
```

A reference variable always refers to the actual variable given at initialization time. The association cannot be changed. Thus, the code

```
int c = 9;
ra = c;       // assignment to a
```

assigns the value of c to a rather than switching ra to refer to c. Both ra and a refer to the same memory location where an integer value is stored (Figure 3.2). When a function takes a reference parameter, the formal reference parameter is considered initialized by the actual parameter being passed each time the function is called.

A function's return value can also be declared a reference — in which case, an lvalue not local to the function must be returned. Consider the function

```
int& maxi(int& x, int& y)
{   return (x > y ? x : y);  }
```

It returns a reference to its maximum argument, allowing usages such as

```
int a = 9, b = 9;
maxi(a,b) = 16;        // assigns 16 to b
maxi(a,b) -= 10;       // decreases b by 10
maxi(a,b)++;           // increases a by 1
```

FIGURE 3.2   THE MEANING OF A REFERENCE

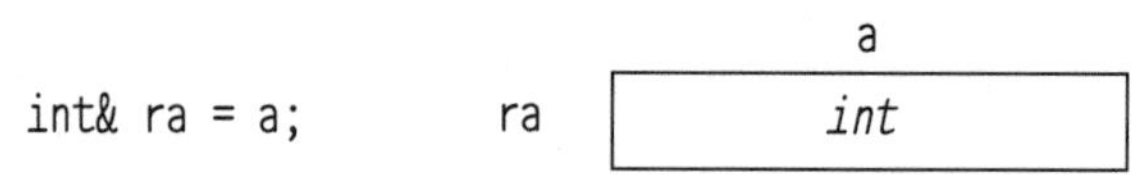

```
                                              a
int& ra = a;        ra   ┌──────────────────────┐
                         │         int          │
                         └──────────────────────┘
```

The major purpose of references in C++ is to pass parameters into functions without copying. Depending on the application, the receiving function may or may not modify an incoming reference. Whether it does is an important piece of information for the caller who passes an actual argument. The read-only nature of variables and parameters can be expressed easily in C++.

3.8 \ READ-ONLY VARIABLES AND PARAMETERS

The type qualifier const expresses the read-only nature of variables. If a type name is preceded by const, it becomes a constant or read-only type. If a variable or an array element is declared read-only, the value of the variable will stay constant and cannot be changed after initialization:

```
const float pi = 3.14159f;
const int lower_limit = 32;
const char greeting[] = "Hello:\n"     // array of read-only char
```

Similarly, the pointer declaration

```
const char *str = "Happy Birthday";
```

prevents any assignments through the pointer variable str. For instance, *(++str) = ´A´ is illegal. However, the pointer variable str itself can still be set. Thus, ++str is perfectly all right.

To declare a pointer variable itself read-only, use

```
char * const ptr = "Happy New Year";
```

To declare a read-only pointer pointing to read-only array cells, use

```
const char * const qtr = greeting;
```

The compiler also disallows assignment of a pointer to read-only data to a regular pointer in order to protect the read-only data. For example,

```
char *s = str;   // error; s not const char*
```

The const qualifier is often used in function declarations. For example, the function header

```
enum Boolean string_match(const char str[], const char line[])
```

means that the entries of str and line are read-only quantities in string_match. The compiler will check for any illegal attempts to modify read-only data.

Similarly, it is important to indicate the read-only nature of reference formal parameters with const not only to prevent accidental modification but also to assure any caller of a function that the reference argument will not be damaged.

For example, the member function `operator-(Fraction&)` can be improved with the code

```
Fraction Fraction::operator-(const Fraction& x);
```

The added const modifier ensures that the reference being passed will not be modified in any way. This code states that the right operand of `Fraction::operator-()` is read-only. But what about the left operand? It is the host object itself and can also be designated read-only with the code

```
Fraction Fraction::operator-(const Fraction& x) const;
```

The const keyword at the end indicates to the compiler that the host object will not be modified by the function.

It is always important to know whether modification is intended on a reference parameter. Passing read-only reference parameters gives you the power/efficiency of pass by reference with the safety of pass by value.

A class data member can also be declared read-only — in which case, its initial value is set at object instantiation time by the class constructor (Section 5.3).

3.9 \ THE typedef DECLARATION

The typedef declaration is used to create new names for basic as well as user-defined types, including classes. The new type name should be either more descriptive or more compact to use. Once a new type name has been established, it can be used just like any other type name. Type names should also be distinct from other identifiers in the same scope:

```
typedef int Enrollment;          // Enrollment is int
typedef unsigned short Age;       // Age is unsigned short
typedef char *String;            // String is char *
typedef Fraction *Fracptr;        // Fraction pointer
```

Note that capitalized identifiers are used for new type names. This convention makes it simpler to distinguish typedef names from other names. With these new type names, clearer codes, as in

```
Age x;
String a, b = "hello there", argv[5];
```

can be used — in this case, to declare x unsigned short; a, b, and argv[0] through argv[4] char *.

Having seen some examples, we are ready for the general syntax of typedef. To establish a new type name *Abc*, just declare *Abc* as though it were a variable of the desired type, then precede the entire variable declaration with the modifier typedef. Hence,

```
typedef char * StringArray[];
```

defines the type name StringArray and allows the main function header to be written as

```
main(int argc, StringArray argv)
```

When a typedef is used only by a class, it can be specified in the class definition so that its name is enclosed by the class scope and will not interfere with other names outside. It must be pointed out that typedef does not actually create a new data type; rather, it simply gives a new name to an existing type. The class declaration, on the other hand, is used to define new types.

Besides aesthetics, the use of typedef simplifies complicated declarations and provides readability and documentation for a program. Clearly, an Age variable is more specific than an arbitrary int variable, and StringArray is more to the point than what it replaces. Later, when we deal with complex declarations, typedef will come in handy.

3.10 \ STORAGE ALLOCATION AND MANAGEMENT

When a variable is defined, storage for it is allocated by the compiler. Thus, variables and arrays declared in a program have storage allocated at compile time. The management of the compile-time allocation depends on the *storage class* of the variable: *automatic* or *static*. We are already familiar with the storage treatment for automatic variables.

Local variables with the static specifier and all global variables, with internal or external linkage, belong to the static storage class. Static-storage variables are initialized to zero by default. They also retain their storage location and therefore value, regardless of entry or exit of functions and blocks.

Compile-time-allocated data storage is managed implicitly, according to the rules just mentioned. Storage allocation at compile time is efficient and convenient but sometimes too restrictive. To avoid such restrictions, certain data storage can also be allocated and managed explicitly at run time.

Run-time storage techniques are often overlooked by beginning programmers. However, they are very important in C++ programming and deserve careful study. Their importance is underscored by the fact that C++ offers the special operators new and delete for treating dynamic storage.

3.10.1   Dynamic Storage Allocation with new

In addition to compile-time storage allocation, it is sometimes necessary in a program to allocate storage dynamically, or at run time. Unlike storage associated with automatic variables, dynamically allocated storage persists until explicitly deallocated. C++ provides the operators `new` and `delete` for the allocation and deallocation of storage at run time.

One frequent reason for dynamic storage is that certain data sizes are unknown at compile time. Consider a function, `array_add`, that takes two `int` arrays, adds them, and returns the sum array. The result, of course, is an array whose size depends on the size of the argument arrays. If the space to hold the answer is to be allocated in the `array_add` function, it must happen at run time. Similarly, if the size of a table is not known beforehand, either a huge table is reserved at compile time (to guard against all eventual sizes) or just enough dynamic storage is allocated for the job at hand. Run-time storage is allocated from a *free pool* reserved for this very purpose.

The operator `new` allocates storage at run time and is used in the form

```
new  typename
```

and `new` returns a pointer to the newly allocated space appropriate to hold data of the indicated type. Needless to say, the pointer returned is of type *typename**. For example,

```
int *i = new int;
float *x = new float;
int *m = new int[20];          // array, space for 20 integers
Fraction *f = new Fraction;    // class object
```

are valid usages. The invalid zero pointer `NULL` is returned if `new` fails to allocate the requested storage, most likely because of lack of free space.

Except for arrays, initializers can be supplied for data storage allocated by `new`, as in

```
int *j = new int(11);          // initial value 11
float *x = new float(3.1416);   // initial value 3.1416
Fraction *f = new Fraction(2,3); // calls constructor
```

For basic types, the optional initializer takes the form of (*expr*). For class objects, the initializer is the argument list to a constructor that is called to perform the initialization.

3.10.2 Dynamic Storage Deallocation with `delete`

Dynamically allocated storage is freed with the operator `delete` when the space is no longer needed. The `delete` operation must be explicitly invoked in a program in the form

```
delete  ptr
```

where *ptr* must be a pointer returned earlier by new. Freed space goes back to the pool of available space for dynamic allocation. Be careful not to free space that has not been dynamically allocated. Otherwise, data and even functions in your program can be destroyed in unpredictable ways. However, C++ guarantees that deleting a pointer with the value zero is not a problem. This means that a pointer to dynamic storage that is initialized to NULL can always be deleted. After delete, the value of ptr is invalid (most likely NULL), and ptr should not be dereferenced again.

Dynamically allocated arrays are freed using

```
delete [ ] arrayname
```

Again, *arrayname* must be a pointer returned by a call to new that created the dynamic array. Thus, the code

```
delete [ ] m;    // delete array m
```

works just fine. The size of the array is known and need not be supplied to the delete call.

When a dynamically allocated object is freed, the delete call automatically calls any *destructor* supplied by the class before freeing up the space. The destructor performs *deinitialization* operations specified for objects of a given class (see Section 5.7).

Applications of new and delete can be found in the circular buffer example given next.

3.11 \ A CIRCULAR BUFFER

To demonstrate some of the key points covered so far, let's consider implementing a *circular buffer* and also apply it in a program to count the total number of words in any given file.

A first-in-first-out (FIFO) character buffer is often useful as a data structure to transfer characters from a producer to a consumer. The provider of characters for the buffer is called the *producer*, and the receiver of characters from the buffer is called the *consumer*. In sequential processing, the producer and consumer are different parts of the same program. In concurrent (or parallel) processing, they can be independently running programs. The buffer is usually represented as a character array of an appropriate size. In the beginning, the buffer contains nothing and is therefore empty.

Normally, head and tail indices are used to keep track of the start of characters yet to be consumed and the start of empty spaces available in the buffer, respectively. The head advances as characters are consumed, and the tail advances as new characters are put into the buffer. When an index reaches the end of the buffer, it wraps around to the beginning of the buffer. This wrap-around property makes the buffer *circular* (Figure 3.3). Obviously, it is an error to consume from an empty buffer or produce into a full buffer.

Let's now define a circular buffer class, Cirbuf, to hide the implementation details and to supply just the right interface for producing into and consuming from a circular buffer object. Our program establishes a Cirbuf object with a given buffer capacity whenever there is a need. The Cirbuf.h header file is included by any file that uses a circular buffer:

```
////// file: Cirbuf.h //////

class Cirbuf                          // circular buffer
{ public:
    enum {D_SIZE = 16};               // default buffer size
    Cirbuf(int size = D_SIZE);        // constructor
    int produce(char c);              // insert c into buffer
    int consume();                    // remove char from buffer
    int is_empty()                    // buffer empty test
    { return(length == 0); }
    int is_full()                     // buffer full test
    { return(length == size); }
    ~Cirbuf();                        // destructor
  private:
    int mod(int x);                   // wrap-around function
    int   head;                       // first char in buffer
    int   tail;                       // first empty slot in buffer
    int   length;                     // number of characters in buffer
    int   size;                       // capacity of buffer
    char *cb;                         // pointer to character array
};
```

FIGURE 3.3   CIRCULAR BUFFER

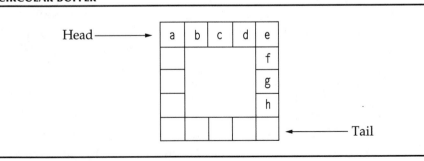

Note that the private data member cb points to the first cell of a character array dynamically allocated by the Cirbuf constructor. A default buffer size of 16 is used. As discussed earlier, the index head points to the first character to be consumed in cb, while the index tail locates the slot for the next incoming character. The number of characters remaining in the buffer is length. The buffer is empty if length is zero. It is full if length becomes equal to size.

These details are only important to you, the designer of the Cirbuf class. Any program that uses a circular buffer object is isolated from these details and uses a Cirbuf object only through its public interface:

```
int produce(char c);
int consume();
int is_empty();
int is_full();
```

Note also that the is_empty (is_full) test should be used before a consume (produce) operation. These operations together with the constructor and destructor are implemented in the file Cirbuf.C:

```
//////   file: Cirbuf.C   //////
#include  <iostream.h>
#include  "Cirbuf.h"

Cirbuf::Cirbuf(int s /* = D_SIZE */)      // constructor
{    head = tail = length = 0;            // initial values
     size = s;
     cb = new char[s];                    // allocate buffer space
}

Cirbuf::~Cirbuf() { delete [] cb; }       // free up space

inline int Cirbuf::mod(int x)             // inline private member
        { return(x >= size ? x-size : x); }

int Cirbuf::produce(char c)               // insert c into buffer
{    if ( is_full() )                     // if buffer full
     { cerr << "produce: buffer full\n";
        return(-1);                       // return error value
     }
     cb[tail++] = c;
     length++;
     tail = mod(tail);                    // wrap around
     return(0);                           // return normal value
}
```

```
int Cirbuf::consume()                       // extract char from buffer
{   char c;
    if ( is_empty() )                       // if buffer empty
    { cerr << "consume: buffer empty\n";
      return(-1);                           // return error value
    }
    c = cb[head++];
    length--;
    head = mod(head);                       // wrap around
    return(c);                              // return character
}
```

In the Cirbuf constructor, the operator new is used to dynamically allocate the character buffer of the desired capacity. Thus, the code

```
Cirbuf a_buf(64);
Cirbuf *d_buf = new Cirbuf(128);
```

establishes a_buf and *d_buf as Cirbuf objects with the indicated capacities. When a Cirbuf object is destroyed, the buffer space should be freed. This is programmed into the destructor ˜Cirbuf (Section 5.7), which is automatically invoked before a Cirbuf object is deallocated. During program execution there are two occasions when a variable is destroyed:

1. When an automatic variable goes out of scope, as in

    ```
    { Cirbuf a_buf(64); /* ... */ }
    ```

    The circular buffer object a_buf is established when the code block is entered and is destroyed when control leaves the block.

2. When dynamically allocated space (through new) is explicitly deleted, as in

    ```
    delete(d_buf);
    ```

By allocating buffer space in the constructor and releasing it in the destructor, the handling of free storage is made transparent to the user of Cirbuf objects, reducing the likelihood of errors related to free storage management.

The implementations of produce and consume are straightforward. Note that each takes care of wrap-around with a call to the private member function mod.

In testing the implementation, use a reasonably small size—say, 5—so that wrap-around happens sooner. Take special notice of the way in which errors are handled. Instead of exiting, a value of −1 is returned. It is up to the calling function of consume or produce to detect the error and treat it appropriately.

When everything is working, establish the object file Cirbuf.o to combine with any file that uses a circular buffer object.

Circular Buffer Application

Let's put the circular buffer to use. Our example program counts the number of words, separated by SPACE, TAB, and/or NEWLINE characters, in the standard input. A producer function readin obtains input characters and deposits them in the circular buffer until it is full. A consumer function word_count then takes characters out of the buffer and counts the number of words until the buffer is empty. These two steps are repeated until the input is finished:

```
//////   file wordcount.C   //////

#include <iostream.h>
#include "Cirbuf.h"                  // use circular buffer

static int wcnt = 0;                 // global count, internal linkage

int readin(Cirbuf& b)                // obtain input from stdin
{   char c;
    while ( ! b.is_full() )          // while circular buffer not full
        if ( cin.get(c) )
            b.produce(c);            // deposit into buffer
        else
            return(0);               // input closed
    return(1);                       // buffer full
}
```

Both of the functions word_count and readin use reference parameters to avoid making copies of the circular buffer object—an important point to remember when you write your own programs:

```
void word_count(Cirbuf& b)          // count number of words
{   int c;
    static word = 0;                 // partial word indicator
    while ( ! b.is_empty() )         // while buffer not empty
        switch( c = b.consume() )    // extract one char
        { case ' ' :                 // word delimiters
          case '\t':
          case '\n':                 // word delimiters
            if( word != 0 ) wcnt++;  // word complete
            word = 0;                // partial word false
            break;
          default:
            word = 1;                // partial word true
        }
}
```

Note how the static partial-word indicator word is used to count one whole word across multiple invocations of word_count and also avoids counting words of length zero.

The main program of wordcount calls readin and word_count repeatedly until input is exhausted. It then makes one final call to word_count before reporting the final result:

```
int main()
{    Cirbuf bf(128);
     for (;;)
     {  if ( readin(bf) )      // readin is producer
              word_count(bf);  // word_count is consumer
         else                  // input closed
         {    word_count(bf);  // count remaining words
              break;           // finish
         }
     }
     cout << "total " << wcnt <<  " words\n";
     return(0);
}
///////    End of File: wordcount.C    ///////
```

Now the program is ready for some sample files. If your computer system has an independent word-count program (for example, the UNIX wc command), it can be used to verify the output of the C++ program.

3.12 \ IMPLICIT AND EXPLICIT TYPE CONVERSIONS

C++ is a strongly typed language that requires all quantities be declared a type before being used in a program. The compiler uses the type information to check for possible argument-passing errors and to generate efficiently running codes. Both basic and programmer-defined types sometimes need to be converted to a related type before an operation can be performed. The conversion is sometimes done *implicitly*, or automatically. Other times, conversions must be *explicitly* requested.

Consider arithmetic operations. An arithmetic operator acting on operands of the same type produces a result of the same type. But if the operands are of different types, then they must be converted to a common type before the operation is performed. For example, an integer must be converted to floating-point before an arithmetic operation with another floating-point number. Such conversions are made automatically according to a set of rules.

Since a char is just a small integer, characters can be used freely in arithmetic expressions involving integers or other characters (as in the previous section). If a char is converted to an int and then back to a char, no information is lost.

In general, implicit conversions are performed for arithmetic operands, function arguments, function return values, and initializers. For example, a function expecting an int argument can be passed any arithmetic type that converts to an int, and the conversion is done by the compiler automatically. Implicit type conversion also takes place whenever the two sides of an assignment have different types; the right-hand-side value is converted to the type of the left-hand side. For instance, if a floating-point number (right-hand side) is assigned to an integer variable (left-hand side), the fractional part is truncated. Therefore, the function

```
int round(float f)
{    int g = f;                  // truncate fractional part
     float fracpart = f - g;
     return ( (fracpart < 0.5) ? g : g+1 );
}
```

performs the rounding of a float to the nearest integer.

When a double is converted to a float, whether the value is truncated or rounded depends on the C++ compiler for your specific machine.

For binary arithmetic operations with operands of two different types, the operand of a *lower* type will be automatically converted to the operand of a *higher* type. (The precise rules can be found in Appendix 7.) If there are no unsigned operands, the rules given in Table 3.2, applied sequentially, will suffice for most applications.

Note that when *integral promotion* is applied, a char, short, enum type, or an int bit field (Section 8.11.3) is converted to an int if int can represent all possible values of the original type. Otherwise, it is converted to unsigned int. (Type conversion rules concerning pointers and references will be discussed later when the need arises.)

TABLE 3.2   ARITHMETIC CONVERSIONS

RULE	IF ONE OPERAND IS	CONVERT OTHER OPERAND TO
1	long double	long double
2	double	double
3	float	float
4	long int	long int
5	*integral promotions*	

In a function call, when an argument has a different type than the corresponding formal parameter, type conversion is also performed automatically. However, the argument conversion takes place only if the function call has been declared by a function prototype supplying the necessary type information. The situation is more complicated when the function is overloaded (Section 3.5). It is best to avoid using this feature and use explicit type-casting whenever an argument in a function call differs from the declared type of the formal parameter.

Explicit Type-Cast

A programmer can also request type conversion *explicitly* to force data of one type to become another. The *type-cast*

```
type name ( expression )
```

converts the given *expression* to the named type. If no expression is given, the result is an undefined value of the named type. With this type-casting, we can recode the round function as follows:

```
int round(float f)
{    float fracpart = f - int(f);          // explicit type-cast
     return ( (fracpart < 0.5) ? int(f)       // round down
                            : int(f) + 1 ); // round up
}
```

Notice that, upon closer examination, we can simply implement the round function like this:

```
int round(float f)
{    return int(f + 0.5);
}
```

This explicit conversion may use any basic type, user-defined enum, and typedef names. For example, the following for loop works because of the explicit casting of the integer j + 1 to Days:

```
for ( j = MON; j < SUN ; j = Days(j + 1) )
   cout << j << "\n";
```

A class is a user-defined type, so it makes sense to talk about converting to a class type. The casting notation

```
ClassName ( expr1, expr2, ... )
```

is used where there can be zero or more argument expressions. The cast actually calls a corresponding constructor defined by the given class to produce the result. For example, the Fraction class (Section 3.3) may support all these conversions:

```
Fraction(1, 2);  // produces Fraction object 1/2
Fraction(3);     // produces Fraction object 3/1
Fraction();      // produces uninitialized Fraction object
```

In fact, how other types are converted into or from a particular class is defined by the class. This subject is not of any immediate concern and will be dealt with in Section 8.7.

For casting a single quantity, the following alternative notations can also be used:

```
float x = 3.2;
(int) x;      // convert to int
(double) x;   // convert to double
(Days) x;     // convert to enum Days
```

3.13 \ HOW TO USE HEADER FILES

The primary purpose of a header file is to make functions, variables, arrays, objects, and other data objects that are defined in one separately compilable source code file accessible from another file. For a file source.C, the convention is to use a corresponding source.h as its header file. Any file, called a *client*, that wishes to use facilities provided by source.C should include the header source.h. Furthermore, the file source.C itself should use a #include line to incorporate its own header file as well. This ensures that declarations stay consistent for the source and clients. Figure 3.4 illustrates this source–client relation.

FIGURE 3.4   SOURCE–CLIENT RELATION

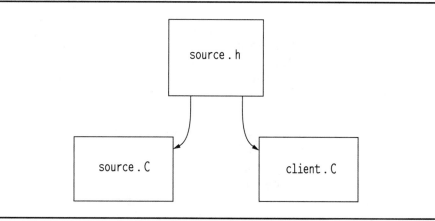

Often in practice, the client file would be using facilities provided by a package consisting of many source code files. In this case, one header file should declare constructs made available by the package. The `iostream.h` is such a header file. This organization allows you to collect information affecting multiple files in one file (the header) so that any modifications can be made easily in one place only. Thus, the impossible question, If I modify this declaration, in what other places do I have to make a similar change?, is completely avoided.

So, which declarations should go in a header file and which belong in the source code file itself? Use the following rules of thumb:

- Declare in the header any function to be accessible from another file with a function prototype (for example, `int gcd(int, int);`).
- Declare in the header any global variables to be accessible from a client with the `extern` modifier. The same global variable should also be defined with an initializer in the source (`.C`) file.
- Put class declarations to be used by clients in the header file.
- Do not put definitions, a declaration that allocates space, in a header file. For example, `int arr[10];` and `float x=3.14f;` are definitions (Section 3.6.1).
- Include any `#define` constants to be used by clients in the header file. The constants `NULL` and `EOF` in `iostream.h` are examples.
- Include enumerations (`enum`), constants (`const`), inline functions, and `typedef` (Section 3.9) declarations to be used by clients in the header file.
- Establish a pair of `.C` and `.h` files for each class or source code module. The `.h` file contains the class and other declarations to be used by a client of the class or module. The `.C` file implements the class or module with member function and other definitions. The `.C` file should also `#include` its own header file.

In summary, a header file is often the *external interface* of a program package. All necessary declarations should be there so that a client just has to `#include` the header file to access all the facilities provided by the package. On the other hand, anything unnecessary for clients should be kept out of the header.

When there are multiple header files that may include other files, there is a distinct possibility that the same header file can be included more than once. Multiple inclusion of the same header file must be avoided (Section 12.7).

The examples given so far conform to these descriptions for header files. Many more examples can be found in later chapters.

3.14 \ SUMMARY

A set of selected features of C++ are presented in detail. They provide a collection of tools and concepts for programming and pave the way for in-depth coverage of C++ and OOP in later chapters.

Identifiers can represent, among others, constants, variables, functions, classes, members, and types in a program. The first important concept related to identifiers is scoping. C++ has one name space for all identifiers. However, the same identifier is distinct in different scopes. There are four types of scopes: file, class, function, and local. Depending on its scope, an identifier can be local to a function, block (internal variables), or class; known to all functions throughout one file but not to anything outside the file; or global and accessible by all parts of the same program in one or more files. Automatic variables are created and destroyed as their program blocks are entered and exited, whereas static variables retain their value independent of control flow.

Identifiers must be declared properly before use. Declarations are instructions to the compiler and do not result in executable code. Filescope declarations are given outside of functions and classes and are used to declare or define global identifiers that may have *external* or *internal* linkage. A global variable is allocated at compile time and initialized to zero by default. There are clear rules for declaring variables in practical terms. The `typedef` feature can simplify declarations by giving meaningful names to complicated declarations.

Identifiers are often used as variables. A C++ variable has three possible storage classes: automatic, static, and dynamic. C++ provides operators `new` and `delete` to dynamically allocate and release storage at run time. It is also possible for an identifier to serve as a reference to a variable or lvalue. A reference must be initialized when declared and thus becomes an alias for the given lvalue. Reference parameters are often used to avoid copying in argument-passing and to collect return values from a function. When a reference or pointer argument does not collect a return value, it should be declared read-only with the `const` specifier to bar modifications on them.

Identifiers also serve as function names. Overloading assigns multiple meanings to the same function name. Different definitions for the same function name must have distinct signatures. The C++ compiler uses a systematic function-call resolution procedure based on the number and types of the actual arguments to pick the correct version of an overloaded function. A function can have optional arguments with default values. Passing a variable number of arguments whose types are known only at run time is possible.

Identifiers and expressions have types. Built-in rules govern conversion of types when an operator is given different data types. Type conversions also take place when passing arguments to a function and when explicitly requested in a program.

The two classes, Fraction and Cirbuf, show how a class encapsulates data and functions to define well-behaved objects. These examples illustrate topics presented in the chapter and demonstrate OOP techniques. Furthermore, they will be revisited frequently in later chapters.

EXERCISES

1. Class member names have class scope and are generally not recognized outside the class without qualification. Can you think of any class members that are recognized without being qualified?

2. Write a gcd that is nonrecursive and that can take any int arguments, not just nonnegative ones.

3. Write a function lcm that takes one or more integer arguments and returns the *least common multiple* of all the arguments (for example, lcm(-15,12) is 60). Modify operator- and operator+ in Fraction to use lcm. (*Hint:* Use gcd.)

4. Add to the class Fraction a member function floor, which returns the largest integer less than or equal to the fraction. (*Hint:* Consider both positive and negative fractions.)

5. A proper fraction lies between −1 and 1. Add to Fraction a member function is_proper().

6. The canonical representation for fractions can be broken if a programmer deliberately invokes Fraction(a,b,0) where it is not known if a and b are relatively prime. Can you design a fix to this "hole"? (*Hint:* Consider another private constructor.)

7. Following the Fraction example, write a class Complex to represent complex numbers with double real and imaginary parts. For Complex, define member binary arithmetic operators that take read-only reference parameters. Use Complex.h and Complex.C files so that the class can be compiled separately. Also, write a program Complextest.C to test the class.

8. Add the member function conjugate() to the class Complex. Is it useful in performing divisions on Complex objects?

9. Add a member to CirBuf so that the capacity of a circular buffer object can be increased dynamically. The member prototype should be int grow(int n), which causes the capacity to increase by n characters. Any unconsumed characters in the buffer remain. A −1 is returned when grow() fails.

10. Examine closely the function partition used in our quicksort (Section 3.2). Can you show that, after the while loop, the element a[i] is not less than pe? Also, is it an improvement to the partition code to modify the exchange call to exchange(a, i++, j--)?

11. Given an array of distinct integers, write an efficient program to find the *median*, the element of the array whose value is in the middle. Namely, roughly half of the elements are over and under the median. (*Hint:* Modify partition.)

12. Write a function sum that produces the total of an indefinite number of arguments uniformly of type either int, float, or double. Make sum always return double for now.

13. Consider the following code for the function swap. Is there any syntax problem here? Does the function achieve its intended purpose? Why?

```
void swap(int& a, int& b)
{    int& tmp = b;
     b = a;
     a = tmp;
}
```

14. In a function header, does it make sense to declare as const any formal parameter other than a pointer or a reference? Why? Is it possible to use the same identifier both as a variable and as a function name? What about an enum tag? A typedef name?

15. Write a program that creates an array frac_arr with new, initializes each element frac_arr[i] with the Fraction object $\frac{1}{i+1}$, displays the array, and then deletes it.

16. A *stack* is a first-in-last-out buffer. If the numbers 1.0, 2.0, 3.0 are entered into the buffer in that order, then they are taken out of the stack in the sequence 3.0, 2.0, 1.0. The operation push enters an item on the top of a stack, and the operation pop removes an item from the top of the stack. These are the only two operations that are allowed to modify a stack. Following the circular buffer example in Section 3.11, implement a class Stack for type float.

17. Use the Stack object in Exercise 16 to implement a program rp to evaluate a *reverse Polish* expression. For example,

rp 3.1 -4.2 / 5.3 6.4 - 7.5 * +

displays the value of 3.1 / -4.2 + (5.3 - 6.4) * 7.5. (*Hint:* Use the library function atof.)

18. Compare and contrast a *file scope declaration* with an extern declaration.

19. (a) If you have a function sum at file scope and a function sum in a class, is the function sum considered to be overloaded? Why? (b) If the file scope sum has a different signature than the class scope sum, can you call the file scope sum from a class member function without using the scope operator ::?

20. A function compare is a natural candidate for overloading. Write versions that compare integers, floating-point numbers, strings, characters, and fractions.

21. In C++, the return type of a function is not considered part of the signature of a function. Does this prevent you from defining functions that, in effect, make the return value part of the signature? If not, explain the mechanism you would use.

22. Consider putting the following declarations in a header file. Are they appropriate? If not, why and where should these declarations be placed?

```
extern int global_flag = 1;
static int in_file_flag = 10;
```

ARRAYS, POINTERS, AND REUSABLE CODE

Arrays are used extensively in C++ programming. Even a string is represented by an array of individual characters. A single array can group many related data items of the same type for easy processing. The arrays we have encountered so far are one-dimensional. Multidimensional arrays are also very useful and are discussed here in detail.

A pointer is a value that *points to* the location of another value. Pointers provide flexibility in organizing and accessing data stored in a program. There is a very intimate relationship between arrays and pointers, which is why they are covered together in this chapter.

Basic concepts of arrays and pointers are presented first. Then, address arithmetic is explained in detail, paving the way to a thorough discussion of two-dimensional arrays. A matrix multiplication routine further illustrates the use of two-dimensional arrays. Next, some well-selected applications, including implementing operations for a polynomial class, demonstrate how arrays and pointers are used effectively in practice. There is also a complete example for text-line sorting with objects, which pulls together many features of C++ programming presented so far.

The chapter also presents more advanced pointer usage and applications in building reusable programs. It covers pointer and reference parameters for functions, read-only and return parameters, multiple indirection, functional arguments, and pointer arrays. The discussion leads to the implementation of a *generic* sorting program that can be reused in different situations. Also discussed is the use of pointers in combination with dynamic storage allocation.

4.1 \ ARRAY CONCEPTS AND DECLARATIONS

The array is the simplest data structure beyond the basic types such as char, int, and float. In earlier chapters, we have already seen some use of arrays. In general, an array is a section of consecutive *memory cells*, each large enough to hold a data element of the same predetermined type. Each cell in an array is also referred to as an *array entry* or *array element*. The declaration

```
char str[10];
```

establishes str as a *one-dimensional* array of 10 entries, str[0], str[1], up to str[9], each of type char. An array can be initialized when declared (Section 1.11). The initializers enclosed in braces ({}) must be constant expressions. Here is an array of two objects with initializers:

```
Fraction frac_arr[] = { Fraction(1,2),
                        Fraction(3,4) };
```

An array declaration, with or without initialization, can occur anywhere a variable declaration can.

The *index* notation str[n] refers to the $(n + 1)$th entry of str. In general, if there are k entries, then the index goes from 0 to $k - 1$. The index notation is used to store and retrieve values in an array:

```
str[0]='A';
cout.put(str[0]);
str[1]='B';
cout.put(str[1]);
```

In other words, each array entry is used just like a variable of the declared type. The advantage is that array entries are indexed and can therefore be used effectively in loops. Although each array entry is like a variable, the array name is a constant representing the address (memory location) of the first entry of the array. Thus, str is a constant whose value is the location of str[0]. Because the array name is a constant, its value cannot be changed. Hence, an array name cannot be used on the left-hand side of an assignment or with a decrement or increment operator such as str++.

As an address, an array name can be assigned to a *pointer variable* of the appropriate type. Thus,

```
char *s;
s = str;
s[0] = 'Z';
```

is a roundabout way to assign the character 'Z' to str[0].

An array name can also be used in a function call as an argument. At the time of the call, the value of the array name (the address of the first entry of the array) is passed to the formal parameter in the called function. Array formal parameters are local variables and are usually used just like pointer variables. The function

```
int strequal(char x[], char y[]);
```

(given in Section 1.11) is an example.

Up to this point, we have used indexing with arrays and pointers. The index notation is easy to read and understand, but pointers can also be manipulated directly, as explained in Section 4.2.

4.2 \ POINTERS AND ADDRESS ARITHMETIC

4.2.1   Basic Pointer Concepts

A pointer variable is a variable whose value is the *address* of a memory location where a specific type of data is stored. When a pointer variable is declared, the data type it points to is specified. The notations

```
int *a, *b;
char *r, *s;
Account *u;
Fraction *f;
```

declare a and b as integer pointer variables and r and s as character pointer variables. The pointers u and f can hold addresses for an Account object and a Fraction object, respectively. Figure 4.1 shows a regular variable p at memory location 1200 and a pointer variable q at location 1204 without an initial value. A pointer declaration merely creates the pointer variable; it neither initializes the pointer variable nor allocates memory space for the variable to point to. *Therefore, before it is used, a pointer variable must be assigned the address of an array, a variable, an object, or some dynamically allocated space.* Figure 4.2 shows q getting the address of p. Therefore, the sequence

```
int *ptr_a;
int m[]={1,2,3,4};            // m is an integer array
```

FIGURE 4.1   REGULAR AND POINTER VARIABLES

```
int p = 7;                        p                              q
int *q;      Address: 1200 ——→ [  7  ]   Address: 1204 ——→ [ ??? ]
```

FIGURE 4.2   A POINTER VARIABLE WITH ADDRESS AS VALUE

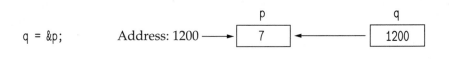

$q = \&p;$ Address: 1200   p   7   q   1200

```
ptr_a = m;                      // pointer ptr_a assigned address of m
ptr_a[3]= ptr_a[0]+5*ptr_a[1]; // entries of m referenced through ptr_a
```

results in m[3] being 11. Since ptr_a is a pointer variable of type int, it can be assigned the address of an integer array m. For a Vector pointer, the same guidelines apply:

```
Vector *v = new Vector[2];    // v points to allocated space
v[0] = Vector(0.0, 1.0);
v[1] = Vector(1.0, 0.0);
```

4.2.2   The Operators & and *

Two unary operators are important in dealing with pointers: &, the address-of operator, and *, the value-of operator. The address-of operator & gives the pointer to (address of) a variable, a class object, or an array entry in memory. The statement

```
int *ap = &m[3];
```

assigns to ap the address of the int array entry m[3] and causes ap to *point to* m[3]. Similarly,

```
Vector *vp = &v[1];
```

assigns the address of the object v[1] to vp. The address-of operator & can be applied only to data stored in memory and will not work with constants, register variables, or expressions such as (a + b).

Taking the address of a reference gives the address of the variable referenced. For example,

```
Cirbuf b(256);         // circular buffer object
Cirbuf& cbuf = b;      // cbuf is reference to b
Cirbuf* b_ptr = &cbuf; // b_ptr == address of b
```

Note that Cirbuf& is a reference type declaration and has *nothing* to do with the address-of operator &.

The value-of operator `*` is used to access a data item through a pointer. The `*` can be used on a pointer variable, a pointer constant, or any expression that produces a valid pointer value. After `int *ptr_a = &a;`, the notation

```
*ptr_a
```

stands for the variable `a` and behaves exactly the same. Thus, `*ptr_a` has the value of `a`, and

```
*ptr_a = 5;
```

is the same as saying `a=5` because it stores 5 at the address where `a` stores its value. Note that the value of the pointer variable `ptr_a` itself is not changed by this assignment. In general, if `ptr` is a pointer of a certain type, then `*ptr` can be used as a variable of that type. The following code further illustrates this concept:

```
*ptr_a = i - 3        // ptr_a is a pointer variable, i integer
*m += 2               // m is an int array
i = 5 * *ptr_a        // multiplication
( i >= *ptr_a )       // relational operation
++*ptr_a              // or (*ptr_a)++, increment *ptr_a
(*m)--                // or --*m, decrement *m
```

The unary operators `*` and `&` have the same precedence as unary arithmetic operators and have higher precedence than binary arithmetic and relational operators. The parentheses are necessary in the last example because unary operators such as `*`, `++`, and `--` *associate right to left*. Hence,

```
*ptr_a--     and     *(ptr_a--)
```

are equivalent and would decrement the pointer variable `ptr_a` rather than the integer `*ptr_a`.

Another general observation that can be made of the `*` operator is that *`*ptr`* is always equivalent to *`ptr`*[0]. In fact, the compiler automatically converts the latter notation to the former. This is another reason why pointers are closely related to arrays.

4.2.3 Double Indirection

For an integer pointer variable `ptr_a`, it is clear what `*ptr_a` means. But, what is `&ptr_a`? By definition, it is the address of `ptr_a`. In other words, `&ptr_a` is a pointer to an integer pointer. Thus, the artificial sequence

```
int k, *ptr_a, **ptr_b;    // ptr_b is a pointer to an int pointer
ptr_b = &ptr_a;            // ptr_b points to ptr_a
ptr_a = &k;                // ptr_a points to k (same as *ptr_b = &k)
**ptr_b = 15;              // k gets 15
```

results in the variable k being assigned the value 15, as illustrated in Figure 4.3. Here is how it works:

1. Since ptr_b points to ptr_a, *ptr_b is ptr_a.
2. Since ptr_a points to k, **ptr_b is k.
3. Thus, **ptr_b = 15 is the same as k = 15.

The same reasoning can be applied to unravel multiple indirections (Section 4.8).

4.2.4 Address Arithmetic

Address arithmetic calculates memory addresses using pointers. Thus, it is also known as *pointer arithmetic*. A pointer is an integer byte count identifying a memory location so many bytes away from a certain reference address, such as the beginning of a program. For instance, 15084 points to byte 15084 from the reference location. A pointer gives the beginning of a *data cell*, which may take 1 or more bytes, depending on the type of data stored there. The exact number of bytes for each data type is implementation-dependent. On 32-bit computers, a char usually takes 1 byte and an int 4 bytes.

In practice, a pointer is often used to access a sequence of data cells stored in consecutive memory locations rather than just a single cell. To get from one such data cell to the next, you can use several convenient address arithmetic operations:

- Pointer + integer, resulting in a pointer.
- Pointer − integer, giving another pointer.
- Pointer − pointer, getting an integer.

A discussion of each of these operations follows.

Pointer + Integer

Adding an integer quantity to a pointer is not as mysterious as it may seem. In fact, we have been using it implicitly all along. The familiar array notation b[3]

FIGURE 4.3   **DOUBLE INDIRECTION**

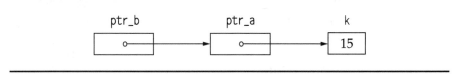

retrieves the desired data by calculating its address based on the information that it is the third item after the cell at b, namely, b[0]. With *explicit address arithmetic*, the same address can be computed by

```
b + 3              // &b[3] or address of b[3]
```

The result of this address addition is a pointer to b[3], as shown in Figure 4.4. Note that this is not adding 3; rather, it is adding 3 times the size of the data cell to the address represented by b.

Thus, if b is an int pointer and b is 15084, then the pointer b+3 has value $15084 + 12 = 15096$, assuming that int takes 4 bytes. But if b is a char pointer, then b+3 becomes $15084 + 3 = 15087$. When an address arithmetic expression such as b+3 is encountered by the compiler, it takes the size of the data cell into account and produces the appropriate code. This arrangement is convenient for programming and makes the program independent of the data type sizes on different computers.

As a result, the general rule holds: If ptr is a pointer and n an integer, then

```
ptr + n
```

is the pointer for the *n*th data cell from the one pointed to by ptr. And the expression

```
*(ptr + n)          // same as ptr[n]
```

is the same as ptr[n], where ptr can be a pointer variable or an array name.

To further illustrate pointer usage, let's consider a pointer version of the standard library function **strcmp** (Section 6.1), which returns an integer value greater than, equal to, or less than zero if the string r is greater than, equal to, or less than the string s, respectively:

```
int strcmp(const char *r, const char *s)
{    while (*r == *s)
     {    if (*r == '\0') return (0);    // strings are equal
          r++; s++;                      // advance pointers
     }
     return(*r - *s);                    // strings are not equal
}
```

FIGURE 4.4   **POINTER + INTEGER**

The definition of strcmp depends on the fact that the string terminator is a zero-valued character.

As another example, consider a pointer implementation of the library function strcpy, which makes a copy of its second argument into the first argument:

```
char *strcpy(char *s, const char *cs)
{   char *tmp = s;
    while (*cs != '\0')
            *(tmp++) = *(cs++);        // copy next character
    *tmp = '\0';
    return(s);
}
```

The pointer variable tmp is first declared and initialized to s. Next, the while loop copies each character on the string cs until '\0' is encountered. Finally, the terminator '\0' is copied, and the pointer s returned. The variable tmp is technically unnecessary because s can serve as a *return parameter* (Section 4.6).

A common source of error in copying by passing pointers is insufficient space to receive the data being copied. In this example, s is assumed to point to the beginning of a reserved space large enough to hold the entire string. The minimum number of bytes needed is

strlen(cs) + 1

where the '\0' terminator occupies the final byte. In this case, it is the responsibility of the calling function to ensure that enough space has been provided. If this is undesirable, the copying function may dynamically allocate space as in the function dstrcpy (dynamic string copy):

```
char *dstrcpy(const char *cs)
{     char *s, *tmp;
      unsigned size = strlen(cs)+1;        // or size_t size
      tmp = s = new(char[size]);           // allocate space
      while (*cs != '\0') *(tmp++)= *(cs++); // copy next character
      *tmp = '\0';
      return(s);
}
```

Note that the pointer returned by dstrcpy can later be freed with delete.

Pointer — Integer

Subtracting an integer from a pointer is the inverse of adding an integer. An example is contained in a pointer implementation of the function match, which compares a string s1 with the name prefix of s2:

```
//   Both s1 and s2 are strings:
//   s1 is the target name to find, s2 is in the form name=value
//   If the names match, value is returned, else NULL is returned.

char *match(char *s1, char *s2)
{   while ( *s1 == *s2++ )
        if ( *s1++ == '=') return(s2);    // field delimiter
    if (*s1 == '\0' && *(s2-1) == '=')
        return(s2);                       // match found
    return(NULL);
}
```

Immediately after the while loop, the last step in determining a match is to pair the terminator of s1 with the field delimiter =, one character before *s2. The pointer subtraction *(s2-1) gives exactly the character needed.

For functions, such as match, that return pointers, it is conventional to return an invalid pointer NULL when the computation fails. The symbolic constant NULL is usually defined as zero in the header iostream.h. Although NULL can be assigned to any pointer variable, dereferencing it with * is a run-time error, which can crash the program.

With pointer subtraction, we have the alternative of going backward on a sequence of data cells. For instance, a loop may go from the end of an array to the beginning. This flexibility and power do not come without danger. Be careful not to *fall off the end* of the data cells by going beyond the proper range.

Pointer − Pointer

It is also valid to subtract one pointer from another. If p and q are pointers to entries of the same array, then

```
n = q - p
```

is an integer n that is the distance between cells p and q. In other words, p + n is q. Note that n can be positive, negative, or zero. Here is a pointer-based version of **strlen** that uses this feature:

```
int strlen(const char *s)    // computes length of string s
{   const char *t = s;
    while( *t++ != '\0' ) {} // go to end of string
    return(t - s - 1);       // length of string without terminator
}
```

In this version of **strlen**, the while loop, with an empty body, increments t until it reaches the end of the string. Then, the return statement computes the correct length of s via pointer subtraction.

Actually, the pointer variable t is incremented to one character beyond the terminating '\0'. So, potentially, t now points to some address that may contain another type of data or may even be outside of the address space of the program. But this is only a problem if access is attempted — say, with *t.

4.2.5 Valid Pointer Operations

In this section, valid pointer operations are summarized for easy reference. The material here also contains some details not previously mentioned, as well as topics yet to come in this chapter.

- *Creation:* The initial value of a pointer has three possible sources: a constant pointer such as an array name, an address obtained with the & operator, or a value returned by a dynamic memory allocation operation.

- *Assignment:* Pointers of the same type can be assigned. Pointers of different types can be assigned only with an explicit cast (Section 3.12). However, a void * variable can be assigned a pointer of any type without explicit casting. An array name is a constant pointer and cannot be used on the left-hand side of an assignment. The NULL pointer (usually zero) can be assigned as a pointer value.

- *p ± integer:* Adding or subtracting an integer from a pointer also includes the operations p++, p--, p += 2, and so on. Such expressions are valid as long as the resulting pointer is within the range of the same array. A pointer is also allowed to go one step beyond the high end of an array. In other words, if p points to the last entry of an array, the pointer p+1 is valid as long as no attempt is made to access the nonexistent entry it points to. Although most compilers do not check whether a pointer falls outside its range, it is good practice to make sure that it stays within the allowed bounds.

- *Pointer subtraction:* Pointers of the same type can be subtracted, yielding an integer that is positive, negative, or zero. In practice, only pointers to entries of the same array are subtracted.

- *Comparison:* Pointers to entries of the same array can be compared with ==, <, >, and so on. Any pointer can be checked for equality with the NULL pointer. A function returning a pointer usually would return NULL as an indication of error or failure. The calling function must compare the returned pointer with NULL to detect such an error.

- *Indirection:* For a pointer ptr of a certain type, *ptr becomes a variable of that type and therefore can be used in expressions and on the left-hand side of an assignment.

- *Indexing:* A pointer p, whether an array name or a pointer variable, can be used with an index subscript as in p[i], where i is a positive or negative integer. The notation is converted by the compiler to *(p+i). Again, it is the programmer's responsibility to make sure that the indexing stays within the bounds of the array.

4.3 \ TWO-DIMENSIONAL ARRAYS

Up to this point, all of the arrays we have seen use a single index or subscript. Such arrays are *one-dimensional*. It is possible to have arrays with more than one subscript. For example,

```
int a[2][4];
```

declares a to be a *two-dimensional* array with the first subscript going from 0 to 1 and the second ranging from 0 to 3. In other words, the array can be thought of as a rectangular grid of two rows and four columns (Figure 4.5). The actual memory organization of a two-dimensional array is still linear: A total of eight entries are allocated in consecutive memory cells (Figure 4.6). The array entries are stored by *rows*, with the first row followed by the second row, and so on. Using pointer arithmetic, the organization by rows also means that the address &a[i][j] is given by

```
&a[0][0] + i*4 + j      // points to cell a[i][j]
```

where the 4 is the number of columns of a. Thus, it is possible to access a[i][j] using the alternative notation

```
int *p = &a[0][0];
*(p + i*4 + j)          // value of a[i][j]
```

or equivalently

```
p[i*4 + j]
```

A two-dimensional array can be initialized as follows:

```
int a[][4]= { {0,1,2,3}, {4,5,6,7} };
```

Note that the range of the last subscript must be given explicitly. The initializer is a list of sublists for the rows. No sublist may contain more elements than the range specified in the declaration. On the other hand, it is always possible to

FIGURE 4.5   **TWO-DIMENSIONAL ARRAY LOGICAL VIEW**

a[0][0]	a[0][1]	a[0][2]	a[0][3]
a[1][0]	a[1][1]	a[1][2]	a[1][3]

FIGURE 4.6   TWO-DIMENSIONAL ARRAY MEMORY ALLOCATION

a[0][0]	a[0][1]	a[0][2]	a[0][3]	a[1][0]	a[1][1]	a[1][2]	a[1][3]

initialize *less* than the full range for any row. Some sublists may even be empty ({}).

One natural question to ask at this point is, Why is the syntax

```
a[i][j]
```

used rather than the common notation for two-dimensional arrays used in other programming languages?

```
a[i,j]           // not used in C++
```

The answer is that a two-dimensional array is really just a one-dimensional array of elements that are themselves one-dimensional arrays. Thus, a[i][j] literally means (a[i])[j], and a[i] is a constant pointer, of type int *, pointing to the $i + first$ row of the two-dimensional array a. The following test program further illustrates many concepts related to pointers and the two-dimensional array:

```
const int RANGE=4;
int main()
{      int a[][RANGE]= { {0,1,2,3}, {4,5}, {8,9,10,11} };
       int *p = &a[0][0];
       int *q = a[0];                    // p and q are the same
       int *r = a[1];                    // pointer to 2nd row
       int *s = a[2];                    // pointer to 3rd row
       cout << *(p+RANGE+1) << endl;     // a[1][1]
       cout << *(q+2*RANGE+2) << endl;   // a[2][2]
       cout << *r << endl;               // a[1][0]
       cout << *(r-2) << endl;           // a[0][2]
       cout << s[3] << endl;             // a[2][3]
       return(0):
}
```

The variable a is created as a 3×4, two-dimensional array of consecutive integers. The second row is partially initialized. The pointers q, r, and s point to the first, second, and third row of a, respectively. A variety of notations have been used to access cells of a to reinforce your understanding of the two-dimensional array representation, as well as pointer arithmetic.

Having a basic understanding of two-dimensional arrays, we are now ready to implement them.

Matrix Multiplication

Using pointer arithmetic, let's write a function matmul to compute the product of two matrices containing integer entries. A matrix is naturally represented by a two-dimensional array. The product of an $r \times s$ matrix X by an $s \times t$ matrix Y is an $r \times t$ matrix Z. (To appreciate this one, *say* the equation.) Each entry $Z_{i,j}$ is given by the inner product of row i of X and column j of Y. Here is a simple example:

$$\begin{pmatrix} 1 & 2 \\ 3 & 4 \\ 5 & 6 \end{pmatrix} \cdot \begin{pmatrix} a & b \\ c & d \end{pmatrix} = \begin{pmatrix} a+2c & b+2d \\ 3a+4c & 3b+4d \\ 5a+6c & 5b+6d \end{pmatrix}$$

The matrix multiplication function matmul is implemented as follows:

```
void matmul(int *x, int *y, int* z, int r, int s, int t)
//   x, y, z are pointers to 1st entries of the 2D arrays
//   r, s, t are array dimensions
{   int rtc(int *row, int *col, int s, int t); // prototype for rtc
    for (int i=0 ; i < r ; i++)
    {   x += i*s;                         // x points to next row
        for (int j=0 ; j < t ; j++)
            *z++ = rtc(x,y+j,s,t);        // y+j points to col j of y
    }
}
```

The function matmul takes the three pointers x, y, and z to the three two-dimensional arrays representing the matrices and takes the int dimensions r, s, and t as input parameters. Nested for loops are used to compute elements of the result array z. Each iteration of the outer loop advances x to the next row. Each iteration of the inner loop takes the row x and multiplies it with the next column of y to produce an entry of z. The row-column inner product is performed by the function rtc (row times column), which takes a row pointer into the array x and a col pointer into the array y and computes the required inner product:

```
int rtc(int *row, int *col, int s, int t) // inner product row . col
{   int sum=0;
    while ( s-- > 0 )
    {   sum += (*row++) * *col;
        col += t;                         // next column entry
    }
    return(sum);
}
```

To get from one entry to the next in the same column of y, the col pointer is incremented by t, the column dimension of y. To test these functions, use the following:

```
int main()
{    int a[2][3]= { {1,-2,5}, {1,2,3}};
     int b[3][2]= { {9,7},{-2,3},{-1,4}};
     int c[2][2];
     matmul(*a,*b,*c,2,3,2);    // pass *a rather than a
     cout <<"( " << c[0][0] << "    " << c[0][1] << " )\n( "
         << c[1][0]   << "    " << c[1][1] << " )\n";
     return(0);
}
```

The output of this program is

```
( 8    21 )
( 2    25 )
```

Using a separate function rtc to compute the row-column inner product adds to the clarity of the programs but incurs the performance penalty of extra function calls at run time. If execution speed is important, you can eliminate the function rtc by coding the inner-product computation as a third, innermost loop in matmul.

In our implementation of matmul, the arrays are passed into the function as pointers of type int. It is also possible to receive two-dimensional arrays as such directly with the function declaration

```
matmul(int a[][3], int b[][2], int c[][2], int r, int s, int t)
```

and to use two-dimensional array indexing in the function body. The disadvantage of using two-dimensional array formal parameters is that the range of the last subscript must be given explicitly in the function header. This means that the function can multiply only matrices with those fixed dimensions — an unreasonable restriction that is avoided by the pointer-based implementation.

At this juncture, let's study some typical applications of arrays and pointers to help sharpen the concepts presented.

4.4 A CLASS OF POLYNOMIALS

Arrays and pointers are now applied in building a polynomial class. It is important that pointers are not studied in isolation but in conjunction with other constructs to solve problems. By doing so, the abstract rules of pointer usage become concrete and easy to grasp. The polynomial class again demonstrates techniques for data abstraction and program encapsulation.

With the exception of numbers, polynomials are the most basic mathematical structures. They are widely used in many fields of study. Consider establishing a class Poly for one-variable polynomials with integer coefficients. Such a polynomial has the familiar form

$$a_n x^n + a_{n-1} x^{n-1} + \cdots + a_1 x + a_0$$

where x is the variable and $a_n, a_{n-1}, \ldots, a_0$ are the coefficients. The polynomial has *degree n*, and the *leading coefficient* $a_n \neq 0$. For example,

$$3x^5 - 10x^2 + 21x - 8 \tag{4.1}$$

is a fifth-degree polynomial with four terms. Each term is a coefficient multiplied by a power of x. Such a polynomial can be represented by an int array recording the power-coefficient pairs of each term. For instance,

```
int pol[] = {5,3,2,-10,1,21,0,-8,-1};
```

gives the fifth-degree polynomial (4.1). The representation pol begins with the highest power, its coefficient, followed by the next highest power, its coefficient, and so on. A minus one (-1) is used as an end marker because no negative power is allowed for a polynomial. To conserve space, terms with a zero coefficient are not included. Table 4.1 shows how this representation works.

The polynomial representation and operations can be encapsulated in a Poly class declared with code similar to the following:

```
/////// 	 File: Poly.h 	 ///////
class Poly
{ public:
        Poly() { pol = NULL; }      // default constructor
        Poly(int *p, int terms);    // constructor
        Poly operator+(Poly q);     // poly addition
        Poly operator-(Poly q);     // poly subtraction
        Poly operator*(Poly q);     // poly multiplication
        void display();             // display host object
        unsigned int deg()          // degree
        { return(pol[0] > 0 ? pol[0] : 0); }
```

TABLE 4.1   A POLYNOMIAL REPRESENTATION

	REPRESENTATION	POLYNOMIAL
	int p1[] = {100,1,50,1,0,1,-1};	$x^{100} + x^{50} + 1$
	int p2[] = {20,9,7,-29,-1};	$9x^{20} - 29x^7$
	int p3[] = {0,8,-1};	8
	int p4[] = {-1};	0

```
    /* other members */
  private:
    int length();              // length of pol
    int *pol;                  // points to free storage
};
```

The constructor makes sure that the incoming terms are copied into free storage. The pointer p supplies n terms with 2*n integers but no end marker, which is strictly for internal use. A zero polynomial is instantiated if n is zero:

```
///////    File: Poly.C    ///////
#include <iostream.h>
#include "Poly.h"

Poly::Poly(int *p, int n)        // constructor
{   n = 2*n;
    pol = new int[n+1];          // dynamic allocation
    for ( int i=0 ; i < n ; i++ )
        pol[i] = *p++;
    pol[n] = -1;                 // terminator
}
```

The private member length() counts how many int's are in the representation pol:

```
int Poly::length()
{ for (int i=0 ; pol[i] > -1 ; i += 2);
  return(i+1);
}
```

The member function operator+() is a little more complicated and can be defined as follows:

```
Poly Poly::operator+(Poly q)             // polynomial addition
{   int *c, *a, *b, *tmp;
    unsigned len, d;
    len = length()+q.length()-1;
    d = 1+2*(1+ MAX(deg(), q.deg()));
    len = MIN(len, d);                   // max length of answer
    tmp = c = new(int[len]);             // temporary space for result
    a = pol; b = q.pol;
    while (*a >= 0)                      // for each term of a
    { while(*b > *a)                     // terms in b of higher power
      {   *c++ = *b++;
          *c++ = *b++;
      }
      *c++ = *a;
```

```
        if (*a == *b)                   // add terms of like power (1)
        {   *c = *++a + *++b;
            if (*c++ == 0) c -= 2;      // terms cancel            (2)
            b++;
        }
        else *c++ = *++a;               // no terms to combine
        a++;
    }
    while (*b >= 0) *c++ = *b++;        // add leftover terms in b
    *c = -1;                            // terminator
    Poly ans(tmp, (c-tmp)/2);           // answer object           (3)
    delete tmp;                         // free temporary space
    return(ans);
}
```

In Poly::operator+(), the maximum size of the result polynomial is computed and then that much space is allocated with new to hold the temporary result. The sum computation now continues depositing terms in tmp using c as a running pointer.

To compute the sum, each term of a is added to the unprocessed terms of b with a power greater than or equal to the current term. The resulting terms are stored in c. When two terms from a and b combine (line 1), a check is made to see whether the new term is zero due to cancellation. If so, the c pointer is decremented by 2 to lose the zero coefficient and its exponent (line 2). The iteration continues until all terms of a and b have been processed. Finally, the −1 terminator is inserted at the end of c.

Now, all we have to do is establish a Poly object with the correct number of terms (line 3), free up the temporary space (which may be too large for the actual result), and return ans.

Note that ans is an automatic variable, so it will be destroyed after operator+() returns. This is not a problem because a copy of the value of ans is returned and not ans itself. The situation is entirely the same as returning an int or a float local variable. However, creating copies of objects containing dynamically allocated storage does present certain complications, a topic discussed later (Section 7.10).

For testing purposes, various polynomials should be added and the results displayed. Having a member function display is handy:

```
void Poly::display()
{   int *p = pol;
    switch ( *p )
    { case -1:                          // zero poly       (A)
        cout << "0" << endl; break;
      case 0:                           // constant poly   (B)
```

```
      cout << p[1] << endl; break;
  default:
    cout << '(';                // display terms
    while ( *p >= 0 )
    {  cout << *p << "  " << *(p+1);
       p += 2;
       if (*p != -1) cout << ", ";
    }
    cout << ")\n";
  }
}
```

Note that a constant polynomial is displayed as an integer (lines A and B). Write a main program to test the Poly class and to display some polynomials.

It is clear that many other members must be defined before the Poly class is complete. Section 4.5 contains another interesting application.

4.5 \ SORTING TEXT LINES WITH OBJECTS

Ordering or sorting lines of text is commonplace in data-processing applications. Let's now consider a simple sort program. The command mysort will be used in the form

mysort [key]

It will read all lines with cin, sort the lines by comparing the given *key* in the lines, and then write out the sorted lines with cout. Each line is assumed to contain one or more fields separated by white spaces (SPACE or TAB). The *key* is an integer indicating which field to use for ordering the lines. If the *key* is unspecified, then whole lines are compared.

For example, suppose there are files containing course grades in the form

```
John Smith      A
Paul Kline      C
Richard Brown   B
```

The command mysort can be used on such files: Use key position 2 to sort by last name and key position 3 to sort by letter grade.

To sort the input lines, the strategy is to read each line into a string (character array) and to put the pointer for each string in another one-dimensional array, forming an array of pointers or a *pointer array*. The entries of the pointer array are sorted and then used in producing the output lines in the right order. The pointer-array approach avoids the actual interchange of text lines by interchanging only the pointers (Figure 4.7). Text-line interchange is expensive because it involves three separate copying operations of character strings.

FIGURE 4.7   SORTING WITH A POINTER ARRAY

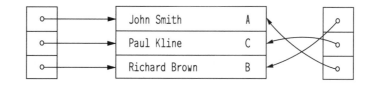

Taking an object-oriented view, we can identify two useful objects:

1. A TextLines object, which holds the input text lines, knows how to interchange any two lines, and can output the ordered lines to standard output.

2. A SortKey object, which compares the designated keys of any two text lines.

With these objects, the implementation of the mysort command consists of the following major steps:

1. Establish a TextLines object, txtobj, to hold the input lines.

2. Establish a SortKey object based on the key position and delimiter characters.

3. Apply quicksort using these objects and then ask txtobj to display itself.

All of this is tied together with a main program which first processes the command-line arguments and then performs the three steps just listed.

This example is more extensive than any we have seen so far. Its description is organized according to the preceding outline. It also shows how to break down a complicated program into independent objects that interact to perform the task at hand.

mysort: Building a Class of Text Lines

After a Textlines object is initialized, lines can be read and stored within the object. The maximum number of lines and characters per line can be specified at object-initialization time. Otherwise, reasonable default values are used. Operations provided include reading text lines (input), interchanging lines (swap), indexing ([]), reporting the number of lines (length), and outputting lines (display):

```
///////     File: TextLines.h     ///////
#include        <iostream.h>
```

```
typedef char * String;
typedef unsigned int Uint;

class TextLines
{ public:
      TextLines(Uint size = 1024, Uint ll = 256);
      Uint length() { return len; }
      void swap(Uint i, Uint j);            // interchange lines
      String operator[](Uint i)             // overloading []
      { return( i < len ? lines[i] : NULL ); }
      void input(istream& in);              // reads lines into object
      void display();                       // output lines
      ~TextLines();                         // destructor
  private:
      String *lines;
      Uint    len;                          // total no. of lines
      Uint    maxlines;                     // max no. of lines
      Uint    linelen;                      // max line length
      int     read_lines(istream& in);
};

inline void TextLines::swap(Uint i, Uint j)
      { String tmp = lines[i];
        lines[i] = lines[j];
        lines[j] = tmp;
      }
```

Overloading the [] operator makes it possible to use indexing on a TextLines object. Thus, if txtobj is a TextLines object, then

```
txtobj[n];          // gives line n
```

is a convenient way to obtain line n. Clearly, a TextLines object is useful whenever a program deals with lines of text from standard input or a file. This is another concrete example of building components that are reusable in many places—a significant advantage of OOP.

A user of TextLines need not know how it is implemented. Access to the header file is enough. Implementation details are hidden in the TextLines.C file, which begins with the constructor and the input function:

```
///////   File: TextLines.C   ///////
#include      <iostream.h>
#include      <string.h>
#include      <stdlib.h>
#include      "TextLines.h"
```

```
TextLines::TextLines
(Uint size /* = 1024 */, Uint ll /* = 256 */)
{    maxlines = size;
     linelen = ll;
     lines = new String[size];
}
```

Notice how the default values are commented out in the constructor header. This is necessary because the default values are first supplied in TextLines.h and resupplying such values is not allowed in C++.

The member input calls the active routine read_lines to read lines. The function read_lines returns the number of lines read if successful. Otherwise, a negative integer is returned: $-j - 1$ means the input line j is too long; -1 indicates other errors.

```
void TextLines::input(istream& in)
{    len = read_lines(in);
     if (len < 0 )
     {  if (len == -1)
           cerr << "TextLines: Input file too large\n";
        else if (len < 0 )
           cerr << "TextLines: Line "
                << -len-1 << " too long\n";
        exit(1);
     }
}
```

The read_lines implementation uses pointers: comparing (line 1), advancing (line 3), and subtracting pointers (lines 2 and 4). To actually read a line, the getline member of the input stream object in is called (Section 6.6).

```
int TextLines::read_lines(istream& in)
{   int k, error=0, m = linelen + 2;
    String buf, s;
    String *lptr = lines, *end = lines + maxlines ;

    if ( (buf = new char[m]) == NULL )
       return(-1);
    while( in.getline(buf, m, '\n') )
    {  k = strlen(buf);                    // line length
       if ( lptr >= end )
       {  error = -1; break; }            // too many lines      (1)
       else if ( k == m-1 )
       {  error = (lines-lptr)-2;  break; } // line too long     (2)
       else if ( (s = new char[k+1])==NULL )
       {  error = -1; break; }            // no free store
```

```
        else                              // copies buffer into s
        {   strcpy(s, buf); *lptr++ = s; }    // puts s on lines[]    (3)
    }
    delete [] buf;
    return(error ? error : lptr-lines);    // error or lines read (4)
}
```

A similar pointer-controlled loop displays all lines contained in a TextLines object. The destructor frees up dynamically allocated storage.

```
void TextLines::display()
{   String *lptr = lines,
        *end = lines + len;
    while(lptr < end) cout << *lptr++ << '\n';
}


TextLines::~TextLines()
{   String *lptr = lines;
    while(len-- > 0)
        delete [] *lptr++;
    delete [] lines;
}
///////    End of file TextLines.C    ///////
```

mysort: Comparing Keys

Line sorting has two aspects: quicksort and key comparison. A SortKey object supplies the capability to identify and compare specific key positions.

When initialized, a SortKey object holds the key position and the delimiter string, quantities used by the private member function key to identify the sort key in a text line (String). An established SortKey object is used to compare two text lines.

Letting the user of mysort specify the key field and implementing a separate key-comparison object provide the kind of flexibility that characterizes good programs. On top of this, the field delimiters are also settable rather than hard-coded. Other useful delimiters include '=', ',', '.', and ':'.

```
///////    File: SortKey.h    ///////
typedef char *String;
typedef unsigned int Uint;

class SortKey
{ public:
    SortKey(Uint pos = 0, String dlm = "\t \r")
    {   delim = dlm;
```

```
        position = pos;
    }
    void set_delim(String s) { delim = s; }   // set delimiter string
    int cmp(const char *a, const char *b);   // compare lines
  private:
    String delim;
    Uint   position;
    const char *key(const char *s);          // identify key
    int is_del(const char* c);               // delimiter test
    int keycmp(const char *a, const char *b); // compare keys
};
```

Selecting the sort keys and comparing them are implemented with pointer operations and string library functions. The string library functions used in key need the <string.h> header file (Section 6.1):

```
///////    File: SortKey.C    ///////
#include <string.h>
#include "SortKey.h"

const char *SortKey::key(const char *s)
{   int i = position;           // key position
    while ( --i > 0 )           // skipping positions
    {   s += strspn(s,delim);   // find start of position (1)
        s += strcspn(s,delim);  // find end of position    (2)
    }
    s += strspn(s,delim);
    return(s);                  // ptr to first char of key
}
```

In the member function key, the call on line 1 skips over delimiters and the call on line 2 skips over a key position. Finally, the desired key position is found, and a pointer is returned. The string library functions strspn and strcspn (Section 6.1) save much extra work.

The cmp member function compares two text lines. Basically, cmp performs a **strcmp** on the two lines or, if a key position has been given, compares the two key fields:

```
int SortKey::cmp(const char *a, const char *b)
{   if (position == 0)
        return( strcmp(a,b));
    return( keycmp(key(a), key(b)) );
}

inline int SortKey::is_del(const char* c)     // private member
        { return(strspn(c,delim) || *c == '\0'); }
```

```
int SortKey::keycmp(const char *a, const char *b)
{   for(; *a == *b; a++, b++)
    {   if ( is_del(a) ) return(0);          // a equal to b
    }
    if ( is_del(a) && is_del(b) )
        return(0);
    if ( is_del(a) ) return(-1);             // a less than b
    else if ( is_del(b) ) return(1);         // a greater than b
    else return(*a - *b);                    // a not equal to b
}
```

An inline function is used to test whether a string begins with a delimiter or
'\0'. Note that keycmp returns positive, zero, or negative for key a greater than,
equal to, or less than key b, respectively. This is consistent with the way strcmp
works and is what the partition routine of quicksort expects.

mysort: Ordering the Lines

The objective of this part of the program is to take the text lines in txtobj and
sort them into order by comparing the appropriate keys.

The approach is to adapt the quicksort procedure used for integer arrays
(Section 3.2) to the TextLines object txtobj. The recursive function quicksort
itself is mostly the same as before. However, now txtobj.swap interchanges
lines. Furthermore, the partition function uses cmp of SortKey to compare two
lines using the user-specified keys:

```
///////    File: mysort.C    ///////
#include       <iostream.h>
#include       <stdlib.h>
#include       "TextLines.h"
#include       "SortKey.h"

int partition(TextLines& txtobj, int l, int r)
{   register int i,j;
    String piv;
    extern SortKey sortkey;       // key-comparison object
    i=l;  j=r;
// choose middle element as pivot
    txtobj.swap((i+j)/2,j);
    piv = txtobj[j];              // overloaded []
    while (i < j)
    {   while (sortkey.cmp(txtobj[i], piv) <= 0 && i < j) i++;
        while (j > i && sortkey.cmp(txtobj[j], piv) >= 0) j--;
        if (i < j) txtobj.swap(i++,j);
    }
```

```
        if (i != r) txtobj.swap(i,r);  // switching lines
        return(i);
}

void quicksort(TextLines& txtobj, int l, int r)
{   int k;
    if ( l >= r ) return;
    k = partition (txtobj, l, r);
    quicksort(txtobj, l, k-1);
    quicksort(txtobj, k+1, r);
}
```

Making txtobj a reference formal parameter is critical to these sorting routines. The basic logic of quicksort and partition stays the same.

The object sortkey is a global quantity set by the main program:

```
SortKey sortkey;    // default global sort key

int main(int argc, String argv[])
{   if (argc > 2)
    {   cerr << "Usage: " << argv[0] << " key_position\n";
        exit(1);
    }
    if (argc == 2)
        sortkey = SortKey(atoi(argv[1]));
    TextLines txtobj;
    txtobj.input(cin);
    quicksort(txtobj,0,txtobj.length()-1);
    txtobj.display();
    return(0);
}
///////    End of File mysort.C    ///////
```

The library function atoi converts a numeric string to an integer.

All the parts are now in place. The main program processes command-line arguments and sets up the sortkey object, which is a file scope quantity used by partition. The program then gets a TextLines object txtobj, reads input lines into it, applies quicksort, and then asks txtobj to display itself. The simple and clear structure of the main program testifies to the advantages of the OOP approach.

Assuming that the binary files TextLines.o and SortKey.o already exist, then mysort is established simply by combining mysort.o with them.

The examples in Sections 4.4 and 4.5 not only show array and pointer usage but also demonstrate how to identify interacting objects that can be programmed independently. Object orientation not only makes programs easier to write but, more importantly, also makes the components useful in many other situations.

4.6 \ POINTERS AND FUNCTION CALLS

Let's now turn our attention to the usage of pointers and arrays in function calls. All aspects of pointer usage related specifically to function calls are collected in this section for easy reference.

Passing Pointer Arguments

When a function call is made, a copy of an actual argument, regardless of its type, is passed to the called function. This is generally known as *pass by value*. The value initializes the corresponding formal parameter that is a local variable in the called function. When a pointer is passed as an argument, a memory address is passed. In most cases, the address is the location of a variable, an array entry, or an object. If x is a variable, ptr a pointer variable, arr an array, arr2 a two-dimensional array, and obj a class object, then the expressions in Table 4.2 are all valid forms of pointers as arguments.

To specify a simple pointer formal parameter y in a function header, the two forms

type *y   and   *type* y[]

are equivalent, and both are commonly used. The second notation implies that y is a pointer to the beginning of an array. Extending the equivalence, the forms

type **y   and   *type* *y[]

TABLE 4.2   FORMS OF POINTERS

&x	Address of x
&obj	Address of class object
ptr	Value of pointer variable ptr
ptr++	Value of pointer variable ptr
arr or &arr[0]	Value of constant array name arr
arr + 2 or &arr[2]	Address of third entry of array arr
&arr2[0][0] or arr2[0]	Address of first entry of two-dimensional array arr2
&arr2[i][0] or arr2[i]	Address of first entry of row $i + 1$ in two-dimensional array arr2

are again the same in function headers. Therefore, the command-line argument

```
char *argv[]          // or String argv[]
```

can, in a function header, also be written as

```
char **argv           // or String *argv
```

When a pointer is passed to a function, the called function knows the type and the starting location of a piece of data but not necessarily where it ends. For example, the formal parameter `int *y` can be used to receive the address of a single integer or an array of integers. Clearly, some other arrangement must be made. Using a special terminator is a convenient way to define the extent of a data item. The conventional terminator `'\0'` for character strings is a good example. Independent of whether there is a terminator, it is always possible to use another integer parameter to pass the size information into a called function, as in `istream::read` of the I/O stream library.

There are two possible purposes for passing a pointer into a function:

1. To give the called function access to data without making a copy.
2. To have the called function initialize or modify the data.

The data in question may be global, local to the calling function, or allocated in the scope of some function in the chain of function calls. More details on these two modes of usage are discussed next.

Read-Only and Return Parameters

A data item passed by pointer is *read-only* if it is not modified in the called function. The parameter of `strlen` is a typical example of a read-only pointer. Counting the number of characters does not modify a string. The `const` modifier (Section 3.8) should be used for such a formal parameter, allowing the compiler to detect any unintended attempt to modify the data. The treatment of such a violation is implementation-dependent, but a warning is usually generated. Furthermore, in making a function call, it is critical to know whether an object passed by pointer will be modified or not. Used consistently, the presence or absence of `const` in a function prototype can convey this important information.

One reason for a function to modify an object passed by pointer is to transmit results computed back to the calling function. Many library functions depend on this feature; `istream::read` is an obvious one. Such a parameter is used to transmit computed results back to the calling function and is known as a *return parameter*. The matrix multiplication routine `matmul` (Section 4.3) uses just such a return parameter for the product matrix. When a function is called with a return parameter, it is the calling function's responsibility to allocate enough space of the correct type to accommodate the returned value.

Functions Returning Pointers

Just like the operator new, a function can also produce a pointer as a return value. However, be careful when you define a function that returns a pointer. The returned pointer must not point to a local variable in the scope of the returning function. An automatic variable in a function is destroyed after the function returns. Certainly, it does not make sense to return a pointer to something that disappears. For example, it is incorrect to use

```
int *bad(int x)
{   int y;
    y = x * x;
    return(&y);      // wrong
}
```

This function will produce no syntax error when compiled and will actually execute. Unfortunately, when the returned pointer is used, it may be pointing to a memory cell that has been destroyed (used for other purposes). A pointer that has lost its object in memory is referred to as a *dangling pointer* and should be avoided.

When a function returns a pointer, make sure that it points to one of the following:

- Memory cells supplied by the calling function.
- External data.
- Static data in the function.
- Dynamically allocated space.

The function Poly::operator+() (Section 4.4) is an example where a pointer to memory allocated by new is returned. When such a pointer is returned, there is the danger of the allocated space not being freed properly later. A class destructor (Section 5.7) can often help in this regard. In other cases, clear documentation of the dynamic nature of the returned pointer must be provided to callers of the function.

4.7 \ ARRAYS, POINTERS, AND REFERENCES

A C++ reference is not a basic data type but an alias for a variable or a class object. In many situations where a pointer formal parameter is needed, a reference parameter can be used instead. Certainly, passing an argument by reference involves no copying, and changes made to a reference modify the original. A reference parameter is sometimes simpler to use than a pointer because there is no need for any indirection notations such as *ptr or ptr->member.

When passing arrays, it is advisable to pass pointers rather than references. An array name, not being an lvalue, actually cannot be passed to a reference parameter or used to initialize a reference variable. A pointer variable should be used instead. Thus,

```
void f(int* &ptr_ref);
int arr[] = {1,2,3,4};
f( arr );               // error; arr is a constant pointer
int* ap = arr;          // pointer variable ap
f( ap );                // o.k.
```

A function can also return a reference (Section 3.7). A local variable in the returning function is a bad choice as a reference return value. The variable will be destroyed after the function returns. Also, there can be neither pointers to references nor arrays of references.

4.8 \ MULTIPLE INDIRECTION

A variable x may be used to access a memory cell *directly* (Figure 4.8). The value of x is stored in its associated data cell. As stated before, the cell of a pointer variable ptr, however, stores the address of another data cell whose content can be accessed *indirectly* through the value of ptr using the value-of operator *. The quantity *ptr can be treated just like a variable and can be used on the left-hand side of an assignment.

A pointer provides one level of indirection. It is possible to have *double indirection* if the value of *ptr is also a pointer. Referring again to Figure 4.8, the value of ptra is the pointer variable *ptra, and the value of *ptra is an int variable **ptra, which has the value 15.

The declaration

```
int *ptr;
```

declares the variable ptr to be of type int *, not *prt of type int as some programmers may mistakenly suppose. Similarly, the declarations

```
char **c;
char ***d;
```

give c type char ** and d type char ***, respectively. A handy example of the type char ** is the array char *argv[] for command-line arguments. Thus,

```
c = argv;
```

is possible. In fact, we have already used a few variables of type char **, including the lines in the sorting example (Section 4.5).

FIGURE 4.8   **MULTIPLE INDIRECTION**

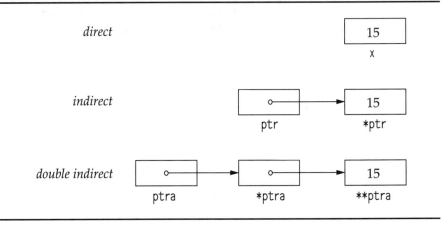

To understand the meaning of d, think of it as the address of an array of different groups of text lines:

d[0] is line_group1
d[1] is line_group2
d[2] is line_group3
.
.
.

Multiple indirection tends to be confusing and error-prone. The situation can be helped by the appropriate application of typedef. Consider

typedef char *String;

typedef String *Lines;

typedef Lines *Groups_of_lines;

Now the variable d can be declared as

Groups_of_lines d;

making it much easier to deal with: The type of *d is Lines, the type of **d is String, and the type of ***d is char. (Section 4.11 contains an example that uses multiple indirection.)

By the way, typedef not only helps to decipher multiple indirections but also to simplify other complicated constructs, as we will see shortly. For the moment, our coverage of pointers continues with the important subject of pointers to functions.

4.9 \ GENERIC PROGRAMS

Normally, functions are written to work on arguments of specific types. Thus, even if there is already a quicksort for an array of integers, there is still nothing to sort character strings, double's, or fractions. However, with a combination of techniques, it is possible in C++ to write a type-independent, or *generic*, function that works for a multitude of different types of arguments.

Our discussions here ultimately lead to an implementation of quicksort that sorts arbitrary data in any caller-specified ordering. To achieve this goal, three distinct but related topics must be presented:

1. Pointers to functions.
2. Formal functional parameters.
3. The type void *.

These same mechanisms also help define generic classes (Section 5.12) where arbitrary types can be treated by objects of the class. Genericness makes programs widely applicable and reusable. C++ also offers a *template* mechanism (Chapter 10) that can be very useful when writing generic programs.

4.9.1 Functional Variables and Arguments

Ordinarily, we think of the values of a variable or formal parameter as some type of data or objects. A whole new dimension opens up when the values can be functions. Functions can be passed as arguments in a call, and the called function can apply the passed function in conjunction with its own preprogrammed procedures. An argument that is a function is known as a *functional argument*. Furthermore, an object can contain variables that are set to names of functions at (or after) initialization time.

The flexibility provided by functional variables/arguments is tremendous. Imagine, now you can write a function that follows different procedures for different invocations. In other words, with functional arguments, a function will not only work with different input data but also utilize different incoming functions. Just consider how much more a sort program can do if it is supplied with the appropriate comparison function each time it is called.

Because the functional variable/argument is an extraordinary feature, not all languages support it. Fortunately, this feature is available in C++, and functional variables/arguments take the form of *pointers to functions*. Let's take a close look at how to use functional arguments, how they work, and what can be achieved with them.

Pointers to Functions

Once a function is defined, the function name preceded by the & operator is a pointer to the function—namely, the address where the function's definition begins in memory. A function pointer, just like any other pointer, can be assigned to pointer variables of the right type and also passed as an argument in a function call.

For example, given a function average defined as

```
int average(int x, int y)
{    return((x+y)/2);}
```

then the following piece of code can be used:

```
int (* fn)(int, int);        // declare function pointer variable fn
fn = &average;               // function variable assignment
int var = (* fn)(14,26);     // function call through pointer
var = fn(14,26);             // shorthand call through pointer
```

First, the functional variable fn is declared to be a pointer to any function that takes two int arguments and returns an int value. (The general syntax for functional variable declaration will be given presently.) Second, fn is assigned the address of the function average. Then, (* fn), or simply fn, can be used as a function name in making a call to average.

To produce a function pointer, the & in front of the function name can also be omitted. Thus,

```
fn = average;                // same as fn = &average
```

is fine, too. This notation is simpler and will be used from now on. In case average is an overloaded function, a pointer to the correct version will be produced by deducing it from the signature used in declaring fn.

Declaring a functional variable may look complicated, but it is really simple. Just use the function prototype with the function name replaced by the notation (* *var*). Specifically, the general form

```
value_type (* var )( args );
```

declares the variable *var* to be a pointer to a function that takes the specified arguments and returns values of the given type.

A functional variable declaration looks strange because it deviates from the normal syntax of variable declarations. What confuses people is the position of the declared variable relative to the other parts in such a declaration. It may take a little getting used to, but the position is perfectly well defined: The variable is put *where the function name would be* in a function prototype. The examples in Figure 4.9 should help as well. More generally, complicated C++ declarations can be deciphered by realizing that *a declaration always spells out* *how the declared variable is used.* For example, the first declaration in Figure 4.9 shows that (*fn_a) (3.5, 6.7) is a function call that returns a float.

Since a functional variable declaration is somewhat long and complicated to look at, we can simplify things greatly by using typedef. For instance,

```
typedef int (* INT_FN)(int, int);
```

defines the type name INT_FN. Note that the type name is placed where the variable would be. INT_FN can then be used to declare any functional variable of that type. In particular, we can declare fn in the average example with

```
INT_FN fn;          // alternative declaration for fn
```

Formal Functional Parameters

The purpose of a function variable, almost exclusively, is to pass a function name to another function or class object. To make things easy to understand, let's examine an artificial example:

```
int mystery(int a, int b, int (* fn)(int, int))
{    return( fn(a,b) );
}
```

Here the function mystery takes three arguments: two integers and a functional parameter fn. The declaration of the formal parameter fn is, as it should be, the same as declaring a variable of the intended type. By using the existing type INT_FN, we can code a simpler-looking version of mystery:

```
int mystery(int a, int b, INT_FN fn)
{    return( fn(a,b) );
}
```

FIGURE 4.9   **DECLARING FUNCTION POINTERS**

Value_type	Var	Arguments
↓	↓	↓
float	(* fn_a)	(float, float);
float	(* fn_b)	(int);
void	(* fn_c)	(char *, int);
char *	(* fn_d)	(void);

The function mystery simply calls the function pointed to by fn and returns the value of the call. Here are some functions, in addition to average, that can be passed to mystery:

```
extern int gcd(int a, int b);

int sqsum(int x, int y)
{    return (x * x + y * y);
}
```

(The gcd function is defined in Section 3.2.)

Here is how to make calls to mystery. Note that the names average, gcd, and sqsum are pointers to the definitions of the functions:

```
int main()
{    cout << mystery(16, 30, average) << endl;    // is 23
     cout << mystery(3, 4, sqsum) << endl;        // is 25
     cout << mystery(312, 253, gcd) << endl;      // is  1
     return(0);
}
```

In fact, any function that takes two int arguments and returns an int can be passed to mystery.

The one topic that remains on our list of discussion topics is the void * pointer, a mechanism to pass data or objects of arbitrary type and a necessary complement to the functional argument facility.

4.9.2   Pointer Type void * and Genericness

To write a function that applies the same algorithm in a variety of situations, we need the functional argument mechanism described earlier. But, in most cases, we also need the ability to receive *data of arbitrary, or unspecified, types*. The ability of a procedure or function to work on different data types is known as *genericness*, and programs exhibiting such capacity are *generic*.

Let's begin with a simple example of determining the length of an arbitrary array. The strategy is to write a function that takes the following two arguments:

1. An arbitrary array.
2. A test function for the end of the array.

The function arblen computes the length of the array any without knowing anything about its type. Thus, arblen is a generic array-length function. The functional parameter is_end is the supplied function that detects the termination of the given array. What arblen does is simply call is_end repeatedly and count the number of calls. The count is then returned when is_end detects the end of the array:

```
typedef int (* END_FN) (void *any, int index);

int arblen(void *any, END_FN is_end)
{    int len=0;
     while ( ! is_end(any, len) ) len++;
     return(len);
}
```

A variable or formal parameter of type void * (pointer to unknown type) can receive a pointer of any type. This provides a way of passing data of arbitrary type into a function. Because the data type is unknown, there are very few allowable operations on a void * variable other than referencing (using the pointer value) and passing it to another function. In particular, indexing, value-of (*), increment, decrement, and other address arithmetic operations are illegal or unsafe on a void * variable. Even so, the void * type is critical to processing arbitrary data, as seen in the function arblen.

To test arblen, we define two terminator detecting functions, int_end and str_end, for nonnegative integer and character arrays, respectively:

```
int int_end(int *a, int i)
{    return( a[i] == -1 );         // true or false
}

int str_end(char *a, int i)
{    return( a[i] == '\0' );
}
```

Now, for testing, we use the following main function:

```
int main()
{    char a[]="abcdefg";
     int b[]={0,1,2,3,4,-1};
     int i = arblen(a, END_FN(str_end) );          // length 7
     cout << "length of string = " << i << endl;
     i = arblen(b, END_FN(int_end) );              // length 5
     cout << "length of int array = " << i << endl;
     return(0);
}
```

Note that explicit type-casting, END_FN(str_end), is used on the function pointers to make the argument match the declared formal parameter is_end of arblen. This also allows passing the void * argument to str_end.

Since void * is so useful, a good question to ask is, Can we also make use of void &, an arbitrary reference? Unfortunately, C++ does not permit void &.

The preliminaries are now finished. We are ready for some practical applications culminating in the implementation of a generalized quicksort.

4.9.3   Sample Generic Functions

Let's consider how void * and functional arguments combine to define generic functions. Our first example is a function that checks to see whether all entries of an array satisfy some given condition. Questions such as

- Is every entry an even/odd number?
- Is every entry positive?
- Is every entry zero?
- Is every character in lower case?

are often asked. We can write one generic function, and_test, that takes care of them all. The and in the name expresses the concept of *logical and*: All tests must be true before the answer is true:

```
typedef int (* BOOLEAN_FN) (void *any, int index);

int and_test(void *any, BOOLEAN_FN test, END_FN is_end)
{     int len=0;
      while ( ! is_end(any, len) )
      {   if ( test(any, len) == 0 ) return(0);
          len++;
      }
      return(1);
}
```

The type name BOOLEAN_FN also documents the fact that functions of this type must be *Boolean,* or one that returns a true or false value. The arbitrary Boolean test is applied to each array entry successively until the end is found by the supplied terminator detector is_end. The first failed test causes and_test to return 0 (false). The value 1 (true) is returned after the array is exhausted. Candidate functions to pass to the parameter test are

```
int even(int *ip, int j)
{  return( (ip[j] & 01)  == 0 );}

int odd(int *ip, int j)
{  return( (ip[j] & 01)  == 1 );}
```

```
int clower(char *cp, int j)
{  return ( islower(cp[j]) ); }
```

The function or_test is similar but is designed to answer questions like

- Is there an even/odd entry?
- Is there a negative entry?
- Is there a zero entry?
- Is there an uppercase character?

Again, the or indicates the *logical or* concept: If at least one test is true, then the answer is true:

```
int or_test(void *any, BOOLEAN_FN test, END_FN is_end)
{      int len=0;
       while ( ! is_end(any,len) )
       {    if ( test(any, len) ) return(1);
            len++;
       }
       return(0);
}
```

4.10 \ A GENERIC SORTING PROGRAM

Our next example further illustrates the flexibility that functional arguments provide. Let's write a sorting program that can rearrange a sequence of items *of any type* into *any specified order,* thus making the sorting program generic and very reusable. The strategy is to modify the quicksort program to use the following three arguments:

1. An arbitrary array.
2. A caller-specified comparison function cmp.
3. A supplied element-interchange function swap.

With the header file

```
///////    File: arbqsort.h    ///////

typedef int (* CMP_FN) (void *, int, int);
typedef void (* SWAP_FN) (void *, int, int);
extern void quicksort(void *any,    // arbitrary array to be sorted
                  int l,            // start index
                  int r,            // end index
                  CMP_FN cmp,       // supplied comparison function
                  SWAP_FN swap      // supplied interchange function
                  );
```

the quicksort function is revised as follows:

```
///////    File: arbqsort.C    ///////
#include "arbqsort.h"

void quicksort(void *any, int l, int r, CMP_FN cmp, SWAP_FN swap)
{    if ( l >= r || l < 0 ) return;
  // call with supplied functions
     int k = partition(any, l, r, cmp, swap);
  // recursive calls
     quicksort(any, l, k-1, cmp, swap);
     quicksort(any, k+1, r, cmp, swap);
}
```

The partition function, which is placed before quicksort in the actual file, now becomes

```
static int partition(void *any, int l, int r, CMP_FN cmp, SWAP_FN swap)
{    register int i=l, j=r;
  // choose middle element as pe
     swap(any,(i+j)/2, r);                    // pe moved to r
     while (i < j)
     { while (cmp(any, i, r) <= 0 && i < j) // use supplied cmp
         i++;
       while(j > i && cmp(any, j, r) >= 0)  // use supplied cmp
         j--;
       if (i < j) swap(any,i++,j);          // use supplied swap
     }
     if (i != r) swap(any,i,r);             // use supplied swap
     return(i);
}
```

Note that indexing of any is not possible in partition because of its type void *. But once its value is passed to the function cmp or swap, the formal pointer parameter there can be used normally.

With these modifications, the generic quicksort can sort arbitrary arrays when given appropriately supplied comparison and swap functions. To sort integer arrays, the following set of functions can be defined:

```
int cmp_bigger(int x[], int i, int j)
{  return ( x[i] - x[j] ); }

int cmp_smaller(int x[], int i, int j)
{  return ( x[j] - x[i] ); }

void intswitch(int a[], int i, int j)
{    int s = a[i];
     a[i] = a[j];
```

```
    a[j] = s;
}
```

The two different comparison functions cmp_bigger and cmp_smaller conform to the type CMP_FN, and intswitch matches the type SWAP_FN. Now sorting can be done with

```
int a[] = {5,3,-1, 9 , 22, 99};

// in increasing order
quicksort(a, 0, 5, CMP_FN(cmp_bigger), SWAP_FN(intswitch));

// in decreasing order
quicksort(a, 0, 5, CMP_FN(cmp_smaller), SWAP_FN(intswitch));
```

It is also a simple matter to convert the text-line sorting program in Section 4.5 to use the generic quicksort. For this purpose, the following functions are needed:

```
int keycmp(TextLines *tl, int i, int j)
{    extern SortKey sortkey;
     TextLines& txtobj= *tl;
     return( sortkey.cmp(txtobj[i], txtobj[j]) );
}

void lineswap(TextLines *tl, int i, int j)
{    tl->swap(i,j);
}
```

Again, the two functions are written to match the types CMP_FN and SWAP_FN, information available from the arbqsort.h header file. With these functions, just use

```
quicksort(&txtobj, 0, txtobj.length()-1,
          CMP_FN(keycmp), SWAP_FN(lineswap));
```

to do the sorting of the TextLines object txtobj. Note that here we are sorting *text lines encapsulated in an object* with the same generalized quicksort function, which drives home the point of handling data of arbitrary type.

The quicksort defined in this section will be used again. Clearly, the basic sorting mechanism is in place and will remain unchanged. The header arbqsort.h provides the interface to client files of the generalized sorting facility. The application of this mechanism in a new area is simply a matter of providing the appropriate comparison and swap functions.

4.11 \ POINTERS AND DYNAMICALLY ALLOCATED STORAGE

We have already seen some uses of the operator new for dynamic storage allocation. In this section, let's consider how dynamic storage is applied in relation to arrays and pointers.

Allocating Two-Dimensional Arrays

Static allocation of two-dimensional arrays is very simple to code. But the syntax for dynamic allocation does not allow direct two-dimensional notations. Thus, codes such as

```
double** arr = new double[m][n];        // syntax error
```

are not possible. However, enough consecutive cells from free storage can accommodate all elements of a two-dimensional array and can be fabricated into the desired array structure.

The function dyn_2d returns a double** that can be used as a two-dimensional double array:

```
double** dyn_2d(int m, int n)
{   double* arr = new double[m*n];      // allocate data cells
    double** a = new double*[m];        // allocate pointer cells
    for ( int i=0 ; i < m ; i++ )       // initialize
    {   a[i] = arr + i*n;               // init m row pointers
        for (int j=0 ; j < n ; j++ )    // init array cells
            a[i][j] = 0.0;              // use as two-dimensional array
    }
    return(a);
}
```

Enough storage for all consecutive data cells is allocated. In addition, storage for pointer cells for each row is also allocated. The array and pointer cells are then initialized before the array name is returned. An overloaded version can also take care of freeing the storage properly:

```
void dyn_2d(double** a)
{   delete [] *a;      // free data cells
    delete [] a;       // free pointer cells
}
```

Dynamic Arrays of Pointers

Let's consider the representation of days in a month. One way to do this is to use short integers for the individual dates, an array of dates for each week, and an array of pointers to the individual weeks as a structure for the month. With a few typedefs, we can define a class Month to create any monthly calendar:

```
////////    File: Month.h    ////////

class Month
{ public:
     typedef short Date;
     typedef Date *Week;      // Week is short *
     enum Day {SUN=0, MON, TUE, WED, THU, FRI, SAT};
     Month(Date ndays, enum Day firstday);
     void display();
     ~Month();
  private:
     Week *month;             // internal representation
};
```

The constructor initializes a month object when given the number of days in the month (ndays) and the day of the week for the first day of the month:

```
Month::Month(Date ndays, enum Day firstday)
{    Week w[7], wk;       // maximum 6 weeks
     short i=0;
     wk = w[i] = new(short[7]);                       // (1)
     for (Day day=SUN ; day < firstday ; day=Day(day+1)) // (2)
         *wk++ = 0;
     for (Date d = 1 ; d <= ndays ; d++)              // (3)
     {   *wk++ = d;
         if (day == SAT)
         {   wk = w[++i] = new(Date[7]);              // (4)
             day=SUN;
         }
         else day = Day(day+1);
     }
     while ( day != SUN )
     {   *wk++ = 0;                                   // (5)
         day = Day( (day+1)%7 );
     }
     month = new(Week[i+2]);                          // (6)
     for (short j=0; j <= i; j++)
         month[j] = w[j];
     month[i+1] = NULL;                  // NULL ptr terminator
}
```

For each week, seven Dates are allocated (lines 1 and 4) to record the days of the week where pointers returned by new are automatically cast to type Week

FIGURE 4.10   THE ORGANIZATION OF Month, WITH POINTERS

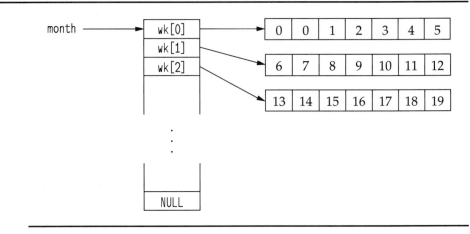

(short *). Days unused in the first and last week are assigned zero (lines 2 and 5). The dates are filled in by the for loop (line 3). Note that arithmetic results involving enum variables are cast properly (lines 2 and 5).

The automatic array w records the weeks created. A dynamic array month is allocated (line 6), and the entries of w are copied into the data member month. Note that month is terminated by a NULL pointer. Figure 4.10 illustrates the organization of month.

To establish a Month object, use something like

```
Month m(31, Month::TUE);
```

Here the class scope notation is used to specify an enum constant defined in the Month class. (Later, in Section 6.6.4, displaying a monthly calendar will again be considered.)

4.12 SUMMARY

The array and the pointer are closely related constructs that help store and manipulate data of any given type. Their mastery is essential for the low-level coding that is required of you. Such details should be encapsulated by objects when possible so that other parts of the program can ignore them.

An array stores elements of the same type in consecutive memory locations. The array name is a constant pointer to the first array cell. A two-dimensional array is actually a one-dimensional array whose elements are pointers to one-dimensional arrays of the same length. This scheme can be generalized into arrays of higher dimensions. Arrays allocated at compile time have fixed maximum dimensions. Arrays whose dimensions are known only at run time can be allocated dynamically.

A pointer provides the ability to manipulate addresses and supplies a level of indirection to data or program access. The unary address-of operator & can be applied to any memory-based variable, class object, or array element to obtain a pointer. The unary value-of operator * is applied to a pointer, ptr, to access the value stored at that memory address. Furthermore, the notation *ptr can be used on the left hand-side of an assignment to store a new value at that location. Hence, the combination *ptr can be thought of and used as a variable of the appropriate type. Both pointer arithmetic and indexing are convenient to step through the cells of an array.

The TextLines class is a substantial OO programming example that uses an array of pointers to represent a sequence of text lines internally. The class supplies access, interchange, input, and output functions for text lines hiding the array and pointer implementation details. The associated SortKey class helps locate and compare keys in text lines. The program mysort uses these objects and quicksort to sort text lines using user-specified keys.

A generic program is one that works for many different types of data items. The function pointer, functional arguments, the void * type, and implicit/explicit-type casting combine to provide one way to write generic functions. With these constructs, a generic quicksort is written to sort arbitrary data items or objects using any supplied comparison function. The generic sort routine is shown reused for integer and text line sorting.

EXERCISES

1. Given the following declaration, what are the values of the expressions (a) a - &a[3], (b) *(a+4), and (c) *(a+5)?

    ```
    int a[]={1,2,3,4,5};
    ```

2. Explain the meaning of each of the following declarations:
    (a) char a[];
    (b) char *b;
    (c) char c[5]="";
    (d) int d[]={0,1,2};
    (e) int *e=d+1;
    (f) int f[20]={0,0,0,0};
    (g) char *g[];
    (h) char *g[]={a,b,c};
    (i) char **a;
    (j) char **a = &b;
    (k) typedef int (* C_FN)(char *, const char *);

3. Write a program to test the use of negative indices for arrays/pointers.

4. Rewrite the circular buffer class given in Section 3.11 with pointers and pointer arithmetic instead of indexing.

5. Consider the SortKey class. In practice, there is a need for a composite key, a key consisting of a primary key, a secondary key, and so on. When two items are compared under a composite key, the primary key is applied first. The secondary key is applied only if the two items are equal under the primary key, and so on. Define a CompKey class.

6. Does the C++ compiler on your computer allow you to increment a void * pointer? If it does, give a good reason why you should not use it.

7. Is it possible to pass a void * actual argument to, say, an int * formal parameter in a function call? If this is not possible, can you specify *two* distinct ways to make such a call by explicit casting? Show your solution with actual working-code examples. (*Hint:* Cast the argument or the function.)

8. Consider references to pointers. Is there anything wrong with the following code? Why? If there is a problem, how do you fix it?

    ```
    int a = 56;
    int*& ptr_ref = &a;
    ```

9. Modify the quicksort routine to remove duplicate entries in the input array. The routine should return the length of the final sorted array, which may be shorter than the given array before sorting. (*Hint:* partition should record positions of duplicate entries.)

10. Modify the sorting program for text lines given in Section 4.5 to use the generic quicksort as suggested in Section 4.10.

11. Consider the address-of operator &. List the type of quantities to which it cannot be applied. Also consider the value-of operator *. List the type of quantities to which it cannot be applied.

12. Discuss the differences and equivalence of the following two notations. In what situations are these notations interchangeable?

    type x[];   and   *type* *x;

13. Discuss the differences and similarities of a two-dimensional array and an array of pointers.

14. Write a simple class `Matrix` with `double` entries. Support the following public operations: (a) to create a matrix, given dimensions m and n, and a two-dimensional array of entries; (b) to delete any rows or columns; (c) to interchange any rows or columns; and (d) to display the matrix.

15. Write a quadruple-precision integer class with arithmetic operations +, -, *, and /; then `display`. (*Hint:* Use `int` array.)

16. Write a function `arr_apply` that takes an array of arbitrary data items and applies a supplied operation on each array cell.

17. Add a multiplication operation to the `Poly` class.

18. Reuse the generic `quicksort` to order polynomials according to their degree.

CLASSES AND OBJECTS

A class builds objects and is, of all constructs in C++, the most central for OOP. A class describes the external behavior and the internal organizations of an object and is used to specify software objects that simulate actual entities found in the problem domain. The class can attach procedures to data structures, thereby achieving encapsulation. It also provides access control to hide internal mechanisms of objects.

Because the class is so important, we have been introduced to it informally early and have used it in many places already. It is now time for a thorough description of the C++ class so that we can see how it is used to implement software objects, learn the design of an object's external interface, and acquire techniques for information hiding.

A complete description of the class definition is followed by an explanation of object creation and initialization. Data hiding and object interface definition using function members and access control are then shown. Constructors and destructors are special members that help build and tear down objects. A good understanding of their functions is crucial to class writing.

Using objects as components to build larger objects is explained through a pocket calculator simulation program. This example also demonstrates how the given problem is broken into interacting objects and how they model entities in the pocket calculator. You should study this example carefully because it will be used as the basis of a sequence of end-of-chapter programming exercises that eventually lead to a substantial OO program.

Furthermore, recursive classes that contain pointers to objects in the same class are described. A linked list example is given.

Other topics covered in this chapter include friend functions and static members. Many examples are given to illustrate the concepts presented. The material leads ultimately to the definition of a generic linked list class that can be used to contain arbitrary data types.

5.1 \ DEFINING CLASSES

The class provides a blueprint for constructing objects and is central to the OOP enterprise. In C++, a class is a user-defined type that has its own scope within which data, functions, typedefs, enums, and other *members* are encapsulated. A class must be declared or defined before it is used. The class definition has the general form

```
class Name
{
        class body
};
```

where the body contains zero or more *member declarations*:

- Data members are declared like variables, but initializers are not allowed.
- Function members are declared by function prototypes in the class body and defined elsewhere. Member functions completely defined in the class body are automatically declared inline. Normally, only very simple member functions are defined inside the class body.
- Other types of members are declared as in other scopes.

The class name is sometimes also referred to as the class *tag*. Function and data member names have *class scope*; they are known throughout the class but not outside the class. Thus, the order in which members are declared is generally not important because every member is known to the whole class. Also, members with the same name in different classes are distinct and do not conflict with one another.

Once established, a class tag can be used to define *objects*, or *instances*, of the class. Thus, a class can be thought of as a blueprint to build objects. An object becomes an independent computing entity with its own memory (data members) and programming (function members). Objects belonging to the same class share the same set of function members but have their own separate data members.

A class envelops its members and controls outside access to them. Thus, the class is the unit of information hiding and access control. The accessibility of a member in the class depends on the location of the code that makes the access. If access to a member is allowed, then that member can be accessed within any instance of the class. Members may be private or public:

- *Private* members are accessible only by member functions in the same class. No other access is allowed. Private members hide data structures and internal procedures of an object.
- *Public* members are accessible from any part of the entire program. The collection of public members forms the external interface through which an object is used.

Unless otherwise designated, members in a class definition are private. We use the keywords public and private (followed by a colon) in the class body to designate the protection modes. A designation affects members following it up to the next designation or to the end of the class. The recommended class format is

```
class ClassName
{  public:
      /* public members    */

    private:
      /* private members    */
};
```

Because public members are the only ones important to a client of the class, they should be given first. The Vector and Fraction classes (Sections 2.4 and 3.3), among others, follow this format.

To further illustrate member access, let's add two more member functions to Fraction (Section 3.3):

```
Fraction Fraction::operator/ (const Fraction& y)
{    return
        Fraction( num * y.denom, denom * y.num );
}


Fraction Fraction::operator* (const Fraction& y)
{    return
        Fraction( num * y.num, denom * y.denom );
}
```

Obviously, these member functions can access not only the private data members num and denom in the host object but also those in another object, y, of the same class.

Class Declaration Styles

It is also possible either to declare class objects without first establishing a class name or to declare objects and the class name at the same time. For example, the two forms

```
class                        and      class Fraction
{                                     {
    /* class body */                      /* class body */
} obj1, obj2, obj3;                   } obj1, obj2, obj3;
```

are equivalent insofar as the declaration of the objects obj1, obj2, and obj3 is concerned. The second form also defines the class name Fraction, which can be used later to declare other Fraction objects. However, these forms, especially the first one, are not very useful in practice. The recommended style for class declaration is to

1. Define the class in a header file *ClassX*.h.
2. Put public members at the beginning of the class definition.
3. Include nonprivate inline member functions in or following the class definition in the header file.
4. Define other member functions in a separate file *ClassX*.C.

This scheme has already been applied in many examples and will be followed throughout the book.

In C++, the keyword struct is also used to define a class. It is the same as class except for one difference: *Members in a class defined by struct are public unless designated otherwise.* We can achieve the same effect with the class keyword by beginning with public members. In practice, struct is seldom used in C++ code and is usually restricted to declaring pure data structures without function members. These two declarations are equivalent:

```
struct Person          and      class Person
{                               { public:
    char* last;                     char* last;
    char  mid;                      char  mid;
    char* first;                    char* first;
};                              };
```

5.2 CREATING AND INITIALIZING OBJECTS

As mentioned before, a class definition is a blueprint for constructing objects. Thus, an object is referred to as an *instance* of a class. A class object is introduced into a program by declaring a variable whose type is the class name (for example, Fraction r;). Such a declaration involves two separate actions to establish the desired object: *instantiation* (allocating memory) and *initialization* (assigning initial values to data members).

There is no complication with instantiation. How objects are initialized, however, depends on whether the class defines an explicit constructor.

Data-Only Classes

Consider objects representing employees in a company. The simplest version would be

```
const int SSN_LENGTH = 12;
const int NAME_LENGTH = 32;

class Employee
{ public:
    char  name[NAME_LENGTH];  // full name
    char  ss[SSN_LENGTH]      // social security no.
    short age;
    float salary;
};
```

The class structures data but supplies no functions. In particular, no explicit constructor is given. Another data-only class definition is

```
class Date
{ public:
    unsigned month, day, year;
};
```

Again, there is no explicit constructor. With these classes, objects and arrays of objects can be established as follows:

```
Date arrival, departure;        // Date objects
Date birthday = {11, 26, 1985}; // array-style initialization (1)
Date vacation = birthday;       // initialize by existing object
Date absence[12];               // array of 12 Date objects
Employee representative;        // Employee object
Employee a_team[6];             // array of 6 Employees
Employee newhire = {"John Doe", // array-style initialization (2)
                    "045-76-5555",
                    24,
                    38000.00
                   };
```

Initializers given inside {} must be constants. An array of Employee objects is initialized in a similar way:

```
Employee pair[] = { { "Pat Brown",  // array-style initialization (3)
                      "000-11-6666" // partial initialization
                    },
                    { "Diana Bell"
                      "000-22-1234"
                    }
                  };
```

The *array-style initialization* (lines 1, 2, and 3) can be used only for objects of a class without any explicit constructors. Furthermore, only public members can be so initialized. In practice, the array-style initializations are used only for classes without function and nonpublic members. The usual method for class initialization is through the appropriate constructors. It is also possible to initialize an object with an existing object of the same class. The initialization is performed by copying each data member. The same *memberwise copy* operation is performed when an object is assigned to another or passed by value in a function call.

The array-style initialization is tedious and rigid and requires constant initializers. Furthermore, nonpublic members cannot be initialized because of lack of access. The class constructor mechanism replaces such initialization with a much easier approach.

5.3 CONSTRUCTORS

A special member function called a *constructor* facilitates object initialization. A constructor defines initial values and automatically carries out operations immediately after object instantiation (Section 5.7, Figure 5.2). Objects of a class with a user-defined constructor are established following rules given in this section. The array-style object initialization (Section 5.2) applies only to classes without explicit constructors.

Adding a constructor to the class Date allows the data members to be private:

```
class Date
{ public:
    Date(unsigned m, unsigned d, unsigned y); // constructor       (1)
    Date();                                   // default constructor (2)
    void display()
    { cout << month << '/' << day << '/' << year; }
  private:
    unsigned month, day, year;
};
```

The constructor Date::Date is overloaded, as constructors usually are. With this constructor, Date objects can be established as follows:

```
Date birthday(mon ,d, y);        // calls constructor with 3 args (i)
Date birthday = Date(mon, d, y); // alternative to (i)

Date appointment;                // calls default constructor  (ii)
```

```
Date appointment = Date();        // alternative to (ii)

Date week[7] = { Date(mon1, d1, y1),
                 Date(mon2, d2, y2)
              };                   // calls default constructor 5 times
```

The alternative forms are usually entirely the same but, depending on the compiler, may involve creating a temporary object and copying. Thus, they can be less efficient and should be avoided.

It is advisable to always define a *default constructor*, one that takes no arguments, for a class with constructors. Without the default constructor, the last three declarations just listed would be impossible.

Be careful: The code

```
Date appointment();               // warning: a function prototype
```

is correct but does not establish an object. Instead, it declares appointment as a function returning a Date value.

For a class named *ClassX*, use the general form to define constructors:

```
ClassX::ClassX( args )
: init-list
{   constructor body
}
```

Unlike other functions, a constructor must be defined without a return type (not even void). A constructor never returns a value. Its exclusive mission is to perform initialization and to set up for a freshly allocated object. If a return statement is used within a constructor, it must be given no argument.

After a single colon (:) and before the function body, an optional *init-list* can be given. The init-list specifies all the desired initializations; the constructor body performs other setup chores. An init-list is a comma-separated list of member initializers, each *mem-initializer* in the form

```
member-id( one or more args )           // a mem-initializer
```

For example, the Date constructor

```
Date::Date(unsigned m, unsigned d, unsigned y)
: month(m), day(d), year(y)        // init-list
{   /* empty body */  }
```

specifies the initialization of all three members of a Date object. Member initialization is performed in *declaration order* (in the class body) independent of the ordering of the mem-initializers in the init-list.

For the Date class, this constructor has the same effect as the more familiar form

```
Date::Date(unsigned m, unsigned d, unsigned y)
{  month = m;        // three assignments
   day = d;
   year = y;
}
```

These two forms, however, are not equivalent in general. For initialization purposes, the init-list is the right choice. Strictly speaking, assignments in the constructor body are not initializations—a point made clear in the following discussion.

Initialization of const and Reference Members

A class may contain const and/or reference members. Outside a class, such variables must be initialized when declared. For a class, const and reference members must be initialized by mem-initializers. This initialization is mandatory. All versions of an overloaded constructor, including the default constructor, must specify such required mem-initializers.

For example, suppose an Account object has a reference member customer:

```
class Account
{ public:

      /* public members */

  private:
      Name&    customer;            // reference member
      unsigned acct_no;             // account number
      double   acct_bal;            // current balance
      /* other private members */
};
```

The constructor must then supply an lvalue mem-initializer for the reference member customer:

```
Account::Account(unsigned id, double amt, Name& n)
:  customer(n)               // init reference member
{     acct_no = id;
      acct_bal = amt;
}
```

Note how the constructor also takes a reference n so that a Name object can be passed into an Account object.

Default Initializations

Data members of objects are generally initialized only through the constructor. A class member declaration must not contain an initializer.

```
class Date
{  public:
      /* ... */
   private:
      unsigned month = 1;     // illegal
      unsigned day = 1;       // illegal
      unsigned year = 2001;   // illegal
};
```

Default values can be supplied to class members through the optional argument mechanism. To do this, the Date constructor can be modified as follows:

```
Date::Date(unsigned m = 1, unsigned d = 1,
           unsigned y = 2001)
: month(m), day(d), year(y)
{   /* empty body */  }
```

Because this definition can take from zero to three arguments, the old default constructor is no longer necessary and must now be removed. As a result, the simple object declaration

```
Date tmp;
```

is the same as

```
Date tmp(1, 1, 2001);
```

Default Constructors

If a class provides no constructors, a default constructor, which takes no arguments and does nothing, is supplied by the compiler. Obviously, not every class can work with just this kind of default constructor. If any constructor is defined for a class, then there is no automatically supplied default constructor. If a constructor that takes no arguments is also needed, which is usual, then one must be explicitly defined in the class.

In summary, instantiation and initialization are two distinct phases in establishing an object. Objects of classes with no constructors or nonpublic members are established in ways similar to built-in types. Constructors help automate object initialization and can perform other operations at initialization time. Objects of classes with user-supplied constructors are initialized only through constructors. A default constructor should accompany other constructors to make declaring objects and object arrays without initializers possible.

5.4 \ THE HOST OBJECT

As independent computing entities, objects have data and function members. Data and operations in one object are distinguished from those in a different object, even if the two belong to the same class. An object is a *host* for its data and function members. Members are usually accessed through a host object:

host.member — for example, sally.acct_bal
host_ptr->member — for example, (&sally)->acct_bal
host.fn(args) — for example, sally.deposit(65.95)
host_ptr->fn(args) — for example, (&sally)->withdraw(19.95)

The same data member in different hosts has different values and memory locations. Function members are shared by all objects of the same class. When a member function is invoked, the address of the host object is also passed to the function through the built-in pointer parameter this (the host pointer). For the called member function, the host object provides an operating environment consisting of the current values of all its data members. Therefore, the same member function can act differently depending on values in the host.

A member function can use a member name without indicating a host object explicitly. We have seen many such uses already. For instance, in the circular buffer class (Section 3.11), the member function Cirbuf::consume() uses the is_empty() function in the same host object directly. Also, the operator-() in Fraction (Section 3.3) refers to denom directly. Such an unqualified member name does not refer to a fixed variable or function. Rather, it refers to a member *in the same host object as the function*. Specifically, the notations is_empty() and denom are really shorthand for this->is_empty() and this->denom, respectively.

Therefore, unqualified member names are interpreted relative to an implicit host object that invoked the member function. A member function can also explicitly refer to its host object through the built-in pointer this. For example, in the class Fraction, the member function operator- returns *this when subtracting zero. (More examples will be given later.)

The Read-Only Host

The host object is an implicit argument to any member function. Sometimes, it is desirable to explicitly specify the read-only nature of this argument. We have already seen how this is done (Section 3.8). The prototype

```
Fraction Fraction::operator-(const Fraction f) const;
```

specifies that the member operator- of the class Fraction takes a read-only right-hand argument f, but the left-hand argument (the host object itself) is also read-only. Thus, if r and s are both fractions, the code

●

r - s

can be used with the assurance that neither r nor s will be modified.

5.5 INTERNAL-EXTERNAL DECOUPLING

An object encapsulates data and programming to form an independent computing entity. It also hides details of internal data structures and mechanisms by providing a public interface through which all outside access to the object is made. The *behavior* of an object is fully defined by its public interface, which you can rely on without knowledge or concern about the internal workings. The decoupling of the internal workings of objects from the rest of the program greatly simplifies the interrelationships among program components and makes modifications much easier.

Public members form the interface, and other members are hidden from outside view. The Account, Vector, Fraction, and Cirbuf classes discussed before are good examples. To further illustrate the importance of information hiding, let's consider again the Poly class (first discussed in Section 4.4). Internally, Poly uses a *sparse representation* (Table 4.1), which excludes missing terms in a polynomial from the data structure. In situations where there are very few or no missing terms, a *dense representation*, listing every coefficient, becomes more compact and efficient. Thus, a polynomial

$$a_n x^n + a_{n-1} x^{n-1} + \cdots + a_1 x + a_0$$

can be encoded by the dense representation

$$(n\ a_n\ a_{n-1} \ldots a_1\ a_0)$$

which uses an int array of length $n + 2$.

What modifications should we make if we want the program to use the dense instead of the sparse representation? If the external behavior of Poly is preserved, then only member functions of Poly are affected; the rest of the program that uses Poly stays the same. How advantageous it is to use OOP!

Here is the modified class definition:

```
///////    File: Poly.h    ///////
#include <iostream.h>
class Poly
{ public:
      Poly();                           // default constructor
      Poly(const int *p, int n);        // p supplies n terms
      void display();                   // display host object
      Poly operator+(const Poly& q) const;  // addition
      Poly operator-(const Poly& q) const;  // subtraction
```

```
      Poly operator*(const Poly& q) const;  // multiplication
      unsigned deg() const                   // degree
      {   return(*pol);  }
      /* other members */
   private:
      void s_to_d(int *buf, const int *p);  // sparse to dense
      int *pol;
};
```

Some const specifiers are added, and some parameters are now reference parameters. These were left out earlier for simplicity. But the public interface of Poly remains the same, so no outside codes need changing.

Inside the class, the inline function deg becomes simpler. A private member s_to_d is added to help convert incoming sparse representation to the dense representation kept internally. These are used in the modified constructor:

```
///////   File: Poly.C   ///////
#include <iostream.h>
#include "Poly.h"

Poly::Poly(const int *p, int n)    // p supplies n terms
: pol( n > 0 ? new int[*p+2]       // initialize pointer pol
            : new int )
{   if ( n == 0 )
        *pol = -1;                 // zero polynomial
    else
        s_to_d(pol, p);            // converted data in pol
}

// sparse-to-dense conversion, a private member
void Poly::s_to_d(int *buf, const int *p)
{    int d = *buf++ = *p;          // degree
     while ( d >= 0 )              // conversion loop
     {   if ( d == *p )
         {   *buf++ = *++p; p++;}  // nonzero term
         else /* ( d > *p ) */
         {   *buf++ = 0;   }       // zero term
         d--;
     }
}
```

With these codes, the same constructor, taking the same arguments as before, now constructs a dense internal representation. Operations on pol must also be revised to use the dense representation. The operator+ function, for example, becomes much simpler than its sparse representation counterpart (Section 4.4):

```
Poly Poly::operator+(const Poly q) const
{   int *c, *a, *b;
    int d = deg(), dq = q.deg();
    if ( d < dq )
    { dq = d;   d = q.deg();
      b  = pol; a = q.pol;            // d=deg(a) >= deg(b)
    }
    else
    { a = pol;  b = q.pol;  }
    a++;  b++;
    while ( d == dq && d > 0
                && *a + *b == 0 )     // leading terms cancel
    { d--;  dq--;  a++;  b++;
    }
    Poly ans;                         // result object
    ans.pol = c = new(int[d+2]);      // allocate space for result
    *c++ = d;                         // degree of result
    while(d-- > dq) *c++ = *a++;      // leading terms
    while(d-- > -2) *c++ = *a++ + *b++; // add corresponding terms
    return(ans);
}
```

The function display produces the same output as before but must work with
the dense internal representation:

```
void Poly::display()
{   int *p = pol + 1;
    int d = deg(), e = d;
    if ( e == 0 )                     // constant poly
    {   cout << *p << endl;
        return;
    }
    cout << '(';                      // display terms
    while ( d >= 0 )
    {   if ( *p != 0 )
        { if ( d < e ) cout << ", ";
          cout << d << " " << *p;
        }
        d--; p++;
    }
    cout << ")\n";
}
```

Compare this display function with the one for the sparse representation (Section 4.4). Convince yourself that it produces the correct display in all cases
including the zero polynomial.

With these and similar modifications, the engine inside the car named Poly (so to speak) can be completely replaced — but you still drive the car the same way. And, the dashboard display looks no different. So, you need not notice the new engine under the hood. The car simply runs faster and more smoothly.

The same code can test the sparse and the dense versions of Poly:

```
#include "Poly.h"

int p[]={5,2,3,3,2,-17};
int q[]={7,2,3,-3,2,15};

int main()
{    Poly p1(p,3); Poly q1(q,3);
     Poly sum = p1 + q1;
     sum.display();
     return(0);
}
```

And, the code results in the same output:

```
(7  2, 5  2, 2  -2)
```

5.5.1 Pocket Calculator Simulation

The power of the C++ class as a data abstraction and encapsulation tool can be greatly magnified by building objects on top of other objects. In other words, larger classes can be specified to contain existing objects as components. This approach is illustrated here by a pocket calculator simulation program.

Suppose we wish to simulate the functions and behavior of a simple hand-held calculator by creating an executable program calc. The program calc supports the arithmetic operations +, -, *, /, and =, as well as the C (clear), A (all clear), and N (sign change) operations.

Here is a typical session with calc:

```
Calc:  0
56 +
Calc:  56
3 −
Calc:  59
5 =
Calc:  54
N
Calc:  -54
```

User input is shown in italic. A session ends when Q is typed.

5.5.2   Program Design

To simulate an actual calculator, it makes sense to implement it as a C++ object containing two component objects, a *compute engine* and a *user interface* (Figure 5.1):

- The user interface object deals with receiving keyboard input and displaying answers.
- The compute engine object executes operations on the given numerical data and stores the results.
- The calculator object controls these components to perform the overall job.

Let's first examine the details of the calculator compute engine.

The CalcEng Class

The calculator compute engine object provides four member functions that constitute its *public interface*:

1. operand is used to enter numeric data into the compute engine.
2. operate is called to perform control and arithmetic operations.
3. opcode is called to obtain the internally kept operator code. (+, *, and so on).
4. output is invoked to produce the argument currently stored.

The calculator compute engine works with three fundamental quantities:

FIGURE 5.1   TWO COMPONENT OBJECTS OF AN OBJECT

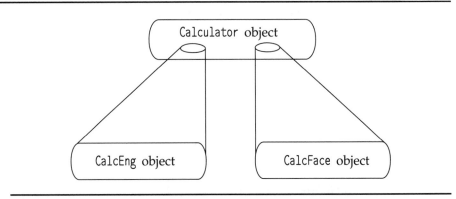

1. ans is the answer, or result of requested computations, initialized to 0.0.
2. op is the operator code (or opcode), one of the characters "+-*/=", whose left operand is always ans.
3. arg is the right operand of op.

Here is the header file for the CalcEng class:

```
///////    File CalcEng.h    ///////

class CalcEng
{   public:
        CalcEng();                  // constructor
        void operate(char c);       // perform operation
        void operand(double in) ;   // enter operand
        char opcode()               // returns current opcode
        {  return op;  }
        double output()             // returns current argument
        { return( argcnt==2 ? (arg) : ans ); }
    private:
        void compute();             // mostly performs ans = ans op arg
        void allclear();
        double ans, arg;
        char op;                    // operation code
        int argcnt;                 // argument count
};
```

The private data member argcnt keeps track of how many operands have been given at any point in time. The public interface makes using a CalcEng object simple and logical while hiding implementation details, which will, however, be exposed at this time.

The member functions of CalcEng are contained in the file CalcEng.C, which begins with some include files and the class constructor:

```
///////    File CalcEng.C    ///////
#include <iostream.h>
#include  "CalcEng.h"

CalcEng::CalcEng()
{   allclear();  }

void CalcEng::allclear()
{   ans = arg = 0.0;
    argcnt = 1;
    op = '=';
}
```

The initialization actions are performed by allclear, a function that also supports the 'A' operation discussed later. Numeric (double) data are entered into a CalcEng object using the member function

```
void CalcEng::operand(double in)
{   if ( op == '=' )
        ans = in;               // as left operand
    else
    {   arg = in;               // as right operand
        argcnt = 2;
    }
}
```

If the previous operation (still kept in op) is '=', then the data is assigned to ans (the left operand of the next operation). Otherwise, it is assigned to arg (the right operand) of the current op (one of "+-*/"). Once the operands are in place, an operation is triggered by calling operate() with the next character code from the user:

```
void CalcEng::operate(char c)
{
    switch( c )
    {   case 'A': // All Clear
        case 'a':  allclear(); return;
        case 'N': // sign change
        case 'n':  if ( argcnt == 1 ) ans = -ans;
                   else arg = -arg;
                   return;
        case 'C': // Clear
        case 'c':  if ( argcnt == 1 ) ans = 0.0, op = '=';
                   else { arg = 0.0; argcnt = 1;}
                   return;
        default : // +-*/=
                   compute();
                   op = c;     // new opcode
    }
}
```

The operations A, N, and C are performed immediately. Others ("+-*/=") trigger computations implemented by compute before being recorded as the new value of op (the next calculation to perform). The compute function checks for the right number of operands and actually carries out arithmetic operations. Of course, its actions are guided by the currently stored value of op:

```
void CalcEng::compute()
{   if ( argcnt == 2 )
```

```
{ switch( op )   // old value of op
  {   case '+':  ans += arg; break;
      case '-':  ans -= arg; break;
      case '*':  ans *= arg; break;
      case '/':  ans /= arg; break;
  }
  argcnt = 1;
}
}
///////   End of file CalcEng.C  ///////
```

Testing CalcEng

Since a class actually defines an independent computing entity, it makes sense to always test a class definition completely and separately. When combining classes into larger programs, all you have to do then is to make sure the objects are interfaced correctly.

To test CalcEng.C, we use a main program such as

```
///////      File: tstCalEng.C    ///////
#include <iostream.h>
#include "CalcEng.h"
int main()
{   CalcEng cal;
    cal.operand(9.8);
    cal.operate('+');
    cal.operand(1.2);
    cal.operate('/');
    cal.operand(2.0);
    cal.operate('=');
    cout << cal.output();
    cal.operate('N');
    cout << cal.output();
    return(0);
}
```

Of course, this simple program falls far short of a comprehensive test for the CalcEng class. Its purpose here is to show some typical test cases. In testing your own program, you should exercise all parts of the code and pay special attention to extreme and unusual cases. Compile CalcEng.C and tstCalEng.C separately to produce the corresponding object files. Once tested, the CalcEng.o file is in place and ready to be combined with other programs.

The CalcEng object is finished. Now let's consider the user interface part of the calculator.

The CalcFace Class

I/O to the user is the responsibility of a CalcFace object. This object reads user input and displays calculator output. Its public interface has two functions:

1. Each call to input consumes a sequence of zero or more digits terminated by a character-coded operation entered by the user. The code and number are deposited in the return parameters c and number, respectively. The return value of input indicates whether no number is supplied (OPONLY) or the input has been terminated (OFF).

2. The function show_number displays a given number to the user.

Here is the header file for the CalcFace class:

```
///////    File CalcFace.h    ///////
#include <iostream.h>
#include <ctype.h>
// number of significant digits
const int PREC=6;

// function input: returns op in c and input number if any
//      return value == OPONLY means only op is entered
//      return value == OFF means no more input

class CalcFace
{   public:
        CalcFace(char* k = "+-*/=NnAaCcQq")
        { keys = k; }
        int input(char& c, double& number);
        void show_number(double number);
        enum {OPONLY = 1, OFF};
    private:
        int inchar() {  return(cin.get()); }
        void extract_number(double&);
        void build_number(char c, int& i);
        int nump(char c);
        char   nbuf[PREC+2];    // buffer for input number
        char*  keys;            // keys recognized
};
```

Internally, the private member inchar produces the next input character or EOF upon end of file. The functions build_number() and extract_number() are used by input() to treat numeric input.

The implementation file CalcFace.C begins with include files, an inline function, and the simple output member function show_number:

```
///////    File CalcFace.C    ///////
#include    <iostream.h>
```

```
#include    <strstream.h>
#include    <ctype.h>
#include    "CalcFace.h"

inline int CalcFace::nump(char c)
    { return( c == '.' || isdigit(c) );  }

void CalcFace::show_number(double number)
{  cout << "Calc:  " << number << "\n"; }
```

Although output is simple, simulating input from a calculator is more complicated. The strategy is to keep reading input characters and accumulating them in a character buffer nbuf (by calling build_number()) as long as they are part of a number. As soon as an operator character is encountered, the number is complete and both the number and the operator are obtained. If the number part is empty, then only an operator is entered. To simulate a calculator, the input number consists of digits with one possible decimal point. The istrstream library facility (Section 6.2) is used to convert a string representation of a decimal number into a double (in function extract_number()):

```
void CalcFace::extract_number(double& number)
{  istrstream tmp(nbuf, PREC + 1);
   tmp >> number;      // converts string in nbuf to double
}

// put function in_string here
int CalcFace::input(char& op, double& number)
{     int c, current_position = 0, num=0;
      while ( (c = inchar()) != 'q' && c != 'Q' )  // (1)
      {  if ( in_string(c, keys) )                  // if c an operator
         {  op = c;
            if ( num )
            {  nbuf[current_position] = '\0';
               extract_number(number);
               return(0);
            }
            else return(OPONLY);
         }
         if ( nump(c) && current_position < PREC )              // (2)
         {  num = 1;
            build_number(c, current_position);
         }
      } // end of while
      return(OFF); // end of input
}
```

The in_string() function used here is defined in Section 1.14. The function input returns three quantities: the operator character code (in reference parameter op), a nonnegative input number (in reference parameter number), and OPONLY, OFF, or zero (as the function return value). Input is terminated when the Q or q key is seen (line 1). Input characters not recognized or beyond the calculator's precision (PREC) are ignored (line 2). The private member build_number accumulates numeric input in the buffer nbuf:

```
void CalcFace::build_number(char c, int& i)
{    static int point_seen = 0;
     if ( i == 0 ) point_seen = 0;       // reset
     if ( i == 0 && c == '0') return;    // ignore leading zeros
     if ( c == '.' )                     // allow at most one decimal point
     {    if ( point_seen ) return;
          else point_seen = 1;
     }
     nbuf[i++] = c;                       // current_position++
}
```

Testing CalcFace

The user interface class CalcFace should be tested independently with a main program such as

```
#include  <iostream.h>
#include "CalcFace.h"

int main()
{    CalcFace cf;
     char op;
     int ind;
     double number;
     while ( (ind = cf.input(op, number))
                  != CalcFace::OFF)
     {    cout << "operator is " ;
          cout.put(op);
          cout << "\n";
          if ( ind != CalcFace::OPONLY )
               cf.show_number(number);
     }
     return(0);
}
```

Note how the enum quantities in CalcFace are referred to outside the class. Once tested, the CalcFace.o file is in place and ready to be combined with other programs.

Now let's see how relatively simple it is to use CalcEng and CalcFace objects in building a Calculator object.

The Calculator Class

Aside from the constructor, the Calculator class has just one publicly callable member, on. Like its real-life counterpart, it turns on a Calculator object:

```
#ifndef Calculator_SEEN__
#define Calculator_SEEN__
///////    File: Calculator.h    ///////
#include    "CalcEng.h"
#include    "CalcFace.h"

class Calculator
{ public:
        Calculator() {} // default constructor
        void on();
   private:
        CalcEng eng;     // CalcEng object
        CalcFace cf;     // CalcFace object
};
#endif
```

Note that the once-only header file feature is shown explicitly (Section 12.7). The private members eng and cf are objects of previously defined classes. To establish a Calculator object, its component objects are automatically built and their default constructors are called.

The on function implements the top-level loop of a pocket calculator. It uses the compute engine and the user interface to make the calculator work in the expected fashion:

```
///////    File: Calculator.C    ///////
#include    "Calculator.h"

void Calculator::on()
{    int ind;
     char op;
     double number;
     cf.show_number(eng.output());       // initial display
     while ( (ind = cf.input(op, number))  // calc loop  (1)
                != CalcFace::OFF )
```

```
    {  if ( ind != CalcFace::OPONLY )
            eng.operand( number );          // operand    (2)
        eng.operate( op );                  // perform op (3)
        number = (op=='c' || op=='C') ? 0 : eng.output();
        cf.show_number(number);             // display    (4)
    }
}
```

As long as there is more user input, the on function repeats these steps:

1. Obtains from the user interface object the next input number and/or operation.
2. Enters the number, if given, as the operand for the compute engine object.
3. Passes the indicated operation to the compute engine.
4. Displays the compute engine output via the user interface object.

To end a session with this calculator, type the character Q or q.

Experimenting with a calculator object is now very simple indeed:

```
///////    File: mycalc.C   ///////
#include    "Calculator.h"

int main()
{   Calculator x;
    x.on();
    return(0);
}
```

Now create the executable program calc by combining the object files CalcEng.o, CalcFace.o, Calculator.o, and mycalc.o. Then, experiment with calc interactively to see how well it simulates a pocket calculator.

5.6 BUILT-IN OPERATIONS FOR OBJECTS

A class gives rise to a user-defined type and objects with operations supported by member functions. A few operations for objects are so basic that C++ performs them without being explicitly programmed. These include

1. Creating an object — instantiation and initialization (Section 5.2).
2. Assignment — for example, frac_a = frac_b + frac_c for fractions.
3. Argument passing — for example, perpendicular(vec1, vec2) for vectors.
4. Return value — for example, return(frac_a);.
5. Address-of — for example, Poly* ptr = &poly_a.

6. Value-of — for example, `*this`.

7. Member-of — for example, `frac_a.num` or `ptr->display()`.

Another built-in operation is object destruction as explained next.

5.7 DESTRUCTORS

While a constructor automates initialization of objects just after instantiation, a destructor, another special member function, automates cleanup actions just before deallocation (Figure 5.2). Unlike the constructor, which is needed by almost every class, the destructor is necessary only when there are cleanup chores to perform before object deallocation. Such chores include resetting variable values, freeing dynamic storage, closing I/O streams, removing temporary files, refreshing windows, deleting menus, and so on. The destructor provides a way to make appropriate actions automatic whenever an object is destroyed. After the destructor call, member objects, if any, are destroyed and their destructors are called in reverse order of initialization.

There are exactly three occasions when an object is destroyed:

1. When a local (automatic) object goes out of scope — for example,

FIGURE 5.2   LIFE CYCLE OF AN OBJECT

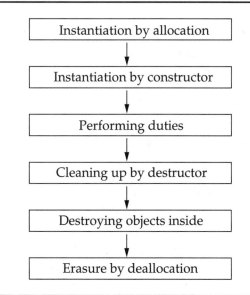

```
{ /* ... */
  Date d(1,14,1998);
  AddrEntry item(n1, a1);
  /* ... */
}
```

This often happens when a function call returns or when a compound statement ends.

2. When an object created by the operator new is specifically destroyed with the operator delete — for instance,

```
Date *d = new Date(1,14,1998);
/* ... */
delete d;
```

3. Just before a program terminates, all global objects (those with static storage) are destroyed.

In any case, the destructor of the object, if defined, is automatically invoked before memory deallocation. The body of a destructor can contain calls to member functions.

The destructor is a member function with a name obtained by prefixing the class name with the character ˜ (tilde). It is illegal for the destructor to specify a return type or to return a value. Furthermore, a destructor takes no arguments and therefore cannot be overloaded.

One example is the destructor for the Cirbuf class (Section 3.11):

```
Cirbuf::˜Cirbuf() { delete [] cb; }  // free up space
```

which frees the character array cb created by the Cirbuf constructor with new. If an object contains a pointer to space allocated by new and if the object is destroyed without first freeing the dynamically allocated memory, then that storage is *lost* to the program. Explicit invocation of delete is tedious and error-prone. The destructor makes freeing of space reached through an object (Figure 5.3) automatic at object destruction time and brings some welcome relief to the programmer who must otherwise free such spaces manually.

FIGURE 5.3   AN OBJECT WITH A POINTER TO FREE STORAGE

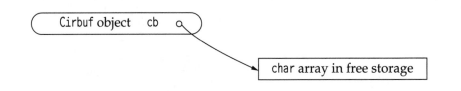

Another example is the class Poly, which can also use a destructor. The class Poly has a member pol, which points to allocated free storage. Thus, consider adding a destructor ~Poly:

```
Poly::~Poly()
{  delete [] pol;  }
```

However, note that adding such a destructor has other implications. It usually means also adding a class-defined assignment operator and a *copy constructor* (Section 7.10.2) to make things work.

In addition to being invoked automatically before object deallocation, a destructor, like other member functions, can be called explicitly (with . or ->). This is useful in situations where cleanup is needed without deallocating the object.

In C++, delete can be given either a pointer returned by new or a NULL pointer. Deleting a null pointer has no effect. For a destructor that frees up space, make sure that delete is applied only to these types of pointers.

When an object containing other objects is destroyed, the host destructor is executed first. The component objects are then destroyed in the reverse order of instantiation. We will examine many more applications of the destructor later.

5.8 \ FRIENDS OF A CLASS

Normally, private members are not accessible by any function outside their class. This is how data hiding is enforced in C++. However, a few situations call for exceptions to this rule. The friend mechanism is used to specify such exceptions. In a class definition, the declaration

friend *function-prototype*

declares a specific function to be a *friend* of the class. A friend has the privilege to access the nonpublic members of the class. The friend declaration can occur anywhere in the class definition and is not subject to access-control designations. It is conventional to place all friend declarations at the beginning of a class definition.

A friend can be an unattached function or a member function of another class. Two friends are now introduced to the class Fraction (Section 3.3):

```
class Fraction
{    friend int compare(int, Fraction);    // a friend function
     friend int compare(Fraction, int);    // another friend function
   public:
     /* ... */
```

```
private:
  int num;               // numerator
  unsigned int denom;    // denominator
};
```

The friend declarations can be added to Fraction.h even after Fraction.C has been compiled and there is no need to recreate Fraction.o. The added friend declarations simply inform the compiler that these two file-scope comparison functions have access to nonpublic members of the Fraction class. The access privilege is necessary for compare to test the relative size of an integer and a fraction:

```
int compare(int i, Fraction r)     // usage: compare(i,r) (A)
{ return(i * r.denom - r.num); }

int compare(Fraction r, int i)     // usage: compare(r,i) (B)
{ return(r.num - i * r.denom); }
```

Of course, the answer of the comparison is positive, negative, or zero, depending on whether the first argument is greater than, less than, or equal to the second one, a widely followed convention.

A good question to ask at this point is, Why not implement compare as a member function of Fraction and avoid the friend mechanism? One reason is that it is not possible to implement both versions A and B as members. Specifically, the member definition

```
int Fraction::compare(int i)     // usage: r.compare(i)
{ return(num - i * denom); }
```

can take the place of version B only. However, it is impossible to make i.compare(r) work because int is not a class.

When comparing two fractions, on the other hand, both the member and the friend options are open. The friend option gives symmetric treatment of the quantities being compared. The member option avoids making access exceptions to nonpublic members. Style dictates which option you choose.

Operators can also be friends. For example,

```
friend Fraction operator-(int, Fraction);
friend Fraction operator-(Fraction, int);
```

can be coded as

```
Fraction operator-(int i, Fraction r)
{   return Fraction(i*r.denom - num, r.denom);  }

Fraction operator-(Fraction r, int i)
{   return Fraction(num - i*r.denom, r.denom);  }
```

Again, it is not possible to implement both of these versions as member functions.

Sometimes, all member functions of a class X must be friends of another class Y. This can be done easily in C++ with

```
class Y
{    friend class X;
    /* ... */
};
```

to make all functions in class X friends of class Y. Also, individual member functions of a class can be made friends without making the whole class a friend. Just precede the selected function names with the class scope operator in the friend declaration.

The friend mechanism bypasses access control and allows nonmember functions access to the nonpublic members of a class. Use this mechanism sparingly and judiciously. While unnecessary use of the mechanism is inadvisable, some situations do require its use (Section 8.1).

Friends should be part of the design of a class. The information-hiding unit extends to include all friends of a class. If the internal workings of a class are modified without changing its public interface, then all that may need modification are member and friend functions. Thus, the friend mechanism is used to facilitate information hiding and not to break it. Let's consider the linked list described next as an example.

5.9 \ RECURSIVE STRUCTURES

It has been mentioned that a class may have members that are also objects. But is it possible or desirable for a class to have a member that, in turn, is an instance of the *same class*? Very much so. Such classes define *recursive structures*. Among recursive data structures, the linked list is one of the most widely used.

The class implementation of a linked list is the topic here. But first, we need to know a little more about the linked list concept.

Linked List

Think of a grocery list as a structure with two members:

1. The name of a grocery item.
2. A grocery list of the remaining items.

In fact, this recursive structure is inherent to any list.

In C++, it is not possible for a class to declare a member of the same class type directly. The reason is that an object cannot be declared with a class tag not completely defined yet. Hence, the declaration

```
class List
{ /* ... */

    List abc;          // List not defined yet
}
```

is incorrect. But, a pointer to the class being defined can be used. Therefore, a recursive class is defined to contain member *pointers* to objects of the same class.

The List Cell

As a first example, consider a *linked list* of characters. Each cell of the list contains a character and a pointer to the rest of the list; that is, each list cell also points to the location of the next cell, like a "chain of elephants" (Figure 5.4). Unlike a rigid array, a linked list affords great flexibility at run time—it is simple to add, delete, and reorder items on the list. Each entry on the linked list is an object of the recursive class ListCell, defined at the beginning of the file List.h:

```
///////    File : List.h    ///////
// linked list of characters
#include <iostream.h>

class ListCell                      // a recursive class
{   friend class List;
  private:                          // all members private
    char item;                      // item is a character
    ListCell* next;
    ListCell(char a = '\0',         // constructor
            ListCell* ptr = NULL)
    : item(a), next(ptr) { }        // constructor init-list
};
```

FIGURE 5.4   A LINKED LIST

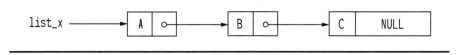

Each ListCell object stores a character in item and a pointer to the next cell in next. Here is how we construct a list:

```
ListCell* list_x = new ListCell('C');      //     (C)
list_x = new ListCell('B', list_x);    //   (B C)
list_x = new ListCell('A', list_x);    // (A B C)
```

A list cell containing the character C is first created with a call to new, and list_x points to this first cell. Another cell is created containing the character B and a pointer to the previous cell. Now list_x points to the second cell and is a list of two characters. This can be done a number of times to create a list of any length.

Linked List Design

The declaration

```
friend class List;
```

makes all member functions of class List friends of ListCell, granting them access to its nonpublic members (Section 5.8). Because all members, including the constructor, are private, the ListCell class is used exclusively by its friend class List, which encapsulates the recursive data structure and all list access and manipulation operations.

Consider how the class List is defined. In designing any class, consideration should first be given to its public interface and external behavior. Internal mechanisms can then be designed and implemented to support the desired external behavior. For a linked list, what should the public interface do?

- Build a list: Establish a new list empty or with one item (constructors); add items to a list (put_on, append, insert).
- Access list cells: Access specific cells and search through a list (first, next, last, and find, each returning an item pointer ListCell* or NULL if no such cell exists).
- Remove items: Delete all cells with a certain item (remove); remove several cells from the front of the list (shorten).
- Substitute items: Replace an existing item with a new item (substitute).
- Display the list: Produce a display of the entire list or a sublist starting at any given list cell (overloaded display).

There can be many good interface designs for the same class. For a list class, there are so many other operations that it is impossible to cover all of them here.

Now let's examine how our design is implemented:

```
class List
{ public:
    List() : head(NULL) { }          // constructor, empty list
    List(char c)                     // constructor, list with one cell
    : head (new ListCell(c,NULL)) { }
    ListCell* first() { return head; } // first cell
    ListCell* last();                // last cell
    ListCell* find(char c);          // first item == c
    int substitute(char r, char s);  // substitute r for first s
    int remove(char c);              // remove c from entire list
    void remove(ListCell* cell);     // remove given cell
    int shorten(int n);              // remove first n cells
    int put_on(char c);              // insert c in front
    int insert(char c, ListCell* cell);// insert c after cell
    int append(int c)                // insert c at end
    { return insert(c, last()); }
    int is_empty() { return(head == NULL); }
    void display(ListCell* p);       // display from p to end
    void display() { display(head); } // display whole list
    ~List();                         // destructor
  private:
    ListCell* head;                  // first cell of list
    void free();                     // free all cells
};
```

The single data member, head, is a pointer to the first list cell. All list cells used are allocated with new. Cells removed are freed immediately, and all cells are freed when a List object is destroyed (~List).

Linked List Implementation

The implementation file List.C begins with the destructor. Because all cells are allocated by new, each list cell must be freed individually with delete at cleanup time. This is the duty of the private member function free:

```
///////   File : List.C   ///////
#include <iostream.h>
#include "List.h"


List::~List() {   free(); }

void List::free()                // private member
{   ListCell *n, *p = head;
    while (p)
    {   n = p->next;
        delete p;
```

```
        p=n;
    }
}
```

The member function shorten removes a number of cells from the beginning of the list. If the list can be shortened by the requested amount, n, then
zero is returned. Otherwise, a negative integer *listlength* − *n* is returned after
removing all list cells:

```
int List::shorten(int n)
{   while (n-- && head)
    {   ListCell* tmp=head;
        head = head->next;
        delete(tmp);               // free up space
    }
    return(- ++n);
}
```

To remove all characters equal to c from the list, the member function
remove(char) first processes all list cells starting with the second cell. Then, the
first cell (head) is treated separately:

```
int List::remove(char c)
{    ListCell *tmp, *p = head;
     int count = 0;
     if ( p == NULL ) return(count);
     while (p->next)              // treat all but head cell
     {  if ((p->next)->item == c)
        {   count++;
            tmp = p->next;
            p->next = tmp->next;
            delete(tmp);          // free up storage
        }
        else
            p = p->next;
     }
     if( head->item == c )        // treat head cell
     {  tmp = head;
        head = head->next;
        delete(tmp);
        count++;
     }
     return(count);              // number of cells removed
}
```

Each cell removed is also freed. The total number of cells removed is returned
by the function.

Inserting a new item at the beginning (put_on) or after a given entry e (insert) is relatively simple:

```
int List::put_on(char c)
{     ListCell* tmp = new ListCell(c,head);
      if ( tmp )
      { head = tmp;
        return(0);
      }
      else return(-1);              // failed
}
```

```
// insert after entry e
int List::insert(char c, ListCell* e)
{     if ( e == NULL )             // insert at head
          return(put_on(c));
      ListCell* tmp = new ListCell(c,e->next);
      if ( tmp )
      { e->next = tmp;
        return(0);
      }
      else return(-1);             // failed
}
```

In each case, if the operator new fails (no more free storage), a −1 is returned. The access functions last and find return a pointer to the list cell found (type ListCell*). Note how last treats an empty list:

```
ListCell* List::last()
{     ListCell* p = head;
      while( p && p->next ) p = p->next;
      return(p);
}
```

```
ListCell* List::find(char c)
{     for( ListCell* p = head; p ; p = p->next )
          if( p->item == c )
              return(p);
      return(NULL);                   // c not on list
}
```

The frequent idiom

```
for( ListCell* p = head; p!=NULL ; p = p->next )   // idiom
```

follows pointers down a linked list efficiently. The member find locates the target character s to be substituted by r:

```
int List::substitute(char r, char s)
{    ListCell* p = find(s);
     if( p == NULL ) return(-1);    // s not on list
     p->item = r;
     return(0);
}
```

The output of display is a list of characters separated by spaces enclosed in parentheses:

```
// display from p to end
void List::display(ListCell* p)
{   cout << "(";
    while ( p )
    {    cout << p->item;
         if ( p = p->next ) cout << " ";
    }
    cout << ")\n";
}
```

The overloaded display functions are

```
void List::display(ListCell* p);   // display from p to end
void display() { display(head); }  // display whole list
```

You may be tempted to use one display function with a default argument instead:

```
void display(ListCell* p = head);  // error
```

This cannot be done because a default argument initializer must be *an expression involving only data at fixed memory locations at compile time*. The location of head depends on its host object at run time. In general, nonstatic class members cannot be default argument initializers.

Try List, ListCell, and some of the member functions using the test file

```
///////    File: tstList.C    ///////
#include <iostream.h>
#include "List.h"

void list_test()
{   List a('B');
    a.put_on('A');                    // (A B)
    a.append('D'); a.append('E');     // (A B D E)
    a.append('F'); a.display();       // (A B D E F)
    ListCell* lp = a.find('B');
    a.display(lp);
    a.insert('C', lp); a.display(); // (A B C D E F)
```

```
        a.remove('F'); a.shorten(2);    // (C D E)
        a.display();
        // destructor called as function returns
}

int main()
{   list_test();
    return(0);
}
```

which, when compiled and executed, produces the following output:

```
(A B D E F)
(B D E F)
(A B C D E F)
(C D E)
```

A complete list class would have other member functions such as concatenating two lists, taking the union or intersection, copying a list, and assigning one list to another. The latter two operations require special member functions, as we will see in Sections 7.9 and 7.10.

The advantage of linked lists is the ability to insert and delete items anywhere in the list with ease. For instance, in a text editor program, each text line can be represented by a linked list of characters to make inserting and deleting characters easy.

This example dealt with characters, but the basic linked list structure and manipulations stay the same for integers, floats, strings, dates, or other data types. In fact, it is possible in C++ to define a list of arbitrary type. Such generality brings to programs much needed flexibility and reusability, as we will see in Section 5.12.

5.10 \ STATIC MEMBERS

Members in an object are known and accessible everywhere within the single object. For example, the num and demon values in a Fraction object are freely accessed by its member functions without being passed as arguments. In general, data and function members are global within their own object. The object allows a limited degree of globalness for members without affecting other parts of the program. The restricted scope provides encapsulation, while the globalness cuts down on unnecessary argument passing.

Extending the degree of globalness, C++ also allows all objects of a class to share certain designated members known as *static members*. A static member is shared among all objects in the class and is therefore not stored inside any single object (Figure 5.5). A static member is global for all objects in a given class but still remains in the scope of the class, so it does not conflict with anything outside the class.

For example, a class may elect to have a static instance_count variable. Then, every constructor call can increment this count by 1, and every destructor call (Section 5.7) can decrement the count by 1. Sometimes, a maximum, a minimum, or some other critical value is made static and accessible to all objects of the same class.

A static member acts as a global quantity for its class objects. Only one instance of a static member is kept no matter how many objects are created. Since a static member is not contained within any single object, it exists and can be used even if there are no established instances of the class.

Other than initialization, a static member can be used and accessed just like a regular member. Because a static member is not associated with any single object, it does not have to be used through a host object. Therefore, the notation

ClassName::static_member

can be used to reference a static member.

Static data members are often used for the following purposes:

- To store constant values or structures shared by all objects in a class.
- To pass data from any object to all other objects.
- To store results computed by collaboration among all objects.

Because a static member is not stored in each object, the storage savings can be significant if the static member is a large table or if many objects are used.

The next example, involving foreign exchange rates, illustrates the use of static members.

FIGURE 5.5   OBJECTS SHARING A STATIC MEMBER

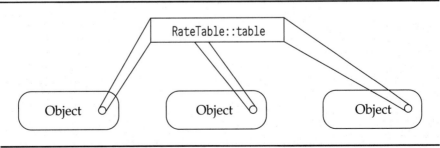

Foreign Exchange

Consider keeping a table of foreign exchange rates. Each table entry is an object of the class Rate:

```
///////   File: Rate.h    ///////
#include <iostream.h>

class Rate
{ public:
     Rate(const char* name = NULL,    // currency name
         double r = 0.0)              // exchange rate
     : cur(name), amt(r) { }
     double amount() { return(amt); }  // retrieve rate
     void rate(double r) { amt = r; }  // set rate
     const char* id() { return(cur); } // retrieve currency name
     void display()
     { cout << cur << "\t\t"
          << amt << endl;    }
   private:
     const char *cur;                 // currency name
     double amt;                      // exchange rate
};
```

A Rate object records the name of a particular currency and its exchange rate. All necessary constructor, retrieval, and update members are provided as inline functions.

The exchange rate table class RateTable specifies two static members: a sorted array of Rate objects and its length:

```
///////   File: RateTable.h    ///////
#include "Rate.h"
class RateTable
{ public:
     RateTable() {}                 // default constructor
     double rate(char *cur);        // find rate for given currency
     new_rate(char *cur, double r); // set rate of cur to r
     void display(char *cur);       // display one entry
     void display();
   private:
     int lookup(char *cur);         // table lookup
     static Rate table[];           // static sorted table
     static unsigned len;           // static table length
};
```

There are also table lookup and modification function members.

The header file contains a symbolic constant (Section 12.4) RATES, which is later used to initialize an exchange rate table:

```
// RATES macro used in RateTable.C to initialize sorted rate table

#define RATES   Rate("Britain (Pound)", 0.5905), \
                Rate("Canada (Dollar)", 1.1802), \
                Rate("Germany (Mark)", 1.6760), \
                Rate("Italy (Lira)", 1233.50),   \
                Rate("Japan (Yen)", 151.17),     \
                Rate("Mexico (Peso)", 2827.01),  \
                Rate("Spain (Peseta)", 104.15),  \
                /*      . . .            */  \
                Rate("Taiwan (NT $)", 24.0)
```

```
///////   End File RateTable.h   ///////
```

A static member is initialized differently than a regular data member is. The initialization is done at file scope as a freestanding declaration. As such, it is contained in the implementation part of the class. For instance, table and len are initialized in the RateTable.C file as follows:

```
///////   File: RateTable.C   ///////
#include <string.h>
#include "RateTable.h"

// initialize two static members
// RATES defined in Rate.h

Rate RateTable::table[] = { RATES };
unsigned RateTable::len = sizeof(RateTable::table)/sizeof(Rate);
```

Here the symbolic constant RATES, which can be modified in the RateTable.h file to add new currency entries and so on, is used to initialize the static member array RateTable::table[].

In general, static member initialization notation is

type ClassName::*static_member* = *initializer*;

where *type* is the type of the *static_member*. The initialization is given at file scope in a .C file. Uninitialized static members are set to zero.

The compile-time operator sizeof (Section 5.11) helps compute the array length. Since the table could be fairly large, it makes sense to keep only one copy.

The member functions rate and new_rate retrieve and set exchange rates, respectively:

```
double RateTable::rate(char *cur)
{     int index = lookup(cur);
      if ( index > -1 )
          return( table[index].amount() );
      else
          return(0.0);   // no exchange rate
}

int RateTable::new_rate(char *cur, double r)
{     int index = lookup(cur);
      if ( index > -1 )
      {   table[index].rate(r);
          return(0);
      }
      else
          return(-1);   // failed
}
```

A single entry or the entire exchange rate table can be displayed with the overloaded display function:

```
void RateTable::display(char *cur)
{     int index = lookup(cur);
      if ( index > -1 )
          table[index].display();
      else
          cout << "Entry " << cur
               << " not found.\n";
}

void RateTable::display()
{ for (int i = 0; i < len; i++)
      table[i].display();
}
```

Table Lookup via Binary Search

A key operation is locating any given currency entry in the array table. Because the exchange rate table is assumed to be already in sorted order, we can use an efficient binary search routine, lookup, to find an entry quickly:

```
// table lookup with binary search

int RateTable::lookup(char *cur)
{     int low = 0, high = len-1, mid, test;
      while (low <= high)
```

```
    {   mid = (high + low)/2;                // midpoint
        test = strcmp(cur, table[mid].id());  // library call
        if ( test == 0 )
            return( mid );
        else if ( test > 0 )
            low = mid + 1;
        else high = mid - 1;
    }
    return(-1);    // entry not on rate table
}
///////    End of file RateTable.C    ///////
```

The library function strcmp (Section 6.1) is used to identify the desired currency. The binary search proceeds by repeatedly going into the middle of the target search range to find the desired entry, which is a particularly efficient search method.

Test the exchange rate table using a simple main function.

```
#include <iostream.h>
#include "RateTable.h"

int main()
{   RateTable exchange_table;
    exchange_table.display();
    exchange_table.new_rate("Taiwan (NT $)", 23.5);
    cout << "revised entry" << endl;
    exchange_table.display("Taiwan (NT $)");
    return(0);
}
```

which, when compiled and executed, produces the output

```
Britain (Pound)      0.5905
Canada (Dollar)      1.1802
Germany (Mark)       1.676
Italy (Lira)         1233.5
Japan (Yen)          151.17
Mexico (Peso)        2827.01
Spain (Peseta)       104.15
Taiwan (NT $)        24
revised entry
Taiwan (NT $)        23.5
```

where the amounts shown are, of course, equivalent to one U.S. dollar.

This example shows how static data members are declared, initialized, and used just like regular members. What remains to be discussed are static member functions and accessing static members without reference to a host object.

Static Member Functions

If a member function contains no references to nonstatic members in the host, then the function can also be declared static. The difference between a static and a regular member function is the existence of the host pointer this:

- A regular member function can be called only through an object (the host) of its class and is instantiated with a pointer to the host (this).
- A static member function can be invoked either through an object or directly using the class scope operator *ClassName*::. It has no host pointer and cannot reference nonstatic members without going through an explicit object.
- Constructors and destructors cannot be static.

For example, we can make all member functions of RateTable static by prepending the keyword static to each of their declarations in the class definition. It is unnecessary, in fact illegal, to add the keyword static to the corresponding member function headers in the .C file:

```
class RateTable
{ public:
    RateTable() {}                      // default constructor
    static double rate(char *cur);      // rate for given currency
    static new_rate(char *cur, double r);
    static void display(char *cur);     // display one entry
    static void display();              // display rate table
  private:
    static int lookup(char *cur);       // table lookup
    static Rate table[];
    static unsigned len;
};
```

With this modification, we can write the main program for testing as follows:

```
int main()
{    RateTable::display();
     RateTable::new_rate("Taiwan (NT $)", 23.5);
     cout << "revised entry" << endl;
     RateTable::display("Taiwan (NT $)");
     return(0);
}
```

In this program, no class objects are used. Thus, the class RateTable is defined not to establish objects but to create a program package or module whose name space is separated from the rest of the program. Although identifiers defined within the module are accessible to other parts of the program, the module name (RateTable in this case) must be explicitly mentioned. In other words, the C++ static member facility also helps support the program module or package concept available in other languages.

5.10.1   enum and typedef Members

Enumerators and typedefs defined in the scope of a class are local to that class and common to all its objects. Although such members are subject to normal access control, they are not regular data members and are not stored in each class instance but in an area shared by all objects of the same class, just like static members. Therefore, enum and typedef members can also be accessed without reference to a host object.

Classwide constants are usually declared as member enumerators to encapsulate information more completely. The familiar ios::in and ios::out are enumerators in the C++ I/O stream library class ios.

Also, despite being names enclosed in their class, enum and typedef members do not exactly have class scope like regular members. Specifically, in a class definition, such members must be declared before they are used.

5.11 \ THE SIZE OF OBJECTS

We have already seen the use of the compile-time unary operator sizeof for computing RateTable::len in Section 5.10. This operator computes the size of built-in or user-defined data types. The expression

```
sizeof( variable or type name )     // parentheses optional
```

is replaced by the compiler with the number of bytes required to store a variable of the given type. Table 5.1 shows the typical values of some built-in types and the rules for computing the size of user-defined types. Using sizeof instead of hard-coded constant sizes makes a program independent of the local system and therefore more portable.

Because some data must be aligned on certain word boundaries in memory, empty space, or *padding*, may be used in storing class members. The initialization of len in class RateTable is a good application of sizeof.

5.12 \ GENERIC LISTS

We are familiar with the class List (presented earlier in Section 5.9). A List object represents a linked list of characters. But what about lists of integers,

TABLE 5.1   SOME sizeof EXPRESSIONS

COMPILE-TIME EXPRESSION	TYPICAL VALUE
sizeof(char)	1
sizeof(short int)	2
sizeof(int)	4
sizeof(long)	4
sizeof(float)	4
sizeof(double)	8
sizeof(*any* *)	4
sizeof(*arrayname*)	*dim* * sizeof(*entry*)
sizeof(*class-tag*)	Total sizes of data members and any padding

fractions, dates, vectors, addresses, and so on? What about lists of objects yet to be defined? Must we reinvent the wheel every time? No, fortunately, there are ways to define such classes once and for all. Two approaches are available to achieve this goal:

1. We can use the *template* facility.
2. We can use the void * type and pointers to functions.

Templates are discussed in Chapter 10. The second approach creates lists storing items of type void * that can contain items of any desired type. Such a list is *generic*, or nontype-specific. A generic list class makes the code for list manipulation *reusable* whenever and wherever a linked list of some type is required. The generic approach presented here works not only for lists but also for any *container class* such as tables, sets, trees, graphs, stacks, and queues — just to name a few items.

Our generic list class ArbList can be defined by modifying the existing class List. You may be surprised at how few changes are needed. To begin with, the code for ArbCell is simply ListCell with char replaced by void *:

```
///////   File: ArbList.h    ///////
// linked list of arbitrary entries
#include <iostream.h>

typedef void *Arbent;        // arbitrary entry

class ArbCell
{ friend class ArbList;
```

```
private:
  Arbent item;                    // item is now arbitrary
  ArbCell* next;
  ArbCell(Arbent c = NULL, ArbCell* ptr = NULL)
  :  item(c), next(ptr) { }   // constructor
};
```

Storing pointers rather than the data items directly is the price for achieving genericness. For items of a basic type, the memory requirement doubles. For larger items such as strings and addresses, the storage increase is not significant at all.

To transform List into ArbList, we make two obvious changes: We replace all ListCell by ArbCell and all char by Arbent. Then, we must provide a way to check equality (for find and remove) of arbitrary items and to display them — tasks that are impossible for void * types. So, an equality tester and a displayer function must be supplied when an ArbList object is initialized. These functions have knowledge of the item type and can therefore perform their tasks easily.

Here is the class ArbList:

```
typedef int (* EQ_FN)(Arbent, Arbent);      // equality tester type
typedef void (* DISP_FN)(Arbent);           // item displayer type

class ArbList
{ public:
    ArbList() : head(NULL) { }                // default constructor
    ArbList(Arbent c, EQ_FN eq, DISP_FN d)   // constructor   (1)
    : head (new ArbCell(c,NULL)),
      equal(eq), dispfn(d) { }
    ArbCell* first() { return head; }         // first cell
    static ArbCell* next(ArbCell* p)
    { return(p ? p->next : p); }              // next cell
    static int is_end(ArbCell* p)
    { return(p == NULL); }                    // end test
    ArbCell* last();                          // last cell
    ArbCell* find(Arbent c);                  // first item equals c
    int substitute(Arbent r, Arbent s);      // r for first s on list
    int remove(Arbent c);                     // c from entire list
    static Arbent content(ArbCell* p)         // content of list item
    {   return p->item;   }
    void remove(ArbCell* cell);               // remove given cell
    int shorten(int n);                       // remove first n cells
    int put_on(Arbent c);                     // insert in front
    int insert(Arbent c, ArbCell* cell);     // insert after cell
    int append(Arbent c)                      // insert at end
    { return insert(c, last()); }
```

```
      int is_empty() { return is_end(head); }
      void display(ArbCell* p);              // display from p to end
      void display() { display(head); }      // display whole list
      ~ArbList();                            // destructor
   private:
      ArbCell* head;      // first cell of list
      void free();        // free all cells
      EQ_FN equal;        // supplied equality tester
      DISP_FN dispfn;     // supplied displayer
};
```

The constructor (line 1) records the supplied equality tester and displayer in the members equal and dispfn. Several static members, next(), content(), and is_end(), are added for a well rounded public interface. The display function now uses dispfn:

```
///////    File:  ArbList.C    ///////

// display from p to end
void ArbList::display(ArbCell* p)
{   cout << "(";
    while ( p )
    {   dispfn(p->item);   // supplied displayer
        if ( p = p->next ) cout << " ";
    }
    cout << ")\n";
}
```

The functions remove and find use the supplied equality tester rather than the == operator:

```
int ArbList::remove(Arbent c)
{   ArbCell *tmp, *p = head;
    int count = 0;
    if ( p == NULL ) return(count);
       while (p->next)                          // treat all but head cell
       {  if ( equal((p->next)->item, c) )  // use equal tester
          {   count++;
              tmp = p->next;
              p->next = tmp->next;
              delete(tmp);                       // free up storage
          }
          else
                p = p->next;
       }
       if( equal(head->item, c) )                // treat head cell
```

```
      {  tmp = head;
         head = head->next;
         delete(tmp);
         count++;
      }
      return(count);                           // number of items removed
}


ArbCell* ArbList::find(Arbent c)
{    for( ArbCell* p=head ; p ; p=p->next )
        if( equal(p->item, c) )                // equal tester
            return(p);
     return(NULL);                             // c not on list
}
```

Other member functions not shown are simple translations from their List counterparts.

Now we can apply the generic ArbList. The example establishes lists of integers from ArbList. The required displayer and equality tester functions are defined early in the file:

```
///////   File: tstAList.C   ///////
#include <iostream.h>
#include "ArbList.h"

// linked list of integers via
//    generic ArbList class

void i_display(int* item)        // displayer for int
{    cout << *item;    }

int i_eq(int* a, int* b)         // equality tester for int
{    return( *a == *b ); }
```

In the following main program, an integer list ilist is an instance of ArbList with the required functions supplied. Then, ilist is used normally as a list of integers. Note that integer pointers rather than integers are always passed in the function calls:

```
static int a[] = {0,10,20,30,40,50};

int main()
{ ArbList ilist(a+1, EQ_FN(i_eq), DISP_FN(i_display) );
    ilist.put_on( a + 3 );      // a+1 and a+3 are int*
    ilist.put_on( a + 5 );
    ilist.display();
```

```
    ilist.put_on( a );   ilist.put_on( a + 2 );
    ilist.append( a + 4 );
    ilist.display();

    ilist.remove( a + 4 ); ilist.remove( a );
    ilist.display();
    return(0);
}
```

Run this program to produce the following output:

```
(50 30 10)
(20 0 50 30 10 40)
(20 50 30 10)
```

We have now successfully built a generic list class that can be applied in many applications.

5.13   SUMMARY

The class is a key construct for encapsulation and data abstraction. A class definition specifies members that are functions, data, typedefs, enum constants, and even classes. Class members are designated private or public for access control. A class is a blueprint for making objects that are instances of the class. Each object can be viewed as an independent computing entity consisting of the members specified in the class. Thus, data and function members are contained in a host object. The special pointer this is available to member functions to refer to its host.

Public members in a class define its interface to the rest of the program and are accessible by any part of the program. Private members are accessible only by member functions in the same object or in an object of the same class. The friend declaration grants specific functions special access rights to the nonpublic members of objects of a class. Certain operations, such as operator-(int, fraction), can be implemented only as friend functions.

A class definition cannot contain initializers for members. A constructor is a special member function for initializing data members and other setup chores. A constructor taking no arguments is called a *default constructor* and is needed for declaring objects without initial values. An object of a class with no constructors whatsoever can be initialized with array-style initializers when declared. A constructor is called automatically when an object is created.

The destructor is another special member function for freeing dynamic storage and other cleanup chores just before an object is destroyed. Not all classes define destructors. Destructors are normally needed only when objects contain dynamic storage.

The OO design and implementation of a pocket calculator show how to break a problem into component objects and combine them to build larger objects. The interactions of these components closely simulate the behavior of actual objects, thus making the program elegant and easy to understand. Building upon existing objects to form larger objects is an important OOP technique. When an object contains other objects, the component objects are instantiated and initialized in declaration order before other members of the host object are initialized. When such an object is destroyed, the object destructor is first executed. Component objects are then destroyed in the reverse order of instantiation.

Except for a few built-in operations, all operations for user-defined types (class objects) must be supplied by a program. The built-in operations are initialization, pass as argument, return as function value, =, ., ->, &, and deinitialization by destructors.

A static data member is shared by all objects of a class and is not stored in any object. A static data member is initialized differently than is a regular data member. A static member is initialized in the same way as a file scope variable. A member function can be declared static if it does not reference nonstatic members in the host.

A recursive structure can be defined with a class containing a pointer to an object in the same class. A linked list is a common recursive structure that affords great run-time flexibility. A generic list class is a typical container class which can be defined using pointers to function and the void * type. Such classes can be reused for applications requiring different and yet-to-be-defined types.

EXERCISES

1. Compare and contrast the two different class declarations class and struct.

2. Consider declaring an array of objects. Is a default constructor absolutely necessary? Illustrate your answer with examples.

3. In what aspects are constructors and destructors special members of a class?

4. Usually, a member is accessed only through a host object. Name all the cases you can think of where this rule does not apply.

5. What is the difference between initializing an object member using a mem-initializer in a constructor init-list and assigning an initial value in the constructor body? Give examples to illustrate your point.

6. Consider static data members of a class. If the static member is private, how can it be initialized? Examine the Poly class (Section 5.5) and the member function s_to_d(). Should it be declared static? Why?

7. Consider a class *ClassX* and an object obj of this class. Assume that this class contains an enumerator member Econst and a typedef Type. Discuss the access notations obj.Type, obj.Econst, *ClassX*::Type, and *ClassX*::Econst.

8. A class has a number of members that are special in the sense that they have predefined meaning. Name the ones you know and explain their functions.

9. In OOP, one important design consideration is which part of the program contains what information. A good segregation of information helps the logic of the design. Consider the placement of information in the pocket calculator example. Which class should possess and provide the *precision* information? Which class should possess and provide the string of keys (+-*/...) allowed? Which other classes need to use this information but should not be the keepers of it? Modify the calculator classes accordingly. (*Hint:* Use static and/or enum.)

10. Define a class TicTacToeBoard that records the game status, allows legal moves, and determines the game outcome. When designing this class, think about other simple board games, such as Othello, and what they have in common.

11. Consider the binary search algorithm used for looking up the foreign exchange table. Follow the generic sorting example in Section 4.10 and build a generic binary search function.

12. Consider objects that are read-only — namely, objects declared const. Does the read-only status of a host object prevent you from using certain member functions? Which ones? Why?

13. Take the Poly class and add all possible read-only declarations to it. (*Hint:* Do not forget the host object.)

14. A binary tree is a recursive structure with a root node that either contains just an item of a certain type (a leaf node) or contains an item, a left binary tree, and a right binary tree (an internal node). Define a BTree class together with appropriate functions.

CHAPTER

6

LIBRARY FUNCTIONS AND I/O STREAMS

Software libraries provide well-written and tested routines for many useful computations. A library is a very efficient way of making high-quality code available to programmers so that they do not have to "reinvent the wheel" every time a need for one of these routines arises.

A library-supplied function or class must have the right declarations, which is done by including the necessary header files. Once declared, the function or class can be used just as one of your own contained in another file. Compiled codes from the basic libraries are usually automatically loaded, as needed, into your final executable program.

Libraries for string manipulation, character operations, and mathematical calculations are described in this chapter. C++ also supplies an I/O stream class library providing object-oriented I/O operations. A systematic presentation of the C++ I/O stream facility is included here so that you learn how to use it effectively.

Many library facilities are available. Some important ones are presented here; others can be found in Appendices 8 and 9.

6.1 OPERATIONS ON STRINGS

Although a string is not a basic type in C++, it remains a frequently used construct in programming. For this reason, a group of library functions for string manipulations is available (Tables 6.1 and 6.2). Familiarizing yourself with these library functions will make programming easier in many situations.

This point is underscored by the fact that several of these functions have already been used in previous examples. Tables 6.1 and 6.2 employ the notation

s   (a character string terminated by '\0'
         to be modified by the library function)
cs   (a const character string not to be modified)
n   (an integer of type size_t)
c   (a single char)

where size_t (size type) is a typedef (Section 3.9) used for sizes of data items. The type size_t usually means an unsigned integer of a certain size, depending on the computer, and is defined in the standard header file <stddef.h>. For most purposes, size_t is the same as unsigned int.

To use any of the string library functions, the header file <string.h> must be included. The functions in Table 6.1 actually alter their first arguments. For copying or concatenating, make sure there is enough room in s to accommodate the incoming characters. The strcmp functions compare strings lexicographically (in dictionary order), returning a negative, zero, or positive value in case the first argument is less than, equal to, or greater than the second. For strncpy, if cs has more than n characters, no '\0' terminator is copied.

The strtok function is a little more involved than the other functions. The purpose of strtok is to scan its first argument and break it up into tokens. A *token* is a sequence of characters forming a word such as a variable name or an arithmetic operator. Tokens in a character string are separated from one another by one or more *delimiter* characters. The delimiters are indicated by the second argument cs. To extract tokens from a string, a series of calls are made to strtok, with each call returning a pointer to the next token as a '\0'-terminated string. The first invocation of strtok supplies a nonempty string s and receives the first token. All subsequent calls pass NULL as the first argument and receive successive tokens.

TABLE 6.1   DESTRUCTIVE STRING OPERATIONS

FUNCTION	DESCRIPTION
char *strcat(s,cs)	Concatenates a copy of cs to end of s; returns s.
char *strncat(s,cs,n)	Concatenates a copy of at most n characters of cs to end of s; returns s.
char *strcpy(s,cs)	Copies cs to s including '\0'; returns s.
char *strncpy(s,cs,n)	Copies at most n characters of cs to s; returns s, pads with '\0' if cs has less than n characters.
char *strtok(s,cs)	Finds tokens in s delimited by characters in cs.

TABLE 6.2   **NONDESTRUCTIVE STRING OPERATIONS**

FUNCTION	DESCRIPTION
size_t strlen(cs)	Returns length of cs (excluding '\0').
char *strcmp(cs1,cs2)	Compares cs1 and cs2; returns negative, zero, or positive for cs1 <, ==, or > cs2, respectively.
char *strncmp(cs1,cs2,n)	Compares at most first n characters of cs1 and cs2.
char *strchr(cs,c)	Returns pointer to first occurrence of c in cs.
char *strrchr(cs,c)	Returns pointer to last occurrence of c in cs.
char *strpbrk(cs1,cs2)	Returns pointer to first character in cs1 and in cs2.
char *strstr(cs1,cs2)	Returns pointer to first occurrence of cs2 in cs1. *All four functions return NULL if the search fails.*
size_t strspn(cs1,cs2)	Returns length of prefix of cs1 consisting of characters from cs2.
size_t strcspn(cs1,cs2)	Returns length of prefix of cs1 consisting of characters *not* in cs2.

The tokens are returned in place by overwriting the first delimiter character after each token with a '\0'. Table 6.3 illustrates how **strtok** breaks "ls   /user/fac/pwang" into tokens. In Table 6.3, ⊔ stands for a space, ⊗ for a '\0'. Naturally, each token returned contains no delimiter characters. A NULL is returned when **strtok** finds no more tokens. Also, the delimiters contained in cs may be different on each call.

Let's examine an actual implementation of **strtok**:

```
#include        <string.h>

char * strtok(char * s, const char * del)
{   char * token;
```

TABLE 6.3   **USING strtok**

	CALL SEQUENCE	TOKEN FOUND IS UNDERLINED
1	strtok(str, del)	<u>ls</u>⊗ ⊔ ⊔/user/fac/pwang⊗
2	strtok(NULL, del)	ls⊗ ⊔ ⊔/<u>user</u>⊗fac/pwang⊗
3	strtok(NULL, del)	ls⊗ ⊔ ⊔/user⊗<u>fac</u>⊗pwang⊗
4	strtok(NULL, del)	ls⊗ ⊔ ⊔/user⊗fac⊗<u>pwang</u>⊗

str = "ls⊔ ⊔ ⊔/user/fac/pwang" and del = "⊔/"

```
    int i = 0;
    static char *spt = NULL;                // starting position
    if ( s ) spt = s;                       // new string
    if ( !spt || spt[0] == '\0' )
        return(NULL);
    while ( spt[i] != '\0'                  // find beginning of token
        && strchr(del, spt[i]) ) i++;
    token = &spt[i];
    while ( spt[i] != '\0'                  // find end of token
        && !strchr(del, spt[i]) ) i++;
    spt[i] = '\0';                          // terminator in place
    spt = &spt[i+1];                        // record position
    return(token);                          // token produced
}
```

A static pointer spt remembers, across calls to **strtok**, the beginning of the string yet to be processed. The library function **strchr** is used to determine whether a character is a delimiter (contained in the string del) or not. This implementation of **strtok** deserves careful study because of its intricacies in index and pointer handling.

To test **strtok**, use the following main program:

```
#include <iostream.h>
const char *WHITE = "\t \n\r";              // TAB SPACE NEWLINE RETURN

int main()
{   char st1[] = "There it is.";
    char st2[] = "\n \t A string\n \r  of 1 or more    \t tokens";
    char* strarr[2] = {st1, st2};
    char * tk;
    for ( int i = 0 ; i < 2 ; i++ )         // process both strings
    {   tk = strtok(strarr[i], WHITE);      // 1st call strtok
        do
        {   cout << tk << "\n";             // output token
        } while ( (tk = strtok(NULL, WHITE)) );
    }
    return(0);
}
```

Run this program to see what output it produces. Because **strtok** modifies its first argument, it is incorrect to pass a *constant* string directly in the function call:

```
strtok("There it is.", WHITE);      // error
```

In the definition of strtok, we could have applied the library functions strspn and strcspn. Subscript notations are used here in manipulating strings. A more concise but less readable alternative is to use pointer arithmetic.

6.2 \ STRING COMPOSITION AND EXTRACTION

At compile time, string constants can be concatenated by juxtaposition (putting them next to each other). At run time, a string can also be composed from a mixture of strings, integers, floating-point numbers, and so on. The *string stream* class, part of the C++ I/O stream class, is designed for this purpose. A string output object produces output similar to cout but in a preallocated character buffer instead.

Here is a simple example:

```
#include <iostream.h>
#include <strstream.h>

int main()
{   const SIZE = 64;
    char buf[SIZE];
    ostrstream mystr(buf, SIZE, ios::out);  // string stream obj
    float amt = 54.95;
    // compose string using mystr object
    mystr << "The price is $" << amt << '.' << '\0';
    // Display string composed
    cout << buf << "\n";
    return(0);
}
```

Note the correct header files to use. In main, a character buffer buf of capacity 64 is allocated. The buffer and its size are used in establishing mystr, an instance of the ostrstream class. The overloaded operator << is used to compose a string in buf through the mystr object.

Compiling and running this program produces the following display:

```
The price is $54.95.
```

The buffer size should be large enough to receive a composed string. Otherwise, only the prefix that fits will be contained in the buffer.

While an ostrstream object helps compose a string from all types of data, an istrstream object does just the opposite — it extracts different data from their string representations. For example, the function str_to_float uses an istrstream object to convert the ASCII string representation of a floating-point number into float:

```
#include <iostream.h>
#include <strstream.h>
#include <string.h>

float str_to_float(char* s)
{   istrstream tmp(s, strlen(s));
    float ans;
    tmp >> ans;
    return(ans);
}
```

Of course, the extraction operator >> does not modify the string s in any way. The conversion fails if the leading part of s does not represent a valid floating-point number.

Similar to using cin, extraction of consecutive quantities separated by white spaces in a string is easy. For example, the main program

```
int main()
{   char *s = "3  -3.1 \t 3.1416";
    cout << s << endl;
    int a;
    float b, c;
    istrstream tmp(s, strlen(s));
    tmp >> a >> b;
    tmp >> c;
    cout << a+b+c << endl;
    return(0);
}
```

produces the following display:

```
3  -3.1        3.1416
3.0416
```

In applications where the extraction of a string is done only once, the creation of the named istrstream object tmp can be omitted in favor of an anonymous object:

```
istrstream (s, strlen(s)) >> a >> b >> c;
```

6.3 STRING INPUT AND OUTPUT

Character string input is easily handled through an I/O stream object. For example,

```
const int LEN = 64;
char buffer[LEN];
cin >> buffer;
```

The char* version of the overloaded input operator >> reads strings separated by white space (SPACE, TAB, RETURN, NEWLINE) into the given buffer. Here white space breaks up a string even inside double quotes. A string terminator ´\0´ (null character) is appended to the end of a string read into buffer. The function read_strings is a good example of how to read multiple strings:

```
#include <iostream.h>
#include <strstream.h>
#include <string.h>

typedef unsigned int Uint;
typedef char * String;

const Uint SIZE = 64;

int read_strings(istream& in, String strs[], Uint dim)
{   Uint k, n=0;
    String s;
    char buffer[SIZE];

    while( in >> buffer )         // read string into buffer (1)
    {   k = 1 + strlen(buffer);
        if (n >= dim || (s = new char[k]) == NULL)
            return(-1);           // error
        else
        {   strcpy(s, buffer);    // copy buffer into s
            strs[n++] = s;        // put s on array strings
        }
    }
    return(n);                    // number of strings read
}
```

Strings are read from the given istream object into the array of string pointers strs of dimension dim. When successful, read_strings returns the number of strings read. Otherwise, it returns −1. Note the use of new and strcpy.

A simple main program to test read_strings is

```
int main()
{   String strs[100];
    int i = read_strings(cin, strs, 100);
    for ( int j = 0; j < i; j++)
        cout << strs[j] << "\n";
    return(0);
}
```

When given the input

```
"To be or not to be?"
        That is the question.
```

this program produces the following display:

```
"To
be
or
not
to
be?"
That
is
the
question.
```

If the input buffer does not have enough room, the trailing portion of the input string will be lost. The library function setw(length) prevents string input overflow. It breaks up a string longer than length - 1 to several strings that just fit. Thus, to be safe, we can modify the input while loop (line 1) as follows:

```
while ( in >> setw(SIZE) >> buffer )
```

6.4 \ OPERATIONS ON CHARACTERS

Since a char is represented as a small integer, it can be used freely in arithmetic expressions involving other characters or integers. For example, the expression

```
'8' - '0'
```

yields the integer value 8 because the values of '0', '1', '2', and so on are consecutive and form an increasing sequence. Also, an expression such as

```
c >= 'A' && c <= 'Z'
```

used to test for c as upper case works because the corresponding uppercase and lowercase characters are a fixed distance apart. Reliance on such features makes the expression dependent on the character set.

The standard header file <ctype.h> defines a group of useful character macros/functions (Table 6.4) that are implementation-independent. Among these, isupper and tolower have already been used (Section 1.6). The various testing functions in Table 6.4 return zero for false and nonzero for true.

TABLE 6.4   CHARACTER FUNCTIONS

FUNCTION	TEST FOR
int isupper(int c)	Uppercase letter (A–Z)
int islower(int c)	Lowercase letter (a–z)
int isalpha(int c)	Uppercase or lowercase letter
int isdigit(int c)	Decimal digit
int isalnum(int c)	isalpha(c) || isdigit(c)
int iscntrl(int c)	Control character
int isxdigit(int c)	Hexadecimal digit
int isprint(int c)	Printable character including SPACE
int isgraph(int c)	Printable character except SPACE
int isspace(int c)	SPACE, FORMFEED, NEWLINE, RETURN, TAB, vertical TAB
int ispunct(int c)	Printable character not SPACE, digit, or letter

FUNCTION	MEANING
int toupper(int c)	Convert to upper case
int tolower(int c)	Convert to lower case

6.5 NUMERIC COMPUTATIONS

Also supported in a standard library are mathematical functions, such as sin, sqrt, and log, for floating-point computations. To use these functions, the header file <math.h> is needed. Appendix 8 contains a list of all mathematical functions.

The library functions work with type double (double-precision floating-point). This means that they take double arguments and return double values. For example, the *cos* function is double cos(double x). For some systems, similar libraries are provided for floats of other sizes as well.

If you use functions supplied by a library, you must link the compiled codes for such functions into the final executable program before it can run correctly. The linker/loader phase extracts the required library functions and combines them with the rest of your program. Usually, the C++ compiler automatically takes care of including functions supplied by the standard libraries and needs no special attention. For library functions not automatically included, such as the mathematical functions on some systems, the C++ compiler must be told what additional libraries to use for a particular compilation. See Appendix 1 or 2 for information appropriate to your system.

6.6 \ THE I/O STREAM LIBRARY

We have already used the standard I/O objects cin, cout, and cerr in some examples. However, since I/O is an important topic, let's take a systematic look at the C++ I/O stream library.

The I/O stream library consists of a number of related classes including

- *Basic I/O:* ios, istream, ostream, and iostream.
- *File I/O:* ifstream, ofstream, and fstream.
- *In-memory I/O:* istrstream, ostrstream, and strstream.

These classes form a hierarchy, building more powerful classes from basic ones. Standard I/O is handled by the iostream class built on top of istream and ostream classes, which in turn depend on the fundamental ios class. Then, file and string I/O are built on top of the standard I/O facilities.

The object cin belongs to the istream class, whereas cout and cerr belong to the ostream class. The unbuffered error stream cerr is also complemented by a buffered stream, clog, used for logging of error and other messages produced by a program.

6.6.1 Opening and Closing Files

For each program, we always have the four ready-to-use objects for standard I/O as mentioned before. I/O objects are connected with specific files with the following:

```
ifstream myin(filename, ios::in);            // for input
ofstream myout(filename, ios::out);          // for output
ofstream myout(filename, ios::app);          // to append at end
fstream myio(filename, ios::in | ios::out);  // for input and output
```

We can also establish a file I/O object without its being attached to any file. The **open** member function is used later to attach such an object to a file. For example,

```
ifstream anyin;          // file input object
anyin.open(filename);    // attach to filename
if ( ! anyin )           // if open failed
{ ...
}
```

Use the member function **is_open()** to test whether an I/O object is still open. To close a file, use **close()**:

```
anyfile.close();
```

To flush (force output) of the buffer of an output object, use `flush()`.

6.6.2   I/O Operators << and >>

The bit-shift operators << and >> are overloaded to serve as output and input operators, respectively. A very simple way to perform output is with

```
cout << var;
anyout << var;
```

The type of the variable var determines the display produced. Besides a single variable, << can also handle any valid expression. In this case, you enclose the expression in parentheses to avoid precedence problems with <<. If var is of type char*, then a `\0`-terminated character string is displayed. The call **endl**(anyout) flushes the buffer and outputs a NEWLINE. It can also be used with <<, as in

```
anyout << var << endl;
```

If << is given a pointer, it displays the address of the pointer in hexadecimal notation. To display the address of a pointer to char, it must first be cast to void* to prevent it from being interpreted as a character string.

The input operator >> deposits input data into a variable of any basic type including char*. For example,

```
float a; int b;
cin >> a >> b;
```

reads correctly the input

```
3.1416  17
```

For >>, input tokens are always separated by white space, which is ignored. Thus,

```
char ch;
while( cin >> ch )
{  ...
}
```

reads, from standard input,

```
uv w
   xy   z
```

as six characters. (White space in the input can be read using other facilities, such as **get** and **getline**, explained later.)

We have already seen how the input operator >> is used to read character strings (Section 6.3). The >> operator is also very convenient to use in reading tabulated data. For instance, the loop

```
float x[3], y[3], z[3];
for ( int i = 0 ; cin >> x[i] ; i++ )
    cin >> y[i] >> z[i];
```

reads correctly the data file

```
1.0     +2.0    3.0
0.1     -0.2    0.3
1.1     +2.2    3.3
```

The expression *obj* >> *arg* (or *obj* << *arg*) always produces a reference to the stream object *obj* as the value of the expression. This explains why << and >> can be concatenated. For example, the lines

```
cout << a << b ;
(cout << a) << b ;
```

are really the same. However, the logical test

```
while( cin >> x[i] )
```

works for a different reason. When cin (the value of cin >> x[i]) is tested, it must be converted from an istream object to a logical value. The istream class defines a special type-conversion rule that converts cin to zero or a positive integer depending on whether cin has been closed or not (Section 8.7).

The I/O operators >> and << can be further overloaded to perform I/O on class objects (Section 8.2), making their use even more general.

6.6.3 Reading and Writing

Several built-in member functions for I/O objects can be used to perform I/O on characters, whole lines, or a sequence of bytes. These are summarized in Table 6.5. Examples using put and get are shown in the table. As another example, consider the function read_lines (Section 4.5) that reads a number of lines into lines, an array of strings:

```
const int linelen = 256;
const int maxlines = 1024;
char* lines[ maxlines ];

int read_lines(istream& in)
{   int k, n = 0, m = linelen + 2;
    char *buf, *s;
```

TABLE 6.5   I/O MEMBER FUNCTIONS

FUNCTION	DESCRIPTION
obj.put(char c)	Outputs c; returns ref to obj.
obj.get(char& c)	Reads character into c; returns ref to obj.
int c = obj.get()	Returns next character or EOF.
obj.write(const char *s, int length)	Outputs string of given length; returns ref to obj.
obj.read(char *buf, int size)	Inputs size number of bytes to buf; returns ref to obj.
obj.getline(char *buf, int n, char delim = '\n')	Puts at most n-1 bytes in buf up to delim or end of file; adds final '\0'; returns ref to obj.
int obj.gcount()	Returns number of bytes read by last getline.

```
        buf = new char[ m ];
        while( in.getline(buf, m, '\n') )
        {   k = strlen(buf);        // line length
            if ( n >= maxlines )    // too many lines
                return(-1);
            else if ( k == m-1 )    // line too long
                return(-n);
            else if ( ( s = new char[k+1]) == NULL )
                return(-1);         // no free storage
            else
            {   strcpy(s, buf);     // copy buffer into s
                lines[n++] = s;     // put s on array lines
            }
        }
        return(n);                  // total number of lines
}
```

A character buffer buf, sufficiently large to detect line length exceeding linelen, is allocated from free storage. After an input line is read by getline(), its length is checked. A new buffer s, just large enough to accommodate the actual line read, is allocated and the line copied with strcpy. Now s is put in the array lines, and the while loop starts over again.

To test read_lines, use the following simple main program:

```
int main()
{    int j = read_lines(cin);
     for ( int i = 0; i < j; i++)
         cout << lines[i] << endl;
```

```
        return(0);
}
```

There are three auxiliary member functions for input:

1. peek() returns the next input character (or EOF) to be examined without consuming it. The character remains to be read later.
2. putback(char c) puts at most one character back into the input stream.
3. ignore(int len = 1, int del = EOF) discards up to len characters until del is reached.

6.6.4 Output Formatting

The C++ output stream defines a standard output format for its objects so that simple output can be performed easily. However, in some applications, the output must be programmed to appear in certain well-defined forms. Formatting is necessary, for example, when you want the entries in a table of numeric data to line up, the credits and charges on a bill to show as positive and negative amounts, or simply to render integers in octal or hexadecimal. How we achieve such effects through a formatting mechanism provided by output objects is our next topic of discussion, which uses the following formatting terminology:

- *Width:* This is the minimum number of character positions (*field*) for the next output item. The item is displayed in a field at least this wide. If necessary, *fill characters* (usually white space) are supplied to make up the width.
- *Justification:* Within a given field, the item is displayed *right* or *left* justified (flush with the right or left end of the field).
- *Base:* The radix base for displaying integers is decimal, octal, or hexadecimal.
- *Precision:* This specifies the number of significant digits displayed for a float or double.

Tables 6.6 and 6.7 show functions and flags provided by output objects to control output format. Default settings are also indicated. The field width is normally zero. When the width is set with the width() function, only the next output item is affected. After that, the width resets to zero again automatically. Other format settings affect all subsequent output. All format functions return the old setting in case it must be restored later.

With precision(), we can improve, for example, the calculator display by modifying the show_number() function of CalcFace (Section 5.5.1) to

```
void CalcFace::show_number(double number)
{    cout.precision(PREC);
```

TABLE 6.6   FORMAT FUNCTIONS

FORMAT REQUEST	MEANING
obj.width(int w)	Sets width to w; returns old width.
int w = obj.width()	Returns current width.
obj.precision(int n)	Sets precision to n; returns old value. Default precision is 6.
int n = obj.precision()	Returns current precision.
obj.fill(char c)	Sets fill character to c; returns old value.
char c = obj.fill()	Returns fill character (default SPACE).

```
        cout << "Calc:  " << number << "\n";
}
```

The function **setf()** sets and retrieves format flag settings, which are bit values that can be combined with logical or. For example, the code

```
cout.setf(ios::uppercase | ios::showpos ); // sets two flags
cout.setf(ios::hex, ios::basefield);       // resets basefield, then sets hex flag
cout << 54321 << endl;
cout << sqrt(2) << endl;
```

gives the following output:

TABLE 6.7   FORMAT FLAGS

FORMAT REQUEST	MEANING
long flag = obj.flags()	Returns current flag.
long flag = obj.flags(nf)	Sets flag to nf, returns old flag
obj.setf(ios::oct, ios::basefield)	Sets base to octal.
obj.setf(ios::hex, ios::basefield)	Sets base to hexadecimal.
obj.setf(ios::dec, ios::basefield)	Sets base to decimal (default).
obj.setf(ios::right, ios::adjustfield)	Selects right justification (default).
obj.setf(ios::left, ios::adjustfield)	Selects left justification.
obj.setf(ios::scientific, ios::floatfield)	Uses scientific notation $[-]m.ddd\mathrm{e}\pm xx$.
obj.setf(ios::fixed, ios::floatfield)	Prevents decimal-point motion (default).
obj.setf(ios::showpos)	Shows both leading + and −.
obj.unsetf(ios::showpos)	Shows leading − only (default).
obj.setf(ios::uppercase)	Uses upper case in numbers.
obj.unsetf(ios::uppercase)	Uses lower case in numbers (default).

```
D431                    // hex with uppercase D
+1.41421                // precision 6, leading +
```

For another example of output formatting, consider displaying a monthly calendar. Since we have already defined a class Month (Section 4.11), we simply add a display member function to Month:

```
#include <iostream.h>

void Month::display()
{    MONTH mon = month;
     cout << "SUN MON TUE WED THU FRI SAT\n";
     while ( *mon )
     {    WEEK wk = *mon++;
          for ( DAY d = Sun ; d <= Sat ; d=DAY(d+1))
          {    if ( wk[d] )
               {    cout.width(3);               // (1)
                    cout << wk[d] << ´ ´;        // (2)
               }
               else cout << "    ";
          }
          cout << endl;
     }
}
```

In Month::display, the exact placements of the calendar dates are controlled with cout.width(3) (line 1) as described. To line up the dates appropriately, we use a width of four characters for each column of the calendar (line 2). Here is a typical display:

```
SUN MON TUE WED THU FRI SAT
              1   2   3   4   5
  6   7   8   9  10  11  12
 13  14  15  16  17  18  19
 20  21  22  23  24  25  26
 27  28  29  30  31
```

6.6.5 File Updating

When the same file is opened for both reading and writing under the mode

```
ios::in | ios::out
```

the file is being updated *in place*; that is, you are modifying the contents of the file. In performing both reading and writing under the update mode, take care when switching from reading to writing and vice versa. The C++ I/O stream library uses a *file-position* indicator (similar to a cursor in a text editor) to keep track of the location for the next I/O byte/character in a file. The file position is moved by each I/O operation. Before switching either way, a file-positioning operation (seekp, for example) may be needed. These remarks will become clear as the update modes are explained.

The ios::in | ios::out mode is most efficient for making one-for-one character substitutions in a file. Under this mode, file contents stay the same if not explicitly modified. Modification is done by positioning and writing the revised characters over the existing characters. A lowercase command based on file updating can be implemented using the following outline:

1. Open the given file with the ios::in | ios::out mode.
2. Read characters until an uppercase letter is encountered.
3. Overwrite the uppercase letter with the lowercase letter.
4. Repeat steps 2 and 3 until end of file is reached.

Here is the implementation:

```
#include <iostream.h>
#include <fstream.h>
#include <ctype.h>
#include <stdlib.h>

int main(int argc, char *argv[])
{    char c;
     if ( argc != 2 )
         cerr << argv[0] << " takes one argument only\n";
     fstream fio(argv[1], ios::in | ios::out);
     if ( ! fio )
     {    cerr << argv[0] << ´:´ << " Cannot open"
                          << argv[1] << " for updating\n",
          exit(1);
     }
     while ((c = fio.get()) != EOF)
         if ( isupper(c) )
         {    fio.seekp(-1, ios::cur);   // position for writing c
              fio.put(tolower(c));
         }
     fio.close();
}
```

After an uppercase character is detected, the file position is on the next character to read. Thus, the position indicator should be moved to the previous character in order to overwrite it. This is done here by

```
fio.seekp(-1, ios::cur);       // back up one byte
```

Then, the lowercase character is output. The rest of the file is processed in the same way.

The prototypes of the file-position-setting member functions are

```
istream& seekg(long offset, ios::seek_dir ori = ios::beg);
ostream& seekp(long offset, ios::seek_dir ori = ios::beg);
```

These two functions are essentially the same except that one belongs to the istream class and the other to the ostream class. For the iostream class, both are available. Note that these two functions set the same unique file I/O position.

After seekg/seekp, a subsequent I/O operation will access data beginning at the new position. The position is set to offset bytes from the indicated origin ori, which is one of the constants

ios::beg   (usually 0: the beginning of the file)
ios::cur   (usually 1: the current position)
ios::end   (usually 2: the end of the file)

Any time during I/O, the current file position can be determined by the member function tellg()/tellp(), which returns an offset from the beginning of the file.

When output is under the ios:app (append at end) mode, output will always be appended at the file's end and will not be affected by repositioning. However, the read position works normally; that is, it is moved by each I/O operation as well as by repositioning.

6.6.6   Binary Input and Output

It is usual to think of I/O as dealing with a sequence of characters. But performing *binary* I/O, where bytes rather than characters are being treated, is also possible. With binary I/O, a block of consecutive memory locations (an entire array or object for example) can be written out, byte for byte, into a file for later retrieval. If a binary file actually contains characters, it is no different from a text file. Otherwise, a binary file contains arbitrary bytes and usually cannot be examined or edited with a text editor. However, it is the most efficient way of reading and writing large amounts of data.

The overloaded member functions for binary I/O are

```
istream& read (const unsigned char *buf, int len);
ostream& write(const unsigned char *ptr, int len);
```

where buf (ptr) points to the data area in memory to receive (provide) len bytes.

To illustrate binary I/O, consider writing an array of Fraction objects to a file and later reading the data back in again. The sequence

```
Fraction uv[] = {Fraction(2,5), Fraction(3,6)};
ofstream out("Fraction.data", ios::out);
```

```
out.write((unsigned char*)(uv), sizeof(uv));
out.close();
```

puts two Fraction objects in the file Fraction.data. Clearly, the output of bytes is very simple and direct. The binary file can later be read back into a program by the code

```
Fraction ab[2];
ifstream in("Fraction.data", ios::in);
in.read((unsigned char*) ab, 2*sizeof(Fraction));
```

The objects read in should work normally. For example, they can be displayed to verify the data:

```
ab[0].display();
cout << "\n";
ab[1].display();
```

Although efficient, binary I/O has its limitations. A binary file is very system-dependent and usually cannot be moved to a different computer and be useful. Even on the same computer, a binary file can be used only by a program written in the same language that knows its data type or class definition. Furthermore, objects containing pointers cannot use binary I/O because the pointers will be wrong when they are read back in again.

6.6.7 Error Conditions

In most cases, a call to an I/O member function returns a reference to its stream object that can be used in a logical test to determine the success or failure of the operation. In addition, an iostream object maintains a set of condition flags recording the ongoing state of the object. Monitoring and setting these flags is done through the four predicate member functions summarized in Table 6.8.

TABLE 6.8   I/O CONDITIONS

FUNCTION	DESCRIPTION
obj.eof()	Returns true if obj has reached end of file.
obj.bad()	Returns true if an invalid operation has been requested.
obj.fail()	Returns true if an operation has failed or bad() is true (ios::badbit set).
obj.good()	Returns true if none of the above is true.
obj.rdstate()	Returns the internal error-state bit vector.
obj.clear(*bv*)	Sets error vector to *bv* or 0 if no argument.

6.7 \ SUMMARY

C++ is more than just a collection of language constructs. It also comes with standard libraries that contain well-written and tested facilities for various useful purposes. Familiarity with the libraries allows you to apply them whenever there is a need.

To use a library facility, remember to include the required header files that provide the necessary declarations. Through the header file string.h, a rich set of standard string-manipulation functions is provided. The header file ctype.h gives access to a collection of character-set-independent operations on characters. Furthermore, through the header file math.h, C++ also has a set of mathematical functions for numeric computation. Other libraries not covered here are listed in several appendices.

Unlike the above-mentioned facilities, the I/O stream is an object-oriented library. The I/O stream classes, their member functions, and the I/O operators >> and << are powerful and efficient tools for handling object-oriented I/O.

Output formatting is done with I/O stream formatting functions and flags. File I/O objects can be established in read (ios::in), write (ios::out), append (ios::append), or a logical combination of these modes. Member functions **get**, **put**, **write**, **read**, **getline**, **peek**, **putback**, and **ignore** are provided for I/O.

Random access I/O is also supported. The current read/write position in a file object can be set (examined) by **seekg/seekp** (**tellg/tellp**). The state of an I/O object is kept in flags accessed by member functions **eof**, **bad**, **fail**, and **good**.

\ EXERCISES

1. Examine the following program. Does it work? If not, can you fix it? If so, can you explain why?

```
#include <iostream.h>
#include <string.h>

main()
{    char foo[]="abcd";
     char bar[]="EFGHABCD";
     strcat(foo,bar);
     cout << foo << '\n';
}
```

2. Write your own implementation of the string functions strspn and strcspn (Section 6.1). Consider the strtok implementation in Section 6.1. Rewrite it using strspn and/or strcspn.

3. Apply the class Month in a program that formats and prints a calendar for a whole year.

4. Consider the pocket calculator program in Section 5.5.1. Modify the calculator display routine to show 16 significant digits.

5. Exercise Cal-1: Take the simple calculator example (Section 5.5.1) and extend it. (a) Add the square root function corresponding to the s(S) key. (b) Add the constant function with the k for "constant in" and K for "constant out." (c) Add one extra memory register and the add-to-memory (M), subtract-from-memory (m), and memory-recall (R) functions. (*Note:* The purpose is to simulate these facilities of a simple pocket calculator.)

6. Exercise Cal-2: Add to calc the ability to save a few intermediate results, in single-letter buffers, and to reuse them in subsequent computations.

7. How would you turn the calc program into one that uses octal numbers?

8. Consider the type double for floating-point computations. How many significant digits (precision) does it support on your computer? On a 32-bit computer?

9. Because the CalcEng class uses double, it can support more precision than the 6 used in the CalcFace class. Modify CalcFace so that an object is initialized with a precision up to the maximum allowed under double. This precision setting should control the number of digits allowed for input and display.

10. Using stream I/O, write a program that reads a text file and appends at the end of the file the length of each word in the file. (*Hint:* ios::in | ios::append.)

11. Add to calc the ability to save itself on disk so that later, when running calc, a user can retrieve the saved state and resume calculations. (*Hint:* Saving the compute engine part should be enough.)

12. Consider the lowercase implementation in Section 6.6.5. Instead of using seekp, can you use the putback feature to achieve the same effect?

13. Read in a file containing x, y, z coordinates on each line. The coordinates are in floating-point with five significant digits and separated by white space. Write

a program to read this file and to produce a well-formatted output file (line up the decimal points in each column) showing y, x, z on each line.

14. Experiment with the error status functions of I/O objects. What happens if you use >> to read some random string into an int variable? What happens if you have too long a string of digits?

INHERITANCE AND CLASS DERIVATION

One of the most outstanding OOP features is *inheritance*, a mechanism that allows the *derivation* of new objects from existing ones. C++ supports inheritance with *class derivation*, defining new classes based on existing ones without modifying them. Such a new class, called a *derived class*, *inherits* the members of one or more existing *base classes* and adds other members of its own. Inheriting from derived classes is also possible, giving rise to inheritance *hierarchies*.

The inheritance mechanism brings several major advantages to progamming:

- *Reuse of existing code:* Avoid recoding what is already available. Simply use inheritance to import working and tested codes as a foundation.
- *Adaption of programs to work in similar but different situations:* Avoid writing largely similar programs all over again because the application, computer system, data format, or mode of operation is slightly different. Simply use inheritance to modify existing codes to suit.
- *Extraction of commonalities from different classes:* Avoid duplicating identical or similar codes/structures in different classes. Simply extract the common parts to form another class and allow it to be inherited by the other classes.
- *Organization of objects into hierarchies:* Form groups of objects that have an "is a kind of" relationship. For example, a savings account is a kind of bank account; a checking account is a kind of account; a sedan is a kind of automobile; a sports sedan is a kind of sedan; a manager is a kind of employee; and a square matrix is a kind of matrix. Such

groupings give a program better organization and, more importantly, allow objects in the same hierarchy to be used as *compatible* types as opposed to completely unrelated types.

C++ supports both single and multiple inheritance. In *single inheritance*, a class is derived from a *single* base class. For example, a class JointAccount can be derived from the class Account, or a Manager from Employee. In *multiple inheritance*, a class is derived from *several* base classes. Skillful use of inheritance through class derivation contributes significantly to a well-designed OO program.

Both conceptual understanding and experience are important to your achieving proficiency in this critical area of OOP. Therefore, this chapter describes class derivation clearly and comprehensively. Your understanding will be enhanced by a vivid mental model of the derived class and objects as well as by good examples. Moreover, principles to guide your application of class derivation are also clearly stated. The important topic of information hiding and member access control under inheritance, often confusing to beginning programmers, is made simple and easy to grasp.

The first topic of discussion is the class derivation mechanism.

7.1 \ CLASS DERIVATION

The class Account, described earlier (Section 2.1), is a simple class. Suppose we now wish to handle joint accounts. Each joint account has two owners instead of just one. Certainly, this is a small change from Account, and we can write a class JointAccount simply by copying the source code of Account and adding a joint owner and some related functions. But there is a better approach — deriving JointAccount from Account without changing it or duplicating the code.

The existing class Account written as a suitable base class for derivation is shown here:

```
///////    File Account.h    ///////

class Account                        // class name
{ public:
    Account() { }                    // default constructor
    Account(unsigned n, double b,    // constructor
            char* ss);
    void deposit(double amt);        // deposit amt into this account
    int withdraw(double amt);        // withdraw amt from this account
    double balance();                // balance inquiry

    /* other public members */
  protected:                         // protected members
```

```
    enum {SS_LEN = 12};
    unsigned  acct_no;              // account number
    char      ss[SS_LEN];           // owner ss no.
  private:
    double    acct_bal;             // current balance
};
```

The member ss records the social security number of the account owner. Members declared protected are just like private members except that they allow certain types of access from derived classes. Designating certain members protected in anticipation of future derivation is an important OOP design consideration. (More will be said about this later.)

Joint Account

Now we can build the new class JointAccount on top of Account by class derivation:

```
///////   File JointAccount.h   ///////
#include "Account.h"

class JointAccount : public Account     // derive from Account (1)
{ public:
    JointAccount() { }                  // default constructor
    JointAccount(unsigned n, double b,  // constructor
        char* owner, char* jowner);
    /* other public members */
  protected:
    char jss[SS_LEN];                   // joint owner ss no.  (2)
};
```

The class header

```
class JointAccount : public Account
```

specifies JointAccount as a derived class of the base class Account.

The general derived-class definition is

```
class Name : base-class list
{
    derived-class body
};
```

A list of comma-separated names of base classes, the base-class list, is given after a colon (:) following the name of the derived class. Each base-class name can be further qualified by one of the keywords public, protected, or private, depending on the type of derivation desired. The keyword private may be omitted. (More will be said about the types of derivation presently.)

Whatever the type of derivation, a derived class *inherits* all* members of its base classes and adds new members of its own. Through inheritance (line 1), members of Account become *inherited members* of JointAccount. The derived class also adds a member jss (line 2) to record the social security number of the joint owner. The owner is recorded in the member ss inherited from the base class. Programming a joint account from scratch is avoided, and codes from Account are reused.

A JointAccount object is initialized by the constructor:

```
///////    File JointAccount.C    ///////
#include <string.h>
#include "JointAccount.h"

JointAccount::JointAccount
(unsigned n, double b, char* owner, char* jowner)
: Account(n, b, owner)              // call base constructor  (3)
{   strncpy(jss, jowner, SS_LEN); } // record joint owner
```

The inherited part of the object, or *base object*, is initialized by calling the base-class constructor (line 3) with appropriate arguments. Base-object initialization is specified in the init-list (line 3).

Now we can establish and use a joint account object. For example,

```
JointAccount bill_mary(123456, 2500,
            "045-22-5555",    // ss of Bill
            "045-33-7777");   // ss of Mary
bill_mary.deposit(450.75);
cout << bill_mary.balance() << endl;
```

With class derivation, much recoding is avoided and joint accounts are established with very little effort. Furthermore, the original Account class stays unchanged, ready to derive other types of accounts. And, perhaps more importantly, any further refinement of Account is automatically reflected in JointAccount. This aspect of OOP is powerful, and its full implications will become clear only after we cover more related topics.

Although the subject of inheritance and class derivation is fascinating, it tends to be confusing because it is difficult to conceptualize. The presentation in Section 7.2 should remedy this situation.

---

*With the exception of constructors, destructors, and operator=.

7.2 \ DERIVED CLASSES AND OBJECTS

7.2.1   Class Scope Nesting

A derived class is a composite class: It has members from the base (*inherited members*) and additional members of its own (*appendant members*). The derived-class scope is *nested* inside the base-class scope, like an inner code block nesting within an outer block. Figure 7.1 shows the scope nesting for JointAccount and Account. The call bill_mary.balance() refers to JointAccount::balance, and it is not defined in the scope JointAccount:: but in the enclosing scope Account::. This is how this particular call gets to the inherited member balance().

In general, consider any derived class *Dd* and the identifier *Dd*::*xyz*. If *xyz* is an appendant member of *Dd*, then it is what *Dd*::*xyz* refers to. Otherwise, the name *xyz* is searched for in the base class of *Dd*. If not found, the search continues up the derivation chain until file scope is reached. The search ends as soon as an identifier is found. Then, its accessibility is determined. The search will not continue even if access is denied.

Consider, for example, the reference bill_mary.acct_bal. It is not found in the scope JointAccount::, so the search continues in the enclosing scope Account::, where the private member acct_bal is found. Thus, JointAccount::acct_bal refers to the inherited member acct_bal. The private status of acct_bal will deny such an access, and the code is incorrect. This happens even if there is a file scope identifier acct_bal that can be accessed if reached.

The scope relation between the derived and the base class is basic to a good understanding of class derivation. Also important are the composition, initialization, and deinitialization of derived objects.

FIGURE 7.1   CLASS SCOPE NESTING

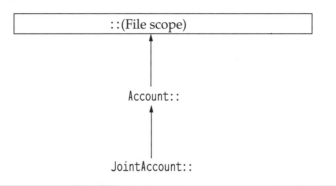

7.2.2　Derived-Object Composition

A *derived object*, such as bill_mary, is an instance of a derived class. For simplicity, consider single inheritance, where there is only one base class. A derived object, then, consists of two parts (Figure 7.2):

1. A *base object* composed of the data and function members as specified by the base class and properly initialized by a base-class constructor. In other words, the base-object part is built using the base class as a blueprint.
2. An *appendant part* consisting of additional data and function members defined in the derived class. The appendant part envelops the base object to form the derived object. Members in the appendant part are referred to as *appendant members*.

All inherited and appendant members are considered members of the derived object. A member function in the appendant part can refer to both types of members directly, using just the member name without mentioning the host object explicitly.

If the base object is itself a derived object, then it contains its immediate base object in exactly the same way. A derived class inherits all members, appendant and inherited, of its base class.

FIGURE 7.2　　DERIVED OBJECT COMPOSITION

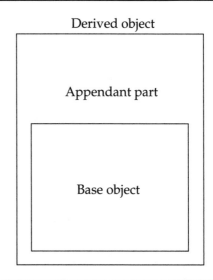

7.2.3   Derived-Object Construction and Destruction

As stated before, neither constructors nor destructors are inherited by derived classes. The initialization (deinitialization) of a derived object is done with a sequence of base and derived constructor (destructor) calls. The different constructors (destructors) collaborate to complete the task.

When a derived object is instantiated, enough memory space is allocated to accommodate all base objects and the appendant part. Then, a derived-class constructor initializes the object in two stages. First, the base-class constructors are invoked to initialize the base objects. For single inheritance, the immediate base constructor is called. For multiple inheritance, the base-class constructors are called in declaration order, the order in which they appear in the base-class list. After all base objects are initialized, the rest of the derived-class constructor is executed to initialize the appendant part.

A derived-class constructor specifies an appropriate base-class constructor call in its init-list. We have already seen how the JointAccount example used this feature:

```
JointAccount::JointAccount           // derived-class constructor
(unsigned n, double b, char* owner, char* jowner)
: Account(n, b, owner)               // init-list
{   strncpy(jss, jowner, SS_LEN); }  // record joint owner
```

If a base constructor call is not specified in the init-list, then the base-class default constructor is called. The init-list may also initialize appendant members. However, it cannot specify the initialization of individual inherited members. Their initializations are done by the base-class constructors. If a base object is also derived, this procedure is applied recursively.

It is possible to initialize a base object by an existing object. For example, we can add a constructor to JointAccount:

```
JointAccount::JointAccount
(Account acnt, char* jowner)
: Account(acnt)                 // init base object by object
{   strncpy(jss, jowner, SS_LEN); }
```

This is useful when turning an existing account (an instance of Account) into a joint account. An initialization object such as acnt can be any object that is converted to the correct type implicitly or explicitly, including user-defined conversions (Section 8.7).

When a derived object is destroyed, base- and component-object destructors are called automatically for deinitialization. The destructors are called in the reverse order of constructor calls.

7.3 \ PUBLIC DERIVATION

Free Checking Account

As another example of inheritance, let's now consider a free checking account that charges a monthly service fee only if the account balance drops below a preset minimum. A class FreeChecking can also be derived from the existing class Account:

```
///////    File FreeChecking.h    ///////
#include "Account.h"

class FreeChecking : public Account     // derive from Account
{ public:
    FreeChecking() { }                  // default constructor
    FreeChecking(unsigned n, double b,  // constructor
        char* owner);
    void fee();                         // charge monthly fee
    int withdraw(double amt);           // withdraw amt
    static void set_minbal(float m) { min_bal = m; }
    static void set_fee(float f) { service_fee = f; }
  private:
    static float min_bal;
    static float service_fee;
    int free;
};
```

Static functions (set_minbal, set_fee) and data members (min_bal, service_fee) are used to record and modify common quantities—minimum balance and service fee. The static variables min_bal and service_fee allow the minimum balance requirement and/or the monthly service charge to be modified without recompiling the program. A private flag free keeps the fee-free status of the account. The flag is maintained by the appendant member function withdraw() and used by fee(), the member function that charges a monthly fee, if any, to the account.

The constructor specifies how the base object and the appendant part are initialized:

```
///////    File FreeChecking.C    ///////
#include "FreeChecking.h"

float FreeChecking::min_bal = 500.0;    // minimum balance
float FreeChecking::service_fee = 18.0; // service fee
```

```
FreeChecking::FreeChecking              // constructor
(unsigned n, double b, char* owner)
:    Account(n, b, owner),
     free(b >= min_bal)                 // init-list
{ }
```

Again, the constructor init-list contains a call to a base-class constructor. Also, the flag free is properly set. A bank normally requires an initial deposit more than the required minimum balance to open a new account. Nevertheless, the constructor checks the initial balance and sets the flag free.

A new withdraw function monitors the account balance and sets the flag free when necessary:

```
int FreeChecking::withdraw(double amt)
{    int ok = Account::withdraw(amt);         // (1)
     if ( ok != -1 && balance() < min_bal )  // (2)
          free = 0;
     return(ok);
}
```

The function calls the base withdraw function (line 1) and, after the withdrawal is made, checks the balance (line 2) and sets free accordingly. An error condition (−1) is returned if withdraw() fails. Two important points are worth noting:

1. The appendant member withdraw() has exactly the same prototype as its counterpart in the base Account. This is good because the same *message* (public function invocation) works for withdrawing from a simple basic account or a free checking account. Any other way would be unreasonable. Imagine asking bank customers to use different messages to withdraw funds from various types of accounts!

2. The free checking withdraw() completes its duty by asking the base withdraw() to perform basic processing and by supplying additional processing itself. Thus, processing common to all types of accounts should be implemented in the base Account; derived accounts will add only their specialized processing.

At the end of every month, the function fee() is called to charge a service fee to the account if required:

```
void FreeChecking::fee()
{  if ( ! free )
       if ( withdraw(service_fee) == -1 )
           cerr << "fee: Insufficient balance for account "
               << acct_no << endl;
     free = (balance() >= min_bal);
}
```

The FreeChecking class is quite simplified as it stands. Test it now with the following code:

```
///////    tstFrCkg.C    ///////
// test FreeChecking
#include <iostream.h>
#include "FreeChecking.h"

int main()
{  FreeChecking susan(555234, 750.0, "034-55-6789");
   susan.deposit(25.50);     // inherited member (a)
   susan.withdraw(250);      // appendant member (b)
   susan.fee();              // appendant member (c)
   cout << "month 1: " << susan.balance() << endl;

   susan.withdraw(30);       // expensive move
   susan.deposit(100);       // too late
   susan.fee();              // charge
   cout << "month 2: " << susan.balance() << endl;
   return(0);
}
```

The account susan starts with a balance of 750.00. At the end of the first month, the account balance should be 525.25 because there is no service charge. But an unfortunate withdrawal of 30 results in a service fee of 18.00 for the following month. The deposit of 100 is too late to avoid the service charge, and the balance becomes 577.50. The program produces the expected output:

```
month 1: 525.5
month 2: 577.5
```

The class FreeChecking, somewhat more complicated than JointAccount, is a more realistic example of class derivation. FreeChecking defines an appendant member function withdraw(), which shields the base-class function with the same name from view, as a result of class scope nesting. Thus, the call on line b invokes the appendant withdraw(), while the code on line a accesses the inherited deposit().

To summarize, a derived class is usually a slight generalization, specialization, or modification of the base class. Often, this means you must add some preprocessing and/or postprocessing to existing functions in the base class. The derived withdraw() function is a typical example of adding some postprocessing after the base withdraw(). Thus, the design technique demonstrated here is that of collecting basic operations in the base class and allowing specialized preprocessing and postprocessing to be added by derived classes.

7.4 \ ACCESS CONTROL UNDER CLASS DERIVATION

The discussion of class derivation introduced us to the protected member category of access control. In addition, there are the three base-class designations: public, protected, and private. C++ has clear and specific rules governing what parts of the program, under what conditions, have access to appendant members (in the derived class) and to inherited members (in the base class). Access to the appendant members of a derived class is governed by normal member access rules. Access to inherited members, those imported from the base class, however, is a different matter altogether.

Access to Inherited Members

1. Access to inherited members by appendant members and friends of the derived class is independent of the base-class designation:

   Access is allowed to all nonprivate (public *and* protected) *inherited members. Access is not allowed to private members in the base class.* For example, an appendant member function of JointAccount has no access to acct_bal in the base object.

2. Access to inherited members from other functions (outside the derived class) depends on the base-class designation:

   public *base:* All inherited public members are accessible as public members of the derived class; all inherited protected members are accessible as protected members of the derived class.

   protected *base:* All inherited nonprivate members are accessible as protected members of the derived class. Thus, there is no access to these members except by appendant functions in a further derivation.

   private *base:* There is no outside access to any inherited members.

These access rules (accessibility) together with class scope nesting (visibility) give rise to some important implications. Private members in a base class are never accessible except to members in the same base class. In a public derivation hierarchy, through each subsequent derived class, the combined set of public interfaces in its base classes is accessible. Furthermore, in a nonprivate derivation hierarchy, each subsequent derived class always has access to the combined set of public and protected members in its base classes. Table 7.1 summarizes access control under derivation.

To achieve finer control, accessibility and visibility of inherited members can be further modified by overriding and exempting individual inherited members:

TABLE 7.1   ACCESS CONTROL UNDER DERIVATION

	INHERITED MEMBER		
ACCESS FROM	public	protected	private
Derived class and its friends	Yes	Yes	No
Subsequent derived class	If public/protected base	If public/protected base	No
Other outside functions	If public base	No	No

- *Overriding:* By defining an appendant member of the same name, an inherited member, otherwise visible, is shielded from view. For example, FreeChecking::withdraw() overrides Account::withdraw(). Thus, the call susan.withdraw(30) invokes the appendant member. Outside access to the base member is possible with the class scope operator. So, susan.Account::withdraw(3) is legal (ill-advised of course). Overriding is a result of identifier scoping under derivation (Section 7.2.1).

- *Exempting:* A nonpublic derivation makes *all* inherited members, accessible under public derivation, inaccessible. There is a way, however, to specifically exempt certain inherited members from this access limitation. Consider a public (protected) member *xyz* of the base class *BaseX* made invisible under nonpublic derivation. The accessibility of *xyz* can be restored by including the line

  BaseX::*xyz* ;

  in the public (protected) section of the derived-class definition. This exemption notation can be used only to restore accessibility to that allowed under public derivation. It cannot be used to promote or demote accessibility beyond that. Thus, a protected member does not become public, or vice versa, through exemption. These remarks will become clear after we see examples of nonpublic derivation.

7.5 \ DERIVATION PRINCIPLES

A question often asked is, When do you use public, protected, or private derivation? The answer is not so simple because it depends on the situation. But here are a few rules of thumb:

1. Use public derivation when a derived object is a kind of base object. For example, a joint account is a kind of account, and a free checking account is another kind of account. The *is-a relationship* usually means that all or most of the public interface of the base object (an Account)

also makes sense for the derived object (a JointAccount). The is-a relationship often also means that derived and base objects may be used together in applications as related/compatible data types. For instance, a list of accounts in a banking system may include many different types of accounts.

A class Manager derived from the base Employee is another example of the is-a relationship. A manager is a kind of employee, so public derivation is appropriate.

Thus, a public base class and a derived class have a type-subtype relationship. This is supported in C++ by implicit type-conversion rules that allow automatic conversion of a derived-type object, reference, or pointer to a corresponding quantity of a base type (Section 7.8).

2. Use private derivation when a derived object is not considered a kind of base object and the base class simply supplies code to make the derived class easier to write. In other words, the appendant functions can use facilities provided by the base class. In this situation, the public interface of the base object makes little sense for the derived object and should be made inaccessible. For instance, a stack or a queue class can be derived from a linked-list class. But neither a stack nor a queue is considered a kind of linked list. Thus, private derivation is more suitable, as we will see in Section 7.6.

In considering a derivation of class Dd from a base class Bb, make sure it is not because a Dd object contains a Bb object as a component. Consider the pocket calculator example. A calculator has two components: a compute engine and a user interface. Thus, the Calculator class has two components: a CalcEng object and a CalcFace object. Hence, the correct design for such a *has-a* or *uses-a relationship* is to employ component objects rather than class derivation.

On the other hand, a stack does not have a list component. It will be internally implemented as a list because it is convenient and the list class has already been defined. When Bb is a private base of Dd, often the relationship is expressed as Dd *"is internally implemented as a"* Bb.

Therefore, a private base class and a derived class have no type-subtype relationship. In general, C++ does not automatically convert a derived object, reference, or pointer to a corresponding private base type (Section 7.8).

3. Use protected derivation when a private derivation is suitable but access from further derived classes to the base class is desirable.

We have already seen examples of public derivation. Now let's focus on a concrete example of private derivation.

7.6 \ PRIVATE DERIVATION

A stack is a common and useful data structure in programming. It is a last-in-first-out (LIFO) buffer like a stack of trays in a cafeteria (Figure 7.3). A *push* operation puts an item on top of the stack, while a *pop* removes the top item from the stack. Basically, these are the only allowable operations on a stack.

Suppose we wish to implement a class for the stack. An array can store the items being pushed and popped. However, an array is limited because it is fixed in dimension. Let's consider using a linked list to store the items. Because we already have a generic list class ArbList (Section 5.12), this approach should be easier. Besides, the list is dynamic and its dimension is not fixed. Furthermore, it does not cost anything to make the stack class generic:

```
///////    File ArbStack.h    ///////
//    generic stack derived from generic list
#include <iostream.h>
#include "ArbList.h"

class ArbStack : private ArbList    // keyword private is optional
{  public:
     ArbStack() { }               // default constructor    (1)
     ArbStack(Arbent z);          // constructor
     int push(Arbent z);
     Arbent pop();
     ArbList::is_empty;           // makes is_empty visible (2)
};
```

As noted, an unqualified base class is private. Also, if a derived constructor does not specify an explicit call to a base constructor, the default base constructor is called automatically. Thus, the code on line 1 is the same as

```
ArbStack() : ArbList() { }        // long version
```

The inherited public member is_empty() is made accessible (line 2) so that it can be used to test whether a stack is empty. The inherited put_on() is used in two inline member functions:

```
inline ArbStack::ArbStack(Arbent z)
     {    put_on(z);    }

inline int ArbStack::push(Arbent z)
     {    return put_on(z);    }

///////    End of file ArbStack.h    ///////
```

FIGURE 7.3   A STACK

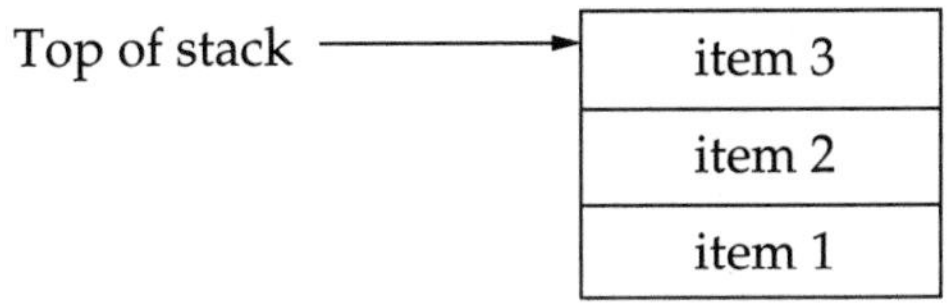

The only function remaining is pop(), which is defined in the implementation file:

```
///////    ArbStack.C    ///////
#include "ArbStack.h"

Arbent ArbStack::pop()
{  if ( is_empty() ) return(NULL);  // pop failed
   Arbent tmp = content(first());   // popped item
   shorten(1);                      // stack popped
   return(tmp);
}
```

Three ArbList functions are used in pop(): first(), shorten(), and content(). Reusing code in the base class ArbList makes ArbStack very simple indeed.

Test ArbStack using code similar to the following:

```
///////    File: tstArStk.C    ///////
// test ArbStack
#include <iostream.h>
#include "ArbStack.h"
// stack of integers via
//      generic ArbStack class

static int a[] = {0,10,20,30,40,50};

int main()
{    ArbStack stack( a + 1);         // 10 on top
     stack.push( a + 3 );            // 30 on top
     stack.push( a + 5 );            // 50 on top
     while ( ! stack.is_empty() )    // pop until empty
         cout << * (int *)stack.pop() << " ";
     cout << endl;
     return(0);
}
```

Note how pop() returns a void * pointer that must be cast before being dereferenced. The program produces the following output:

```
50 30 10
```

A queue can be derived using techniques similar to those used for ArbList.

7.7 SPECIALIZATION OF GENERIC CLASSES

Generic classes such as ArbList and ArbStack are general but awkward to use directly. It would be better, for example, to push and pop an Employee on a stack and not to constantly fuss with void * pointers, type-casting, and dereferencing.

With class derivation, we can easily *specialize* ArbStack to a type-specific stack — say, EmpStack. We can then use EmpStack to directly push and pop Employee items:

```
///////    File EmpStack.h    ///////
// employee stack derived from arbitrary stack

#include "ArbStack.h"
#include "Employee.h"

class EmpStack : private ArbStack
{ public:
      EmpStack() { }            // default constructor
      EmpStack(Employee& x)     // constructor
      : ArbStack(&x) { }
      int push(Employee& x);    // push Employee
      Employee& pop();          // pop Employee
      ArbStack::is_empty;       // make is_empty() visible
};
```

Note how reference parameters are used to avoid copying objects. The fact that EmpStack is implemented as an ArbStack is hidden via private derivation. Therefore, the public interface of the base does not surface.

The appendant members push() and pop() are so simple that they are inline:

```
inline int EmpStack::push(Employee& x)
      { return ArbStack::push( (Arbent) &x); }

inline Employee& EmpStack::pop()
      { return *(Employee *)ArbStack::pop(); }
```

Because there is no automatic type-casting between Employee* and Arbent (void*), we must use explicit type-casting. With the EmpStack class defined, pushing and popping employees on a stack is much more intuitive and less error-prone.

The class specialization technique shown here is completely general and can be applied whenever a generic class must be made type-specific.

The derivation chain ArbList, ArbStack, and EmpStack demonstrates a simple inheritance hierarchy. Having layers of derivation and function calls is the price you pay for better software organization, reliability, and reusability. Declaring functions inline will help, and a good compiler will significantly reduce the overhead involved.

7.8 \ TYPE RELATIONS UNDER INHERITANCE

Inheritance and class derivation offer a powerful way to organize programs and group related objects. Indeed, a derivation hierarchy creates a set of related types that are compatible in use. The different types of accounts illustrate this point very well. In general, when type *DerivedX* is a type *BaseX*, it is logical to be able to use a *DerivedX* object in place of a *BaseX* object. The reasoning is similar to using a short or an unsigned where an int is expected. In this situation, the type *DerivedX* becomes a *subtype* of *BaseX*.

Actually, such compatible uses have already been applied without being explained explicitly. In Section 2.6, the function

```
void doio(istream& in, ostream& out);
```

is called either with standard I/O objects cin and cout or with file I/O objects:

```
doio(cin, cout);
doio(infile, ofile);
```

The reference parameter out can take on cout or ofile. This works because cout and ofile are objects derived from the same base (Section 7.13); the same goes for cin and infile. Type compatibility under inheritance provides this convenience and flexibility.

C++ supports type compatibility through type conversions. In addition to the conversions already discussed in Section 3.12, C++ performs implicitly a set of reasonable type conversions for objects related by inheritance. Other conversions among such related objects require explicit casting and/or user-defined conversion codes (Section 8.7). The kinds of implicit conversions performed are described next.

Inheritance-Induced Implicit Conversions

In argument passing, initialization, and assignment, implicit type conversions for inheritance-related objects are performed in the following cases:

1. Converting a derived object, reference, or pointer to a corresponding *public base type:* This implicit conversion supports the is-a relationship. It is the reason cout and ofile can be passed to the doio() parameter out.

   It is safe to convert a derived object to a base object because there is always an instance of the base class in the derived object and the public interface of the base object is accessible.

   This implicit conversion is important for OOP because it allows the same function parameter to receive different objects in an inheritance hierarchy. For example, a function Account::transfer() should be able to take any account object in a hierarchy rooted at Account.

2. Converting a *public base opm* (offset pointer to member, Section 8.10.2) to a derived opm: Again, because the base member is present within a derived object, the implicit opm conversion is safe.

3. Inside the appendant part of a derived class, conversions listed in items 1 and 2 are performed implicitly even if the base class is nonpublic.

In these cases, a base class can be accessed directly or indirectly through layers of class derivations.

Keep in mind that an object pointer is implicitly converted to void* when necessary (independent of class derivation). A void* pointer can be converted to an object pointer only through explicit casting.

Inheritance-Related Explicit Conversions

Conversion of a base object or reference to a derived type is not possible without user-defined conversion codes. Conversion of a base pointer to a derived pointer requires explicit casting. For example,

```
Account* bp;                              // base pointer
FreeChecking fc(. . .);                   // object with public base
bp = &fc;                                 // implicit conversion
FreeChecking *fcp = (FreeChecking *) bp;  // explicit conversion
```

Here the base can be either public or nonpublic. Thus,

```
ArbStack *ap;                             // base pointer
EmpStack x(. . .);                        // object with private base
ap = &x;                                  // implicit conversion
EmpStack * ep = (EmpStack *)ap;           // explicit conversion
```

also works. Note that it is possible to cast a true base pointer to a derived pointer. Through such a pointer, it is even legal syntax to access an appendant member that is really not there. Of course, executing such codes is disastrous:

```
Account susan(. . .);                    // base object
JointAccount *jp;
jp = (JointAccount *)&susan;             // explicit conversion
strncpy(jp->jss, "032-55-1234", SS_LEN); // disaster !
```

But susan does not contain the member jss. The disastrous assignment over-writes a memory location not in the object susan. Such bugs are usually not detected immediately, and they make debugging difficult. So, be very careful with explicit casting.

7.8.1 Inheritance and Overloading

When an overloaded function takes arguments that are objects or object point-ers, the same call-resolution rules as listed in Section 3.5 apply. However, those rules must now be interpreted with the type conversions among inheritance-related objects in mind.

Let *arg_type* and *par_type* be the argument object type and the declared formal parameter type, respectively. The call-resolution rules as they relate to object arguments are restated here for clarity:

- Exact match: *par_type* is *arg_type*, *arg_type&*, or const *arg_type&*.
- Standard promotion: Not applicable to objects.
- Standard conversion: Any inheritance-induced implicit conversion.
- User-supplied conversion: Class-defined conversion as described in Section 8.7.
- No match or ambiguous match (more than one): An error.

7.9 \ ASSIGNMENT OF OBJECTS

7.9.1 Built-in Object Assignment

C++ understands how to assign one class object to another. Built-in assignment works only if the right-hand-side object has, or can be converted to, the same type as the left-hand-side object. The actual assignment is done *memberwise*; that is, data members are assigned individually. Consider the assignment of fractions

```
Fraction a, b(3, 4);
a = b;
```

or of compatible accounts

```
Account a1( . . . );
FreeChecking a2( . . . );
a1 = a2;
```

For a = b, the individual assignments a.num = b.num and a.denom = b.denom are performed. And for a1 = a2, the base part of a2 is assigned to a1 in a similar memberwise fashion. Of course, the right-hand side can also be a computation or function call that results in an object:

```
a = a - b;    // class Fraction member operator-
```

Combination assignment operators such as += and *= have no built-in meaning when applied to class objects even if the arithmetic operators operator+ and operator* are defined in the class. The only operators with prescribed meanings for objects are

&   (address-of)
.   (member-of)
=   (assignment)

Any other operator must be explicitly defined for objects of a class before it can be given such arguments. The general topic of operator overloading is discussed in Section 8.1. The focus here is assignment of objects.

Conceptually, object assignment is implemented by an assignment operator that is either defined by the programmer or generated by the compiler. Built-in assignment is supported by the compiler-generated assignment operator and works fine for many classes. But there are situations that require programmer-supplied assignment operators.

7.9.2 Class-Defined Object Assignment

For assigning objects containing pointers, built-in assignment is usually inadequate. Consider two objects obj1 and obj2 in some class. Suppose obj1.str points to a character string string_1 and obj2.str points to a second character string string_2 (Figure 7.4). If the assignment

```
obj1 = obj2;
```

is performed, what is the result? Because obj1.str gets the value of obj2.str, both pointers now point to the second string, and it may well be that the address to the first string is lost (Figure 7.4). Furthermore, modification to string_2 via obj1.str affects obj2, and vice versa. Such coupling of objects as a side effect of assignment is almost always unexpected and unwanted.

FIGURE 7.4   SIDE EFFECT OF obj1 = obj2

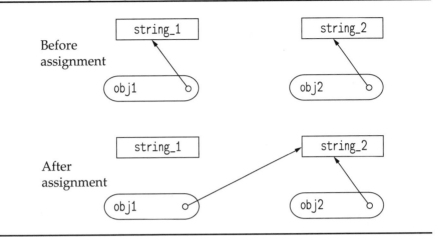

The situation becomes much worse if obj1.str and obj2.str each points to dynamically allocated space that is freed automatically by the object destructor. Suppose obj1 is destroyed first and it frees (deletes) string_2. When obj2 is destroyed later, it also attempts to free string_2, resulting in a serious error that destroys the consistency of the free pool from which dynamic storage is allocated.

The preceding discussion points out a grave problem with using built-in assignment semantics for objects with pointer members. The same problem exists for objects with reference members. What is the solution to this problem? The built-in assignment semantics can be avoided by defining operator=() in the class. To make things clear, let's look at an example of user-defined operator=().

The Class-Defined operator=()

Recall the circular buffer class described in Section 3.11. A Cirbuf object contains, among other members, a cb pointer to a dynamically allocated character buffer. This buffer is freed by the destructor ~Cirbuf. These characteristics make it necessary to define operator=() if assignments of Cirbuf objects are required.

We can modify the Cirbuf class by adding a new member to the Cirbuf class definition:

```
Cirbuf& Cirbuf::operator=(const Cirbuf& b);   // Cirbuf assignment
```

This is a particular case of the general assignment prototype

```
ClassX& ClassX::operator=(const ClassX&);
```

for class-defined operator=(). Here is the actual function definition:

```
///  add to Cirbuf.C  ///
Cirbuf& Cirbuf::operator =(const Cirbuf& b)
{   if (&b == this) return(*this);      // check for a = a        (1)
    head = 0;                           // set member values
    tail = length = b.length;
    if ( size != b.size )               // buffer size different (2)
    {   delete [] cb;                   // free old buffer
        size = b.size;
        cb = new char[size];            // new buffer
    }
    for (int i=0 ; i < length ; i++)    // copy all unconsumed chars
        cb[i] = b.cb[(b.head+i) % size];
    return(*this);                      // return host object      (3)
}
```

The purpose is, of course, to assign the given object b to the host object. First, a check is made (line 1) to determine whether the object is assigned to itself (for example, a = a) — in which case, nothing needs to be done, except to return the host object. Then, head, tail, and length are assigned appropriate values. If the assignment involves two buffers of different sizes (line 2), the old buffer is freed and a new one with the correct size is allocated. All that is needed now is to copy the characters remaining in the buffer of the object b into the buffer of the host object. Finally, *this is returned.

The function header, trivial assignment check (line 1), and return statement (line 3) constitute a formula for defining operator=().

Test the user-defined assignment of Cirbuf objects with the following code:

```
#include <iostream.h>
#include "Cirbuf.h"

int main()
{ Cirbuf b1(64);                    // set up b1
    b1.produce('A');
    b1.produce('B');
    b1.produce('C');
    char c = b1.consume();          // B C remain in b1
    { Cirbuf b2, b3;                // b2 and b2  capacity 16
      b2 = b1;                      // calling operator=()
      cout << (c = b2.consume());
      cout << (c = b2.consume())
          << endl;
      c = b2.consume();            // consume empty buffer
      if (c > 0 ) cout << c;
```

```
      b3 = b2;                    // another = call
   }                              // b2 and b3 destroyed
   cout << "from b1 ";            // use b1 some more
   cout << (c = b1.consume());
   cout << (c = b1.consume()) << endl;
   return(0);
}
```

The code tests not only the assignment operator but also its correct operation in conjunction with object destruction. The test should produce the following display:

```
BC
consume: buffer empty
from b1 BC
```

7.10 \ COPYING OF OBJECTS

During the execution of a C++ program, there are many occasions when a copy of an object must be created. Such copies are often established automatically by the compiler without programmer intervention. Generally, a copy is needed as follows:

1. When an object is passed by value in a function call. For example, in the call

   ```
   vec1.inner(vec2)
   ```

   a copy of the Vector object vec2 is made and passed to the member function inner in vec1 (Section 2.4).

2. When a function returns an object by value. For instance, the function

   ```
   Vector Vector::operator -(Vector)
   ```

   returns a copy of a local Vector variable.

3. When an object is initialized by another object. For example,

   ```
   Vector vec3 = vec1;
   Vector vec4 = vec2 - vec1;
   ```

   where vec3 and vec4 are the copies made.

7.10.1　Built-in Object Copying

In each of the situations just listed, a copy is made of an existing object. Unless otherwise specified, C++ creates a copy of an object by copying each and every nonstatic data member, of basic or user-defined type, in the object.

The memberwise copying actions are entirely similar to those for built-in object assignment. Object copying is performed by the *copy constructor*, a special class member that can be generated by the compiler or supplied by the programmer. Built-in copying is supported by the compiler-generated copy constructor. And, for the same reasons as detailed in Section 7.9.2, the built-in copy semantics may not be adequate for certain objects with pointer members.

7.10.2　Class-Defined Object Copying

When the built-in object copying semantics are not adequate, the correct actions can be specified by the class. This is done by *defining the copy constructor* explicitly.

The Copy Constructor

Consider again the class `Poly` discussed in Section 4.4. The member `pol` points to a sequence of integers in free storage. To make the class work better, we should add a destructor:

```
Poly::~Poly() { delete [] pol; }
```

Also, it is clear that the class needs an `operator=()` and a copy constructor. So, we add the following lines to the class declaration:

```
~Poly();                        // destructor
Poly& operator =(const Poly& p);  // overload =
Poly(const Poly& p);            // copy constructor
```

In general, a copy constructor is a constructor with the special prototype

```
ClassX::ClassX(const ClassX&);    //copy constructor
```

or the equivalent but less restrictive alternative

```
ClassX::ClassX(ClassX&);
```

The `Poly` copy constructor must allocate free storage and copy the polynomial representation:

```
Poly::Poly(const Poly& p)       // copy constructor
: pol(new int[p.deg() + 2])     // allocate free storage
{
```

```
        for (int i=p.deg()+1 ; i > -1 ; i--)
            pol[i] = p.pol[i];                // copy representation
        cout << "copy constructor called"   // only for testing
            << endl;
}
```

Some display code is included just for testing purposes. The assignment must also be specified in the class:

```
Poly& Poly::operator =(const Poly& p)
{   if ( this == &p) return(*this);
    unsigned pd = p.deg();
    if ( deg() < pd )                       // space not enough
    {   delete [] pol;
        pol = new int[pd + 2];
    }
    for (int i=0 ; i < pd + 2 ; i++)
        pol[i] = p.pol[i];
    cout << "= called" << endl;             // testing only
    return(*this);
}
```

With these improvements, we can test the Poly class again. Use the following main program, which is designed to show the effect of the copy constructor:

```
#include "Poly.h"

int p[]={7,-2,3,3,2,-15,1,-3,0,-9};
int q[]={7,2,3,-3,2,15,1,3,0,9};

Poly test_fn(Poly p, Poly q)             // value arguments
{   p.display(); q.display();
    Poly sum = p + q;                    // init by object
    sum.display();
    return(sum);                         // return value
}

int main()
{    Poly p1(p,5);
     Poly q1(q,5);
     p1.display();
     q1.display();
     p1 = test_fn(p1, q1);               // overloaded =
     p1.display();
     return(0);
}
```

Running the program should produce the following output:

```
(7  -2, 3  3, 2  -15, 1  -3, 0  -9)
(7   2, 3  -3, 2   15, 1   3, 0   9)
copy constructor called
copy constructor called
(7  -2, 3  3, 2  -15, 1  -3, 0  -9)
(7   2, 3  -3, 2   15, 1   3, 0   9)
copy constructor called
(0  0)
copy constructor called
= called
(0  0)
```

When you test this program, your output may show a different number of copy constructor calls because different C++ compilers have different levels of optimization to avoid making copies.

Note that there is a very close relationship between user-defined assignment and copying. In some situations, the copy constructor can simply be a call to assignment. For example, the Cirbuf copy constructor is simply

```
inline Cirbuf::Cirbuf(const Cirbuf& b)      // copy constructor
     { *this = b; }
```

This technique works only when the operator=() is appropriate. Otherwise, the copy constructor can always be coded independently.

In summary, objects containing pointer, reference, or const data members usually cannot use the built-in object assignment or copying semantics. Classes with pointers to free storage should usually have all of the following defined:

- Destructor for freeing storage.
- Assignment operator=().
- Copy constructor.

7.11 DERIVED-OBJECT ASSIGNMENT AND COPYING

As stated earlier, neither the assignment operator nor the copy constructor is inherited by a derived class. A derived class may define either or both explicitly. If a derived class does not supply an explicit copy constructor, one is generated for it that copies base and member objects by calling their copy constructors and copies other data members directly. An explicit copy constructor must specify desired base- and member-object copy constructor calls on its init-list. (Again, default constructor calls can be omitted.)

The treatment of derived-object assignment is similar. If a derived class does not supply an explicit assignment operator, one is generated for it that calls base- and component-object assignment operators and assigns other data members individually. An explicit assignment operator takes care of calling (or not calling) base- and component-object assignment operators itself.

Let's consider a simplified example. The following base class has both copy constructor and assignment operator:

```
class BaseX
{ public:
     BaseX() {}                        // default constructor
     BaseX(int a, int b)               // constructor
     : i(a), j(b) {}
     BaseX(const BaseX& obj)           // copy constructor
     { i=obj.i; j=obj.j; }
     BaseX& operator=(const BaseX& obj);  // assignment
   private:
     int i, j;
};

BaseX& BaseX::operator=(const BaseX& obj)  // assignment
{ if (this == &obj)
     return(*this);
   i = obj.i; j = obj.j;
   return(*this);
}
```

The derived class also defines an explicit copy constructor and assignment operator:

```
class DerivedX : public BaseX
{ public:
     DerivedX() { }                    // default constructor
     DerivedX(int a, int b, int c)     // constructor
     : BaseX(a,b), k(c) { }
     DerivedX(const DerivedX& obj)     // copy constructor
     : BaseX(obj)                      // base copy constructor call
     { k=obj.k;   }
     DerivedX&
     operator=(const DerivedX& obj);   // assignment
   private:
     int k;
};

DerivedX& DerivedX::
operator=(const DerivedX& obj)         // assignment
{ if (this == &obj)
     return(*this);
```

```
        BaseX::operator=(obj);                // base assignment call
        k = obj.k;
        return(*this);
}
```

Notice the base copy constructor call and the base assignment operator call. The integer data members really do not require copy or assignment operators, but they simplify the example.

If a base class does not have properly defined assignment and copying, these operations can be supplied in a derived class as explained next.

7.12 \ OBJECT ASSIGNMENT AND COPYING VIA DERIVATION

A class such as ArbList does not contain properly defined assignment and copy operations, which is all right as long as these operations are not required. When we want to make the class more robust, we can define a derived class that adds the desired operations.

For example, a generic list class ArbList_ac with proper assignment and copy operations is derived as follows:

```
////////    File: ArbList_ac.h    ////////

// generic list with assignment and copy
// a friend class of ArbList
#include "ArbList.h"

class ArbList_ac : public ArbList
{ public:
     ArbList_ac() { }                         // default constructor
     ArbList_ac(Arbent c, EQ_FN eq, DISP_FN d)
       : ArbList(c, eq, d) { }                // constructor
     ~ArbList_ac() { }                        // destructor
     ArbList_ac& operator =(const ArbList& x); // assignment     (1)
     ArbList_ac(const ArbList_ac& x)          // copy constructor (2)
     {   copy(x); }
     ArbList_ac(const ArbList& x)             // conversion      (3)
     {   copy(x); }
   private:
     void copy(const ArbList& x);
};
```

ArbList_ac is quite simple. Other than trivially defined functions, there are just the assignment (line 1), the copy constructor (line 2), and a constructor for type conversion (line 3). Each of these will also call the private function copy() for copying data members.

To allow copy() access to all data members, ArbList_ac can be made a friend of ArbList, unless the nonpublic data members of ArbList have already been declared protected to allow access from the derived class.

The operator=() is examined first:

```
///////   File: ArbList_ac.C   ///////
#include "ArbList_ac.h"

// assignment
ArbList_ac& ArbList_ac::operator =(const ArbList& x)
{   if ( &x == this ) return(*this);
    if ( ! is_empty() ) free();  // free list entries
    copy(x);                     // copy x into host object
    return(*this);
}
```

The type of the formal argument x is ArbList&, instead of ArbList_ac&, so that the assignment operator can take either an ArbList or an ArbList_ac object as the right-hand argument. An ArbList_ac argument will be converted automatically by inheritance-induced implicit type conversion. As a result, the following codes are possible:

```
ArbList_ac aa( /* . . . */ );
ArbList_ac bb( /* . . . */ );
ArbList    cc( /* . . . */ );
aa = bb;              // rhs is ArbList_ac
bb = cc;              // rhs is ArbList
```

Note that converting a base object to a derived object is not done without user-supplied rules (Section 8.7). The type-conversion member (line 3) allows an ArbList_ac variable or parameter to be initialized by or passed an ArbList object:

```
ArbList_ac dd = cc;
```

The actual copying is performed by the member function

```
void ArbList_ac::copy(const ArbList& x)
{   equal = x.equal;          // copy data members
    dispfn = x.dispfn;
    ArbCell* lx = x.first();
    head = NULL;              // empty list
    ArbCell* p = head;
    while ( ! is_end(lx) )    // copy list
    {    insert(ArbList::content(lx), p);
```

```
        p = ArbList::next(p);
        lx = ArbList::next(lx);
    }
}
```

This copy member is also used in the copy constructor. It is good practice to share a piece of common copying code between the copy constructor and the assignment operator when possible.

With the assignment, copy constructor, and conversion constructor in ArbList_ac, assignment, initialization, and argument passing between objects of the two types ArbList and ArbList_ac can be done without any exceptions.

7.13 \ THE I/O STREAM CLASS HIERARCHY

The C++ I/O stream library provides a good example of OOP with classes and inheritance. The I/O stream class hierarchy is outlined in Figure 7.5 to give you a better idea of how the different I/O stream objects relate to one another and to show how class derivation can be used effectively in practice. At the base of Figure 7.5 is the ios class whose enum members ios::in, ios::out, and so on are familiar quantities. Derived from ios are the istream, ostream, and fstreambase classes. Adding object assignment (class-defined operator=()) to istream (ostream), the class istream_withassign (ostream_withassign) is derived, which gives rise to the standard cin (cout, cerr, and clog). Thus, it is possible to assign other appropriate I/O objects to these standard ones to redirect I/O through them. (The _withassign class names are abbreviated in Figure 7.5. I= for istream_withassign, etc.)

FIGURE 7.5   I/O STREAM CLASS HIERARCHY

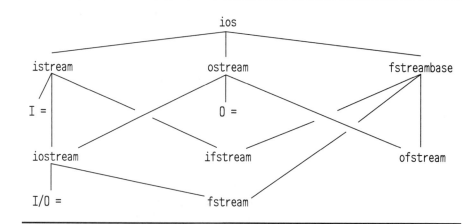

Multiple inheritance is used to derive iostream from both istream and ostream. There is also a class iostream_withassign.

The ifstream (ofstream) class is derived from the two base classes fstreambase and istream (ostream). These are additional examples of multiple inheritance. An fstream object can perform both input and output to a file and is derived from the two classes iostream and fstreambase.

The derivations in Figure 7.5 are all public. The actual derived-class declarations are listed here for easy reference:

```
class fstreambase : virtual public ios ;  // virtual base (0)
class ifstream : public fstreambase, public istream ;
class ofstream : public fstreambase, public ostream ;
class fstream : public fstreambase, public iostream ;
class istream : virtual public ios ;       // virtual base (1)
class ostream : virtual public ios ;       // virtual base (2)
class iostream : public istream, public ostream ;     // (3)
class istream_withassign : public istream ;
class ostream_withassign : public ostream ;
class iostream_withassign : public iostream ;
```

Designating a base class virtual (lines 0–2) avoids duplicating the same base object in a derived object when multiple inheritance is involved. Thus, in an iostream object (line 3), there is only one ios object. Virtual bases will be explained in detail later (Section 9.1.1).

The complete picture of the I/O stream classes also includes string-handling classes and other manipulations. But the outline here is sufficient for most purposes and rich enough as a source of examples for topics still to come.

7.14 \ CLASS SCOPE NESTING UNDER MULTIPLE INHERITANCE

In single inheritance, the scope of a derived class is nested in its unique base class. When there are several direct base classes, a derived class is considered nested in each of the base scopes. To find an identifier under multiple inheritance, all the direct bases are searched at once. For example, let JtFrChecking be derived from JointAccount and FreeChecking (Figure 7.6). If an identifier used in the scope JtFrChecking:: is not found there, both base scopes (scope FreeChecking:: and scope JointAccount::) will be searched at once. If there is only one match, then the identifier is found. Multiple matches result in ambiguity and an error. If there is no match, then all bases of the base classes are searched at once, and so on.

FIGURE 7.6   NESTING OF MULTIPLE SCOPES

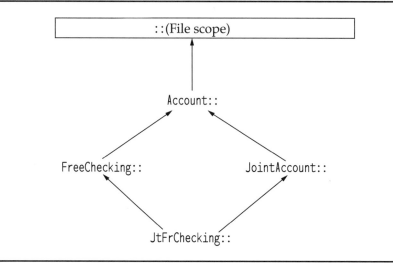

7.15 SUMMARY

Class derivation is the C++ mechanism that supports inheritance by adding to or modifying existing classes without changing their code. A class can be derived from one or several base classes. A base class can be designated public, protected, or private, giving rise to three different types of derivation. Repeated derivation results in class hierarchies.

A derived class inherits all members of its base classes except constructors, destructors, and assignment operators. The derived-class scope is nested inside the scopes of its direct base classes. A derived-class identifier hides a base-class identifier of the same name. An identifier is located in the nested scope of a derivation hierarchy by following the derivation chain toward the root base class, searching base classes at the same level simultaneously, and ending at file scope. An identifier is first found; its accessibility is then determined. If more than one identifier is found, ambiguity results.

A derived object is composed of base objects and an appendant part containing added members. The derived-class constructor and base-class constructors collaborate to initialize a derived object. Similarly, the derived-class destructor and base-class destructors cooperate to deinitialize a derived object.

Appendant members and friends of a derived class can always access the nonprivate inherited members. Access to inherited members from outside the derived class depends on the base-class designation. Section 7.4 contains a summary of access control rules under derivation.

Public derivation expresses the is-a relationship, whereas private or protected derivation facilitates code reuse and supports the is-implemented-as-a relationship. The has-a or uses-a relationship should be modeled with component objects within a class. The C++ implicit conversion rules between inheritance-related types are designed to support these relationships.

C++ defines only a few operations generally applicable to all objects: assignment, copying (initialization, argument passing by value, function return by value), address-of (&), and member-of (.). Most other operations on objects must be programmed explicitly. Built-in assignment and copying work fine for objects without pointers, references, or const members. Other objects may require a user-defined assignment operator

```
ClassX& ClassX::operator=(const ClassX&);
```

and a copy constructor

```
ClassX::ClassX(const ClassX&);
```

When objects contain pointers to free storage, these operations are programmed to cooperate with the constructors and destructors for a well-rounded class. Assignment and copy constructors are not inherited, and an explicit derived-class definition must specify calls to appropriate base-class counterparts. Class derivation can be used to add the necessary assignment and/or copy constructor to an existing class.

EXERCISES

1. What is the fine and important distinction between an "inherited member" and a "member in the base class"? Consider the derived class JointAccount and the additional member

```
int JointAccount::operator > (Account& a)
{    return(acct_no > a.acct_no);    }
```

Is anything wrong with this member function other than the fact that it is a contrived example? Explain.

2. Does a friend of a base class have any special access privilege to members, inherited or not, of a derived class?

3. Which members of a base class are not inherited by a derived class? When a member is not inherited, what difference does it make? Explain and give an example. (*Hint:* Consider assignment.)

4. Is it possible to list the same base class more than once on the base-class list of a derived class? Is it possible to have a circular derived-base relationship: Class *RR* is derived from class *SS* and class *SS* is derived from class *RR*? If not, what prevents it from being done?

5. Enumerate the differences between a public and a private class derivation.

6. Consider the two member functions *BaseX*::*xyz*(int) and *DerivedX*::*xyz*(char *). If obj is an object of *DerivedX*, which function does the call obj.*xyz*(5) invoke? Explain.

7. Under what situations can a derived object (reference, pointer) be passed to a base-type parameter? Under what situations can a base object (reference, pointer) be passed to a derived-type parameter?

8. Consider C++ built-in object assignment. If you assign objects that themselves contain member objects, how would the assignment proceed?

9. For class objects, list all the situations you can think of under which the built-in assignment may be inadequate and explain why. (*Hint*: const, reference.) Do the same for built-in copying.

10. Is it possible to pass an ifstream object to an istream formal parameter in a function call? What about an istream& parameter? Why?

11. Follow the ArbStack example (Section 7.6) and derive ArbQueue from ArbList.

12. Derive EmpQueue, a queue of employees, from the generic queue in Exercise 11.

13. Exercise Cal-1: Consider the improvements suggested for the pocket calculator program (Chapter 6, Exercise Cal-1). Instead of adding these new capabilities in the existing calculator classes directly, consider achieving the same with class derivation. Specifically, derive NewEng from CalcEng to add the new capabilities to the compute engine (change private to protected in CalcEng). The public interface of NewEng should be kept the same as CalcEng. Also, operations already implemented in CalcEng should not be duplicated in NewEng. It should simply add preprocessing and/or postprocessing to the base CalcEng::operate(). The CalcFace class should need no modification. The simple Calculator class can be modified to take a NewEng object.

14. Exercise Cal-2: Use the improved calculator program in Exercise 13 and further derivation to implement the calculator suggested in Chapter 6, Exercise Cal-2.

15. Extend the two-dimensional Vector class to n dimensions using dynamic storage allocation in the constructor. Also, define the proper destructor, assignment, and copy constructor.

16. Follow the ArbList_ac example and derive the class Poly_ac (Section 7.10.2).

OPERATOR OVERLOADING AND ADVANCED TOPICS

Objects, classes, and inheritance provide enormous power for program organization, complexity reduction, and code reuse. However, as stated earlier, there are very few ready-made operations for objects. This is not an oversight on the part of C++; few operations make sense for all the varied kinds of user-defined types. Thus, to make a class of objects work well, your program has to define many of its operations, often through overloading operators. This is especially true for sophisticated classes.

Operator overloading is an integral part of OOP and helps make programs generic. Therefore, rules for operator overloading are clearly stated in this chapter, and the practical value and critical role of operators in OOP are demonstrated. Examples include =, +=, I/O by >> and <<, iteration with (), and smart pointers with ->, as well as free storage management with new and delete.

Adding appropriately defined operators and other special members to a class tends to make classes more robust. The concept of robust classes is highlighted here. Ultimately, a user-defined object can behave almost as built-in types.

C++ provides many features for making objects easy to use, flexible, and versatile. Some of these features are somewhat advanced and thus less frequently used, but the discussion of C++ would be hopelessly incomplete without them.

A special pointer type known as the *offset pointer to member* (opm) provides additional program flexibility. The chapter makes a logical and clear presentation of this topic by explaining the declaration, assignment, and dereference of opms (with .* and ->*). Examples show their power and utility. Other topics include user-defined type conversions, unions, and bit fields, as well as nested and local classes.

8.1 \ OPERATOR OVERLOADING

Making the same operators work for different user-defined types increases the genericness of programs. Only three operators (&, ., =) have built-in meaning for class objects. Other operators do not work with objects unless definitions are supplied. Properly defining the meaning of appropriate operators for class objects is an important aspect of OOP.

C++ provides a mechanism for specifying the meaning of an operator such as +, <<, and [] for objects. It is done by defining *operator functions*. An operator function named "operator *op*" overloads the operator *op*. We have already seen some operator functions, including operator - for fractions and operator + for polynomials. Note that there are two tokens in an operator function name and it does not matter if they are separated by white space (operator +) or not (operator+). Either style can be used to improve readability in a given situation.

Operator overloading helps OOP, for example, by making arithmetic operators such as + work for both basic types and objects such as fractions. We can thus write generic codes that work for all such arithmetic types. And, by making I/O operators such as << work for basic and user-defined types, we can write sophisticated I/O codes that work generically.

Table 8.1 shows all the operators that can be overloaded as well as the four that cannot be. However, there are certain restrictions to operator overloading:

1. At least one operand (argument) of the operator must be of user-defined type — that is, an object. Therefore, the meaning of an operator for built-in data types cannot be changed.
2. Operator functions cannot have default arguments.
3. The number of operands (or *arity*) for an operator cannot be changed.
4. Brand-new operators cannot be introduced. Thus, it is not possible to introduce a new operator like **.
5. Operator precedence is built-in and fixed.
6. The four operators =, [ ], ( ), and -> can be overloaded only with member operator functions.

Member or Nonmember

For all except four operators, the operator function can be defined as a class member or just as a file scope function. For example, consider adding

TABLE 8.1   **OPERATOR OVERLOADING**

OVERLOADABLE OPERATORS							
/	%	^	|	~	!	<	>
+=	-=	*=	/=	%=	^=	&=	|=
<<	>>	<<=	>>=	==	!=	<=	>=
&&	||	++	--	,	->*	new	delete

UNARY AND BINARY				MEMBER ONLY			
+	-	*	&	=	[ ]	( )	->

NOT OVERLOADED							
				.	? :	::	.*

the operator += for the class Fraction. The intended meaning of f1 += f2 is f1 = f1 + f2. It is not illegal to use += for completely unrelated purposes, but it is usually ill-advised.

Taking the member route, we add the declaration

```
Fraction& operator +=(const Fraction&);
```

to the Fraction class declaration and the code

```
Fraction& Fraction::operator +=(const Fraction& fra)
{    *this = *this + fra;    // operator+ already exists
     return(*this);
}
```

to the Fraction.C file.

Taking the nonmember route, we define a file scope function

```
Fraction& operator +=(Fraction& f1, const Fraction& f2)
{    f1 = f1 + f2
     return(f1);
}
```

to perform the desired operations. Either style works fine in this case. The member function is declared with only one argument because the host object is always the implicit left operand; that is, the two expressions

```
f1 += f2               // member operator +=
f1.operator +=(f2)
```

are the same. The nonmember operator function takes two arguments. Thus,

```
f1 += f2               // nonmember operator +=
operator += (f1, f2)
```

are equivalent expressions.

In general, the expression x *op* y can access either the member or the non-member implementation of *op*. When both forms are present, argument matching determines which one, if any, is called. Ambiguity results if there are several matches. Similar remarks can be made for unary operators.

Because direct invocations are possible, it is not an error to keep both the member and nonmember versions in a program even if they may cause ambiguity. One form is usually sufficient. When all operands are objects of the class, take the member route.

There are situations when the nonmember route is your only choice. Consider overloading * for the Fraction class to take care of fraction-integer multiplication:

```
Fraction * int    (case I)
int * Fraction    (case II)
```

Case I can be treated by a member operator function, but case II cannot because a class object must be the left operand in order to invoke its member function with the operator notation. Everything else being equal, you should define both cases as nonmember functions. Here case I is coded as a friend:

```
inline Fraction operator *(const Fraction& fra, int i)
{
    return(Fraction(fra.num * i, fra.denom, 1));
}
```

Case II can be similarly defined.

It is not necessary to discuss the overloading of each and every operator in Table 8.1 because most follow the rules already presented. However, a few important cases have yet to be mentioned.

8.2   STREAM I/O FOR OBJECTS

The stream operators >> and << are convenient for I/O operations. Each of the two operators takes an I/O stream object as the left operand. The operators already perform I/O for all built-in types because the stream library defines operator functions for all basic-type right operands. If these operators are also made to work for user-defined objects, then I/O operations can be made extremely easy—just apply these operators. A systematic approach is described here for overloading >> and <<.

To display fractions, for example, we can define a friend operator<<() of the class Fraction:

```
ostream& operator <<(ostream& out, const Fraction& cf) // (1)
{   out << cf.num << '/' << cf.denom;
```

```
    return(out);
}
```

With this operator function, output of fractions can be done using <<

```
fraction r(1,2), s(-3,4);
cout << r << ", " << s << endl;
```

just as easily as displaying strings or integers. The function header (line 1) is a frequent idiom:

- The left operand is an ostream object and should be the return value.
- Reference parameters are used to avoid copying objects.
- The object to be displayed is read-only.

If we write the public member function Fraction::display as

```
void Fraction::display(ostream& out = cout) const
{    out << num << '/' << denom;
}
```

then we can simplify operator<<() to

```
ostream& operator <<(ostream& out, const Fraction& cf)    // (2)
{    cf.display(out);
     return(out);    // always return left operand
}
```

This version does not need to be a friend of Fraction and can be declared inline for more efficiency. The definition (line 2) is almost universal for all class types. Change one word and the operator function is adapted to another class. How much simpler can it get (Section 10.2)?

Now consider how >> is overloaded to input fractions:

```
istream& operator >>(istream& in, Fraction& f) // (3)
{   int num, denom;
    char c;
    in >> num >> c;
    if ( c == '/' ) in >> denom;
    else            // set error state        (Section 6.6.7)
    {   in.clear( ios::badbit | in.rdstate() );
        return(in);
    }
    f = Fraction(num, denom);                  // (4)
    return(in);   // always return left operand
}
```

The function header (line 3) is another idiom. The reference object f is a return parameter receiving the input fraction through memberwise assignment (line 4). A file of fractions can now be read with >>:

```
3/4   18/19   -20/52
2/5   3/6     5/8
```

We can add an input function read to the Fraction class as a public member:

```
void Fraction::read(istream& in /* = cin */)
{   int num, denom;
    char c;
    in >> num >> c;
    if ( c == '/' )
        in >> denom;
    else                             // clear() set error state
    {   in.clear( ios::badbit | in.rdstate()); return; }
    *this = Fraction(num, denom);  // call constructor
}
```

We then simplify >> to

```
istream& operator >>(istream& in, Fraction& f)
{   f.read(in);
    return(in);
}
```

Hence, if a class is built with the appropriate display and read functions, then overloading >> and << becomes quite trivial. Follow these conventions consistently to make I/O of objects just as easy as built-in types.

8.3 \ A REFERENCE-COUNT STRING CLASS

For objects with member pointers to free storage, one approach the user-defined copy constructor and the operator=() can take is to make copies of data in free storage. Another approach involves *reference counting*.

In many applications, multiple objects with members pointing to the same free storage address present no problem. It is only the freeing of this storage by the destructor that causes difficulty. Consider an application where many strings in free storage will be used and the storage required should be minimized. Much space is saved by not making copies of the same string every time it is assigned, passed in a call, or returned from a function. This can be done by creating Cell objects that bind a reference count with a string in free storage. The count keeps track of how many pointers can access the Cell object. The string is freed only when the count drops to zero:

```
class Cell
{ friend class Refstr;
  private:
    Cell( char *s );                   // constructor
    char *str;                         // free storage string
    unsigned cnt;                      // reference count
    ~Cell()                            // destructor
    {   cout << "~Cell\n";             // for testing only
        delete [] str;
    }
};

Cell::Cell( char *s )
: str(new char[strlen(s)+ 1])
{    strcpy(str, s);                   // str in free storage
     cnt = 1;                          // reference count
}
```

The Cell class is used exclusively by its friend class Refstr, which manages strings with a reference count. Thus, the Cell code is kept in the file Refstr.C for better information hiding. The Refstr.h file provides the reference string class:

```
///////    Refstr.h    ///////
#include<iostream.h>
#include<string.h>

class Cell;    // defined in Refstr.C file

class Refstr
{ public:
    Refstr(char *str = "");                // constructor
    Refstr(const Refstr& s);               // copy constructor
    Refstr& operator =(const Refstr& s);   // assignment
    int cmp(const Refstr& s) const;        // compare two strings
    unsigned count()                       // retrieve count
    {    return(ptr->cnt);  }
    void display();
    ~Refstr();                             // destructor
  private:
    Cell *ptr;                             // ptr to ref count str
};
```

A new Refstr object is initialized by

```
///////   File: Refstr.C   ///////
Refstr::Refstr(char *s)
: ptr(new Cell(s)) { }
```

When a Refstr object is destroyed, the destructor is called:

```
Refstr::~Refstr()
{  cout << "~Refstr" << ptr->str << " cnt="
       << ptr->cnt << "\n";
   if ( --ptr->cnt == 0 )              // decrement cnt
       delete ptr;                     // call ~Cell
}
```

Note that the storage is freed only when the reference count is zero. The output is used for testing only. The Refstr copy constructor and assignment operator increase the reference count rather than make copies:

```
Refstr::Refstr(const Refstr& s)       // copy constructor
{   ptr = s.ptr;                      // assign pointer
    ptr->cnt++;                       // increment count
}
```

```
Refstr& Refstr::operator =(const Refstr& s)
{   if ( this == &s || ptr == s.ptr )
        return(*this);                // trivial assignments
    cout <<  ptr->str << " = "
        << s.ptr->str << "\n";
    s.ptr->cnt++;                     // increment count
    if ( --ptr->cnt == 0 )           // last pointer gone
        delete ptr;
    ptr = s.ptr;
    return(*this);
}
```

These functions show you how to avoid copying to improve efficiency in your program. Again, the output is for testing only. Other members for dealing with reference strings can be defined. For example,

```
int Refstr::cmp(const Refstr& s) const
{   if ( s.ptr == ptr )               // same pointers
        return(0);
    else
        return(strcmp(ptr->str, s.ptr->str));
}
///////   End of Refstr.C   ///////
```

compares two strings. It is interesting to track Refstr objects and see how their reference counts change. Use the following test program:

```
///////    File: tstRfstr.C    ///////
#include "Refstr.h"

int callcmp(Refstr a, Refstr b)
{     return(a.cmp(b));  }

main()
{     Refstr s1("There"); Refstr s2("Here");
      Refstr s3("Hello");                      // 3 constructor calls
      Refstr s4 = s3;                          // copy constructor only
      s2 = s1;                                 // assignments
      s1 = s2;
      if ( callcmp(s1,s2) == 0)
          cout << "A\n";
      s1 = s3;
      if ( callcmp(s3,s2) == 0)
          cout << "B\n";
      cout << "main finishing\n";
}
```

Running this program produces the following output:

```
Here = There
~Cell
~Refstr There cnt=4
~Refstr There cnt=3
A
There = Hello
~Refstr There cnt=2
~Refstr Hello cnt=4
main finishing
~Refstr Hello cnt=3
~Refstr Hello cnt=2
~Refstr There cnt=1
~Cell
~Refstr Hello cnt=1
~Cell
```

The destructor ~Cell is called three times to free the three strings (s1, s2, and s3) that are allocated dynamically. Other strings in the program are just pointers to one of these three strings.

The techniques presented here can also be used to build a reference-counting class from any given class — say, Abc. A pair of classes are needed:

1. A class AbcCell containing a reference count, a pointer to Abc, a constructor, and a destructor.

2. A class RefAbc with a pointer to AbcCell in free storage, and appropriately defined constructor, destructor, copy constructor, and assignment operator.

These two classes combine to give reference-count objects for Abc without modifying class Abc at all. In fact, class Abc may be a library facility whose source code is inaccessible.

8.4 \ OVERLOADING ++ AND --

The increment and decrement operators ++ and -- are special because they can be used as prefix or postfix operators. Overloading ++ is discussed here. (Overloading -- is the same.)

To overload the prefix version of ++, use

```
type ClassX::operator ++();        // prefix ++ as class member
type operator ++(type arg);        // prefix ++ as nonmember
```

To overload the postfix version ++, a special signature must be used:

```
type ClassX::operator ++(int);     // postfix ++ as class member
type operator ++(type arg, int);   // postfix ++ as nonmember
```

The artificial second int argument does not even need a paramenter name because it is just there to tell the C++ compiler that the postfix version of ++ is being overloaded.

Here is an example for the preincrement of a fraction:

```
Fraction Fraction::operator ++()
{   num += denom;
    return(*this);
}
```

8.5 \ SMART POINTERS

Of the two member selection operators . and ->, only the latter can be overloaded and it is treated specially. Normally, -> is a binary operator taking a pointer as the left operand and a member name as the right operand. However, if its left operand is an object instead of a pointer to an object, the notation invokes the unary member function operator->(). Specifically, the code

obj->mem

is interpreted as

(*obj*.operator->())->*mem*

The function operator->() must return either a valid object pointer or an object
with an overloaded ->.

As mentioned before, operator->() can be defined only as a member function. A typical application of the overloaded -> is in creating *smart pointer*
objects — pointers that also perform additional work as programmed. To keep
track of how often customers access their bank accounts, for example, we can
define an AccountPtr class to access accounts:

```
#include "Account.h"

class AccountPtr
{  public:
        AccountPtr(unsigned n, double b)
        : ptr(new Account(n,b)), cnt(0) { }

        Account* operator -> ()    // overloaded ->
        { cnt++;
            return(ptr);
        }
    private:
        unsigned cnt;
        Account* ptr;
};
```

Then, we can use codes like

```
AccountPtr john(123456,640.75);
john->deposit(24.50);
cout << john->balance() << endl;
```

so that john.cnt keeps track of the number of times John's account has been
accessed.

There are four operators (=, [], (), ->) that must be overloaded as member
functions. Three of these have now been described. (See Section 4.5 for [].) The
function-call operator () is covered next.

8.6 ITERATORS

In OOP, objects hide their internal workings and therefore reduce software
complexity. But are there any downsides to this approach? Specifically, are
any operations made harder or impossible to perform without knowledge of
the internal structures? One is the operation of visiting every item contained

in an object. Consider, for example, the circular buffer class (Section 3.11). Suppose there is a need to inspect each character still in a Cirbuf object without consuming any character. One way to achieve this is to provide another public member function for the iteration:

```
int Cirbuf::next(char& c)
{    static int ind = -1;
     if ( ind == -1 ) ind = head;
     if ( ind == tail ) return(ind = -1);
     c = cb[ind++];
     ind = mod(ind);
     return(ind);
}
```

A static variable ind is used to remember the index of the last character examined. The reference parameter c receives the next character. A nonnegative value is returned unless the end is reached. With the next function, a typical iteration can be written as follows:

```
Cirbuf mybuf(64);
char c;
/*   ... */
while ( mybuf.next(c) > -1 )
     cout << c;
```

The example is an attempt to iterate over items inside an object without knowledge of internal structures. The method is of limited use because *one iteration must be completely finished before another begins* and *calls to next from different host objects interfere with one another.*

A more general solution involves defining an *iterator class*, a special friend class, to provide systematic access to internal elements of a target object. Consider a CirbufIterator:

```
class CirbufIterator              // friend class of Cirbuf
{    public:
         CirbufIterator(Cirbuf& buf);    // constructor
         int operator ()(char&);         // () as operator
     private:
         Cirbuf& b;                       // reference member
         int ind;                         // index
};
```

With this iterator class, iterations are performed as follows:

```
CirbufIterator next(mybuf);       // iterator object
while ( next(c) )                 // next.operator()(c)
     cout << c;
```

Also, multiple iterations can be ongoing without mutual interference. The constructor initializes the iterator:

```
CirbufIterator::CirbufIterator(Cirbuf& buf)
: b(buf), ind(buf.head)
{ }
```

The operator() deposits the next item in its reference parameter and returns nonzero unless the end is reached:

```
int CirbufIterator::operator ()(char& c)
{    if ( ind == b.tail ) return(0);      // end reached
     c = b.cb[ind++];                     // next char
     ind = b.mod(ind);
     return(1);                           // nonzero
}
```

The iterator friend class is an important technique for hiding internal structures of objects while still providing necessary access from the outside. In some situations, the iterator can also be given other functions to perform as it scans through all the elements. Such chores include removing, adding, or substituting an element.

Functors

The iterator is also an example of a *functor*, a function embodied in an object. Unlike ordinary classes that attach manipulation routines to data structures to build higher-level structures, a functor uses auxiliary data kept internally to help a specific operation. For the iterator, the operation involves *going through a set of elements systematically*, and the data member ind helps to perform the operation. In defining functors, the member operator() makes a functor object simulate a function, as in

```
next(c)
```

While this code looks like a call to a function next, it is actually invoking the "operator ()()" member in the object next.

8.7 \ USER-DEFINED TYPE CONVERSIONS

Standard conversions for built-in types are applied implicitly and explicitly according to well-defined rules (Section 3.12). Automatic type conversions significantly reduce the number of overloaded operators and functions needed. Without conversions, x *op* y must be supported by many definitions covering all possible/desirable type combinations. For example, after defining the two friend functions

```
Fraction Fraction::operator+(const Fraction&, int);   // (1)

Fraction Fraction::operator+(int, const Fraction&);   // (2)
```

we can add a Fraction object not only to an int but also to a short, an unsigned, a char, and so on — all thanks to implicit conversions.

C++ knows about conversions among built-in types and among inheritance-related objects (Section 7.8). Other conversions for class objects are undefined unless appropriate type-conversion rules are specified. These user-defined type conversions can then be applied by the compiler when needed. Thus, *user-defined type conversions* help extend implicit and explicit type conversions to class objects. Conversions to and from a class type are discussed separately next.

Outward Conversion

A type-conversion class member

```
operator type ();       // convert host to type
```

is used to specify conversion of the host object to data of the given *type*. For example to convert fractions to double, we add the following code to the class Fraction:

```
operator double()
{  return( double(num)/double(denom) );
}
```

With this member, a Fraction object fra can be explicitly converted to double using either of the two notations

```
double(fra)            // convert Fraction to double (3)
(double) fra           // same as double(fra)
```

Then, we can use codes like

```
Fraction fra(22, 7);
if ( x > 3.1416 && x < double(fra) )
/* ... */
```

where x is a variable of type double. Type-conversion members can also be invoked using normal object syntax. Therefore,

```
fra.operator double()
```

works as expected.

The explicit conversion request in x < double(fra) is not necessary all the time. It can be omitted, and the code

```
x < fra                    // implicit conversion of fra
```

works fine because implicit conversion turns fra into type double.

Inward Conversion

The mechanism for converting data of another type into an object of a class is a constructor that takes exactly one argument of the foreign type. For example, to convert an int into a Fraction, we simply add the following constructor:

```
Fraction::Fraction(int j)    // (4)
: num(j), denom(1) { }
```

The explicit conversion notation is exactly that of a constructor call:

```
int i = 7;
fra = fra * Fraction(i);
/* ... */
```

Of course, an inward conversion, such as int to Fraction, is also applied implicitly. In fact, with the conversion specified on line 4, the mixed-arithmetic functions (lines 1 and 2) can be omitted without adversely affecting the codes

```
fra + i              // works without (1), given (4)
i + fra              // works without (2), given (4)
```

which call the member operator+(fraction) by implicitly converting i to Fraction using the constructor (line 4). However, if the Fraction-to-double conversion (line 3) is also defined, ambiguity results.

Conversion Ambiguity

The expression fra + i becomes ambiguous when fra can be converted to double and i can be converted to Fraction. Since both conversions are possible and there is no mechanism to indicate which to do first, the expression results in a compile-time error.

When multiple conversions are possible in a given situation but there is only one exact match, then there is no ambiguity. Thus, adding a Fraction-to-float conversion does not make the expression double x = fra ambiguous. Sometimes, there is more than one exact match. Consider classes Xyz and Abc. If

Xyz defines an outward conversion to Abc and Abc defines an inward conversion from Xyz, then the code

```
Xyz var1;
Abc var2 = Abc(var1);      // ambiguous explicit conversion
Abc var2 = var1;           // ambiguous implicit conversion
```

is ambiguous because either Abc(Xyz) or Xyz::operator Abc() can be invoked. The classic-style cast

```
(Abc) var1                 // invokes Xyz::operator Abc()
```

is, however, not ambiguous because it is not confused with a constructor call.

Besides extending the applicability of operators and functions, user-defined conversions can also supply a convenient way for error handling as described next.

I/O Stream Conversions

User-defined conversion can be applied to report error or exception conditions. The common I/O stream conditions

```
while ( cin.get(c) )       // while input c successful (A)

while ( cin >> x )         // while input x successful (B)

ofstream ofile(/* ... */);
if ( ofstream )            // if open successful      (C)
```

involve logical tests on istream and ostream objects. When a class object is used in a logical expression, it must be converted either to some arithmetic type or to a pointer type. Thus, its class must define an unambiguous conversion to an arithmetic or a pointer type.

The I/O stream classes use a conversion generally defined as follows:

```
operator void*()           // convert to void pointer
{   if ( /* internal fail bits set */ )
        return NULL;
    else
        return this;
}
```

It is this kind of user-defined conversion that allows the convenient coding shown on lines A through C. To make this conversion work, in case the object being tested is declared const, simply add the following conversion code:

```
operator const void*() const;
```

It does the same thing. The void* conversion is better than arithmetic conversions because it tends not to introduce ambiguity. Consider the conventions presented here in establishing your own error-reporting objects.

8.8 ROBUST CLASSES

When writing C++ code, we may define a class so that it works only for a limited range of applications. Errors may occur when its objects are used for unintended purposes. For example, the Cirbuf class works well without a user-defined copy constructor as long as the copying of Cirbuf objects is avoided. Since there is no perceived need to initialize one Cirbuf object with another and since passing/returning circular buffers by reference is always easier and more efficient, copying is indeed easily avoided. However, if another programmer comes along and uses Cirbuf in unforeseen ways that involve copying, built-in copying will be invoked and lead to errors. Similar comments can be made for the assignment operator.

Calculator, CalcEng, and CalcFace (Section 5.5.1) are typical examples of limited-application classes. Their objects are not intended for passing as arguments or for assignment to one another. Adding special members for such purposes does not make sense for them.

A user-supplied destructor, a copy constructor, overloaded operators such as =, +, -, *, and / as well as the I/O operators >> and << are features that help user-defined types behave increasingly like basic types (int for example). Adding these features makes a class more *robust*.

For a class without pointer, reference, or const data members (Fraction for example), it is relatively easy to achieve robustness. In other situations, appropriately defined special members and operators must be supplied.

8.9 MANAGING FREE STORAGE

The special C++ operators new and delete make free storage convenient to use. Each performs a sequence of appropriate operations to complete its duty. For example, new computes the memory size needed, allocates the storage, and returns a pointer properly cast to the desired type. Auxiliary information is also kept to help delete later. To provide flexibility, special redefinable operator functions are used for actual allocation/deallocation of memory:

- new relies on the global (file scope) special operator function operator new() to allocate memory.
- delete uses the file scope operator delete() to deallocate storage.

For example, `new int` will eventually make the call

```
operator new( sizeof(int) )
```

which returns a `void*` pointer to the requested amount of space. More generally, the code

```
new(args) type
```

results in the call

```
operator new( sizeof(type), args)
```

activating the appropriate version of the overloaded `operator new()`.

The global `operator delete()` takes a `void*` argument and returns nothing. It cannot be overloaded. The expression `delete ptr` calls `operator delete( ptr )` to free space pointed to by `ptr`.

These special operator functions employ lower-level routines, such as `malloc` and `free`, or some other operating-system-supplied procedures to manage free storage.

However, the built-in operations can be inadequate or inefficient for certain applications. In such situations, you, the programmer, can take over the management of free storage entirely or partially:

- By redefining the functions `operator new()` and `operator delete()` at file scope, you take over memory management completely.
- By overloading `operator new()`, additional modes of free storage allocation can be supplied.
- By overloading `operator new()` and `operator delete()` as members, a class can assume its own memory management.

Global new and delete

Consider an application where two programs running concurrently must share memory to achieve a common task. To allocate and free storage in the shared memory area, library functions, such as `shmalloc` and `shfree`, are provided. The operators `new` and `delete` can work with shared memory by redefining `operator new()` and `operator delete()` globally:

```
void* operator new(size_t nb)    // global operator new()
{  void* p = shmalloc( nb );
   return( p );
}

void operator delete(void* p)    // global operator delete()
{  if ( p ) shfree( p );         // delete NULL is safe
}
```

With these definitions, memory management through the operators new and delete deals with shared memory.

In general, operator new() must have a first argument of type size_t, a typedef (usually unsigned) contained in stddef.h, and it must return a void* pointer to the space allocated. The signature and return type for operator delete() are fixed.

Redefining the global new and delete is often too drastic a measure to take. In many applications, controlling the way certain objects are dynamically allocated is enough.

Member new and delete

When new (delete) is applied to allocate (deallocate) an object in free storage, the compiler will use an appropriate member operator new() (operator delete()) if defined in the class. (Otherwise, the global instance will be invoked.) These special member functions are automatically declared static because they are called either before an object is formed or after it has been destroyed.

Suppose dynamic allocations of fractions are to be done in shared memory. The goal is achieved simply by defining these operators for the class Fraction:

```
void* Fraction::operator new(size_t nb)    // member operator new()
{  void* p = shmalloc( nb );
   return( p );
}

void Fraction::operator delete(void* p)    // member operator delete()
{  if ( p ) shfree( p );
}
```

Like the global operator, the member operator new() can be overloaded. The member operator delete() cannot be overloaded, but it may take either of two forms:

```
void ClassX::operator delete(void* p);            // case I
void ClassX::operator delete(void* p, int size);  // case II
```

For case II, the correct size of the space to be reclaimed will be passed as the second argument.

For allocating and deallocating an array of objects, however, the global, not the class-defined, operator new() and operator delete() are used.

Reusing Space of Unwanted Objects

Consider a while loop in which objects are generated with new and discarded with delete. It is more efficient in certain situations to overlay a new object on top of one to be discarded without reallocation of free storage. One way to achieve this effect is to define an instance of `operator new()` that returns a pointer to the space to be overlaid. For example,

```
void* Fraction::operator new(size_t nb, Fraction* p)
{  return (void*) p;
}
```

allows the writing of codes like

```
static Fraction fr;          // global variable
new(&fr) Fraction(i,j);      // reuse space
```

so that the space for `fr` can be reused.

8.10 \ POINTERS TO MEMBERS

Ordinary pointers represent the address of a variable, an array cell, or even a function. Their use makes programs more general. However, the pointer concept has yet to be applied to members of objects or classes. Two cases can be distinguished:

1. An ordinary pointer is used for an individual data member within a specific object or a static member.
2. An *offset pointer* is used to point to *a member in a class* that can be associated with any instance of the class.

These cases are discussed separately next.

8.10.1   Ordinary Pointers

Recall the `Employee` class

```
#define SIZE 32

#define ss_SIZE 12

class Employee
{  public:
      char     name[SIZE];      // full name
      char     ss[ss_SIZE];     // social security no.
      unsigned age;
      float    salary;
};
```

and the object newhire of this class. Pointers to members of newhire can be established as follows:

```
float *f_ptr = &newhire.salary;    // declare f_ptr
unsigned *u_ptr = &newhire.age;
char *str_ptr;                     // declare str_ptr
str_ptr = &a.ss;
```

Here the code is no different from that of ordinary pointers. In general, the address of any data member in a specific object can be assigned to (or initialize) an ordinary pointer variable.

8.10.2   Offset Pointers

For any object (for example, Fraction fr(3,5)), the member selection notations

```
fr.num
(&fr)->denom
```

always require explicitly stated member names (num and denom in this case). Is it possible or desirable to use something like

```
fr.var
```

where *var* is a *variable member name*? The expression produces either fr.num or fr.denum, depending on the value of *var*. The flexibility is desirable, and C++ supports this through the *offset pointer to member*, or *opm*, mechanism.

An opm is a special pointer that gives the offset, or distance, relative to the beginning address of an object. Given an object and an opm, a specific member in the object is located. C++ extends the syntax for ordinary pointers to opms. For example,

```
int Fraction::* nd_ptr;         // opm variable nd_ptr
nd_ptr = & Fraction::num;       // assigns opm value
nd_ptr = & Fraction::denom;     // assigns new opm value
```

Here an opm variable nd_ptr is established that can hold either of the two possible opm values. The offset pointer declaration is formed by simply prefixing the usual * with a class scope operator *ClassX*:: to indicate the class involved. Thus, an opm has both a type and a class name attribute. The opm nd_ptr can point to any Fraction member of type int. The value obtained by the notation

```
& Fraction::num               // produces offset value
```

is not a regular memory address but an offset (or relative position) from the beginning location of any Fraction object where the int member num would be stored. The general offset value notation is &ClassX::*member*. An offset is computed only if access to the member is allowed.

After being set to the offset of either num or denom, nd_ptr can then be used to access that member within any given Fraction object with the C++ operators .* and ->*, respectively:

```
Fraction r(1,2), s(6,15);      // two Fraction objects
int a = r.*nd_ptr;             // same as r.num or r.denom
Fraction *fp = & s;
a = fp->*nd_ptr;               // same as fp->num or fp->denom
```

In general,

- *obj*.*opm* dereferences the given *opm* in the given object *obj*.
- *obj_ptr*->*opm* dereferences the given *opm* in the object pointed to by *obj_ptr*.

To appreciate the flexibility afforded by the opm, consider a function prod that takes an opm pointer parameter:

```
int prod(Fraction fa[], int dim, int Fraction::* opm)
{   int ans=1, i;
    for ( i=0 ; i < dim ; i++ )
        ans *= fa[i].*opm;
    return(ans);
}
```

The function prod takes a fraction array fa, its dimension dim, and an opm as arguments. It computes the product of either the numerators or the denominators of the given fractions, depending on the value of opm.

A simple demo function illustrates how prod is called:

```
void opmdemo()
{  Fraction ar[] = {Fraction(1,2),        // array of fractions
                    Fraction(2,5),
                    Fraction(3,7)};
   int np = prod(ar, 3, & Fraction::num);   // friend access (1)
   int dp = prod(ar, 3, & Fraction::denom); // friend access (2)
   cout << np << endl;                      // prod of num = 6
   cout << dp << endl;                      // prod of denom = 70
}
```

The function opmdemo must be made a friend of Fraction before the offsets (lines 1 and 2) of the private members can be taken. Note that the function prod() does not need the friend status.

The discussion so far has focused on pointers to data members. Pointers to function members are also useful. Only opms, not ordinary function pointers, can point to regular member functions as described next.

8.10.3   Pointers to Member Functions

To appreciate the utility of pointers to member functions, consider the movement of a chess piece or a cursor on a game board displayed on a computer screen. A Board class keeps the board status and supplies member functions for making the basic moves. Let there be four basic moves: up, down, left, and right. There is also a general move function that combines a number of basic moves to achieve its goal.

To simplify things, a typedef is used:

```
class Board;
typedef void (Board::* B_MOVE)(unsigned);
B_MOVE opmf;   // offset pointer to member function
```

A B_MOVE variable opmf is an offset pointer to a member function. It can point to any member function of the class Board that takes one argument of type unsigned and returns nothing. Because a regular member function needs a host object for its invocation, it cannot be accessed through the ordinary function pointer mechanism.

The Board class looks something like this:

```
class Board
{ public:
      Board(unsigned x0, unsigned y0);
      void up    (unsigned n = 1);  // basic moves
      void down  (unsigned n = 1);
      void left  (unsigned n = 1);
      void right (unsigned n = 1);
      void move(int m, B_MOVE h, int n, B_MOVE v);
   /* other members */
   private:
      unsigned int x;            // current x position
      unsigned int y;            // current y position
   /* other members */
};
```

The general move function applies the specified basic moves a given number of times:

```
void Board::move(int m, B_MOVE h, int n, B_MOVE v)
{  (this->*h)(m);   // use opm to member function
   (this->*v)(n);
}
```

TABLE 8.2   **OFFSET POINTER TO MEMBER NOTATIONS**

NOTATION	DESCRIPTION
Type ClassX::* opmd;	Declares *opmd* data opm.
Type (ClassX::* opmf)(···);	Declares *opmf* function opm.
& ClassX::xyz	Gets offset value of member.
obj.*opmd	Dereferences *opmd* in *obj*.
objptr->*opmd	Dereferences *opmd* in **objptr*.
(obj.*opmf)(···)	Calls function in *obj* via *opmf*.
(objptr->*opmf)(···)	Calls function in **objptr* via *opmf*.

The parentheses in the expression (this->*h) are necessary to use it as a function. Here is a piece of code that uses the general move:

```
B_MOVE u = & Board::up;          // & cannot be omitted
B_MOVE d = & Board::down;
B_MOVE l = & Board::left;
B_MOVE r = & Board::right;
Board ab(7,10);
ab.move(2, u, 3, r);             // moves up 2 and right 3
```

For better encapsulation, it is possible in this case to make B_MOVE a typedef member and to define u, d, l, and r as properly initialized static members of Board.

Because opms are not ordinary pointers, they do not obey type-conversion rules for pointers. In particular, an opm cannot be converted to a void*. The offset pointer to member notations are summarized in Table 8.2.

Pointers to Static Members

Pointers to static data or function members are ordinary pointers, not opms. Therefore, the opm notations are not used for static members. The address-of (&) and value-of (*) operators work with normal pointer syntax for pointers to static members.

8.11 \ UNIONS

8.11.1   Basic Concepts

An int variable holds integer values, and a double variable holds double data. Is it possible or desirable for a variable to hold one type of value at certain times and other types of values at other times? Yes, and a union variable has exactly this property. A union is declared with the same syntax as a class. Once a *union tag* is established, it can be used to define objects of that type. The declaration

```
union IntDouble
{       int    ival;      // public members
        double dval;
}
```

creates the union tag IntDouble, which can be used in

```
IntDouble x;
```

to declare a union variable x, which can hold *either* int *or* double values:

```
x.ival = 9;       // x as int variable
x.dval = 4.321;   // x as double var, overwrites int value
```

In effect, a union object is a struct object that stores all its data members at the same location (offset zero relative to the beginning of the object). A union object is given enough space to hold the largest of its data members. Thus, a union object holds only one type of value at a time. The member notations x.dval and x.ival are used not to get different offsets but to get different interpretations of data stored at the same location. Hence, the compiler treats x.ival as an int variable and x.dval as a double even though both occupy the same memory address. It is your responsibility to access a union object correctly to retrieve the most recently assigned value.

Consider dividing one integer by another. To make things interesting, let's define a function that returns either an integer or a double, depending on whether the division is even:

```
IntDouble divide(int a, int b, int& evenflag)
{    IntDouble ans;                   // union object
     if ( (evenflag = !(a % b)) )     // even division
         ans.ival = a/b;             // ans is int
     else                            // otherwise
         ans.dval = a/double(b);     // ans is double
     return(ans);
}
```

The reference parameter evenflag is set correctly so that a calling function of divide can examine its value to determine whether an int or a double has been returned. Thus, we can write a test function as follows:

```
void test(int a, int b)
{    int flag;
     IntDouble x = divide(a,b,flag);
     cout << a << '/' << b << " = ";
```

```
        if ( flag )
            cout << x.ival << "\n";
        else
            cout << x.dval << "\n";
}
```

Then, when we run the program, the calls

```
test(8, 4);
test(2, 3);
```

should produce the following output:

```
8/4 = 2
2/3 = 0.666667
```

Union objects can occur in arrays and other objects just as class objects can. The notations for a union are the same as for a struct. In fact, a union could be redefined as a struct and used without change. The only difference would be the space needed; a union uses less storage because all members are stored at the same location.

Because of the nature of a union, not all types of classes can be union members. In particular, any class with a constructor, destructor, or user-defined assignment operator cannot be a union member.

The artificial example here illustrates the basic concepts of unions. Let's now examine a few actual applications of unions.

8.11.2   Heterogeneous Data Structures

The primary purpose of a union is to create *heterogeneous* structures — that is, data whose elements are not of the same type. This ability allows you to use, for example, either an array of numbers and strings or a list of various types of items.

Consider an array of grades for a student's academic record in a course. Each grade can be either a percentage (a score out of 100) or a letter grade. We first introduce a union PorL:

```
union PorL
{    short score;     // percent grade
     char  letter;    // letter grade
};
```

We then define a class Grade:

```
class Grade
{ public:
     enum G_Type {PERCENT, LETTER};
```

```
    unsigned short score();         // retrieve score
    void score(unsigned short);     // set score
    char letter();                  // retrieve letter grade
    void letter(char);              // set letter grade
    G_type type() { return t; }
  private:
    G_Type  t;        // type info
    PorL    grade;    // union object
};
```

We now create an array of grades:

```
Grade mary[10];         // array of 10 Grade objects
mary[0].score(89);      // percent score
mary[1].letter('A');    // letter grade
```

We use the type flag t to maintain consistency of grade interpretation:

```
unsigned short Grade::score()
{   assert( t == PERCENT );  // insist on percent type
    return grade.score;
}
```

```
void Grade::score(unsigned short g)
{   t = PERCENT;            // set grade type flag
    grade.score = g;
}
```

With this kind of public interface, the union value is never interpreted incorrectly.

Now let's look at an example where the union mechanism is used to build nested lists. Consider lists of the form

```
(A B C D E)
((A B) C (D E))
((A (B C)) (D E))
```

These are nested lists of characters. A *nested list* of characters is a list containing zero or more characters and/or nested lists. Therefore, items in a nested list are objects of type NItem:

```
class NItem
{   friend class NList;
  private:
    enum Boolean {LIST, CHAR};
    union
    {   char    ch;
        NItem*  lis;
```

```
     };                                  // anonymous union
     Boolean l_c;                        // LIST or CHAR indicator
     NItem* next;
     NItem(char c = '\0', NItem* ptr = NULL)
       : l_c(CHAR), ch(c), next(ptr) { }    // constructor
     NItem(NItem* l = NULL, NItem* ptr = NULL)
       : l_c(LIST), lis(l), next(ptr) { }    // constructor
};
```

As you can see, NItem is a modification of the ListCell class discussed before
(Section 5.9). The value cell in NItem now becomes a union storing either a single
character or a NItem* pointer. Correct interpretation of the union is ensured
through proper use of the Boolean indicator l_c.

If a union is given neither a tag nor a variable to declare, then it is an *anonymous union*. Member names in an anonymous union surface to its enclosing
scope and can be used directly there. Thus, for the NItem example, the code
fragment

```
NItem a('F');
if ( a.l_c == NItem::CHAR ) cout << a.ch;
```

shows direct access of the union member ch. Anonymous unions cannot have
nonpublic members or member functions.

Actual nested lists are objects of the friend class NList whose definition is
outlined here:

```
class NList
{ public:
     NList() : head(NULL) { }            // empty list constructor
     NList(char c)                       // list with first cell
       : head (new NItem(c,NULL)) { }
     int put_on(char c);                 // put on a char          (1)
     int put_on(NList& c);               // put on a nested list   (2)
     void display(NItem* p, int r = 0);  // display from p to end (3)
     void display() { display(head); }   // display whole list
     /*   many others not shown   */
  private:
     NItem* head;                        // first cell of list
     void free();                        // free all cells
};
```

The second version of the member function put_on (line 2) helps construct
nested lists:

```
int NList::put_on(NList& nl)
{  NItem* tmp = new NItem(nl.head, head);
      if ( tmp )
```

```
        { head = tmp;
            return(0);
        }
        else return(-1); // failed
}
```

It puts the given nested list nl at the beginning of the host object. Other member functions may provide insertion at other places in a list.

The display function is recursive in order to process nested sublists. It can also be given a second argument to control the display of a final NEWLINE:

```
void NList::display(NItem* p, int r /* = 0 */)
{   cout << "(";
    while ( p )
    {   if ( p->l_c == NItem::CHAR )
            cout << p->ch;       // access union member
        else
            display(p->lis, 1); // recursive call
        if ( p = p->next ) cout << " ";
    }
    cout << ")";
    if (r == 0 ) cout << "\n";  // final NEWLINE
}
```

Only a few functions are shown here to give you the flavor of dealing with nested lists. A complete nested list class is much more complicated. However, enough is given here so that you can run a simple test program:

```
int main()
{ NList aa('A'), bb('B'), cd('D');
        cd.put_on('C');
        bb.put_on(cd);
        aa.put_on(bb);
        aa.display();      // ((((C D) B) A)
        return(0);
}
```

The union saves space by storing different data members at the same location. In addition to the union, C++ offers another way to save space used in a program as explained next.

8.11.3   Bit-Packing Members

A class member can be declared to occupy a few bits in a single word. This ability allows you to pack information more tightly for certain applications.

FIGURE 8.1   **BIT FIELD MEMBERS**

31	30	29	24	23	16	15	0
← q →		← rgn →		← div →		← dept →	

Such members are known as *bit fields* and are either signed or unsigned integer types with the number of bits specified after a colon (:).

For example, consider a departmental quarterly report class. It can have, among others, four bit fields:

```
typedef unsigned int Bit;

Bit dept  : 16; // department code, lower 16 bits
Bit  div  :  8; // division id, next 8 bits
Bit  rgn  :  6; // region designation, next 6 bits
Bit   q   :  2; // 1st, 2nd, 3rd, or 4th quarter, next 2 bits
```

When given consecutively, these four members fit into a 32-bit word (Figure 8.1). Bit field members, except for storage, are no different from other data members of a class.

Enough said about space-saving mechanisms. What about saving the programmer's time? Is this not the most costly aspect of today's software business? Encapsulation should be used to hide low-level details such as union and bit-field to make a program easier to handle.

8.12 \ NESTED AND LOCAL CLASSES

When a class is defined within the scope of another class, then it is a *nested class*. When a class is defined inside a function or a block, then it is a *local class*.

A local class is known only to its local scope, and all its functions must be defined within the class itself. Normally, all members of a local class are public. Static members are not permitted; neither are references to automatic variables. The local class is seldom used or required.

A nested class, however, is sometimes useful as an encapsulation mechanism. Take the reference string class Refstr discussed in Section 8.3 for example. The auxiliary class Cell can alternatively be enclosed within Refstr as a nested class. One approach places the Cell class definition "as is" in the public part of Refstr. This works fine. Another approach involves making all Cell members public and nesting the code in the private section of Refstr — in which case,

Refstr does not have to be a friend class to Cell anymore. Here is the modified Refstr using the latter approach:

```
///////    Refstr.h    ///////
#include<iostream.h>
#include<string.h>

class Refstr
{ public:
      Refstr(char *str/* = ""*/);              // constructor
      Refstr(const Refstr& s);                 // copy constructor
      Refstr& operator =(const Refstr& s);     // assignment
      int cmp(const Refstr& s) const;
      void display();
      ~Refstr();
   private:
      class Cell                               // nested class
      { public:
            Cell( char *s );
            char *str;
            unsigned cnt;
            ~Cell() { cout << "~Cell" << endl; delete [] str; }
      };
      Cell *ptr;   // Cell must be seen before
};
```

These modifications are all that you need for the Refstr class to work as before.

The only effect of class nesting is that a class is defined in the name scope of another class. The enclosing class does not have any automatic special-access privilege to members of a nested class.

Consider class nesting when the only client of a class is its enclosing class (and possibly classes derived from the enclosing class). Now where and how can member functions of the nested Cell be defined? The functions are still defined at file scope (in Refstr.C), but the member names must be qualified to be inside Refstr. Thus, the constructor Cell::Cell becomes

```
Refstr::Cell::Cell( char *s )      // extended class scope operator
{    str = new char[strlen(s)+ 1];
     strcpy(str, s);
     cnt = 1;
}
```

Note that the only change is the added prefix Refstr:: to the function name. The extended class scope operator can be used to access members of a nested class (subject to access control) from the outside.

An identifier used but not defined in a nested class is looked for first in its enclosing classes and then in file scope. Scope operators can be used to access identifiers specifically.

8.13 \ SUMMARY

In C++, most operations on objects must be programmed explicitly, often through operator overloading. With the exception of four operators, all can be given user-supplied meanings by defining operator functions.

You have the choice of implementing an operator function as a member or a nonmember. When one (the left) or both operands are objects, the operator invokes the corresponding operator function (either the member or the non-member implementation). When both exist within the same scope, argument matching is used to select the correct operator function.

Most operators follow the same overloading rules; =, [], (), and -> can only be overloaded by members. Also a set of useful conventions may be followed to overload the I/O operators >> and <<. Reference counting is a novel approach to dynamic memory management that also involves the overloading of =.

To enhance information hiding, you can use iterator objects for systematic access to components of an object. An iterator exemplifies a functor, an object representing operations rather than data. The operator () can make a functor look like a function in usage. By adding appropriate operators and other special members, you can make a class more robust and its objects behave almost like basic types.

Overloading `new` and `delete` is different from overloading other operators. Only part of their operations can be modified through defining global or class scope operators (`operator new()` and `operator delete()`). By defining these special operator functions, you control free store management.

Implicit and explicit type conversions can be extended for objects by class-defined type conversion rules. User-defined type conversion cuts down on the number of functions necessary to cover different argument type combinations. It can also be used for error reporting as demonstrated by the I/O stream class.

An ordinary pointer is used for a static member or a data member in a single object because there is a unique memory address where the member is stored. Offset pointers (opms), on the other hand, can point to class members within any instance of the class. An opm specifies the location of a member relative to the beginning address of an object. Opms provide the ability to use variables and formal parameters whose values are names of class members. Thus, a program is not limited to explicitly stated member names. The operator `&ClassX::` returns offset values and the operators `.*` and `->*` dereference opm variables.

A union is a special struct that stores all its members at the same location in the object. Therefore, a union object requires just enough room to store the largest data member, thereby saving space. Member functions and flags can be used to make sure that union members are set and retrieved consistently. Because the union provides a variable of multiple types, it is useful in constructing heterogeneous structures. Bit-field members help information packing at the bit level.

Although not often used, nested and local classes can help information hiding and program encapsulation.

EXERCISES

1. Consider the member versus nonmember implementation of overloaded operators. Both implementations are shown for Fraction += in Section 8.1. Suppose both are included in a program. Confirm that the program can be compiled without error. Would f1 += f2 still work? If not, how do you invoke each of the two operator functions?

2. Is it possible to overload >> or << for I/O as member functions in a class such as Fraction? Why?

3. Modify the Fraction class by adding read and display and overloading >> and << as suggested in Section 8.2. Write a test program to read a file of fractions and display them to verify the results.

4. Define += and *= for fractions. Also, make +, -, *, and / work as binary operators for mixed int and Fraction operands.

5. Modify the display member for the class Poly. Add the member read and the operators << and >> for Poly objects.

6. As indicated in Section 8.10.3, modify the Board class to contain the type B_MOVE and the appropriately initialized static members u, d, l, and r. With these modifications, show what a call to move now looks like.

7. Consider the unary address-of operator & applied to class member functions. Can it be applied to a constructor? A destructor? An overloaded member function? Explain how it works.

8. Define a class Amount that represents nonnegative amounts expressed in double. Make sure appropriate conversion is defined so that Amount objects can be used just like a double.

9. Add error indication for the CalcEng object through user-defined type conversion to allow such tests as if (*engine*).

10. A member function always has the host object as an implicit argument. Do automatic type conversions apply to this argument? What implications can you think of as a result?

11. Add to the nested list class NList a member function depth that returns the maximum level of nesting in an NList object.

12. Derive a generic binary tree class BTree from a generic nested list class ArbNList.

13. Consider user-defined free storage management (Section 8.9). If you define the two-argument

    ```
    void* Fraction::operator new(size_t nb, Fraction* p);
    ```

    without also defining the one-argument

    ```
    void* Fraction::operator new(size_t nb);
    ```

    what would happen? Why?

14. Verify that if a class defines operator void*() correctly as suggested in Section 8.7, then conditions if (*obj*) and if (! *obj*) both work as expected.

OOP TECHNIQUES

This chapter focuses on two major topics: multiple inheritance and polymorphism. Multiple inheritance makes derivation from multiple base classes possible and is effective in many situations. The practical use of multiple inheritance, the problem of base-class duplication, and the C++ countermeasure, the *virtual base* (shared base), are clearly described here.

There is much more to object-oriented programming than establishing and deriving individual classes and objects, although these are important basic activities. At a higher level, OOP involves programming and manipulating objects as "black boxes"—that is, making uniform interfaces for related objects and establishing generic programs for all *plug-compatible* objects. These topics are central to OOP and require a combination of C++ features.

By establishing common interfaces, related objects can be treated as black boxes that are manipulated the same way from the outside. Thus, these black boxes become interchangeable parts that are pluggable into another program. The ability to work with different black-box objects is generally known as *polymorphism*. The C++ *virtual function* is the mechanism that plays a key role in providing polymorphism, and it is described in detail. The practical use of plug compatibility is demonstrated by several examples.

A uniform public interface of plug-compatible objects takes careful planning. Designing base classes for inheritance is important. The C++ *abstract base class* facilitates the extraction of common operations and the preplanning of uniform interfaces. An ordered-sequence class is presented to serve as a schematic for building objects that can store, order, and retrieve arbitrary elements simply and efficiently. Then, the generic ordered-sequence object is applied to handle ordered lines in text files.

Finally, the concept of an *object-family class*, one whose objects represent different but related quantities, is introduced. Such classes encapsulate polymorphic objects and aid in writing generic routines. A Number object-family class whose instances represent fractions, integers, and other types of numbers illustratesO this technique.

9.1 \ MULTIPLE INHERITANCE

We have already seen several examples of single inheritance deriving from just one direct base class. Some situations call for more than one base class. Multiple inheritance is a convenient way to define new objects that are combinations of existing types. For example, a TeachingAssistant can be derived from an Instructor and a Student class; MotorCycle from MotorVehicle and Bicycle; and IceCream from DairyProduct, Dessert, and FrozenFood. Although not as frequently used as its single-base counterpart, multiple inheritance provides a powerful dimension to OOP for both code reuse and program organization.

The easiest way to understand multiple inheritance is by studying an example. So, let's apply multiple inheritance to derive a joint free checking account JtFrChecking from the existing JointAccount and FreeChecking, each of which happens to be already derived from the basic Account class:

```
///////   File JtFrChecking.h   ///////
#include "FreeChecking.h"
#include "JointAccount.h"

class JtFrChecking                         // multiple inheritance
: public JointAccount, public FreeChecking // order insignificant
{ public:
   JtFrChecking() { }                      // default constructor
   JtFrChecking(unsigned n, double b,      // constructor
         char* owner, char* jowner);
};
///////   End file JtFrChecking.h   ///////
```

Note that including the header files and defining the constructor do not take much work and we easily obtain a new class. We now establish a joint, free checking account:

```
JtFrChecking peter_lucy(23456, 750.0, "034-55-1111", "052-44-7777");
```

But there is a slight complication: Both the JointAccount and the FreeChecking base objects contain an Account object (Figure 9.1). This means that peter_lucy contains two instances of Account. The duplication is legal but often unnecessary

FIGURE 9.1   NONVIRTUAL MULTIPLE INHERITANCE

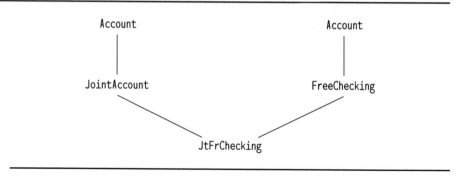

or even unworkable as is the case here. Certainly, an account with two different balances is not right.

9.1.1   Shared Bases

The C++ *virtual base* is the mechanism that is designed for the purpose of avoiding duplication of base objects. Simply declare virtual the base class whose instance should not be duplicated within a derived object. For JtFrChecking, we modify the declarations of JointAccount and FreeChecking as follows:

```
class JointAccount : public virtual Account     // (1)
{   /* class body as before */   };

class FreeChecking : public virtual Account     // (2)
{   /* class body as before */   };
```

The term *virtual base*, although less intuitive than *common base* or *shared base*, means exactly that. In the derived object JtFrChecking, there would be just one

FIGURE 9.2   VIRTUAL MULTIPLE INHERITANCE

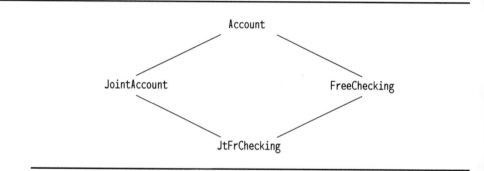

Account object common to (shared by) the two base objects JointAccount and FreeChecking (Figure 9.2). If both virtual and nonvirtual instances of a base class exist (omitting the keyword virtual from line 2 but not from line 1 for example), then there is a unique shared virtual instance plus other nonshared instances.

Since a virtual-base object (Account for example) is shared, should it be initialized by one of the derived class (JointAccount or FreeChecking)? Or should each of the immediate derived classes perform its initialization as programmed by the following code?

```
FreeChecking::FreeChecking
(unsigned n, double b, char* owner)
:  Account(n, b, owner),              // init virtual base (1)
     free(b >= min_bal)               // init-list
{ }
```

```
JointAccount::JointAccount
(unsigned n, double b, char* owner, char* jowner)
: Account(n, b, owner)               // init virtual base (2)
{   strncpy(jss, jowner, SS_LEN); }
```

The answer is none of the above. C++ actually shifts the duty of initializing a virtual-base object to the *most derived class*, the class at the end of the derivation chain in question. Thus, the JtFrChecking constructor

```
///////   File JtFrChecking.C   ///////
#include "JtFrChecking.h"
```

```
JtFrChecking::JtFrChecking
(unsigned n, double b, char* owner, char* jowner)
:  Account(n, b, owner),                  // init virtual base (3)
     JointAccount(n, b, owner, jowner),   // (4)
     FreeChecking(n, b, owner)            // (5)
{ }
```

```
///////   End of JtFrChecking.C   ///////
```

should contain a call to the Account constructor (line 3). If the explicit call is not given (line 3), the default Account constructor will be called to initialize the virtual-base object. Other initializations (lines 1 and 2) are skipped entirely. Specifically, the calls on lines 4 and 5 will skip their respective Account calls. Later, if a class is derived based on JtFrChecking, then it takes over the initialization of the virtual base Account.

To test the joint free checking account, use the following simple main program:

```
int main()
{    JtFrChecking peter_lucy(23456, 750.0, 034-55-1111, 052-44-7777);
     cout << peter_lucy.balance() << endl;    // initial balance
     peter_lucy.withdraw(400);
     cout << peter_lucy.balance() << endl;    // after withdrawal
     peter_lucy.deposit(300);
     cout << peter_lucy.balance() << endl;    // after deposit
     peter_lucy.fee();
     cout << peter_lucy.balance() << endl;    // after service fee
}
```

Running this program produces the following output:

```
750
350
650
632
```

9.1.2   Base-Member Access under Virtual Derivation

Access to members in a virtual-base object obeys the same public-private derivation rules as given before (Section 7.4). Making the base object unique actually reduces possibilities for access ambiguity. The call peter_lucy.balance() would be ambiguous if Account were not a virtual base because the compiler could not choose between JointAccount::balance() and FreeChecking::balance(). With Account as a virtual base, these versions of balance() become the same, thus eliminating the ambiguity. The same can be said about deposit() in the object peter_lucy.

The situation for peter_lucy.withdraw() is slightly different: It is redefined in the class FreeChecking but not in JointAccount. Thus, the call accesses the version defined in FreeChecking whether or not Account is made a virtual base.

Through multiple inheritance with a virtual base, we can access a unique base member via different routes: Getting to Account::balance() either through JointAccount or FreeChecking is one example. What if these routes involve different types of derivation that affect access permissions? For example, what if Account is a private base of JointAccount? In C++, if at least one of the multiple routes to arrive at the unique member is permissible, then access is granted.

9.1.3   Virtual-Base Object Initialization

A virtual-base object is not stored in a section of contiguous memory inside the derived object as are regular-base objects. It is stored independently, and its address is included in a derived object. This arrangement allows a virtual-base object to be easily shared by multiple subobjects within a derived object.

When a derived object is initialized, immediate virtual-base objects are initialized before other virtual-base objects. Other constructors are called in well-understood order after all virtual objects have been initialized. Destructor calls are always carried out in the reverse order of constructor calls.

9.2 \ PROGRAMMING WITH PLUG-COMPATIBLE OBJECTS

One enormous advantage of OOP is the ability to treat objects as "black boxes" and to deal with them only through their interfaces. If a set of similar or related black boxes supports a common interface, then we can write codes to work on all boxes without change.

The concept of building and operating on *plug-compatible* objects is commonplace in daily life. Consider cars for example. Having learned to drive one car, you can drive most other cars without changing your method of driving. Many different types of cars become interchangeable as far as you are concerned. The fact that one car's accelerator controls the fuel injection and another the carburetor does not affect the way you drive.

How C++ builds plug-compatible objects (cars) and defines *polymorphic* operations (driving) on them is our focus here. To illustrate this important technique, we will make bank accounts plug-compatible for certain well-defined operations such as transferring funds between accounts and producing a list of accounts.

9.2.1   Compatible Types and Polymorphism

By putting all different accounts in a public derivation hierarchy rooted at the base class Account, the different accounts become compatible types through class derivation. Because the derived types are considered a kind of Account, there is at least a chance of making them interchangeable. Since there already are a few types of account objects thus derived, the task at hand is simplified.

To make interchangeable use meaningful, these different account objects must support *either a uniform public interface or certain critical common operations*. To a degree, this has been done also: Account, FreeChecking, JointAccount, and JtFrChecking all support the same prototypes for balance(), deposit(), and

FIGURE 9.3   POLYMORPHISM AND PLUG-COMPATIBLE OBJECTS

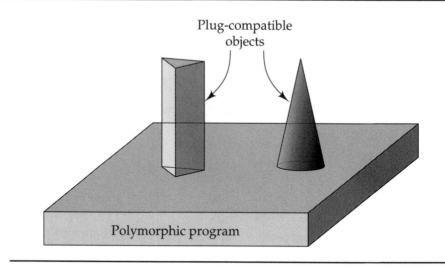

Polymorphic program

withdraw(). Therefore, a piece of code that uses only the uniform interface has a chance to work for all these types of account objects.

Now we can write a transfer function to work on all different account types:

```
int transfer(float amt, Account& from, Account& to)
{    int flag = from.withdraw(amt);
     if ( flag != -1 )
          to.deposit(amt);
     return(flag);
}
```

The ability for the same program to work for more than one type of object is known as *polymorphism* (Figure 9.3). Consider transfer() for example. Each of the parameters from and to can receive multiple types of account objects (Account, JointAccount, FreeChecking, and so on) instead of just one fixed type (*monomorphism*). The correct transfer procedure is performed by using the proper withdraw() and deposit() operations in different types of accounts.

Two key techniques help the polymorphic transfer achieve plug compatibility:

1. *Using base-type pointer or reference parameters:* Here from and to are base references, so accounts of any type can be passed into transfer(). This is a result of type compatibility under inheritance (Section 7.8).

2. *Using only the uniform public interface:* Here withdraw() and deposit() are uniform, so the code makes sense for all different types of accounts.

But there is one difficulty: An actual argument — say, of type FreeChecking — referenced through the formal parameter from, which is of type Account&, causes the code from.withdraw(amt) to perform

from.Account::withdraw(amt)

rather than the desired

from.FreeChecking::withdraw(amt)

The reason is that the type of the parameter from is used at compile time to determine which class member to invoke. Because the type of from is Account&, from.withdraw() naturally invokes the member in Account, which is very disappointing indeed. The true type of the argument referenced by from would lead to the *correct* member function, but that true type is not known at compile time.

This difficulty must be overcome before a *polymorphic* function, such as transfer(), can work correctly on plug-compatible objects. Any solution must somehow make the code

from.withdraw()

use the actual type of the argument referenced by from at run time.

9.2.2   Virtual Functions

The C++ *virtual function* is the mechanism that allows the designation of certain member functions as virtual to enable special run-time handling of their invocations*.

If a virtual function is invoked through a public base reference or pointer, then the actual type of the object, not that of the reference or pointer, is used to determine which one of a group of compatible virtual functions to call. Suppose a FreeChecking object fc is passed to the public base reference from of the transfer function. The call from.withdraw(amt) would indeed become fc.withdraw(amt) if withdraw() has been designated virtual. Similar effects take place if &fc is passed to an Account* pointer. However, the virtual mechanism cannot work if fc is passed by value to a parameter of type Account.

Thus, a virtual function really represents a group of functions, with identical prototypes, in a derivation hierarchy. A call to a virtual function is done through a base reference or pointer and treated specially at run time (Figure 9.4). Unlike regular functions, a virtual function call involves selecting one in a group of virtual functions to invoke, according to the actual host-object type at run time.

---

*Do not confuse virtual functions with virtual (shared) bases. Unfortunately, the same keyword is used for both purposes.

FIGURE 9.4   DYNAMIC VIRTUAL FUNCTION SELECTION

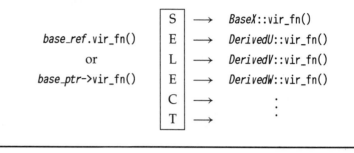

Now let's consider how virtual functions are declared and used. To make plug-compatible objects work, all uniform interface functions should be virtual. By declaring a base prototype virtual, any member function with the same prototype in a derived class (direct or indirect) is also automatically virtual and put in the same group of virtual functions. Thus, to make plug-compatible accounts, we revise the base class Account as follows:

```
#include <iostream.h>

class Account
{ public:
      Account() {}
      Account(unsigned n, double b,
              char* ss);
      virtual void deposit(double amt);
      virtual int withdraw(double amt);
      virtual double balance() const;
      virtual void display(ostream& out = cout) const;       // (1)
      /* other public members */
  protected:
      enum {SS_LEN = 12};
      unsigned  acct_no;
      char      ss[SS_LEN];
  private:
      /* other members */
      double    acct_bal;
};
```

Declared virtual are the three existing interface functions deposit(), withdraw(), and balance() as well as a new function display(). As a result, there are four distinct virtual function groups here. These are the only changes to Account. The corresponding interface functions, if any, in the derived account classes are now automatically virtual and included in their respective groups. While it is not necessary to add the virtual keyword to their declarations, there is no harm in doing so.

For Account, we implement the virtual display() function as follows:

```
// in Account.C

void Account::display(ostream& out /* = cout */) const
{   out << "Account No: " << acct_no << "\n"
        << "Owner SS:   " << ss << "\n"
        << "Balance:    " << acct_bal << endl;
}
```

Once given (line 1), the virtual keyword need not be repeated when defining the function. Here are some counterparts of Account::display() in derived accounts:

```
void JointAccount::display(ostream& out /* = cout */) const
{   out << "Account No:     " << acct_no << "\n"
        << "Owner SS:       " << ss << "\n"
        << "Joint Owner SS: " << jss << "\n"
        << "Balance:        " << balance() << endl;
}


void FreeChecking::display(ostream& out /* = cout */) const
{   out << "Free Checking Account\n";
    Account::display();                      // inherited member (2)
}


void JtFrChecking::display(ostream& out /* = cout */) const
{   out << "Free Checking Account\n";
    JointAccount::display();                 // inherited member (3)
}
```

Each display function serves the need of its class. Clearly, they all have the same function prototype. Some enlist the help of inherited functions (lines 2 and 3).

To test the plug-compatible account objects, construct a simple test program as follows:

```
#include <iostream.h>
#include "acc.h"

// put the transfer function here

void show(Account* a[], int n)
{   for (int i=0; i < n; i++)
    {   a[i]->display();
```

```
        cout << endl;
    }
}

int main()
{   JtFrChecking jfc(23456, 750.0, "025-72-5555", "024-88-3333");
    JointAccount ja(55123, 1600.0, "043-12-4444", "034-21-2222");
    FreeChecking fc(66432,  600.0, "098-02-1111");
    transfer(300, fc, jfc);      // (4)
    fc.fee();
    transfer(200, ja, fc);       // (5)
    Account* acnt[3];
    acnt[0] = &jfc;
    acnt[1] = &ja;
    acnt[2] = &fc;
    show(acnt, 3);               // (6)
}
```

Here the header file acc.h includes all headers for the Account class hierarchy.
Three different account objects jfc, ja, and fc are used to demonstrate plug
compatibility. The function transfer is a polymorphic procedure that works
for all types of accounts (lines 4 and 5). The function show is another polymorphic procedure that displays an array of pointers to various types of accounts
(line 6). Such procedures will work for all existing types of accounts and any
additional types of accounts established in the future. As long as the public
interface is preserved, the procedures will work without modification.

Running this program produces the following output:

```
Free Checking Account
Account No:    23456
Owner SS:      025-72-5555
Joint Owner SS: 024-88-3333
Balance:       1050

Account No:    55123
Owner SS:      043-12-4444
Joint Owner SS: 034-21-2222
Balance:       1400

Free Checking Account
Account No: 66432
Owner SS:   098-02-1111
Balance:    482
```

We have seen the power of plug compatibility and how this OOP technique
works. And, it works in many situations. We can make the Calculator class,

for instance, polymorphic by using a CalcEng pointer instead of a CalcEng object directly. We can then use compatible derived compute engines in a Calculator object and create different calculator models by installing different engines inside.

9.2.3   Keys to Plug Compatibility

Programming with plug-compatible objects is achieved by a combination of OOP mechanisms and techniques. Its key ingredients, which represent the essence of OOP, are as follows:

1. *Interchangeable objects:* It must be possible to represent a collection of similar objects that are interchangeable under certain operations. Such objects usually have an is-a relationship and can be organized into a public derivation hierarchy under C++.

2. *Uniform public interfaces:* The interchangeable objects must have certain identical public interfaces to allow the same polymorphic procedure to work on all of them. This is achieved by maintaining a set of public interface functions with uniform prototypes throughout the class hierarchy.

3. *Polymorphic parameters:* A polymorphic function that operates on the interchangeable object must declare formal parameters capable of receiving arguments of any plug-compatible type. The parameters should be public base reference or pointer types.

4. *Dynamic access of interchangeable operations:* By declaring the uniform interface functions virtual, the correct derived member function can be accessed through a polymorphic parameter. Declaring internal functions virtual allows derived classes to supply appropriate internal routines later.

As a further illustration, consider overloading the operator << for displaying any plug-compatible account:

```
ostream& operator <<(ostream& os, Account& a)
{    a.display(os);
     return(os);
}
```

Notice how this short function works to allow output of any type of account object acnt_obj to any output stream by using the following deceptively simple code:

```
out << acnt_obj;
```

9.3 \ Planning Uniform Public Interfaces

Section 9.2 showed us how to write polymorphic codes that work for all plug-compatible objects. One key aspect is maintaining a consistent set of public interfaces for the derived classes, which is the main topic here.

A uniform public interface does not happen all by itself. It takes careful analysis, planning, and skillful coding. It often involves trial and error before a final design emerges. In C++, achieving uniform interfaces involves the following strategy:

- Begin with a desire to have a certain set of common operations defined for a collection of related objects.
- Design, in the base class, a set of virtual function prototypes to be followed by all derived classes. The set defines a uniform public interface and, often, interactions between the base and derived classes. The goal is to make the desired common operations possible on the planned set of plug-compatible objects.
- Supply, in the base class, definitions for all or just some of the virtual functions. Supply missing definitions and redefine others in derived classes.

Thus, we can use the base class and its set of virtual functions to preplan derived classes. The base class serves both as a source of derivation and as a schematic for building derived classes.

9.3.1   Abstract Base Class: Ordered Sequences

Consider items such as integers, names, dates, foreign exchange rates, or any other objects that can be ordered into a linear sequence for easy manipulation and retrieval. Imagine creating objects representing such ordered sequences. An ordered-sequence object contains a number of elements and presents an external view of these elements organized in linear order. The external view is supported by the ability to refer to each element through an associated index $(0, 1, 2, \ldots)$.

Externally, an ordered sequence is characterized by the following public operations:

- Adding an element.
- Removing an element.
- Finding the index of an element by key.
- Retrieving an element by indexing.
- Detecting the length of the ordered sequence.

These operations should be part of the public interface for any type of ordered sequence. Internally, an ordered sequence requires at least the following operations:

- Effectively sorting elements into order.
- Efficiently retrieving elements.

This analysis reveals that different ordered sequences have a great deal in common. The challenge is to extract the commonalities and form a single class from which each specific ordered sequence can inherit. If we let OrderedSeq be such a base class, then OrderedSeq must deal with elements and keys of unknown type. A derived class will specialize the element type and the key, if any.

More analysis and our experience with generic sorting (Section 4.10) soon lead us to the conclusion that sorting and searching can be done with common routines contained in the base if a derived class supplies appropriate element interchange, element comparison, and key-to-element comparison operations with uniform call syntax. Adding and removing elements can be done with a combination of base and derived operations.

Abstract Base Class

If our strategy is to have a set of common operations defined in the base class OrderedSeq and a complementary set of operations supplied by a derived class to form a fully operational class, then we write OrderedSeq in the form of an *abstract base class*:

```
///////   File OrderedSeq.h   ///////
typedef unsigned Uint;

class OrderedSeq  // abstract base class
{ public:
    OrderedSeq() : ordered(0) {}              // default constructor
    virtual int  enter(void* any);            // add any, -1 failed
    virtual void remove(Uint i)         =0;   // remove by index (PURE)
    virtual int  index(void* key);            // -1 if not found
    virtual Uint length()               =0;   // current length of seq (PURE)
  protected:
    virtual int  append(void* any)      =0;   // add any at end, -1 failed (PURE)
    virtual void sort();                      // sort into order
    virtual Uint sorted() { return ordered;} // 0 if arr is not sorted
    virtual void sorted(Uint s)
    { ordered = s;}                           // set sorted flag
  private:
    virtual void swap(Uint i, Uint j)   =0;   // interchange elements (PURE)
    virtual int  cmp(Uint i, Uint j)    =0;   // compare elements (PURE)
```

```
        virtual int   cmp(void* key, Uint j) =0;   // compare key to element (PURE)
        void quicksort(int l, int r);
        Uint partition(int l, int r);
        Uint ordered;                              // sorted flag
};
```

The abstractness of OrderedSeq comes from *pure virtual functions*, such as

```
virtual void remove(Uint i) =0;              // remove by index
virtual void swap(Uint i, Uint j) =0;        // interchange elements
```

which are made undefined by the =0 notation. No objects can be established for a class with undefined pure virtual functions. Because pure virtual functions are inherited, a derived class is also abstract unless it supplies real definitions for all the pure virtual functions. Therefore, a pure virtual function forces a derived class to supply a real definition with the given prototype.

Thus, an abstract base class serves as a schematic for building derived classes rather than for establishing objects of its own. Without the proper operations supplied by a derived class, the base class OrderedSeq is useless. The abstract base prescribes interfaces and operations required of derived classes.

Note that the abstract OrderedSeq contains only one data member, the flag ordered, used by sorting and searching operations, but no sequence of elements. No assumption is made on how the sequence of elements will eventually be stored. The base is designed to work together with all properly derived classes.

Extracting Common Operations

What common operations can we define in OrderedSeq when neither the elements of the sequence nor their type is known? Quite a few. In fact, you may be surprised at how many nontrivial operations can be supplied given the right interface design between the base and the derived class.

To begin with, consider searching:

```
///////   File: OrderedSeq.C   ///////
#include "OrderedSeq.h"

// binary search returns index of desired entry
int OrderedSeq::index(void* key)
{    if ( ! sorted() ) sort();      // sort when necessary
     int low = 0, mid, test;
     int high = length()-1;
     while (low <= high)            // binary search
     {   mid = (high + low)/2;
         test = cmp(key, mid);      // call virtual cmp (1)
         if ( test == 0 )
             return( mid );
```

```
        else if ( test > 0 )
            low = mid + 1;
        else high = mid - 1;
    }
    return(-1);                    // entry not found
}
```

Note that if the sequence is not already in sorted order, it is sorted first. Then, an efficient binary search algorithm is employed to locate the desired element, calling upon the key-to-element comparison function (line 1). The pure virtual cmp(key, n), defined in a derived class, returns a positive, zero, or negative value, depending on whether the key is greater than, equal to, or less than the key contained in the element with index n. Either the index of the element found or -1 is returned.

Now consider sorting using the quicksort algorithm:

```
// basic sorting using quicksort
void OrderedSeq::sort()
{   if ( sorted() ) return;
    quicksort(0, length()-1);    // virtual length()
    sorted(1);
}
```

```
void OrderedSeq::quicksort(int l, int r)
{   if ( l >= r || l < 0 ) return;
    int k = partition(l, r);
    quicksort(l, k-1);
    quicksort(k+1, r);
}
```

The virtual function length(), defined in a derived class, gives the length of the sequence. The function partition(), where all the actual sorting work is done, relies on properly defined element comparison (cmp(i,j)) and interchange (swap(i,j)) virtual functions:

```
Uint OrderedSeq::partition(int l, int r)
{   register int i=l, j=r;
    swap((i+j)/2, r);                             // pe moved to r
    while (i < j)
    { while (cmp(i, r) <= 0 && i < j) i++;        // virtual cmp
      while (j > i && cmp(j, r) >= 0) j--;        // virtual cmp
      if (i < j) swap(i,j);                       // virtual swap
    }
    if (i != r) swap(i,r);                        // virtual swap
    return(i);
}
```

Having common searching and sorting defined in the abstract base class is already quite good, but more can be done:

```
// enter puts new element at end of array and
// invalidates ordered flag
int OrderedSeq::enter(void* any)
{   int i = append(any);              // virtual append
    if ( i != -1 ) sorted(0);        // append failed if i == -1
    return(i);
}
```

The common enter() asks the virtual function append() to put a new element at the end of the sequence and invalidates the flag ordered. Multiple elements can be entered without resorting the sequence after each enter() call. Reordering is deferred until the next retrieval from the sequence.

Some pure virtual functions are not part of the public interface but part of the internal operations required by member functions. For example, the element interchange and comparison functions are required by partition, and append is needed by enter.

To fully appreciate the power and convenience of OrderedSeq, let's use it to form a specific sequence. The following example shows how to derive from an abstract base class and how to use it as a schematic for building uniform interfaces.

9.3.2   Derived Class: Ordered Dates

Consider applying the abstract base class OrderedSeq to form a sequence of dates. A simple date object is an instance of the class:

```
///////   File Date.h   ///////
#include <iostream.h>

class Date
{  public:
       Date();
       Date(unsigned m, unsigned d, unsigned y)
       : month(m), day(d), year(y)  { }      // constructor
       int cmp(const Date& d) const;         // date comparison
       void display()
       { cout << month << '/' << day << '/' << year; }
   private:
       unsigned month, day, year;
};
```

The class provides Date objects that can be compared for ordering. Objects of the Date_OS (date ordered-sequence) class represent sequences of dates that can be ordered:

```
////////    File Date_OS.h    ////////
#include "Date.h"
#include "OrderedSeq.h"

class Date_OS : public OrderedSeq        // derive from abstract base
{ public:
    Date_OS() : len(0) { }               // default constructor
    Uint  length() { return(len); }      // current length of seq
    Date* operator[](Uint i);            // overloading []
    void  remove(Uint i);                // remove by index
  protected:
    int   append(void* date);            // add any at end, -1 failed
  private:
    void  swap(Uint i, Uint j);          // interchange elements
    int   cmp(Uint i, Uint j);           // compare elements
    int   cmp(void* date, Uint j);       // compare key to element
    enum  {Max=256};                     // maximum size
    Date* dates[Max];                    // pointer array
    Uint  len;                           // total no. of dates
};
```

All of the member functions follow the prototype set forth by the abstract base class OrderedSeq.

   An array of Date pointers is kept internally. The array is statically allocated to simplify our example. Interchange of elements on the pointer array is very easy. Comparisons are simply done by calls to Date::cmp(), as shown by the following inline functions:

```
inline void Date_OS::swap(Uint i, Uint j)      // interchange
    { Date* tmp = dates[i];
      dates[i]  = dates[j];
      dates[j]  = tmp;
    }

inline int Date_OS::cmp(Uint i, Uint j)        // compare elements
    { return dates[i]->cmp(*dates[j]); }

inline int Date_OS::cmp(void* date, Uint j)    // key to element comparison
    { Date* tmp = (Date*) date;
      return tmp->cmp(*dates[j]);
    }
```

Two more member functions, append() and remove(), that are dictated by the abstract base are just slightly longer. Note that append casts the incoming void* into a pointer of known type. It also checks whether the array is full. In a more flexible implementation, the pointer array could be dynamically allocated and extended when full:

```
///////   File Date_OS.C   ///////
#include "Date_OS.h"

int Date_OS::append(void* date)              // append entry at end
{   if ( len < Max )
    {   dates[len++] = (Date*) date;
        return(0);
    }
    return(-1);                              // pointer array full
}
```

Removing an element from the ordered sequence is done by moving all entries below it up one notch:

```
void Date_OS::remove(Uint i)                 // delete entry i
{   if ( i < len )
    {   for ( int j=i ; j < len ; j++ )
            dates[j] = dates[j+1];
        len--;
    }
}
```

Again, these operations must be implemented in the derived class where a member function has access to the pointer array and its type.

Another part of the overall public interface of Date_OS is the index access notation:

```
Date* Date_OS::operator[](Uint i)
{   if ( i >= len) return(NULL);
    if ( ! sorted() ) sort();
    return(this->dates[i]);
}
```

It allows elements in an object ds of Date_OS to be retrieved by index:

```
Date* pta = ds[i];
```

This is, of course, important to applications requiring ordered dates.

Following the abstract base makes it relatively straightforward to get Date_OS implemented correctly. Now test it with some typical operations:

```
#include "Date_OS.h"

int main()
{    Date d[10] =
         {Date(2,12,1949), Date(4,20,1949),
          Date(3,15,1949), Date(11,6,1986),
          Date(7, 4,1996), Date(2,12,1959),
          Date(4,20,1959), Date(3,15,1959),
          Date(11,7,1986), Date(7, 3,1996)};
     Date_OS mydates;                          // enter 10 dates
     for ( int i=0; i < 10; i++)
         mydates.enter(d+i);
     for (i=0; i<mydates.length(); i++)
     {   mydates[i]->display();
         cout << "\n";                         // display date list
     }
     i = mydates.index(d+6);
     mydates.remove(i);
     cout << "\nEntry " << i << " removed\n";
     i = mydates.index(d+6);                   // access should fail
     (d+6)->display();
     if ( i == -1 ) cout << " entry not found\n";
}
```

Running the program produces the following output:

```
2/12/1949
3/15/1949
4/20/1949
2/12/1959
3/15/1959
4/20/1959
11/6/1986
11/7/1986
7/3/1996
7/4/1996

Entry 5 removed
4/20/1959 entry not found
```

Through this example, we have seen how the abstract base class OrderedSeq is applied and how the base and derived functions cooperate.

Ordered Bank Accounts

Now let's consider an example in which we establish a sequence of ordered bank accounts. The only difference here from our sequence of dates is that, while there is just one kind of date, there are many kinds of accounts. However, we should not encounter any major difficulty.

Here is all that we need to do:

1. Make sure the base class Account has a virtual function cmp() for comparing accounts. Ordering can be based on social security number, name of owner, and so on.
2. Derive Account_OS from OrderedSeq with an internal Account* pointer array. Follow the Date_OS model.

That is it. Done! Consider what has been achieved. An instance of Account_OS is an object in the OrderedSeq hierarchy, and it reuses all the common codes in the base. Account_OS, in turn, contains a sequence of plug-compatible accounts all in the Account hierarchy. An Account_OS object can be used to establish a sequence of accounts of any single type or mixed types. And, common banking operations can be applied to all accounts in a sequence.

9.4 \ DESTRUCTION OF PLUG-COMPATIBLE OBJECTS

Recall that a destructor performs deinitialization just before an object is de-allocated. When plug-compatible objects have no user-supplied destructors, no complications occur because of object destruction. The problem that user-defined destruction causes and its solution are described next.

Consider a revised FreeChecking that defines its own destructor, perhaps to free up dynamically allocated transaction records. Such a destructor would look like

```
FreeChecking::~FreeChecking()
{   delete transac;  }
```

where transac is a pointer to free storage of type Transactions* for example.

This destructor is invoked every time a FreeChecking object is destroyed, except when the object is destroyed through a base pointer (Account*). To see the problem clearly here, consider show(), the account display routine, which deletes each object after it has been displayed:

```
void show(Account** a, int n)
{   for (int i=0; i < n; i++)
    {   a[i]->display();
        cout << endl;
```

```
        delete a[i];    // delete object via base pointer
    }
}
```

Because delete is given a pointer of type Account*, the destructor called is ~Account() and not ~FreeChecking() as desired. The C++ *virtual destructor* mechanism solves this problem. When a base destructor is designated virtual, as in

```
virtual ~Account() {}
```

for example, then all derived destructors, explicitly supplied or not, are automatically virtual. The effect is familiar: If an object with a virtual destructor is destroyed through a base pointer, the destructor associated with the actual object is invoked. This happens despite the fact that a derived destructor has a name different from that of the base destructor. It is interesting to note that this fact alone distinguishes virtual destructors from other virtual functions. Destructors, virtual or not, are always invoked in the reverse order of constructor calls.

With an understanding of the virtual destructor, we can now see that the abstract base class OrderedSeq should also declare a virtual destructor

```
virtual ~OrderedSeq() {}
```

It is normally a good idea to declare a virtual destructor for any base class with virtual functions.

9.5 ORDERING TEXT LINES

Arranging lines of text in sorted order for easy retrieval and update is important in many practical applications. Text lines are usually ordered by a user-supplied key field contained in each line. We have already seen one application of sorting text lines (Section 4.5). Now, let's write a much more complete program by deriving from the abstract base class OrderedSeq:

```
///////    File: TLine_OS.h    ///////
#include    <iostream.h>
#include    "SortKey.h"
#include    "OrderedSeq.h"

typedef char * String;
typedef unsigned int Uint;

class TextLine_OS : public OrderedSeq
{ public:
```

```
            TextLine_OS(Uint  pos  = 0,          // key position
                        Uint size = 1024,        // max lines
                        Uint ll = 256,           // max line length
                        String dlm = DELIM);     // field delimiters
            String operator[](Uint i);           // overloading []
            void remove(Uint i);                 // delete entry i
            Uint length() { return(len); }       // no. of lines
            void input(istream& in);             // read in lines
            void display(ostream& out=cout);     // output lines
            ~TextLine_OS();                      // virtual destructor
        protected:
            int append(void* line);              // append entry at end
        private:
            int cmp(Uint i, Uint j);             // compare lines
            int cmp(void* k, Uint j);            // compare key to line
            void swap(Uint i, Uint j);           // interchange lines
            String *lines;                       // text lines
            SortKey key;                         // sort key
            Uint    len;                         // total no. of lines
            Uint    maxlen;                      // max no. of lines
            Uint    linelen;                     // max line length
            int read_lines(istream& in);         // input function
        };
```

Here we modify an earlier class definition, TextLines (Section 4.5), which already has many of the required functions. However, TextLine_OS provides much better encapsulation: All I/O, sorting, searching, retrieval, and update functions are contained in the class and its base.

The constructor sets the key position and allocates storage:

```
///////    File: TLine_OS.C    ///////
#include      <string.h>
#include      <stdlib.h>
#include      "TLine_OS.h"


TextLine_OS::TextLine_OS
(Uint pos, Uint size, Uint ll, String dlm)
: key(pos, dlm)                              // initialize key
{    maxlen = size;
     linelen = ll;
     lines = new String[size];              // dynamic allocation
}
```

Notice that the private member object key is initialized by calling its constructor on the init-list.

Functions dictated by OrderedSeq are also defined:

```
int TextLine_OS::append(void* line)        // append entry at end
{   if ( len < maxlen )
    {   lines[len++] = (char*) line;
        return(0);
    }
    return(-1);                            // pointer array full
}

void TextLine_OS::remove(Uint i)           // delete entry i
{   delete [] lines[i];
    for(int j=i ; j < len ; j++)
        lines[j] = lines[j+1];
    len--;
}
```

These two functions are simple and straightforward. So are the two required comparison functions:

```
int TextLine_OS::cmp(Uint i, Uint j)       // compare lines
{ return key.cmp(lines[i], lines[j]); }

int TextLine_OS::cmp(void* k, Uint j)      // compare key to line
{ return key.cmp(k, lines[j]); }
```

While these four functions are new, some functions are modifications of those in TextLines. These functions add a check of the ordered flag and call sorting when necessary:

```
String TextLine_OS::operator[](Uint i)     // item retrieval
{   if ( ! sorted() ) sort();              // ordering
    return( i < len ? lines[i] : NULL );
}

void TextLine_OS::display(ostream& out)    // output
{ String *lptr = lines,
        *end = lines + length();
    if ( ! sorted() ) sort();              // ordering
    while ( lptr < end )
        out << *lptr++ << '\n';
}
```

Other members of TextLine_OS not shown are the same as those in TextLines.

The only change we make to the class SortKey is that of adding a public comparison function:

```
int SortKey::cmp(void *a, const char *b)
{   if (position == 0)
        return( strcmp((char *)a,b));
    char *k = (char *)a;
    b = key(b);
    return(keycmp(k,b));
}
```

This compares a key passed in as a void* to a line pointed to by b and supports the index() functions in the abstract base OrderedSeq.

Now our fully functional class for handling ordered text lines is complete. We can test these facilities with a simple main function:

```
///////    File: tstTLnOS.C    ///////
#include        <iostream.h>
#include        <fstream.h>
#include        <stdlib.h>
#include        "TLine_OS.h"

int main(int argc, String argv[])
{    if (argc > 3)
     {   cerr << "Usage: " << argv[0] << " [ key ] file\n";
         exit(1);
     }
     int keypos=0;
     if (argc == 3)
     {    keypos=atoi(argv[1]);
          argv[1] = argv[2];
     }
     ifstream myin(argv[1]);
     if ( ! myin )  cerr << "Cannot open file "
                         << argv[1];
     TextLine_OS txtobj(keypos);            // object
     txtobj.input(myin);                    // read lines
     txtobj.display(cout);                  // display sorted lines

     cout << "\nInput search key:";         // input sort key
     char key[16];
     cin.getline(key, 16);
     int i = txtobj.index(key);             // retrieve line
     cout << "index for " << key << " is "
          << i << endl;
```

```
        return(0);
}
```

After checking command-line arguments and obtaining the key position, a `TextLine_OS` object `txtobj` is established. Lines of text are read into `txtobj` from the given file, and the sorted version is displayed. Then, the program asks the user to input the search key of some entry to retrieve. The index of the line found is also displayed. When run on a file of grades, the program produces such output as the following:

```
Joe  Brown      C
Susan Gray      I
George Lee      S
John Smith      A
Mary Taylor     B

Input search key:Lee
index for Lee is 2
```

9.6 \ Understanding Virtual Functions

We have seen how useful and powerful plug-compatible objects are. We know what a critical role virtual functions play in the overall scheme of a derivation hierarchy. However, the concept of a virtual function can still be somewhat difficult at first. The following points should help sharpen your mental picture of virtual functions:

1. Once a base prototype is designated `virtual`, all derived functions with the same prototype are automatically virtual, with or without explicit virtual declaration, and form a set of functions to be selected at run time.

2. When a virtual function is invoked through a base-type pointer or reference, the actual run-time type of the object determines which virtual function to call.

3. A direct call of a member virtual function by another member function is considered to be an invocation through the host pointer `this`. (The calls to `swap` and `cmp` in the `partition()` function of the `OrderedSeq` class are examples.) This feature allows functions in the base class to call virtual functions to be supplied in derived classes.

4. Only member functions can be virtual. Constructors, `new`, and `delete` are the only members that cannot be virtual. However, destructors can be virtual despite having different names.

5. A pure virtual function can be left undefined but must be defined by a derived class before instances can be established.

6. The access protection designation (`public`, `protected`, or `private`) of a virtual function is determined by the base class (the pointer/reference type), not the class of the actual object.

7. Inline functions can be virtual, but this is seldom useful. Virtual functions cannot be static.

8. There are three situations when a virtual-function invocation is fixed at compile time:

   • When a virtual function is invoked through an object instead of a pointer or reference. Here the call loses its virtualness and is just like any regular-member function call.

   • When a virtual-function call explicitly specifies the class scope. (The call `JointAccount::display()` in the function `JtFrChecking::display()` is an example.)

   • When a virtual function is called within either a constructor or a destructor, the version defined by the class itself is always invoked since the derived object is either not yet constructed or already destroyed.

9.7 \ INHERITANCE PLANNING

For a class, the `public` members represent an interface to outside functions. The combined `public` and `protected` members represent an interface to a derived class. When writing a class as a base for further derivation, this second interface, as well as certain other factors, must be considered carefully. Without proper planning, derivation from an existing class will quickly run into problems. Often, we can solve these problems by revising the base classes in question, assuming we have access to the base source code and are allowed to make modifications to it. The situation is quite different when modifying the base is not possible.

The essential principle in planning for inheritance is a well-formed model of the overall behavior of the base object in relation to derived objects. This model facilitates decisions in the following critical areas:

1. *Protected or private:* Consider whether a `private` member should be designated `protected` instead to allow access by a derived class.

2. *Virtual or nonvirtual:* Decide whether a function should be designated `virtual`. If a function is expected to be redefined by a derived class, then it should be designated `virtual`. Ideally, virtual functions should

also be written so that preprocessing, postprocessing, or both can be easily added in a derived class. When in doubt, always make a base function virtual. Usually, the only price you pay is some performance degradation. A base destructor is almost always designated virtual.

3. *Shared base or not:* When the base class is itself derived, like JointAccount, whether its base is shared (virtual) affects future multiple inheritance. For a public derivation hierarchy, there is normally no need for duplicated base objects, and declaring base classes virtual usually makes good sense. The way a virtual base can be initialized should be clearly documented in a derived class because further derived constructors must call the correct virtual-base constructor.

4. *Member function overloading:* When the base class contains an overloaded member and a derived class redefines one version of it, then the remaining versions in the base class become hidden and no longer form part of the accessible interface for a derived object. Take this into account when naming base-class members.

5. *Pure virtual functions:* Use these to preplan derived-class interfaces and virtual functions to be supplied by a derived class.

Virtual-Function Composition

A derived class often redefines a base virtual function to augment its capabilities. For example, the FreeChecking member

```
int FreeChecking::withdraw(double amt)
{   int ok = Account::withdraw(amt);        // call base withdraw
    if ( ok != -1 )                          // added processing
        if ( free && balance() < min_bal )
            free = 0;
    return(ok);
}
```

first calls the base withdraw() and then performs some additional processing. In general, a derived class may add either *preprocessing*, *postprocessing*, or *both* to a base virtual function in order to achieve more complicated behavior. This method of composing functions via derivation is an important inheritance technique. However, we must do a certain amount of planning to use it effectively.

Consider the top-level loop of the pocket calculator:

```
void Calculator::on()
{     int ind;
      char op;
```

```
        double number;
        cf.show_number(eng.output());
        // calculator top-level loop
        while ( (ind = cf.input(op, number))    // loop control
                  != CalcFace::off )
        { if ( ind != CalcFace::oponly )        // loop body
                eng.operand( number );
            eng.operate( op );
            number = (op == 'c' || op == 'C') ? 0 : eng.output();
            cf.show_number(number);
        }
}
```

As it stands, it is impossible for a derived class to augment the loop body unless we rewrite the complete function on(). To allow for future composition, we extract the loop body from the loop control to form another virtual function perform():

```
void Calculator::on()
{     int ind;
      char op;
      double number;
      cf.show_number(eng.output());

      while ( (ind = cf.input(op, number))    // loop control
                  != CalcFace::off )
      { perform(ind, op, number);
      }
}
```

```
// extracted loop body
void Calculator::
perform(int ind, char op, double number)    // virtual
{    if ( ind != CalcFace::oponly )
          eng.operand( number );
      eng.operate( op );
      number = (op == 'c' || op == 'C') ? 0 : eng.output();
      cf.show_number(number);
}
```

In this way, preprocessing and/or postprocessing can easily be added to the loop body in a derived class of Calculator. The loop control part can also be replaced or modified without affecting the loop body.

For maximum efficiency, we should plan even further ahead. The added preprocessing and/or postprocessing parts should also be defined in virtual functions so that future derived classes can augment or modify these parts, thus allowing full flexibility in composition in a derivation chain.

9.8 OBJECT-FAMILY CLASSES

With plug-compatible objects, programs are more generic and the same code can be applied to various objects through base pointers and references. Compatibility through pointers or references is very handy. However, in some situations, related quantities should be treated as instances of the same class so that they operate correctly and combine into new instances in the same class. In other words, we need *a class to encompass a family of objects*.

Consider different kinds of numbers for example: integers, fractions, real, imaginary, and complex. In some applications, it would be convenient to treat different numbers as objects of the same Number class. When two fractions are added, an integer may result. Representing this result as an integer is nicer than representing it as a fraction that is equal to an integer. When two complex numbers are multiplied, a real number may emerge. Again, representing such an answer by a real number is nicer than representing it as a complex number with a zero imaginary part. In other words, arithmetic operations should work on mixed kinds of numbers. The actual type of the result depends on its value.

Such a Number class allows us to build, for instance, a class of polynomials with Number coefficients, or a class of matrices with Number entries. Such classes are of course much more generic.

A family class such as Number can be achieved in C++ with a combination of mechanisms. Here is the overall strategy:

- Number is defined as an *envelope* class whose objects represent many different subtypes of numbers and whose functions supply operations for all subtypes in the family. Mixing of subtypes is allowed.
- Distinct subtypes of numbers are defined as derived classes of Number.
- A Number object has an internal (private) pointer of type Number*, which can point to different derived objects of Number.
- Operations requested through the envelope class Number are *forwarded* to the actual objects to be carried out by virtual functions.
- The forwarding mechanism is also used by derived virtual functions to resubmit requests that need more type information.
- Results computed are again instances of Number, which supplies constructors to build numbers of various kinds.

To see how this strategy works exactly, let's consider a simplified example involving three classes:

1. Number, the envelope class for the family.
2. Fraction, derived from Number.
3. Integer, derived from Number.

9.8.1 The Number Envelope

The Number class serves both as an envelope containing the various subtypes of numbers and as a base class for the derived subtypes. Let's first examine the header.

The Header File Number.h

The public interface includes constructors, a destructor, a copy constructor, and assignment, display, arithmetic, and other usual operations involving numbers. Those functions declared virtual are redefined by various types of numbers as derived classes of Number. The actual number is represented by a base pointer. So, a Number object is represented internally by a Number* pointer, which can point to any derived object of Number and thus allows Number objects to represent many different subtypes of numbers (Figure 9.5). (How subtypes of numbers are created, operated on, and destroyed will be explained later.)

FIGURE 9.5   ENVELOPE AND SUBTYPE OBJECTS

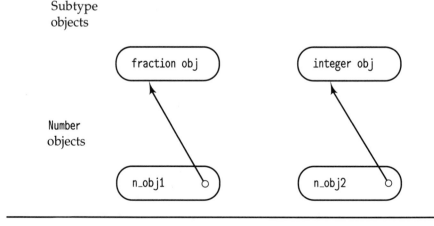

Note that the macros OP, VT, and CS are used to make the code fit better on a page for easier reading. While this practice may be all right in a textbook, it is not recommended for actual coding. Here is the header:

```
///////    Number.h    ///////
#define OP operator
#define VT virtual
#define CS const

class Number
{ public:
     Number() {}                            // default constructor
     Number(int a);                         // integer constructor
     Number(int a, int b);                  // fraction constructor
     Number(CS Number&);                    // copy constructor
     Number& OP =(CS Number&);              // assignment
     VT void display()                      // virtual display
     { ptr->display(); }
     VT Number OP +(CS Number& n) CS        // virtual
     {   return ptr->OP +(n);  }            // arithmetic  (1)
     VT Number OP /(CS Number& n) CS        // operations
     {   return ptr->OP /(n);  }            //             (2)
   /* other public members */
     VT ~Number(){ delete ptr; }            // destructor
  private:
     VT Number* copy() const                // utility function
     {  return ptr->copy() ;}
     Number* ptr;                           // ptr to actual number
```

To keep things simple, only addition and division operations are considered. Generalizations will become obvious.

Arithmetic involving two objects of the type Number is difficult unless the exact subtype of each object is known. In other words, an arithmetic operation must first deduce whether two fractions, two integers, or an integer and a fraction are being treated. The key is to use the virtual mechanism twice, once to deduce the subtype of each operand.

Consider two Number objects, n_i and n_f, where n_i is actually an integer and n_f a fraction. This means that n_i.ptr points to a derived object of subtype Integer, and n_f.ptr points to a derived object of subtype Fraction. Let's trace how the division operation

n_i / n_f

is performed. The operation is directly interpreted as the call n_i.operator/(n_f) (line 2), which leads to another call

```
n_i.ptr->operator/(n_f)
```

This second call forwards n_f, through the virtual function mechanism, to the operator/() function in the object *n_i.ptr, which happens to be of type Integer. At this point, the subtype of the left-hand operand n_i has been deduced.

A set of protected virtual functions in the class Number is central to the determination of the actual type of the right-hand operand (n_f, for example):

```
// class Number continued
   protected:
      VT Number AddFra(CS Number& n) CS        // host is Fraction
      { return n.ptr->AddFra(*this); }         // n + *this
      VT Number DivFra(CS Number& n) CS        // host is Fraction
      { return n.ptr->DivFra(*this); }         // n / *this
      VT Number AddInt(CS Number& n) CS        // host is Integer
      { return n.ptr->AddInt(*this); }         // n + *this
      VT Number DivInt(CS Number& n) CS        // host is Integer (3)
      { return n.ptr->DivInt(*this); }         // n / *this      (4)
      /* other protected members */
};
```

Again, only functions for addition and division are shown. Each of these protected functions is called only by a specific derived class of Number. For example, Number::AddFra(n) knows its host object is a Fraction, and Number::DivInt(n) knows its host is an Integer (line 3). In the latter case, for example, to find the subtype of n, the call (line 4)

```
n.ptr->DivInt(*this)     // arg is Integer (5)
```

is made through n.ptr leading to the virtual function DivInt() in the derived object *n.ptr. Thus, the call (line 5) knows the type of its host and its operand (an Integer) and can therefore simply carry out the desired operation and return a Number result. (This will be considered again after the codes for DivInt() in the derived classes are shown, and we will also return to n_i / n_f.)

The remainder of the Number.h file contains some inline functions:

```
// Number.h (continued)
#include "Fraction.h"                          // (A)
#include "Integer.h"

inline Number::Number(int a)                   // make integer
      : ptr(new Integer(a)) { }
```

```
inline Number::Number(CS Number& n)          // copy constructor
       : ptr((&n)->copy()) { }
```

```
///////    End of Number.h    ///////
```

Because of the mutual reference among Number, Fraction, and Integer, all headers must be *once-only* (Section 12.7). In Number.h, some #include lines (such as line A) must be put in an appropriate place in the middle of the file rather than at the beginning.

Implementation of Number

Most functions of Number are simple enough to be inline. Two functions, a class-defined assignment and a fraction-or-integer constructor, are placed in Number.C:

```
///////    Number.C    ///////
#include "Number.h"
#include <stdlib.h>

Number& Number::OP =(CS Number& n)          // assignment
{   if (&n == this) return(*this);
    delete(ptr);
    ptr = (&n)->copy();
    return(*this);
}


Number::Number(int n, int d)                // constructor
{   if (d == 0) exit(1);
    if ( d < 0 )
    {   n = -n;  d = -d;  }                  // make d > 0
    int c = gcd(n,d);
    if ( c != 1 )                           // remove gcd
    {   n /= c;
        d /= c;
    }
    if ( d == 1 ) ptr = new Integer(n);
    ptr = new Fraction(n,d);
}
```

These functions are straightforward. Let's now examine the Fraction class.

9.8.2   The Fraction Subtype

The derived class Fraction takes care of the actual representation of a fraction number and supplies operations exclusively on fractions, as well as procedures involving a fraction and a number of another subtype. To ensure that all numbers are created and used uniformly through the envelope class Number, a derived subtype, such as Fraction, contains no public members. Each is used by Number and other derived classes in the family through friendship:

```
///////   Fraction.h    ///////
#include "Number.h"

class Fraction : public Number
{    friend class Number;
     friend class Integer;
  protected:
     Fraction(int n, int d)                  // constructor
     : num(n), denom(d) { }
     Number OP   +(CS Number& n) CS;         // n subtype unknown
     Number OP   /(CS Number& n) CS;         // n subtype unknown
     Number AddFra(CS Number& f) CS;         // f + *this (1)
     Number DivFra(CS Number& f) CS;         // f / *this (2)
     Number AddInt(CS Number& i) CS;         // i + *this (3)
     Number DivInt(CS Number& i) CS;         // i / *this (4)
     void display();
  private:
     int num;                                // numerator
     unsigned int denom;                     // denominator
     Number* copy() const
     { return (new Fraction(num, denom)); }
};
```

Except for the constructor, all Fraction functions are virtual following the interface set down by the base class Number. Arithmetic operations are forwarded from Number to Fraction operator functions like these:

```
inline Number Fraction::OP +(CS Number& n) CS
      { return Number::AddFra(n); }


inline Number Fraction::OP /(CS Number& n) CS
      { return Number::DivFra(n); }


///////   End of Fraction.h   ///////
```

Knowing the host object is of type Fraction, these operator functions can call type-encoded functions *Opr*Fra() in Number. These base-class functions will forward the operands to the corresponding type-encoded functions, such as those on lines 1–4, in a derived class.

The member Fraction::DivInt() divides an Integer by the host Fraction, as shown in its implementation in Fraction.C:

```
//////// Fraction.C ////////
#include <iostream.h>
#include "Number.h"

Number Fraction::DivInt(CS Number& i) CS    // i / *this
{   Integer& ii = (Integer&) i;
    return Number(ii.val * denom, num);
}
```

The reference parameter i is first explicitly cast before computing the answer and returning a Number object.

Similarly, Fraction::AddInt() is coded as follows.

```
Number Fraction::AddInt(CS Number& i) CS        // i + *this
{   Integer& ii = (Integer&) i;                 // cast to known type
    return Number(ii.val * denom + num, denom);
}
```

9.8.3   The Integer Subtype

To complete the picture, let's examine the Integer class. It is similar to Fraction, so the rules for adding more subtypes to the Number family should become very clear:

```
//////// Integer.h ////////
#include "Number.h"

class Integer : public Number
{   friend class Number;
    friend class Fraction;
  protected:
    Integer(int i) :val(i) {}             // constructor
    Number OP   +(CS Number& n) CS        // n subtype unknown
    { return Number::AddInt(n); }
    Number OP   /(CS Number& n) CS        // n subtype unknown
    { return Number::DivInt(n); }
    Number AddFra(CS Number& f) CS;       // f + *this
    Number DivFra(CS Number& f) CS;       // f / *this
```

```
    Number AddInt(CS Number& i) CS;        // i + *this
    Number DivInt(CS Number& i) CS;        // i / *this
    void display();
  private:
    int val;
    Number* copy() const
    { return (new Integer(val)); }
};
```

The integer division operation Integer::DivInt(), which computes (i / *this), is coded as follows:

```
///////     Integer.C     ///////
#include "Number.h"


Number Integer::DivInt(CS Number& i) CS
{ Integer& ii = (Integer&) i;
    return Number(ii.val, val);
}
```

All three classes — Number, Fraction, and Integer — have been described. We can now summarize the n_i / n_f computation:

```
n_i / n_f                    // invokes Number::operator/()
n_i.operator/(n_f)           // forwards n_f to Integer::operator/()
n_i.ptr->operator/(n_f)      // calls Number::DivInt()
n_i.ptr->Number::DivInt(n_f) // calls Fraction::DivInt()
n_f.ptr->DivInt(*n_i.ptr)    // divides *n_i.ptr by *n_f.ptr
```

To see how things work together, we can run a test program:

```
#include <iostream.h>
#include "Number.h"


int main()
{   Number f(4,6);
    Number i(3);
    Number g(-3,2);
    Number k = f + i;
    k.display(); cout << endl;
    k = f + g;
    k.display(); cout << endl;
    k = f / g;
    k.display(); cout << endl;
    k = k / f + f;
```

```
    k.display(); cout << endl;
}
```

Compiled and run, this program produces the following display:

```
11/3
-5/6
-4/9
0
```

The material in Section 9.8 deserves careful study. Many subtleties exist that you may miss in a first reading. Experiment with the code so that you get a feel for its nuances and an appreciation for its sophistication.

9.9 SUMMARY

In multiple inheritance, an indirect base class may become duplicated—a problem we usually want to avoid. The C++ virtual (shared) base is the mechanism that takes care of such unwelcome repetition of base objects. Under such situations, the initialization of the virtual-base object shifts to the most derived class.

Polymorphism is a higher form of OOP activity that involves making generic operations apply to different types of objects that are plug-compatible. Several techniques are involved in polymorphism: uniform public interfaces, is-a relationships with class derivation, implicit conversion of derived reference/pointer to base reference/pointer, and run-time routing of function calls via the virtual function mechanism.

A class presents one interface to the public and another to its derived classes. Careful planning is necessary to alleviate potential problems in future derivations. The abstract base class with pure virtual functions can be used to make planning for uniform interfaces easy. The technique is demonstrated by an OrderedSeq class, which results in a program reusable in all situations that involve searching and sorting. In planning classes for derivation, careful consideration should be given to how functions are written so that virtual-function composition can be easily and effectively achieved.

The compatible-object idea extends to the object-family class, which collects related plug-compatible objects within one single class. This organization also allows operations that construct new instances of such objects. The Number class illustrates this sophisticated concept.

EXERCISES

1. Consider the declaration of a virtual-base class. Can the keyword virtual be put in front of public? private? protected?

2. Consider the nonvirtual version of JtFrChecking. Can a JtFrChecking constructor call the Account base constructor in this case? Why?

3. Consider multiple inheritance and a virtual base that is a public base following one branch of the derivation chain and a private base following another. How does this affect the derived object's ability to access members in the virtual-base object?

4. If a base class is declared virtual for some but not all derivations, what happens if you derive from these derived classes mixing virtual and nonvirtual versions of the same base class? Explain and give examples.

5. Add a pure virtual function display() to OrderedSeq and supply its proper definition in Date_OS.

6. Consider the ordered dates example and the class Date_OS. Modify the class definition so that the pointer array dates is not fixed in length. It is initialized to zero length and becomes longer by a predetermined increment every time a new element comes into a full array. Make sure you free all dynamically allocated storage properly.

7. The sort() provided by OrderedSeq is the quicksort, one of the most efficient sorting algorithms known. Nevertheless, the fact that sort is virtual means it can be replaced by another sorting routine in a derived class if desired. Try to supply another sorting routine this way.

8. The OrderedSeq class is array-oriented. Create an OrderedList class that is similar to it but is linked-list-oriented.

9. Consider the improvements to the calculator program (Chapter 7, Exercises Cal-1 and Cal-2). Make the derived compute engine objects plug-compatible. Modify the Calculator class so that it uses a plug-compatible compute engine derived from CalcEng. Run Calculator objects initialized with different engines. Also, break up the main computation loop of the calculator to allow derived classes to add preprocessing/postprocessing to each loop iteration. (*Hint:* Use a CalcEng* member.)

10. Consider virtual destructors (Section 9.4). When delete is applied to an Account*, which points to a FreeChecking object, what destructors are called and in what order?

11. What friend functions, if any, can be virtual?

12. Is it allowable to have the base version of a virtual function declared public and a derived version protected or private. If so, what effect, if any, is there when the virtual function is used?

13. Consider the object-family Number. What functions must be added to Number, Fraction, and Integer to support the additional binary arithmetic operations * and -?

14. Add the function prototypes in Exercise 13 to the appropriate class declarations.

15. Define the functions needed in Exercise 14 and test the revised object-family.

16. Take the polynomial class defined in Section 4.4 and make its coefficients Number objects. See how simple it is to work on polynomials with integer and fraction coefficients.

10

TEMPLATES

$\mathbf{O}$ne way to make programs generic is to allow *type parameters* in a language. Similar to a formal parameter for a function, a type parameter can take on *types as values*. Thus, if T is a formal type parameter, the declaration

```
T x, y, z;
```

declares three variables whose type depends on the value of T. Allowing functions, classes, and other constructs to contain type parameters gives a programmer the ability to write *program templates*, which turn into fully completed codes when the type parameters take on values.

The C++ template facility supports type parameterization and was added to the language late in its evolution. As a result, there is considerable variation in the level of support for templates among different C++ implementations. As usage experience increases and implementation standardizes, the template facility will become a major feature for writing reusable code.

This chapter introduces basic template concepts and then describes both function templates and class templates. Complete example templates are given and put to use. The template technique is applied, in combination with other C++ features, to define a widely applicable generic hash table class. The pros and cons of the template versus the void* approach for genericness are also discussed.

10.1 \ BASIC CONCEPTS

A C++ *template* is a program skeleton specified by putting "placeholders" into ordinary program codes. Once the placeholders are filled, a template produces actual definitions or declarations. By filling the placeholders with different quantities, many different codes can be produced from a single template. Each specific version thus produced is known as an *instantiation* of a template. Thus, a template is a mechanism for generating programs.

The placeholders are *template formal parameters* that take on different values including type names such as int and Fraction. C++ supports templates for producing definitions and declarations of functions and classes.

With templates, we can write functions and classes that work for any appropriate basic and user-defined types. Consider, for example, the power() function discussed in Section 3.5. Such power functions can be defined once and for all by the template

```
template <class T>          // T is type parameter
T power (T a, int exp)
{     T ans = a;
      while ( --exp > 0 )
              ans *= a;
      return(ans);
}
```

Clearly, the power() definition involves the type parameter T. T can be given the value int, double, Fraction, Complex, or any other type including those yet to be defined. Of course, the function will work only for those types where the operator *= is defined.

The general form of a template is

```
template < type1 T1, type2 T2, ... >
normal declaration or definition
```

The *template header* begins with the keyword template followed by one or more *template formal parameters* in angle brackets. A template header controls the immediately following declaration or definition, which must make use of the template formal parameters. A template parameter can be one of the following:

- *Type parameter:* The special notation class *T* means *T* is a type parameter. The borrowed keyword class here means "any type."
- *Nontype parameter:* Normal function-style parameters, such as int i or CMP_FN cmp, specify nontype parameters.

For function template definition, nontype template parameters are unnecessary and illegal.

A template tells the compiler how to make an actual declaration or definition once the type parameters are bound. For example, the code

```
Fraction x, y(1,2);
x = power(y, 3);        // triggers template instantiation
```

causes the compiler to instantiate the power() template with T replaced by Fraction, resulting in the complete definition of a Fraction version of power(). To perform such instantiations, the compiler must access the source code for the power() template and the header Fraction.h at the time of instantiation.

The following simple main function causes three more instantiations:

```
main()
{      int i = 5, j = 2;
       float r = 0.5;
       double b = 12.345;
       cout << power(j,i) << endl;    // T is int
       cout << power(r,i) << endl;    // T is float
       cout << power(b,i) << endl;    // T is double
}
```

With these basic concepts in mind, let's examine function and class templates in detail.

10.2 \ FUNCTION TEMPLATES

One technique we can use to make functions generic involves the void* pointers mentioned in Section 5.12. This technique has its strengths and its drawbacks. The function template mechanism offers us an alternative that can be very attractive because it defines a potentially unbounded set of overloaded functions with a single construct. Each function in this set is a *template function* and an *instance* of the function template. An appropriate template function is produced automatically by the compiler when needed.

10.2.1 Function Template Definition

To see the power of function templates, consider, for example, a generic binary search. The header file provides the function prototype and documentations:

```
#ifndef bsearch_SEEN__
#define bsearch_SEEN__
///////    File: bsearch.h    ///////
// Generic binary search template prototype

template<class T1, class T2>     // template header
int bsearch(T1 arr[],            // ordered array of any type T1
         T2 key,                 // search key of any type T2
         int low, int high,      // inclusive search range
         int (* cmp)(T1, T2)     // comparison function
         );

// cmp(arr[i], key) compares arr[i] with key and returns -1, 0, +1
```

```
// bsearch returns the index of the entry found or -1 if not found
#endif
```

Any client program that wishes to use the binary search simply includes this header and calls bsearch() with an appropriate cmp argument. The #ifndef once-only feature (Section 12.7) is shown here to underscore its importance when you are using the template mechanism.

In the bsearch template, both template parameters, T1 and T2, are type parameters. For function templates, nontype parameters are not allowed. The actual implementation of the function template is in a different file:

```
///////    File: bsearch.C    ///////
// Generic binary search template
#include  "bsearch.h"

template<class T1, class T2>                      // template header
int bsearch(T1 arr[], T2 key, int low, int high,
        int (* cmp)(T1, T2)  )
{    int mid, test;
     while (low <= high)
     {    mid = (low + high) / 2;
          test = cmp(arr[mid], key);              // -1, 0, +1
          if (test > 0)
               high = mid - 1;
          else if (test < 0)
               low = mid + 1;
          else
               return(mid);                       // found
     }
     return(-1);                                  // not found
}
```

The binary search algorithm is implemented for an array of type T1 using search keys of type T2. Since these are known types for any instance, variables of type T1 or T2 are treated no differently in the function body than are any other quantities of known type.

To write function templates effortlessly, follow these three steps:

1. First, write a specific version of the function with all fixed types.
2. Then, compile and test the function.
3. Finally, replace selected types in the function with type parameters and add the template header.

Now let's apply the binary search function template:

```
#include <iostream.h>
#include <string.h>
#include "bsearch.h"                    // need template prototype

char *names[] = { "George M. Blum", "Ruth B. Boland",
                  "Bill C. Johnson", "David P. Moses",
                  "Debra S. Rice",   "John A. Smith",
                  "Paul S. Wang"};

const int LEN = sizeof(names)/sizeof(char*);

char *getkey(char *s, unsigned int i)
{    for ( int j = 1; j < i; j++)       // skipping fields
         while ( *s++ != ´ ´ );         // delimiter is single space
     return(s);
}

int cmp_lastname(char *ent, char *key)
{    char *k = getkey(ent, 3);
     return(strcmp(k, key));
}

main()
{
     int j = bsearch(names, "Rice", 0, LEN-1, cmp_lastname);  // (1)
     if (j >= 0 ) cout << names[j] << "\n";
     j = bsearch(names, "Doe", 0, LEN-1, cmp_lastname);       // (2)
     if (j < 0 ) cout << "Doe not found\n";
}
```

The simple application here shows the use of bsearch() to retrieve a name from an ordered array of names with the last name as a key. The first invocation (line 1) triggers the instantiation of the template with T1 = char* and T2 = char*. The second call (line 2) simply invokes an existing function.

10.2.2 Function Template Instantiation

Template parameters are *formal* in the sense that there is no difference between the following declarations:

```
template <class A, class B>
int func_1(A, B);
```

```
template <class T1, class T2>
int func_1(T1, T2);
```

The template header for a nonmember function involves only type parameters (of type class). Furthermore, *each template parameter must appear, in some form, within the function signature at least once.* Remember, the return value type is not part of the signature.

The C++ compiler instantiates function templates automatically. When the compiler encounters a particular template function call for the first time, the function is still undefined. However, the function template together with the function call signature provides enough information to build the needed function right then and there (Figure 10.1).Values for the template parameters are discovered by comparing the function template signature with the function call signature, using the following procedure:

1. The formal parameters in the function template signature are examined in turn.
2. Each formal parameter involving a type parameter is matched with the corresponding actual argument in the function call. A successful match binds the type parameter.
3. All matches must be consistent. Only trivial promotions to produce a match are allowed (int& to const int&, for example).
4. Formal parameters not involving type parameters must also be matched without nontrivial conversion/promotion.

If all formal parameters match the incoming arguments and the match produces consistent type parameter values, then template instantiation takes place.

Function-Call Resolution

Since a function template simply defines a set of overloaded functions, we can further overload the set with individual nontemplate functions or even additional function templates.

FIGURE 10.1   FUNCTION TEMPLATE INSTANTIATION

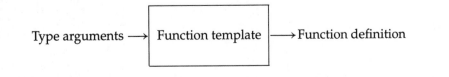

Type arguments ⟶ Function template ⟶ Function definition

When resolving a function call, the compiler examines the *nontemplate* versions first. Specifically, three steps are used:

1. Examine all nontemplate versions of the function, if any. If there is one exact match, call that version. If there is more than one exact match, display a compilation error message.
2. Examine all template functions, if any, for an exact match. If one is found or can be instantiated, then call it. Display an error message if there are two or more exact matches.
3. If steps 1 and 2 do not resolve the call or produce an error, then reexamine all nontemplate versions of the function using call-resolution rules for regular overloaded functions.

Thus, we can replace selected template functions with specialized individual versions that override their template function counterparts. We often do this when we want to handle special cases or increase code efficiency.

Note that optional arguments and variable-length arguments are generally not supported under function templates.

10.3 \ CLASS TEMPLATES

Templates can also make classes generic and useful in a wide variety of situations. One important application of a class template is establishing generic container classes such as vectors, lists, ordered sequences, and hash tables. A class template simply involves a template header followed by a normal class definition.

10.3.1 Class Template Definition

A class template parameter can be either a type or a nontype parameter. Consider a template for vectors of any type and length:

```
#ifndef Vector_SEEN__
#define Vector_SEEN__
////////   File: Vector.h   ////////
// n dimensional vector of type T elements

template <class T, int n>          // type and nontype parameters
class Vector
{   public:
        Vector() { }               // default constructor
        Vector (T v0);             // init elements to v0
        T& operator [](int i);     // vector index notation i >= 1
```

```
        void display();
        Vector<T,n> operator+(const Vector<T,n> v) const;
        /* other members */
    private:
        T vec[n];                       // internal array of type T (1)
};
#endif
```

The once-only header construct is explicitly shown here because it is indispensable for class templates. The practice has long been recommended, however, for *all header files*. The template parameter n allows us to use static allocation for the internal array vec (line 1). The class template defines a set of *template classes*, each of which is denoted by Vector<*T*,*n*>. For example,

```
Vector<int,2>    iv(0);        // 2-dimensional int vector
Vector<double,3> dv1(0.0);     // 3-dimensional double vector
Vector<double,16> dv2(0.0);    // 16-dimensional double vector
```

The value passed to the template parameter n must be a constant expression of a type that matches the declared type of n exactly. Thus, passing an unsigned 16U would be disallowed unless it is explicitly cast into the correct type.

Member functions are, as usual, defined in a separate file, which begins with the constructor:

```
///////    File: Vector.C    ///////
#include <iostream.h>
#include <stdlib.h>
#include "Vector.h"

template <class T, int n>
Vector<T,n>::Vector(T v0)        // constructor
{
    for ( int i=0 ; i < n ; i++ )
        vec[i] = v0;
}
```

The scope operator Vector<T,n>:: puts the constructor in the scope of the template class Vector<T,n>. We can similarly define the operator+() member:

```
template <class T, int n>
Vector<T,n> Vector<T,n>::operator+(const Vector<T,n> a) const
{
    Vector<T,n> ans;
    for ( int i=0 ; i < n ; i++ )
        ans.vec[i] = a.vec[i] + vec[i];
    return(ans);
}
```

Normal vector subscript notation is supported by

```
template <class T, int n>
T& Vector<T,n>::operator [](int i)      // base 1 indexing
{   if ( i > 0 && i <= n )
        return vec[i-1];                // internal base 0 indexing
    else
    { cerr << "Vector index out of range\n";
      exit(1);
    }
}
```

which returns a reference T&. As these examples show, the only differences between a template member function and an ordinary member function are the template header and the template class name (Vector<T,n>).

Now let's put the Vector class template to use:

```
///////    tstVect.C    ///////
#include "Vector.h"

int main()
{   Vector<double,3> dv1, dv2;       // Vector objects
    for ( int i=1 ; i <= 3 ; i++ )   // assign to components
    {   dv1[i] = i/2.0;
        dv2[i] = -i/4.0;
    }
    Vector<double,3> dv = dv1 + dv2;  // Vector addition
    dv.display();
}
```

As usual, Vector.C and tstVect.C are separately compiled. When combining Vector.o and tstVect.o into the final executable program, make sure the template source files are available for the compiler. On UNIX systems, for example, this means that the sources are either in the current directory or in a directory given by the -I option for CC.

Run the program to produce the following vector display:

```
(0.25  0.5  0.75)
```

10.3.2   Class Template Instantiation

A *template class* is a class built from a class template. When the compiler encounters a template type specifier such as

```
Vector<double,3> dv;
```

FIGURE 10.2   CLASS TEMPLATE INSTANTIATION

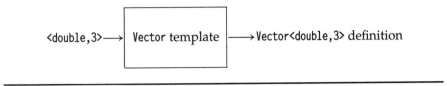

for the first time, it takes the given template arguments and builds a proper class definition automatically (Figure 10.2). The template type specifier can be used just like an ordinary type specifier.

Member functions of a class template are function templates with the same template header as the class. A template member function is instantiated when the compiler first sees a call to it.

10.4 \ A List Template

We have already seen an implementation of a generic linked list using void* and function pointers (Section 5.12). A template provides us with a simpler alternative. The idea is straightforward: Make the value type of a list cell a type parameter. Most of the existing codes for the linked list will then stay unchanged. We only have to put them in a template setting.

Three classes are involved: Cell, List, and ListIterator:

```
#ifndef TmpLIST_SEEN__
#define TmpLIST_SEEN__
////////   File: List.h    ////////
// linked-list template
#include <iostream.h>

template <class T> class List;              // (1)
template <class T> class ListIterator;      // (2)

template <class T>
class Cell
{    friend class List<T>;                  // (3)
     friend class ListIterator<T>;          // (4)
   private:
     T& value() { return(*item); }
     void value(T& v) { item = &v; }
     T* item;                               // (5)
     Cell<T>* next;
```

```
        Cell(T& c, Cell<T>* ptr = NULL)          // (6)
           : item(&c), next(ptr) { }
};
```

Forward declarations for class templates simply are given without the class body (lines 1 and 2). The friend declarations (lines 3 and 4) work as expected — List<int> is a friend class of Cell<int>, and so on. The item is now of type T* (line 5), so only a pointer to type T is stored instead of a copy, which could be large since T can be any type. Note that making and storing copies should be avoided in template writing because the sizes of the parameterized types can be large. Using reference parameters in templates (line 6) is thus common practice.

The template version of the list class is simpler because function pointers are no longer needed. Instead, element comparison and display functions now depend on overloaded operators associated with the parameterized type T:

```
// type T must define operator== and overload <<

template <class T>
class List
{   friend class ListIterator<T>;
  public:
    List() : head(NULL) { }                  // empty list constructor
    List(T& c)                               // list with first cell
      : head (new Cell<T>(c)) { }            //                        (A)
    Cell<T>* first() { return head; }        // first cell             (B)
    static Cell<T>* next(Cell<T>* p)         // next cell              (C)
       { return (p ? p->next : p); }
    Cell<T>* find(T& c);                     // first item equals c
    int put_on(T& c);                        // insert in front
    int insert(T& c, Cell<T>* cell);         // insert after cell
    /*  other members */
    ~List();                                 // destructor
  private:
    Cell<T>* head;                           // first cell of list
    void free();                             // free all cells
    int equal(T& r, T& s)                    // equality test
    {  return( r == s ); }
};
```

The class definition is shortened here to show just a few members with various class template notations: dynamic allocation (line A), template class pointer (line B), and static function (line C).

The list iterator class also shows reference template type notation (lines E and F):

```
template <class T>
class ListIterator
{  public:
      ListIterator(List<T>& x) : l(x)        // (E)
      { cur = pre = x.first(); }
      int operator()(T& n);                  // returns next entry in n
      void del();                            // erases last retrieved item
   private:
      List<T>& l;                            // (F)
      Cell<T>* cur;
      Cell<T>* pre;
};
#endif
```

The file List.C consists mostly of member functions with the added template header

```
template <class T>
```

and the class scope operator List<T>::. A few typical definitions are shown here:

```
///////    File: List.C    ///////
#include "List.h"

template <class T>                           // destructor
List<T>::~List() {    free();  }

template <class T>
int List<T>::substitute(T& r, T& s)
{   for( Cell<T>* p = head; p ; p = p->next )
       if ( equal(p->value(), s) )           // call inline equal (i)
       {   p->value(r);                       // set value
           return(0);
       }
    return(-1);                              // s not on list
}

// display from p to end
template <class T>
void List<T>::display(Cell<T>* p)
{   cout << "(";
    while ( p )
    {   cout << p->value();                   // overloaded <<    (ii)
        if ( p = p->next ) cout << " ";
```

```
    }
    cout << ")\n";
}

template <class T>
void ListIterator<T>::del()
{    l.del( pre );          }
```

The codes on lines i and ii show the use of overloaded operators associated with the type T. This is an advantage of the template implementation over the void* method, which requires function pointers.

10.4.1   Applying the List Template

Consider manipulating lists of employees. The List class template makes this simple:

1. Make sure the Employee class has the operator==() and overloaded <<.
2. Use List<Employee> to instantiate list objects.

Here is a simplified Employee class:

```
#ifndef EMPLOYEE_H__
#define EMPLOYEE_H__
///////    File: Employee.h     ///////
#include   <iostream.h>
#include   <string.h>

class Employee
{  public:
      Employee() {}
      Employee(char* n, unsigned a, char* s)
      :   name(n), age(a), ss(s)  { }
      char * id() { return(ss); }
      int operator ==(Employee a)
      { return(strcmp(ss, a.ss) == 0); }
      void display(ostream& out = cout) const ;
   private:
      char*    name;         // full name
      unsigned age;
      char*    ss;           // social security number
      float    salary;
};

ostream& operator<<(ostream& out, const Employee& e);
```

```
ostream& operator<<(ostream& out, const Employee* e);
#endif
```

Actual overloading of << is done in the implementation file:

```
///////    File: Employee.C    ///////
#include <iostream.h>
#include "Employee.h"

void Employee::display(ostream& out) const
{    out << name << "  age=" << age
          << "  ss=" << ss;
}

ostream& operator<<(ostream& out, const Employee& e)
{   e.display(out);
    return(out);
}

ostream& operator<<(ostream& out, const Employee* e)
{   e->display(out);
    return(out);
}
```

To see how employee lists are created and used and to test the List template, consider the following code:

```
///////    File: tstList.C    ///////
#include <iostream.h>
#include "List.h"
#include "Employee.h"
// linked-list of employees via
//       List template

static Employee a[] =
     { Employee ("Big Mac", 39, "023441288"),
       Employee ("John Doe", 32, "083467890"),
       Employee ("Joe Smit", 24, "333451282"),
       Employee ("Joe Smi", 27, "333451228"),
       Employee ("Joe Sm", 28, "333452128"),
       Employee ("Joe S", 29, "333415228") };

int main()
{    List<Employee> weekly( a[1] );
     weekly.put_on( a[3] ); weekly.put_on( a[5] );
     weekly.display(cout);
```

```
                   weekly.put_on( a[0] ); weekly.put_on( a[2] );
                   weekly.append( a[4] ); weekly.display(cout);

                   weekly.remove( a[4]); weekly.remove( a[0] );
                   weekly.display(cout);

                   weekly.shorten(3); weekly.display(cout);
                   weekly.shorten(1); weekly.display(cout);
                   return(0);
            }
```

Here Employee objects, through reference parameters, are put on the list. Just as easily, Employee* pointers can be put on the list:

```
List<Employee *> weekly( a+1 );
```

To put copies, not the objects themselves, on the list, copying can always be done first:

```
Employee copy = a[1];
weekly.put_on( copy );
```

10.5 \ TEMPLATE CLASS SPECIALIZATION

The list template works for many built-in and all user-defined types. However, some cases require more than simply using List<*type*>. Consider List<char*> for example. Since it is impossible to overload == for the type char*, certain list operations, such as substitute(), will work incorrectly (line i).

This difficulty can be overcome in C++ with the template specialization mechanism. If the following member function

```
inline int List<char*>::equal(char*& r, char*& s)
      { return (! strcmp(r,s));  }
```

is defined before List<char*> is used, then it overrides the template-supplied member function of the same exact signature. One or a few member functions — even the entire class — can be redefined for particular type values to make things work correctly or more efficiently.

The reason the list template had the equal() function in the first place was to allow the above-mentioned specialization. It is not a bad idea to include the specialized List<char*>::equal() at the end of the file List.C.

10.6 \ DERIVED-CLASS TEMPLATE

For an example of class templates involving derivation, consider an implementation of Stack<T>, a template class derived from List<T>:

```
///////     Stack.h     ///////
//   stack derived from list<T>
#include "List.h"

template <class T>
class Stack : private List<T>          // keyword private is optional
{  public:
      Stack() { }                      // default constructor
      Stack(T& z) { put_on(z); }       // constructor
      int push(T& z) { return put_on(z); }   // pushes reference z
      int pop(T& z);                   // returns -1 if failed
      List<T>::is_empty;               // makes is_empty visible
};
```

Obviously, transforming the Stack class in Section 7.6 into a template is almost
a mechanical procedure. The pop() requires special attention for correct error
handling. It returns -1 as a failure indication and puts the popped item in the
reference parameter.

```
///////     Stack.C     ///////
#include "Stack.h"

template <class T>
int Stack<T>::pop(T& z)
{  if ( is_empty() ) return(-1);        // pop failed
   z = content(first());                // popped item
   shorten(1);                          // stack popped
   return(0);                           // pop succeeded
}
```

When the Stack template is instantiated, with Stack<int> for example, it also
causes instantiation of the base template class List<int> if it has not been
instantiated already.

   To see how the Stack template is used, consider the following simple test
routine:

```
///////     File: tstStack.C     ///////
#include <iostream.h>
#include "Stack.h"
// stack of integers via
```

```
//        Stack class template

static int a[] = {0,10,20,30,40,50};

int main()
{    Stack<int> mystack(a[1]);              // instantiation
     mystack.push(a[3]);
     mystack.push(a[5]);
     int i;
     while ( mystack.pop(i) != -1  )
         cout << i << " ";
     cout << endl;
     return(0);
}
```

Run the program to produce the following output:

```
50 30 10
```

With Stack<T>, other types of stacks should be just as easy to handle.

10.7 \ A GENERIC HASH TABLE

A *hash table* is an ingenious method to store and retrieve data that avoids sorting and searching and provides direct random access to the items stored. In this section, by applying a combination of OOP techniques, we will implement a hash table template for all types of records.

Basic Concepts

A hash table stores a data item, called a *record*, by taking a part of the record, known as a *key*, and computing an index from it. The index determines where in the hash table a particular record is stored or retrieved. For instance, the name part of an address record can be a key that is transformed into an integer index by, say, adding the integer representation of its characters together.

The action of turning a key into an integer index is called *hashing*. A *hash function* takes a key and computes an integer index called the *hash code* whose value lies in the proper range. The hash function is designed to give different hash codes for different keys, but this cannot be guaranteed. Normally, there is a chance of two different keys producing the same hash code. When this happens, we say that the two records have *collided*.

The linked list offers a good solution to the problem of collision: The hash table entries are linked lists, and records with the same hash code are stored in the same linked list, located at the hash address. If the hash table is large enough and if the hash function is well designed, collision should occur infrequently, and the linked lists are kept very short.

Thus, when properly used, the hash table offers a data organization in which most records are accessible directly at their hash code location. Only once in a while will a sequential search down a very short list be necessary to locate a record. With the hash table, the need to keep records in sorted order is avoided entirely. Adding new records and removing old ones are simple operations that do not involve reordering or other time-consuming operations.

10.7.1   A Hash Table Template

Since the hash table is so ingenious, we should apply it wherever appropriate. Thus, it would be very convenient if a template HashTable is defined to allow codes such as

```
HashTable<Rate> rate_table(size);
HashTable<Employee> third_shift(size);
```

The HashTable supports several basic operations:

1. Adding a record.
2. Retrieving a record matching a given key.
3. Removing a record.
4. Inquiring whether a record is already on the hash table.
5. Finding the number of records contained on the table.

These are reflected by the public interface of HashTable:

```
#ifndef HashTable_SEEN__
#define HashTable_SEEN__
///////    File: HashTable.h    ///////
#include "List.h"
typedef unsigned Uint;

template <class T>
class HashTable
{ public:
    enum {noe, H_MULT=2640025017u};    // no entry and hash multiplier
    HashTable(Uint k = 8,              // constructor
              Uint m = H_MULT);
    void put(T& a);                    // enters record a
    int  get(const char *key, T& r);   // returns record in r
```

```
        int  rid(const char* key);          // removes a record
        int  is_on(char* key);              // checks if record is on table
        Uint length() { return len; }       // returns length of table
        ~HashTable();
    private:
        List<T>** ht;                        // table of linked lists
        Uint hash(const char*);              // built-in hash function
        static int on_list                   // record on list 1?
            (List<T>& l, char* key);
        Uint len;                            // no. of entries on table
        Uint mult;                           // hash multiplier
        Uint bits;                           // hash table 2^bits
};
```

Internally, a pointer array ht is used whose entries point to linked lists that store the records (Figure 10.3). Unused entries of ht contain NULL pointers.

The size of the dynamically allocated pointer array ht should be set depending on how many records the hash table is expected to handle. If we expect up to 500 records, a size slightly larger — say, 600 to 700 — can be used to reduce the chance of collisions.

When a hash table object is established, two arguments are passed to the constructor:

1. **k**: The table size is set to 2^k or a default of 256. Keeping the size a power of 2 makes hashing much easier.
2. **m**: The *multiplier* m is used in the internal hash function to produce the hash code. The default multiplier is a good choice.

FIGURE 10.3   A HASH TABLE

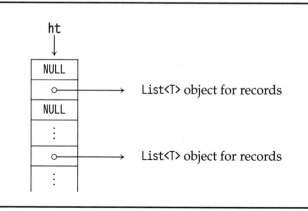

The key is assumed to be a character string, and any application that uses HashTable<T> will also define a key extraction function getkey() that can be called to obtain a key from any record of type T. This function can always transform any nonstring key into a string by turning bytes into characters. Prototypes for getkey() and a nontemplate utility function str_to_u() are also included in HashTable.h:

```
template <class T>
char* getkey(T& item);              // required key function

Uint str_to_u(const char *str);     // common utility function
```

```
///////     End of HashTable.h    ///////
#endif
```

10.7.2   Hash Table Implementation

The constructor initializes bits, mult, and len:

```
///////     File: HashTable.C    ///////
#include <iostream.h>
#include <string.h>
#include "HashTable.h"

template <class T>
HashTable<T>::HashTable
(Uint k /* = 8 */, Uint m /* = H_MULT */)
:  bits(k), mult(m), len(0)
{
    int size = 1 << bits;
    ht = new List<T>*[size];
    for ( int i = 0; i < size; i++ )
        ht[i] = NULL;
}
```

It also allocates the pointer array (List<T>** ht) and initializes all entries to NULL. The destructor frees each list pointer, triggering the list class destructor. Then, the ht pointer array is freed:

```
template <class T>
HashTable<T>::~HashTable()
{
    int size = 1 << bits;
    for ( int i = 0; i < size; i++ )
        if ( ht[i] ) delete(ht[i]);        // triggers List<T>::~List()
```

```
        delete(ht);
}
```

Now let's examine the design of the private member function hash(), which produces a hash code from any given character string key. The hashing is done in two stages:

1. First, convert the character string into an unsigned int.
2. Then, randomize the unsigned int into a hash table index.

The file-scope function str_to_u takes a string and converts it into an unsigned int value. This is done by treating the string as a sequence of unsigned int quantities and multiplying them together with a selected constant — 7u here:

```
Uint str_to_u(const char *str)
{     Uint value = 7u;
      char c;
      while ( (c = *str) != '\0' )
      {    value *= c;
          str++;
      }
      return(value);
}
```

The actual hash index is then produced by unsigned multiplication of the value produced by str_to_u() with the hash multiplier mult and right-shifting the result so that only bits of its leading bits remain. The hash code thus produced is random and falls within the proper range:

```
#include <limits.h>

template <class T>
Uint HashTable<T>::hash(const char* key)
{    Uint val = 0;
     val = str_to_int(key);
     return( (val*mult) >> (CHAR_BIT*sizeof(Uint) - bits));
}
```

The symbolic constant CHAR_BIT, usually 8, is defined in <limits.h>. There is much depth to the selection of the hash multiplier.* The one used here is based on *Fibonacci hashing* and should work well for all 32-bit computers.

---

*See D. E. Knuth, *The Art of Computer Programming* (Reading, MA: Addison-Wesley, 1973), vol. 3.

Hash Table Operations

The private function hash() is used by the public members put(), get(), and rid(). The member put() enters a record into the hash table:

```
template <class T>
void HashTable<T>::put(T& r)          // enter record r
{    char *key = getkey(r);           // obtain hash key
     Uint hc = hash(key);             // compute hash code
     List<T>* l = ht[hc];
     if ( l == NULL )                 // location not used before (1)
     {   ht[hc] = new List<T>(r);     // make a new list
         len++; return;
     }
     if ( ! on_list(*l, key) )        // if not already on list    (2)
     { len++;  l->put_on(r); }        // put record on list
     return;
}
```

To enter a record r, its hash code hc is computed first. If the pointer ht[hc] is NULL, then r is put on a new list, and the address of the new list is assigned to ht[hc] (line 1). Otherwise, collision occurred, and r is put on the existing list if it is not already on that list (line 2). Note that since on_list() is a static member function within a template, it is shared by all instances of HashTable<T> for any specific type T.

The member rid() removes a record from the hash table:

```
template <class T>
int HashTable<T>::rid(const char* key)    // removes a record
{    Uint code = hash(key);
     List<T>* a = ht[code];
     if ( ! a ) return(noe);
     ListIterator<T> next(*a);
     T item;
     while ( next(item) )
        if ( strcmp (key, getkey(item)) == 0 )
        { next.del();  len--;
           if ( a->is_empty() )          // if no more records
               ht[code] = NULL;          // reset to NULL    (3)
           return(! noe);
        }
     return(noe);
}
```

After a record is removed via a list iterator object, the pointer is reset to NULL if the list of records becomes empty (line 3).

The retrieval function get() is similar:

```
template <class T>
int HashTable<T>::get(const char* key, T& rval)
{    List<T>* a = ht[hash(key)];
     if ( ! a ) return(noe);
     ListIterator<T> next(*a);
     T item;
     while ( next(item) )
        if ( strcmp (key, getkey(item)) == 0 )
        {    rval = item;
             return( ! noe);            // entry found
        }
        return(noe);                    // not found
}
```

It returns the enum constant HashTable<T>::noe if the requested entry is not found. With these codes, other member functions are easy to write.

Using the Hash Table Template

Now let's use the hash table template for a table of Employee. The source code files involved are

- Employee.h and Employee.C, for employee objects (Section 10.4.1).
- List.h and List.C, for the list template (Section 10.4).
- HashTable.h and HashTable.C, for the hash table template (Sections 10.7.1 and 10.7.2).
- tstHsTbl.C, for the application.

To test the hash table template, consider the following code:

```
///////   File: tstHsTbl.C   ///////
#include <iostream.h>
#include "HashTable.h"
#include "Employee.h"
#define HT_E HashTable<Employee>

char* getkey(Employee& e)      // required getkey function
{ return( e.id() );    }

main()
{    Employee a("Big Mac", 39, "023441288");
     Employee b("John Doe", 32, "083467890");
     Employee c("Joe Smit", 24, "333451282");
     Employee d("Joe Smi", 27, "333451228");
```

```
        Employee e("Joe Sm", 28, "333452128");
        Employee f("Joe S", 29, "333415228");
        Employee z;

        HT_E ht(1);      // very small hash table for testing
        ht.put( b ); ht.put( a ); ht.put( c );
        ht.put( d ); ht.put( e ); ht.put( f );
        if ( ht.get("333415228", z) != HT_E::noe )
            cout << z << endl;
        else
            cout << "333415228 not found \n" ;


        ht.rid(getkey(a));
        if ( ! ht.is_on(getkey(a)) )
            cout << "023441288 not found \n" ;


        if ( ht.get("083467890", z) != HT_E::noe )
        {    cout << z << endl; }
        else
            cout << "083467890 not found \n" ;


        cout << ht.length() << "=len\n";
        ht.rid(getkey(d)); ht.rid(getkey(e));
        cout << ht.length() << "=len\n";
}
```

Compile and run this program to produce the following output:

```
Joe S   age=29   ss=333415228
023441288 not found
John Doe   age=32   ss=083467890
5=len
3=len
```

10.8 \ TEMPLATE VERSUS void*

Previous chapters demonstrated the combined use of void* and function pointers to make programs generic. The technique depends on the conversion of void* pointers to pointers of known types, usually through function calls. Applying such a program for new types of data often means supplying the right functions with the desired type conversions. The scheme forces the use of pointers, even for simple built-in types. For example, a void*-based arbitrary list (Section 5.12) handles ints or doubles only through int* or double*,which is, of course, less efficient.

The template mechanism avoids many of the above-mentioned problems by building a new function or class for each new application. Thus, a template function or class can be just as efficient as a regular function or class. However, the template approach, as it currently stands, has three major drawbacks:

1. Even after separate compilation, the source code for the template files must be present at link time of a program.
2. A template duplicates many similar functions among multiple instantiations and can make a program much larger than necessary.
3. Without standardization of the template facility, template codes can have portability problems.

These shortcomings are not present for the void* method. On the other hand, nontype parameters provide a degree of freedom for templates unavailable under any other technique. As alternatives, these approaches complement each other for writing generic and reusable codes.

10.9 SUMMARY

The C++ template facility supports type parameterization for writing generic programs. There is considerable variation of template support among C++ compilers.

Generally, both function and class templates can be written. The template header specifies a list of template formal parameters within angle brackets, and its scope extends to the end of the immediately following declaration or definition. Type parameters can be used just like an ordinary type name within the template code.

For function templates, all template parameters must be type parameters, of type class, and each must appear at least once in the function signature. A function template defines a potentially unbounded set of overloaded functions. The first call to a template-made function instantiates the template and defines the function. A function can be overloaded in the ordinary way and have one or more template definitions supplying additional instances. The C++ compiler follows specific rules in resolving calls to such functions.

For class templates, both type and nontype (ordinary) template parameters are allowed. A template class name takes a form like Vector<int,2> and can be used wherever a normal type name is used. Encountering a new template class type triggers the instantiation of the required class from the template. Member functions of a template class are instantiated when first called. For particular values of the parameters, the template class or certain members of it can be specialized to work differently from what the template dictates.

In most cases, both the template mechanism and the void* technique can be used to achieve the desired genericness. The former avoids complicated pointer casting, while the latter avoids duplication of run-time codes.

EXERCISES

1. The template facility of C++ may not be supported uniformly by all versions of C++ compilers. In particular, there is considerable difference in the support of typedef templates. Check your compiler to see whether this feature is implemented.

2. Write a function template for swap() used in sorting.

3. Consider the following code:

```
#include <iostream.h>

template <class T1, class T2>
T2 myfunc(T1 x, T2 y) {  return(x-y); }

int mycall()
{ int uu = 8;
  return myfunc(uu,uu);        // call myfunc
}

int myfunc(int y, int x)       // redefine myfunc
{  return(x+y); }

int main()
{    cout << mycall();  return(0); }
```

Would this code compile successfully? If it runs, what output would you expect? Explain.

4. A function template does not allow the use of nontype template parameters. If you really need such a feature, how can you get around the restriction?

5. Is there an easy way to declare all instances of a certain function template to be friends of a class? Of all classes derived from a template?

6. Does your C++ compiler allow operators to be defined as templates? Can templates be written for inline and static functions? (*Hint:* Experiment.)

7. In a class template, is it possible to have a `typedef` member that involves the formal type parameters? If so, construct an example.

8. Does the `sizeof` operator work with template formal types?

9. Consider template class specialization. The list template in Section 10.4 depends on the overloaded `<<` for display. Does this work for all types T? If not, what types would cause difficulty? How do you propose to fix it?

10. Take the test program for the hash table template (Section 10.7.2) and modify it for a hash table of text lines as character strings.

11. Write a more complicated test program for the hash table template that involves more than one type of hash table.

12. Follow the `str_to_u()` example and write a function template

    `key_to_u(T key, int len)`

    that takes a key of any type and of size `len` and computes an unsigned result. Also, explain why `str_to_u()` is implemented as a file-scope function instead of as a member function.

CHAPTER 11

OBJECT-ORIENTED DESIGN

Just because C++ provides good support for OOP does not mean that simply using C++ constructs will lead to well-organized object-oriented programs. On the contrary, without a good design created with an object-oriented view, the resulting program will most likely possess little object orientation, if any.

Object orientation requires a whole new approach to software design. The well-known life cycle model divides software construction into several phases:

1. Requirements analysis.
2. Design specification.
3. Implementation.
4. System testing.
5. System maintenance.

The first two phases produce a set of design specifications that guide the implementation (actual coding) phase. The life cycle model gives a somewhat rigid top-down view of the software creation process. Object-oriented design usually involves an incremental and iterative process.

One technique shared by all software design methodologies is "divide and conquer," whereby the problem at hand is decomposed into smaller and more manageable pieces. After each individual piece is solved, the individual solutions are put together to achieve the overall goal. Starting with large pieces and breaking them down into smaller ones is considered a *top-down* approach. Collecting small chunks and combining them into larger chunks of the solution follows the *bottom-up* style. How a problem is broken apart is limited only by the experience, creativity, and ingenuity of the designers.

In object-oriented design, the given problem is broken into interacting objects that correspond to actual or logical entities in the problem domain. A detailed study of OO design would take us beyond the scope of this book. This chapter will, however, give some basic principles, suggest concrete steps to follow to identify objects, explain the CRC design method, and provide an example. The chapter concludes with considerations on error and exception handling.

11.1 \ DECOMPOSITION APPROACHES

Before the design process begins, there must be a clear understanding of the requirements and purposes of the software to be constructed. The first step of the design process usually involves breaking down the whole problem into manageable chunks and defining the interrelationships among them. Decomposition forms a basis for design specifications that in turn govern implementation. The three major decomposition methods are listed here:

1. Procedural decomposition.
2. Data decomposition.
3. Object-oriented decomposition.

11.1.1   Procedural Decomposition

One way to solve the given problem is to look at the steps required for its solution. This method of decomposition produces interrelated procedures that combine to form the desired solution.

Taken from the top down, a problem is divided into several major procedures. Each procedure is then decomposed in the same manner. Common procedures are identified, and eventually the procedures are implemented as functions. The bottom-up approach to procedural decomposition considers basic steps necessary in the solution and how they combine to form larger procedures.

With any methodology, after a problem is decomposed sufficiently, we always arrive at a point where procedures are necessary to carry out the computation. The design of efficient procedures (*algorithms*) to solve given problems is a major topic in computer science.

11.1.2   Data Decomposition

Another way to break up a problem is to look at the usage of data. This method of decomposition considers what parts of the solution system deal with which data, how data flow through the system, and which pieces of data are shared by what parts. The data considered include input to the system, information generated for internal use, and results for output. This analysis identifies self-contained pieces and defines their interrelationships.

A need-to-know view should be applied to data decomposition. A system component possesses knowledge of required data only and nothing else. This design principle helps isolate data to restricted parts of the system and therefore reduces the overall complexity.

11.1.3   Object-Oriented Decomposition

The OO view is to decompose a system into autonomous computing agents that correspond to the interacting mechanisms in the given problem. These agents are then modeled by software objects. In a banking system, for example, the objects are customers, accounts, loans, CDs, passbooks, statements, and so on. At a finer level, objects could be addresses, charges, credits, overdrafts, payments, and fines.

Each object represents some tangible entity and behaves in a well-defined way. The internal organization of the object can be anything that supports its external behavior. The major advantage of OO decomposition is its flexibility and close relation to the problem domain. Clearly, once objects are identified and put into place, they can support, for example, one particular banking system just as easily as another.

Procedural decomposition and OO decomposition take orthogonal views: One highlights the sequencing of logical solution steps; the other focuses on the interacting entities. Both views are important for the overall design process, but it is perhaps best to first apply the OO view to identify the objects and define their behaviors. Then, the sequencing-of-events view can be applied to the interactions of these objects.

The data decomposition view can also help identify the objects, define their relations, and set limits on knowledge and access of data. The need-to-know principle of data decomposition is enforced very well with OO decomposition. Protected and hidden from unnecessary outside view are not only data structures but also internal procedures. To the rest of a program, an object is completely characterized by its behavior, which is important to good design.

Thus, in one sense, the OO organization is like setting up a company that contains a number of autonomous divisions, departments, factories, centers, and so on. Some of these entities contain other entities, and all have well-defined external behaviors and internal organizations. A company can adapt to many different tasks and react to a changing marketplace because these entities can adapt to different patterns of interaction without major reorganization.

11.2 OBJECT-ORIENTED DESIGN PRINCIPLES

OO design, like other creative activities, does not follow any fixed recipe. There is no magic formula to create a software design. The recommended OO design approach involves an iterative process called the *round-trip gestalt design*, a style that views the system as a whole and emphasizes incremental development and stepwise refinement. A preliminary design is based on what is known and doable; improvements, modifications, and redesigns take place thereafter.

But this does not mean that OO design is completely unstructured. Although the design follows an evolutionary path, the design process usually involves a sequence of tasks:

1. Identify classes and objects in the entire system.
2. Characterize external behavior of each object.
3. Specify the data and operations within each object.
4. Identify requests answered by each object.
5. Identify services required of other objects by each object.
6. Establish the visibility of each object in relation to other objects.
7. Group similar objects together and develop inheritance relations and class hierarchies.
8. Implement the design specifications.

Often the most crucial step is the first one — in this case, to identify classes and objects.

11.2.1   Identifying Classes and Objects

The design process begins with just the problem and a vague notion of the tasks to be achieved. The software designer examines and reexamines the problem at hand; becomes familiar with the terminologies, conventions, assumptions, and solution methods in the problem domain; and forms a high-level computation model of the solution. The interacting entities (real and logical) become candidates for objects, and the nouns used in the problem description, such as account, loan, and mortgage, are considered as potential class names.

At this point, the problem is just starting to be decomposed, and the boundaries are not yet fixed. Often, the closer the computation model is to reality, the better the decomposition. The process not only formulates a high-level abstract view of the software to be constructed but also sharpens the problem definition and the attributes of the final software product. Note that the list of classes and objects identified should be discussed among a few designers to provide checks and balances and to seek different perspectives.

11.2.2   External Behavior of Objects

Once classes and objects are identified and listed, each object on the list must be characterized by its external behavior. In other words, each object is considered a "black box," and its actions and reactions to the outside world are prescribed. To do this, the designer acts like a detached customer, demanding functionalities from these black boxes with little concern over how the functions are achieved.

To help the design, a script can be written for each object that describes its role in the overall scenario and includes its introduction, its typical actions, and its exit. It is also important to look at different scenarios and how the objects interact through their external interfaces in each scenario. These activities may suggest modifications or refinements of the OO decomposition produced earlier.

Finally, a list of objects with external behavior specifications is produced.

11.2.3   Designing Objects

With the external behavior defined, an object's public interface functions, data structures, and internal workings are then considered. When an object represents a high-level abstraction, it can often be further decomposed using the same OO design methods. Additional objects are then introduced into the evolving design. For each different object, a class is specified to support data hiding and encapsulation. Arguments for public function members should reflect the information necessary to achieve the functionality at hand. Requiring too little information will obviously not work. However, requiring too much information will lead to unreasonable designs.

The design produced at this stage serves as a blueprint for the eventual implementation of classes.

11.2.4   Relationships among Objects and Classes

The goal now is to obtain a comprehensive picture of how the objects in the system interact to perform the desired overall functionalities. By examining requests answered by each object, services required of others by each object, and the direct/indirect relationships among objects, groups of closely related objects can be formed. The behavior patterns and characteristics of objects and classes are then compared to detect any additional is-a, has-a, uses-a and can-be-implemented-as-a relationships. Objects that can be made plug-compatible are identified. The visibility and invisibility of objects help package classes into files and modules.

In the process of discovering such relationships, certain adjustments of the characterization of the objects may suggest themselves. Thus, the design process is evolutionary.

11.2.5   Implementation

Implementation is the coding phase. The designed classes, modules, and objects are set down in C++ code. But this process is not a simple transcription of the design specifications into codes. Often, implementation exposes unforeseen problems and opportunities that make rethinking parts of the design necessary or desirable. Thus, the design process is iterative.

11.3 \ THE CRC METHOD

A particularly effective technique for identifying objects and defining their relationships is the CRC (class, responsibility, collaboration) method. It is especially good for helping beginning programmers learn OO design.

For CRC, a set of regular index cards is used. On each card, the name of a class, its responsibilities, and collaborators (other classes/objects) are recorded (Figure 11.1). Completing these cards is an iterative and evolutionary process; many cards will be revised or rewritten before a design emerges:

- *Class names:* It is important to find the right names for the classes to be created. Names should be natural, conventional (using accepted terms

FIGURE 11.1   A SAMPLE CRC INDEX CARD

Class: CalcEng	
Responsibilities	**Collaborators**
Stores operands, opcode, result.	☐ Calculator
Performs arithmetic operations.	
Carries out control operations.	☐ Derived engines
Produces quantity stored.	
Reports error.	

from problem domain), and easy to understand and remember. They should not be misleading. Using nouns for class names is recommended.

- *Responsibilities:* These are actions assigned to an object. Responsibilities should be described with short verb phrases. Again, it is important to use the right words.
- *Collaborators:* For each class, names of related objects should be recorded. All objects required to fulfill the responsibilities are obvious collaborators. Classes that require/supply services or data from/to the class under consideration should also be recorded.

With a set of index cards so marked, the designers then proceed to play out execution scenarios and spot omissions or corrections for the descriptions. They also ask "what if" questions to anticipate all conditions that might arise. They can break up complicated classes into more components if necessary. A clear understanding of the problem domain is very helpful because domain knowledge should be used to check and verify the OO design.

11.4 \ INTERFACING TO EXISTING SYSTEMS

When a complete system is built from the ground up, the OO design techniques that have been discussed work well. Often, however, a software project must use existing systems that are large, old, and not easily changed. Such *legacy* systems affect how the overall system is designed and how object orientation is applied.

The recommended approach is to encapsulate any existing legacy system with a specially designed class that captures and formalizes the outside behavior of that system. In this way, the rest of the system can still be thoroughly object-oriented. The interface to the legacy system is made through objects of the interfacing class, thus isolating the legacy system from the rest of the software and reducing potential complications significantly.

Let's examine this approach by considering the class encapsulation of curses, a package of two-dimensional terminal screen I/O routines, and then using the legacy system to provide screen I/O for the pocket calculator discussed earlier (Section 5.5.1).

11.4.1   Using a curses Interface Class

The curses Package

The curses package, a screen-updating library of C functions, is available on UNIX workstations and on PCs and supplies many efficient terminal output operations such as updating the screen, cursor-motion optimization, and so on. The package uses *windows*, which are logical data structures capable of representing the entire terminal screen or a portion of it. If a window is as large as the entire terminal screen, then it is referred to as a *screen*. After initialization, curses establishes two built-in *screens:*

1. curscr: The *current screen* is for the current state of the terminal screen.
2. stdscr: The *standard screen* is for the next state of the terminal screen.

A program controls terminal display by making modifications to the stdscr and then calling a curses function to refresh the terminal screen. All the necessary computations to update the terminal and the curscr are performed automatically. The user is not limited to these screens. In fact, any number of named screens and windows can be established to help manipulate and update the terminal screen. This makes it relatively easy to maintain multiple windows on a terminal screen.

To use curses in a program, follow these four basic steps:

1. *Initializing:* Call initscr() to properly initialize curses (obtain terminal-specific characteristics, establish the screens curscr and stdscr, and record the current terminal I/O control modes for later use). Among other things, the global variables LINES and COLS are set to the number of lines and columns of the terminal. After calling initscr(), change the terminal input modes to suit the application. Often, automatic echoing of user input is suppressed and input-line buffering is disabled, allowing a window-oriented program to have each character typed on the keyboard immediately and arrange its own appropriate reactions to the input character.

2. *Establishing windows:* After initialization, establish additional windows, if needed. The library function call newwin(line, col, y, x) establishes a new window, whose upper left corner is at position (y, x), with the given number of lines and columns and returns a window identification (wid) for future operations to reference the window. Note that curses uses (y, x) for the position line y column x in a window.

3. *Performing input/output:* The basic functions that modify stdscr are move(y, x) to move the current position to location (y, x) and addch(c) to add the character c at the current position. The two operations can be combined to mvaddch(y, x, c). A call to refresh() will update the terminal screen according to stdscr. The function getch() reads a character from the stdscr. For other windows, waddch(wid, c) adds a character and wgetch(wid) gets a character.

4. *Finishing:* Before the program terminates, the routine `endwin()` should be called to restore normal terminal I/O modes and perform other cleanup chores.

The CursesWindow Class

To encapsulate the legacy `curses` package, a class named `CursesWindow` is designed. It initializes properly with constructors, cleans up at the end with a destructor, and supplies member functions that call the set of **curses** library functions.

A **curses** window or screen now becomes an object, an instance of `CursesWindow`. Data related to a particular window are kept in the object, and all manipulation routines are accessed as members. The header file begins with constructors:

```
////////   File CursesWindow.h   ////////
// a class interface to the legacy curses package

#include   <curses.h>    // C++ header for the C curses library

class CursesWindow
{ public:
     CursesWindow(WINDOW* &window);       // useful only for stdscr (1)

     CursesWindow(int lines,              // number of lines        (2)
                  int cols,               // number of columns
                  int begin_y,            // line origin
                  int begin_x);           // col origin

     CursesWindow(CursesWindow* par,      // parent window          (3)
                  int lines,              // number of lines
                  int cols,               // number of columns
                  int by,                 // absolute or relative
                  int bx,                 //   origins:
                  char absrel = 'a');     // if `a', by & bx are
                                          // absolute screen pos,
                                          // else if `r', they are
                                          // relative to par origin

     ~CursesWindow();                     // destructor
```

The header `<curses.h>` supplies declarations that make C-defined functions and identifiers accessible from C++. It may not be standard for all C++ implementations. See Appendix 10 for easy ways to construct such headers yourself.

The three constructors establish the standard stdscr (line 1) as an object, obtain a window of given size and location (line 2), and make a subwindow within a parent window (line 3). The destructor takes care of cleanup actions such as releasing subwindows and restoring normal terminal I/O modes, as required.

The class definition continues with many public member functions that provide access to the full complement of **curses** functions. Only a few function members are listed here to give you an indication of what is involved:

```
//////// CursesWindow public functions

// window status
  int  Height();                    // number of lines in host window
  int  Width();                     // number of cols in host window
  int  Begy(){ return w->_begy;};   // smallest y coord in host window
  int  Begx(){ return w->_begx; };  // smallest x coord in host window

// reading
  int Getch();                      // read character in host window
  int Getstr(char *str);            // read string in host window
  /* . . . */

// writing
  int Addch(const char ch);         // write character to host window
  int Addstr(char * str);           // write string to host window
  /* . . . */

// screen control
  void        Refresh();            // display host window
  int         Standout();           // highlighting begin
  int         Standend();           // highlighting end
  /* . . . */

// many other function members not shown
```

All nonpublic members are protected and accessible in derived classes. A count of all **curses** windows established is also kept:

```
//////// CursesWindow data members
protected:
    static int      count;      // count of all active windows
    WINDOW *        w;          // the curses WINDOW
    int             alloced;    // 1 if allocated by constructor
    CursesWindow*   par;        // parent, if subwindow
    CursesWindow*   subwins;    // head of subwindows list
    CursesWindow*   sib;        // next subwindow of parent
```

```
   void      kill_subwindows();      // release all subwindows
};
extern CursesWindow std_win;       // global object encapsulates stdscr
/* more inline function definitions */
```

///////   End of CursesWindow.h   ///////

Every public member function simply encodes a call to the appropriate **curses** library function. The inline feature can make the interface more efficient. For example,

```
inline int CursesWindow::Height()     // host window height
     {  return w->_maxy;     }
```

```
inline int CursesWindow::Getch()      // read one character in host window
     {  return ::wgetch(w);  }
```

The full CursesWindow class is contained in the code disk available via the order form at the back of this book. The class can be used to improve the pocket calculator example of Chapter 5 by providing a simulated liquid crystal display window, as we see in the next section.

11.5 \ POCKET CALCULATOR SIMULATION

For our design example, let's revisit the pocket calculator simulation. Since Chapter 5, we have considered many aspects of this problem in a sequence of exercises. Now we are interested in designing and implementing a more realistic pocket calculator with a simulated liquid crystal display (LCD) window (Figure 11.2). By applying the design principles explained in this chapter and following the CRC method, we can formulate a design.

11.5.1 CRC Design

The CRC descriptions for the calculator simulation contain five classes:

FIGURE 11.2   **POCKET CALCULATOR SIMULATED LCD WINDOW**

1. *Compute Engine*

   - Responsibilities: Stores operands, operation codes, and results; performs arithmetic operations; carries out control functions such as clear, all clear, and sign change; produces quantity stored in the compute engine upon request; keeps an internal state for error reporting to the outside.
   - Collaborators: *Calculator Control*, derived plug-compatible compute engines with additional features.

2. *User Interface*

   - Responsibilities: Receives input keystrokes; recognizes operations and numeric operands; produces next operation and operand from user input; displays operation code; displays operand; displays result; displays error; restricts input under error.
   - Collaborators: *Calculator Control*, derived plug-compatible user interface classes.

3. *Display Window* derived from `CursesWindow`

   - Responsibilities: Establishes simulated LCD window of proper size; shows given character string in LCD window; shows given single-character opcode; clears LCD window; restores normal I/O to user.
   - Collaborators: *LCD Interface*, `CursesWindow`.

4. *LCD Interface* derived from *User Interface*

   - Responsibilities: Uses *Display Window* for I/O; echoes each input keystroke as typed; (otherwise, has same responsibilities as base class).
   - Collaborators: Base *User Interface, Calculator Control, Display Window*.

5. *Calculator Control*

   - Responsibilities: Runs any plug-compatible compute engine and user interface; performs calculator top-level loop; turns calculator on and off; detects internal error; requests display of results and errors.
   - Collaborators: *Compute Engine, User Interface*, and their plug-compatible derivations.

Note that the *Display Window* object can be a customized `CursesWindow` object in order to better simulate a real calculator display. This is simply done by publicly deriving from `CursesWindow`.

11.5.2 Implementation

The C++ implementation of the pocket calculator program involves five classes: CalcEng, CalcFace, CalcWindow, LcdFace, and Calculator. The CalcWindow class uses the CursesWindow class that encapsulates the legacy **curses** library. The CalcEng class implements the compute engine and, other than some additional error handling, is not different from that presented in Section 5.5.1. The user interface is modified through inheritance to use a CalcWindow for realistic simulation.

The CalcFace Class

The base CalcFace class now supports these basic operations: input of numbers and operations, display of number, display of opcode, display of error, and handling of input under error.

The member input() normally returns the next operation and the operand in the reference parameters op and number, respectively. The return value indicates OPONLY if only an operation but no operand has been entered, OFF if the calculator is being turned off, or zero otherwise.

```
#ifndef CalcFace_SEEN__
#define CalcFace_SEEN__
////////    File CalcFace.h     ////////
#include    <iostream.h>
#include    <ctype.h>

// The function input returns op and nonnegative
//     numeric input, if given, in number
// Return value OPONLY means only op is entered.
// Return value OFF means no more input.

class CalcFace
{   public:
        CalcFace( const int digs,         // calculator precision
                   const char* k           // operation keys recognized
             );
        virtual int input(char& op, double& number, int err);
        virtual void show_number(double number);
        virtual void show_error(char* err)
        {   cerr << err << endl;   }
        virtual void show_op(char op) { }
        virtual int err_input(char& op);   // input under error
        enum {OPONLY = 1, OFF};
        ~CalcFace() { delete nbuf;  }
    protected:
        virtual int inchar()
```

```
            {  return(cin.get()); }
            virtual void extract_number(double&);
            virtual void build_number(char c, int& i);
            int nump(char c);
            char*         nbuf;              // buffer for input number
            const char*   keys;             // keys
            const int     prec;             // precision
};
#endif
```

CalcFace serves as a base for the window-oriented user interface class LcdFace, which adds mechanisms to use a **curses** window object for better simulation of a pocket calculator:

```
#ifndef LcdFace_SEEN
#define LcdFace_SEEN
///////    File LcdFace.h    ///////
#include    <iostream.h>
#include    "CalcFace.h"
#include    "CalcWindow.h"

class LcdFace : public CalcFace
{   public:
        LcdFace( const int digs,          // calculator precision
                const char* k             // operation keys recognized
            );
        void show_number(double number);  // virtual
        void show_error()                 // virtual
        {   cw->show_op('E');    }
        void show_str(char* str)          // virtual
        {   cw->show_str(str);  }
        void show_op(char op)             // virtual
        {   cw->show_op(op);  }
        ~LcdFace();
    protected:
        void build_number(char c, int& i);  // virtual
        CalcWindow*  cw;                     // ptr to window object
        int inchar()
        { return(cw->Getch()); }            // direct char input
};
#endif
```

The constructor dynamically allocates a calculator window of the right size to accomodate the maximum number of digits allowed. An in-memory register nbuf is used to store characters (including . and '\0') for numeric input:

```
///////    File LcdFace.C    ///////
#include  "LcdFace.h"
#include  <iostream.h>
#include  <strstream.h>
#include  <string.h>

LcdFace::LcdFace(const int d, const char* k)
: CalcFace(d, k)                          // base constructor
{
    cw = new CalcWindow(d);               // LCD for calculator
}


LcdFace::~LcdFace()
{   delete cw;
    delete stdwptr;
}
```

Dynamically allocated spaces are freed by the destructor.

The show_number() function is now defined to display a number in the LCD window. This is done by turning the double number into a string and asking the display window to display the string:

```
void LcdFace::show_number(double n)
{     static int width = prec+2;
      cw->clear_lcd();                    // clears window
      if ( n == 0.0 ) show_str("0.");
      else
      {   ostrstream os(nbuf, width, ios::out);
          os.precision(prec);
          os.width(width);
          os << n << "";                  // put n as string in buf
          show_str(nbuf);                 // through LCD window
      }
}
```

Now the input number must be displayed as it is being entered just as it would be in a real calculator. This is done by supplying a new definition for the virtual build_number() to display the number as it is being built:

```
void LcdFace::build_number(char c, int& i)
{     static int leading_0 = 0;
      static int before_point = 1;
      if ( i == 0 )                       // reset
```

```
        {   leading_0 = 0; before_point = 1;
            cw->clear_lcd();
        }
        if ( leading_0 && c == '0' )
            return;                              // ignore extra leading zero
        if ( i == 0 && c == '0' )
            leading_0 = 1;                       // first leading zero
        else
            leading_0 = 0;
        if ( before_point )
        {   if ( c == '.' )
            {   before_point = 0;
                if ( i == 0 ) nbuf[i++] = '0';
                nbuf[i++] = c;
            }
            else if ( i == 1 && nbuf[0] == '0' )
                nbuf[0] = c;
            else
            {   nbuf[i++] = c;
                nbuf[i] = '.';
            }
        }
        else  // after point
        {   if ( c == '.' ) return;
            nbuf[i++] = c;
        }
        if ( before_point ) nbuf[i+1] = '\0';
        else nbuf[i]= '\0';
        show_str(nbuf);
    }
```

The build_number() function receives characters one at a time and builds a valid decimal number in nbuf. The argument c is the next input character, and reference argument i is the total number of characters accumulated so far for the number. The function contains logic to ignore extra leading zeros and to allow numbers with at most one decimal point. Only valid characters become part of the number being built; other characters are ignored. The accumulating buffer nbuf always contains a proper string.

The CalcWindow Class

The LCD window is represented by an object of CalcWindow, a class derived from CursesWindow. The object shows a string and indicates an opcode, as well as clears the LCD window:

```
///////    File: CalcWindow.h    ///////
#include <iostream.h>
#include <strstream.h>
#include "CursesWindow.h"

class CalcWindow : protected CursesWindow
{ public:
     CalcWindow(int digits, CursesWindow* parent = &std_win);
     ~CalcWindow();
     void show_op(char c);              // show operation
     void show_str(char* str);         // show given string
     void clear_lcd();                 // clear window
     CursesWindow::Getch;              // reads input char: char Getch()
  private:
     int x0, x1;                       // internal positions
     void lcd(int i, char* str);       // actual output
     void init();
     void clean_up();
};
```

The constructor establishes a base **curses** window at a fixed position of just the right size (line 1). It also draw a box around the LCD and enters the direct window I/O mode:

```
///////    File: CalcWindow.C    ///////
#include "CalcWindow.h"

CalcWindow::CalcWindow(int d, CursesWindow* p)
: CursesWindow(p, 5, d+14,  5, 16, 'r'),    //   (1)
{    int width = d+4;
     x0 = 5; x1 = x0+width-1;               // begin and end of LCD
     Box('#','#');                          // draw box around LCD
     init();                                // init direct window I/O
}

void CalcWindow::init()
{    fflush(stdin);
     fflush(stdout);
     noecho();                              // do not echo input characters
     crmode();                              // set to direct input mode
}

CalcWindow::~CalcWindow()
{ clean_up(); }

void CalcWindow::clean_up()
```

```
{    Clear();
     Refresh();
     fflush(stdin);
     fflush(stdout);
}
```

The destructor does proper cleanup and restores the terminal screen. The basic output routines are

```
void CalcWindow::show_op(char op)        // display opcode
{   Mvaddch(3, x1 + 2, op);
    Refresh();
}
```

```
void CalcWindow::show_str(char* b)       // display string in lcd window
{   lcd(x1-strlen(b)+1, b);
}
```

```
void CalcWindow::lcd(int x, char* str)   // output to lcd window
{    Standout();
     Mvaddstr(2, x, str);
     Standend();
     Refresh();
}
```

The given string str is displayed in standout mode. (Again, the complete calculator simulation program is available on the code disk.)

The Calculator Class

The Calculator class is defined to take plug-compatible compute engine and user interface objects. The calculator object is initialized with pointers to given compute engine and user interface objects:

```
///////    File: Calculator.h    ///////
// a polymorphic calculator

#include    "CalcEng.h"
#include    "CalcFace.h"

class Calculator
{ public:
    Calculator
      ( CalcEng*  e,          // plug-compatible engine
        CalcFace* f           // plug-compatible interface
      )
```

```
        : eng(e), cf(f) { }
        virtual void on();
    protected:
        virtual void perform(int ind, char op, double number);
        virtual void treat_error();
    private:
        CalcEng*    eng;            // plug-compatible engine
        CalcFace*   cf;             // plug-compatible interface
};
```

The calculator top-level loop executes a body that is a separate function
(perform()). This design allows the virtual perform() and the virtual treat_error()
to be modified later with added preprocessing and postprocessing through
class derivation:

```
///////    File: Calculator.C   ///////
// a simple calculator
#include    "Calculator.h"

void Calculator::on()
{    char op;
     double number;
     cf->show_number(eng->output());
     // top-level cycle
     int ind;
     while ( (ind = cf->input(op, number, ! *eng))
                != CalcFace::OFF )
     {  perform(ind, op, number);
     }
}

void Calculator::perform(int ind, char op, double number)
{    if ( ind != CalcFace::OPONLY )
            eng->operand( number );
     eng->operate( op );
     number = (op == 'c' || op == 'C') ? 0 : eng.output();
     if ( ! *eng )  treat_error();    // error testing (1)
     else
     {   op = eng->operation();
         if ( op == '=' )
             cf->show_op(' ');
         else
             cf->show_op(op);
          cf->show_number(number);
     }
}
```

```
void Calculator::treat_error()
{    cf->show_error();
}
```

Error testing reported by the compute engine is achieved through class-defined `void*` conversion (line 1).

11.6 \ ERROR AND EXCEPTION HANDLING

For practical software projects, one important consideration is the handling of errors during program execution. Possible sources for run-time error include arithmetic overflow/underflow, division by zero, argument not within legal domain, results out of allowable range (too large or small), unexpected arguments, illegal pointers, array index out of range, free storage exhausted, no such file, disallowed file access, and I/O error.

11.6.1 Arithmetic and Mathematical Computation Errors

Overflow (underflow) occurs when a computation result is too large (small) and exceeds the limited precision of the data type used. For example, consider adding a positive integer to the largest positive `int`. What is the expected answer? Of course, the result will be incorrect because of overflow. Try it with your C++ program. You may very well find that the result is a negative `int` and that the program continues as if nothing wrong has happened. Generally, it is the programmer's responsibility to detect such errors when necessary.

The header files `<limits.h>` and `<float.h>` contain symbolic constants for the largest and smallest integral and floating-point values, respectively. For example, `INT_MAX` is the maximum `int` quantity, and `INT_MIN` the minimum (most negative). Thus, for `int` a and b, the test

```
if ( a > 0 && (MAX_INT - a) < b )
```

predicts that `a + b` will overflow.

Error Indications from Mathematical Functions

The standard mathematical functions (Appendix 8) indicate domain and range errors. A *domain error* occurs when a function is passed an argument whose value is outside the valid interval for the particular function. For example, only positive arguments are valid for the `log` function. A *range error* occurs when the computed result is so large or small that it cannot be represented as a `double`.

The global variable errno defined in the header <errno.h> is used by system-supplied routines (library and system calls) to indicate error. When a domain error happens, errno is set to EDOM, a symbolic constant defined in <errno.h>, and the returned value is implementation-dependent. For example, the call sqrt(-9.0) results in errno being set to EDOM. On the other hand, when a range error takes place, errno is set to ERANGE, and either zero (underflow) or HUGE_VAL (overflow) is returned. When an error occurs, an error message may also be generated by the library function.

11.6.2   Error Values

Standard library functions return standard error values when they fail. The error indication returned must be consistent with the return value type declared for the function. At the same time, the error value must not be anything the function would ever return without failure. For library functions, the standard error values are

- EOF, usually −1, used by functions normally returning a nonnegative integer.
- NULL, usually 0, used by functions normally returning a valid pointer (nonzero).
- Nonzero, used for a function that normally returns zero.

Again, it is up to your program to check for such a returned value and take appropriate actions. The following idiom is in common use:

```
if ( (value = call(...)) == errvalue )
{       // handle error here
        // output any error message to cerr
}
```

In your program, you can follow this error value technique. For example, the gcd(a,b) function normally returns a valid greatest common divisor that is a positive integer. Thus, zero or negative integer values can be used to report error conditions such as "both a and b are zero."

11.6.3   Error States

When a member function wishes to indicate error, an error flag or state variable in the host object can be set to a predefined value. This state variable is made accessible through the public interface of the object to determine whether an error or some exception condition has occurred. Error examination can be made even simpler by the class-defined conversion to void* (Section 8.7). The

C++ I/O stream classes provide good examples (Table 6.8) for error states and error reporting.

The error state technique should be part of your class design when appropriate. For example, consider the CalcEng class. It should contain an error flag set internally to indicate overflow, underflow, square root of a negative quantity, and so on. Correct error reporting to the calculator user is thus made very easy.

11.6.4   Error Treatment and Recovery

After detecting an error or exception condition, a program has basically four alternatives:

1. To ignore the error: The program continues to execute as if nothing has happened. Normally, this is neither doable nor acceptable.
2. To call exit(n): If n is zero, this is a normal termination of the running program. If n is nonzero (usually positive), this is a normal exit with an abnormal *exit status*, a value transmitted to the invoking environment of your C++ program.
3. To call abort(): This call causes immediate program termination without cleanup actions associated with normal termination. On some systems, abort() may save information for a postmortem.
4. To recover from the error: The setjmp and longjmp functions (Appendix 8) can be used for error recovery but are not recommended because longjmp does not destruct automatic objects. Instead, the C++ exception-handling mechanism should be used.

When a C++ program terminates normally (returning from main or calling exit()), destructors for static objects are called. The atexit() function (Appendix 8) can be used to specify additional actions to be taken before program termination. This allows a program to release a lock, to remove a temporary file, or to perform some other critical action before termination. The abort() call causes immediate termination without any of these actions at exit.

11.6.5   C++-Defined Exception Handling

The C++ keywords try, catch, and throw are reserved for the exception-handling facility, a new feature that is still undergoing standardization. As a result, some C++ compilers may not fully support the exception mechanism described here.

The keyword try controls a code block (compound statement) whose execution errors can be caught and handled by codes supplied with the keyword catch. If you put all statements in the main program in a try block, then error from any part of the program will be caught. The call throw(obj) transfers control from the point of call up the function-call chain to the nearest enclosing try block, which will receive the argument object obj and perform exception handling.

Consider a simple example where we catch the "wrong argument" error:

```
int main()
{    try                                    // try block
     {    return( mymain() ) ;
     }
     catch ( WrongArg& a )                  // error catch (1)
     {    cerr << a.error_msg() << endl;    // handling    (2)
          return(1);                        //    codes    (3)
     }
     catch ( Overflow& a )                  // error catch (4)
     { /* overflow handling code */
     }
     return(0);
}
```

For every error type to be caught and handled differently, a distinct class must be defined to supply objects used in the throw and catch mechanism:

```
class WrongArg
{    public:
        WrongArg(char* msg)
        : err(msg) {}
        char* error_msg() { return err; }
     private:
        char* err;
};
```

With the WrongArg class, a function (gcd for example) performs exception handling as follows:

```
int gcd(int a, int b)
{    if ( a==0 && b==0 )
        throw(WrongArg("gcd: gcd(0,0) undefined"));

     // rest of nonrecursive gcd code
}
```

This throw will be caught by the matching catch (line 1) after the try block in main, and the corresponding codes (lines 2 and 3) will be performed. If the program does not then terminate, control skips to the first statement after all the catch phrases, thus allowing the program to continue after the error. If throw() were given an Overflow argument, it would be caught by the catch on line 4.

11.7 SUMMARY

Good OO programs require a combination of thoughtful design and skillful implementation. The two processes form a feedback loop and help programs evolve. The central issue in OO design is the identification of objects and classes in a given system. Decomposition methods break up the entire problem into easier-to-handle pieces. The CRC method is particularly helpful during the OO design process. Effective use of the CRC method has been demonstrated with the pocket calculator simulation program design.

For practical projects, incorporating legacy systems and handling run-time errors are important design and implementation considerations. A class can be used to encapsulate an entire legacy system. The CursesWindow example illustrates this approach by encapsulating the legacy curses package.

System-supplied functions give standard error indications that must be examined by a program to detect run-time errors and exceptions. The C++ keywords try, catch, and throw are part of an exception-handling system that is still being standardized.

EXERCISES

1. Consider the CRC design of the pocket calculator simulation program. Add the CRC description for a derived compute engine class.

2. Experiment with the curses package on your system. Test the CursesWindow class on it.

3. Add error detection to the base CalcEng class. Detect both overflow and under-flow for the operations +, -, *, /, and ^.

4. Add error reporting through void* conversion for CalcEng.

5. Modify the handling of the opcodes A (all clear) and C (clear) in relation to error handling in CalcEng. Note the behavior of C after an error on a real pocket calculator.

6. Write a class Menu whose objects are initialized with several strings for a menu title and several menu items. The object uses the curses library, through the CursesWindow encapsulation, to display the menu and to allow user selection.

The member function show() displays the menu, and select() returns the user's final selection as an index. The interactive user selection should provide normal feedback to the user as different items are visited before the selection is finalized.

7. What happens on your system when int i = INT_MAX + 7; is done? What is the value of i now?

8. What happens on your system when the library function sqrt() is called with a negative number? Or when log() is given zero?

9. Write a program that creates a temporary file under a special name. Use the atexit() function to cause the program to delete this temporary file before termination. If the program calls abort(), does it still delete the file?

10. Complete the pocket calculator implementation with sophisticated derived compute engines, proper error handling, a simulated LCD window, and a Calculator control that can establish any combination of compute engine and user interface.

11. Apply the CRC method and the OO design approaches suggested in this chapter to design a program for playing Othello. Identify the objects in this game and write the CRC cards for them. Think about the game pieces, game board, moves, board positions, players, move generator, user interface, board display, and so on. Make the design general so that it works for most board games.

12. Take the Othello program design and consider its implementation. Apply inheritance planning and polymorphism. Take into account future extensions and modifications to create other games. Do you find points overlooked in the design phase? Fix the design and start over.

COMPILING AND PREPROCESSING

To program effectively in C++, a good understanding of how a program is treated by the compiler is fundamental. However, many aspects of the compiler will be implementation-dependent and somewhat different on different operating systems. For example, Unix System Laboratories (USL) C++ is implemented as a *front end* of C, translating C++ code into corresponding C code for an existing C compiler to process. Other compilers, such as the GNU g++, are *native-language* compilers, translating C++ source code directly into assembly code for a particular machine. On PCs, C++ tends to be an interactive code development environment with editor, compiler, debugger, and other facilities.

It is not possible to cover all these systems here. Our discussion is based on general compilation principles for C++. Details of compiling and running your program on UNIX and PC systems (Borland and Microsoft C++) can be found in Appendices 1 and 2.

After providing an overview of the entire compilation process, this chapter focuses on the preprocessing phase. The use of preprocessing is an integral part of C++ programming and is standardized across all systems. Important preprocessing features include header files, symbolic constants, macros, and conditional text inclusion. The practical uses of these features are explained.

12.1 COMPILING AND RUNNING C++ PROGRAMS

The compiler takes *source code* files in C++ and produces *object code* files in machine language. This process may produce intermediate files in C or assembly code. Object files can then be combined into an executable file, which is a program that can run on your computer. The compiler treats each source code

TABLE 12.1   FILENAME SUFFIXES

SUFFIX	FOR
.C	C++ source file
.c	C source file
.h	C++ or C header file
.s	Assembly code file
.o	Object code (compiled) file

file separately, and each source code file is known as a *compilation unit*. Distinct compilation units are treated independently by the compiler.

To the compiler, a compilation unit consists of tokens, separated by white space. *Tokens* are the smallest, unbreakable units used to build a program, and they include keywords (class and int for example), operators (such as + and =), variables, separators/terminators (like ; and {), constants, and so on. *White space* includes SPACES, TABs, RETURNs, and NEWLINEs.

Files for different purposes are usually named with conventional suffixes. These suffixes may be different depending on the computer system used. Examples in this book consistently follow the suffix convention given in Table 12.1.

12.1.1   The Compilation Process

A compiler not only translates programs into machine code to run on a particular computer, but also takes care of arranging suitable *run-time support* for the program by providing I/O, file access, and other interfaces to the operating system. Therefore, a compiler is not only computer-specific but also operating-system-specific.

Generally, there are two types of C++ compilers: The *native-mode* compilers take C++ source code and generate object code directly; the *translator-mode* compilers transform C++ source code into equivalent C code and then use a C compiler to generate the .o files. The original USL C++ software uses the translator approach. Other C++ compilers, such as the GNU g++, work in native mode. Still others, such as the HP-UX C++ compiler, can work in either mode.

The C++ compilation process consists of five phases (Figure 12.1):

1. *Preprocessing:* Preprocessing removes comments and handles constant definition, macro expansion, file inclusion, and conditional compilation.

FIGURE 12.1   **COMPILATION PHASES**

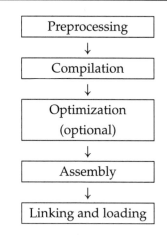

2. *Compilation:* Taking the output of the previous phase as input, the compiling phase performs syntax checking, parsing, and assembly code generation.

3. *Optimization:* This optional phase improves the efficiency of the generated code for speed and compactness.

4. *Assembly:* The assembly phase creates an object file containing binary code and relocation information to be used by the linker/loader.

5. *Linking/loading:* The link/load phase combines all object files and links in necessary library subroutines to produce an executable program.

The descriptions here give only a rough idea of the process. At this point, it is sufficient to know that the C++ compiler performs all five phases automatically.

12.2 \ PREPROCESSING

Preprocessing is the first phase of the C++ compilation process. Your program goes through preprocessing before the main translation phases of compilation. Preprocessing supplies certain well-defined text transformations on the compilation unit (Figure 12.2). C++ preprocessing is the same as ANSI C preprocessing, except for the treatment of C++ // comments and recognition of the additional C++ tokens ::, .*, and ->*.

FIGURE 12.2   C++ PREPROCESSING

Generally, preprocessing performs two types of text transformations: *automatic* and *requested*. There are four automatic transformations: (1) Every trigraph is replaced (a *trigraph* is a special three-character sequence — see Exercise 2), (2) every comment is replaced by a single space, (3) every BACKSLASH–NEWLINE pair is deleted, and (4) every predefined macro is expanded.

Other than the automatic ones, preprocessing makes no other transformations unless specifically requested. You use preprocessing *directives* to request transformations. A directive is given with a # as the first nonblank character on a line followed by a keyword. File inclusion with #include and symbolic-constant definition with #define are the two most widely used directives. A directive for preprocessing will be deleted after being processed.

12.3 \ HEADER FILES

The preprocessing directive #include is used to include another file in a source code file. The line

```
#include <iostream.h>
```

which includes the C++ I/O stream header, has appeared in many programs already. In general, the directive

```
#include <filename>
```

is used to include system header files. The given *filename* should be located in one of a list of standard system directories kept by the CC command.

When a #include line is encountered in a file (current file), preprocessing does the following:

1. Locates the requested file (target file) to be included.
2. Reads and processes the target file, which may contain other preprocessing directives itself. In particular, it may #include other files.
3. Inserts the resulting target file into the current file in place of the #include line and continues to read the current file.

Therefore, the effect of a #include directive is almost as if the target file were physically inserted in place of the #include line.

To make a call to the operating system (a system call) or a C++ library function in a program, certain specific system header files usually must be included. Required header files will be part of the documentation of a library or system call. Not including the necessary header files will cause errors and compilation failure.

In addition to standard header files, it is also possible to include header files of your own. The preprocessor directive

```
#include "filename"
```

is used to include the file specified. The double quotes are part of the directive. This feature is used to include nonstandard header files. For instance, the wordcount program (Section 3.11) includes the Cirbuf.h header:

```
#include "Cirbuf.h"
```

If *filename* is not found in the same directory as the input file, the standard system directories are searched.

12.4 SYMBOLIC CONSTANTS AND MACROS

The preprocessing directive #define is used to define *symbolic constants* and *macros*. For example, after the definition

```
#define TABLE_SIZE 1024
```

the symbolic constant TABLE_SIZE can be used in all subsequent source code instead of the integer 1024. This makes the program much more readable and easier to modify when the table size must be changed. The general form is

```
#define identifier token ...
```

Preprocessing will replace the identifier with the given tokens everywhere in subsequent source code, except in string and character constants. Although using any identifier is allowable, using all capitals for symbolic constants and reserving all lowercase identifiers for variables, function names, and so on is advisable. It is then easy to distinguish symbolic constants from other identifiers in a piece of C++ code. Table 12.2 gives some examples of symbolic constants that also show the various forms of numeric constants. In Table 12.2, note how a character (FORMFEED) can be specified with its octal ASCII code, a bit pattern (LOW_BIT) by an octal number, and a special zero pointer (NULL) by zero.

Whereas a *symbolic constant* provides a fixed substitution, a *macro* is a variable text-substitution mechanism. A macro is defined with parameters in the form

```
#define name(arg1, arg2, ...) definition
```

TABLE 12.2 **EXAMPLES OF SYMBOLIC CONSTANTS**

#define PI 3.14159	#define NEWLINE '\n'
#define DELTA 0.1e-8	#define TAB '\t'
#define MAXSIZE 200	#define NULLCHAR '\0'
#define EOF -1	#define BACKSLASH '\\'
#define TWELVE 014	#define TWELVE 0xc
#define TRUE 1	#define FORMFEED '\014'
#define FALSE 0	#define NULLSTRING ""
#define NULL 0	#define LOW_BIT 01

For example, the macro SQUARE

```
#define SQUARE(x)  ((x)*(x))
```

has one parameter and can be used in such forms as

```
area = SQUARE(side);    // becomes area = ((side)*(side));
r = c/SQUARE(a+b);      // becomes r = c/((a+b)*(a+b));
```

Macros are *expanded* by preprocessing using the definition and the supplied parameters.

Another macro MIN

```
#define MIN(x, y)    ((x)>(y) ? (y) : (x))
```

takes two arguments x and y and is defined by a conditional expression. The macro call

```
MIN(a + b, c - d)
```

is expanded into

```
((a + b)>(c - d) ? (c - d) : (a + b))
```

Although a macro call looks like a function call, it is just an abbreviation to be replaced by its full definition through preprocessing. Note the use of the extra parentheses around x and y in the definition of MIN. This is necessary because x and y can be arbitrary expressions in a macro call. If the definition were given without the extra parentheses, would the example just given still be expanded correctly?

Another commonly used macro is absolute value:

```
#define ABS(a)    ((a)>=0 ? (a) : -(a))
```

Technically, a symbolic constant is just a macro with no arguments. Also, the right-hand side of a macro may involve other macros that may or may not be defined yet. When a macro expansion is performed, the result will be scanned again for any macros to be expanded until no more expansion is encountered.

Redefining Macros

Once a macro is defined, it normally should not be defined again. While re-defining with the same definition may be allowed, using a different definition will produce a warning message. Often, redefining a macro with the same definition is caused by multiple inclusions of the same header file. (Avoiding duplicate inclusion is the subject of Section 12.7.)

Sometimes, it is also useful to undefine a macro, removing its definition entirely with the #undef directive:

```
#undef ABS
```

Once undefined, a macro can then be defined again with no problems. A macro definition persists from the point of definition to the end of the compilation unit.

12.5 \ INLINE FUNCTIONS VERSUS MACROS

Preprocessing macros are convenient but error-prone — there is no syntax checking until after substitution, and there is no argument-type checking either. Besides, run-time errors caused by macros are very hard to find. Furthermore, expressions with side effects are dangerous in macros. For example,

```
MIN(i, j++)      (side-effect-in-macro-call trap)
```

looks innocent enough but in fact expands to

```
((i)>(j++) ? (j++) : (i))
```

which is certainly incorrect.

In C++, const variables and inline functions should be used instead of #define constants and macros wherever possible. Thus, the following codes are preferred:

```
const int TABLE_SIZE = 1024;

inline int MIN(int x, int y)
      {   return(x > y ? y : x);   }
```

They can be used without loss of efficiency or the side-effect trap. In addition, the compiler performs all the normal checking for an inline function as for a normal function.

Remember, an inline function definition must be seen before a call to it can be compiled. Also, member functions actually defined within a class declaration are automatically inline.

12.6   CONDITIONAL TEXT INCLUSION

Preprocessing also provides a mechanism to include/exclude certain parts of a program. This facility is useful in many ways. For beginning programmers, the primary use would be in debugging and testing programs.

If #define is given just one token,

```
#define name
```

then *name* becomes *defined* (as opposed to *undefined*). You can include or exclude sections of code in your program, depending on whether certain special names are defined or undefined.

Conditional inclusion can be specified in the form

```
any-if-condition
    source code lines A
#else
    source code lines B
#endif
```

where *any-if-condition* can be #if, #ifdef, or #ifndef. The #else clause is optional. If the condition is satisfied, then part A will be included; otherwise, part B (if given) will be included. Table 12.3 lists the possible conditions.

Conditional inclusion can be used to include debugging code. For example, the factorial function (Section 1.4) can be revised as follows:

```
int factorial(int i)
{     int ans = 1;
#ifdef DEBUG
    cerr << "entered factorial with i = " << i << "\n";
#endif // end DEBUG
    /* the rest of factorial */
}
```

The point is to perform the diagnostic output only when the program is being debugged. Therefore, such lines do not have to be deleted for regular execution. Note that a comment is supplied after the #endif to mark the end and make it easier to see where the conditionally included code starts and ends. Although not required, this is a highly recommended practice.

To activate such conditional debug statements, either add a line

```
#define DEBUG
```

TABLE 12.3   PREPROCESSING CONDITIONALS

if CONDITION	MEANING
#if *constant-expression*	True if *expression* is zero
#if defined(*identifier*)	True if *identifier* is #defined
#ifdef *identifier*	True if *identifier* is #defined
#ifndef *identifier*	True if *identifier* is not #defined

at the beginning of the source code file or tell the compiler to define the symbol when it is invoked. For instance, the UNIX CC command supplies a -D option for this very purpose. See Appendix 1 or 2 for information appropriate to your system.

Another frequent use of conditional inclusion is to handle system- or hardware-dependent code. For example,

```
#ifdef SUNOS
/*  for SUN Operating System */
#define TABLE_SIZE    256
#endif  // end SUNOS

#ifdef HP700
/* for Hewlett-Packard 700 series */
#define TABLE_SIZE    128
#endif  // end HP700
```

Here the symbolic constant TABLE_SIZE is defined differently depending on whether the symbol SUNOS or HP700 is defined (with #define).

You can also position extra code for program testing right in the source file itself. For example, the lines

```
#ifdef TEST
int main()
{   Fraction x(1,30), u(-1,60), v(-1,60);
    Fraction y;
    y = x + u + v;
    y.display();
    return(0);
}
#endif  // end TEST
```

could be put in the file Fraction.C (Section 3.3), which can then be tested by compiling it with the symbol TEST defined.

The expression for the #if directive may involve integer and character constants, macros, arithmetic operators, bitwise operations, shifts, relational operators, as well as the two logical operators && and ||. If the expression involves an undefined token, the token is treated as zero.

Also, the directives #else and #elif can be used between a pair of #if and #endif in the obvious way:

```
#if FLAG == 1
   . . .
#elif FLAG == 2
   . . .
#else   // default case
   . . .
#endif  // end else
```

You can also use conditional inclusion to exclude code without deleting it, as in

```
#if 0
// This code no longer needed -- John Doe, Date

  .

  .

  .

#endif // end 0
```

This technique gives you an easy way to reinstate the code later or to see what has been removed by whom and when.

12.7 \ ONCE-ONLY HEADER FILES

In programs, it is common practice to have many source code and header files. The header files often have #include lines to include other headers. The inclusion relations among header files can be complicated and may cause certain header files to be included more than once during the preprocessing phase. This is not only wasteful but also introduces preprocessing and other errors. For example, a duplicated class declaration results in a compilation error. An inline function declared more than once is also incorrect. The situation is especially true when using the C++ template mechanism (Chapter 10).

To avoid possible multiple inclusion, a header file can be written as a big, conditional inclusion construct:

```
//  A once-only header file Cirbuf.h

#ifndef Cirbuf_SEEN__
#define Cirbuf_SEEN__

  .

  .

  .
```

```
/* the entire header file*/
    .
    .
    .
#endif // Cirbuf_SEEN__
```

The symbol `Cirbuf_SEEN__` becomes defined once the file `Cirbuf.h` is read. This fact prevents it from being read again because of the `#ifndef` mechanism. This symbol uses the underscore suffix to minimize the chance of conflict with other macros or constant names. It is recommended that all header files be coded in the once-only form suggested here. To keep our examples uncluttered, the once-only feature in header files may not always be shown.

12.8 STANDARD MACROS

C++ preprocessing also maintains a number of built-in macros to make programming easier. The built-in macros are implementation-dependent, but the standard macros shown in Table 12.4 should be available. Since these are preprocessing-defined quantities, the word *current* in Table 12.4 refers to the time when the predefined macro is being interpreted. The base file is the compilation unit given to CC when invoked. The current input file can be any file being read because of file inclusion.

Values of some standard macros will change as preprocessing proceeds. They are handy in diagnostic messages such as

```
cerr << "Reached line " << __LINE__ << " in file "
     << __FILE__ << "\n";
```

or in greetings such as

```
cout << "Welcome to WonderProgram Created " << __DATE__
     << __TIME__ << "\n";
```

To further aid program diagnostics, the macro assert defined in the header <assert.h> is available. It is useful for testing various *assertions* (conditions that should hold), at different places in a program. This is done by calling assert with any C++ expression that produces a logical value. If the value is zero (false) at run time, an error message is produced, and execution is aborted. Here is a small test program to show you how to use assert:

```
#include <iostream.h>
#include <assert.h>

int main()
```

TABLE 12.4   STANDARD MACROS

MACRO	MEANING	TYPE	EXAMPLE
__FILE__	Current input file	String	"iostream.h"
__BASE_FILE__	Main input file	String	"Fraction.C"
__LINE__	Line number in current file	Integer	109
__DATE__	Current date	String	"Jan 31 2000"
__TIME__	Current time	String	"21:45:03"
__cplusplus	C++ flag	Integer	#ifdef __cplusplus

```
{    int x=9, y=8;
     assert(x == (y+1));
     cout << "first\n";
     assert(x > y);
     cout << "second\n";
     assert(x < y);
     cout << "third\n";
}
```

Note that the assert macro is only active when the symbolic constant NDEBUG (no debug) is not defined. This gives you a convenient way to disable the diagnostics for the production version of the program.

The assert macro invokes the standard library function abort() to terminate the program abnormally without certain cleanup actions usually performed when a program ends (Section 11.6.4).

12.9 SUMMARY

The C++ compiler is available on a multitude of computers and operating environments. Both native-mode and C-front-end compilers exist. Five distinct phases can be identified for the C++ compilation process: preprocessing, compilation, optimization, assembly, and linking/loading. System-specific information for compiling and running your C++ programs can be found in Appendices 1 and 2.

Preprocessing, the first phase of compilation, performs some important program transformations before the output is sent to the compiling phase. Automatic transformations are trigraphs, comment deletion, BACKSLASH–NEWLINE deletion, and expansion of built-in macros (Table 12.4). Other operations can be requested using preprocessing directives.

Each directive takes one line and begins with a # followed by the directive keyword. Line continuation is allowed. The #include directive includes system- and user-supplied header files that may themselves contain #include directives.

The directives #if, #ifdef, #ifndef, #endif, #elif, and #else supply the flexibility to include/exclude portions of a source code file, depending on certain conditions. Multiple inclusion of the same header can be avoided through the once-only technique. It is recommended that all C++ headers be once-only.

There is also a macro mechanism to define symbolic constants and to use abbreviations for code sequences. The #define and #undef directives define and undefine macros. Constant variables (const) and inline functions (inline) should be used whenever possible instead of macros. The built-in macro assert(*expr*) is convenient for checking conditions that must hold at key points in a program.

EXERCISES

1. Consult and learn how to use the documentation for your C++ compiler. Compare it with the general description given in this chapter and with Appendices 1 and 2; note any differences.

2. For systems using a reduced character set, preprocessing allows the use of the following nine trigraph sequences for the corresponding single character:

??(	[	??)	]	??=	#
??<	{	??>	}	??/	\
??´	^	??!	|	??-	~

The preprocessing escape sequence ?? takes effect everywhere (including inside single and double quotes) and is processed before any other preprocessing transformation. Try a test program with ?? inside a string and see what happens. Trigraphs are normally not a concern for anyone using a full character set such as ASCII.

3. Will preprocessing handle circular file inclusion where file1.h includes file2.h, which in turn also includes file1.h? What happens in this situation on your system?

4. Will preprocessing handle recursive macro definitions where the definition of a macro xyz directly or indirectly involves xyz itself?

5. Most C++ compilers allow you to process a compilation unit with preprocessing only, leaving the results in a file for inspection. Find out how this is done with your compiler.

6. Consider the following code fragment:

```
#define BUFFER_SIZE 1024
#define TABLE_SIZE BUFFER_SIZE/4
#undef BUFFER_SIZE
#define BUFFER_SIZE 512

cout << TABLE_SIZE;
```

What TABLE_SIZE will be displayed?

7. Consider multiple files, each containing a test main program used for testing the particular file. The test main program is conditionally included with #ifdef. Devise a convenient scheme that allows you to exclude all but a specific main program for any particular test run.

8. Consider the inline declaration. If a function is declared inline, where should you put its definition? In a .h file or a .C file? Why?

9. Find out whether the standard macro __TIME__ actually changes as preprocessing proceeds.

10. Consider the following inline function:

```
inline void error(char *msg)
{
    cerr << msg << ": error at line " << __LINE__ << endl;
}
```

Does this function have the intended effect? If not, why?

COMPILATION AND EXECUTION UNDER UNIX

The two types of C++ compilers on UNIX systems are (1) a native-mode compiler, such as the GNU **g++** from The Free Software Foundation or a proprietary implementation from a vendor, and (2) a front end to the C compiler, such as the Unix Systems Laboratories (USL) **CC** compiler. The use of these compilers is very similar. The **CC** command is described here in detail. Even if your compiler is not **CC**, the information presented will apply in most situations.

Compilation with CC

The compiler is invoked at the UNIX shell level with the **CC** command:

CC *option* or *filename* . . .

The command takes one or more arguments, each in the form of a UNIX *filename* or a compiler *option*. The filenames specify which files to compile, and the options control compiler actions.

A filename ending in .C (on some systems, .cc) is taken as a C++ source file, and a corresponding object file (.o) will be produced. A filename ending in .o is taken as an object file and is loaded into the final executable module. When compiling a single .C file into an executable module, the .o file produced is automatically deleted.

The executable program produced is named a.out unless a name is specified using the -o option. The name of the executable module is used as a UNIX command at the shell level to run the compiled program. Arguments supplied on the command line are accessible by the main program through argv

(Section 2.3). With CC, you should always use the +a1 option to compile your C++ programs.

If your program reads standard input (cin), then input data comes from the keyboard. You can type multiple lines of input and when the input is done, enter ^D (control-D) as the first character on the last line of input. Output from cout is displayed on the screen.

UNIX also allows *I/O redirection* with the notations

```
mysort < infile
mysort > outfile
mysort < infile > outfile
```

In this case, cin reads the given *infile* instead of the keyboard, and/or cout outputs to the given *outfile* instead of the screen.

When dealing with a program consisting of multiple source code files, it is usual practice to compile .C files separately into corresponding .o files. The object code files can later be combined with others (with CC) to form the executable program. The command

```
CC -c filename.C
```

produces *filename*.o.

Linking object codes from the standard library (<stdlib.h>) and I/O stream library (<iostream.h>) is automatic. Other libraries, such as those containing mathematical functions (<math.h>), are indicated by the -l option. For example,

```
CC -o calc CalcEng.o CalcFace.o Calculator.o calctest.C -lm
```

asks for the mathematical functions library libm.a.

Consult your computer manual to see all the available options for your C++ compiler. Online manual pages can be easily displayed, for example, with

```
man CC
man g++
```

A few often-used options for CC are listed here:

-c	Suppresses the loading phase and produces .o files only. No executable module will be produced.
-o *name*	Names the executable module with the specified *name* instead of the default a.out.
-E	Applies preprocessing only and sends results to standard output.
-O	Invokes the optional code optimizer phase. Used to produce faster running code, it is generally used only when producing final, production versions of a program.

`-lname`	Specifies the library file `libname.a` to load additional library functions.
`-Dname=str`	Initializes the preprocessing macro *name* to the given string *str*. If *=str* is omitted, *name* is initialized to 1 (same as `#define name`).
`+d`	Treats inline functions as regular functions to help debugging.
`+i`	Leaves intermediate C code files (`..c`) in the appropriate directory.
`+a1`	Requests translation into ANSI C code rather than traditional C. This is recommended unless your installation does not have an ANSI C compiler. The option +a0 requests translation into traditional C code and compilation by a traditional C compiler.

These options are used by the USL **CC** compiler. Other C++ compilers have similar options. The GNU **g++** compiler is a native-mode compiler and supports these options plus others. The -g option of **g++** is important to know because it asks **g++** to compile a program for debugging with an interactive debugger such as **dbx** (Appendix 5).

Compiler Error Messages

The C++ compiler lists errors encountered when processing a file. Errors involve grammar problems, function-call mismatches, redeclaration of variables, missing punctuation, and so on. Each error is indicated with a filename and a line number. The actual mistake that leads to this error is either on this line or just before it.

COMPILATION AND EXECUTION ON PCs

The two major C++ environments on PCs—Borland C++ and Microsoft C/C++, which offer a combined C and C++ development environment—are (1) the Borland IDE (Integrated Development Environment) and (2) the Microsoft PWB (Programmer's Workbench). Generally, the environment provides a window-mouse-menu-oriented interface to text editing, compiling, linking/loading, debugging, and other facilities.

On PCs, a filename usually consists of two parts: a *name of one to eight characters* and an *extension of one to three characters* separated from the name by a period. Note that there is *no distinction* between uppercase and lowercase characters in filenames. Filenames used in this book are sometimes much longer than eight characters. When using such a file on a PC, truncate the filename to the first eight characters. (The code disk available for PCs also follows this convention.) On PCs, filenames use standard extensions:

EXTENSION	FOR
.CPP	C++ source file
.C	C source file
.H or .HPP	Header file
.OBJ	Object code (compiled) file
.EXE	Executable file
.LIB	Library file
.PRJ	Borland C++ project file
.MAK	Microsoft C/C++ project file

BORLAND C++

Compiling and Running a Simple Program

The IDE makes it very simple to create, compile, and run a simple C++ program that is contained in one file — say, PROG.CPP. Assuming you are in the IDE editor window and you have entered PROG.CPP and saved it on disk, then just press control-F9 to compile and run the program. You will see, in a status box, the progress of the compilation. When the compiler is done, the *user screen* appears automatically. This is where you can interact with the running PROG.CPP as if you were running it from DOS. You are back in the editor window after PROG.CPP terminates.

Compiling and Running A Multiple-File Program

Within IDE, you create a project file (.PRJ) to manage compilation and execution. The project file contains source filenames, file dependencies (order of compilation), and other information. The project file is not necessary for dealing with a single source code file. The Compile menu is used for compilation and generation of an executable (.EXE) file. Follow these steps to create a project file:

1. Use the Project option from the main IDE menu to access the project management functions. Then, use the Open command from the Project menu to open an existing project or create a new project file.
2. Use other options on the Project menu to add or delete source, header, and library files. Be sure to list all files needed by the program.

Under IDE, a multiple-file C++ program consists of source files, header files, and a project file. To compile this program, first open the project file with Project Open, then press the F9 key or choose Compile Make. This starts the compilation. If errors are detected by the compiler, a message window is created to display such information and to make corrections easy.

To correct a compilation error, first change to the message window and select one of the errors. If you select with the arrow keys, press the Enter key to place the cursor at the point where the error was detected. If you select with the mouse, a double-click does it all.

After a successful compilation, run your program by pressing control-F9 or select the Run command from the Run menu. Pass any command-line arguments with the Argument command on the Run menu.

It is good practice to compile source code files separately. This can be done by selecting the Compile-to-OBJ option on the Compile menu. The Link-EXE-file option creates an executable file from the object and library files indicated in the project file without recompiling.

An interactive debugger and run-time libraries are provided. Most library functions are automatically linked into your executable file. Consult your programmer's guide for more details.

Microsoft C/C++

There are two modes in which to use the C++ compiler: within PWB and outside PWB. The latter is the only option on PCs without windows. Although PWB is not as completely visual and interactive as Borland C++, the Microsoft Visual C++ product does offer visual PWB, which improves on PWB.

Compiling and Running from the DOS Level

Working outside PWB, you give DOS commands to compile and run your C++ program. For example, the command

```
cl /c FILENAME.CPP
```

produces the compiled object file `FILENAME.OBJ`. The `/c` is an option (or switch) that tells the compiler `cl` to produce `.OBJ` files only and not to make them executable. If you have a complete program in a single source code file, then using the `cl` command without the `/c` option produces the executable file `FILENAME.EXE`.

And, the command

```
cl TSTCALC.CPP CALCENG.OBJ CALCFACE.OBJ CALCULAT.OBJ MATH.LIB
```

produces the executable file `TSTCALC.EXE`. Then, you can run the program by giving the name of the executable file (`TSTCALC`) on the command line and supplying any appropriate command-line arguments. Clearly, the command `cl` takes source, object, and library files as arguments. Use the online help facility or consult the run-time library manual for names of header files to include and library files, if any, to specify.

Compiling and Running under PWB

For single source file programs, you simply select the Build command from the Project menu. This generates an `.EXE` file.

Within PWB, you create a project file (`.MAK`) to manage compilation and execution of a multiple-file program. The project file contains source, header, and library filenames, as well as other information.

To access the project-management functions, use the Project option from the main PWB menu. Select the New Project option from the Project menu to create a new project file. Use the Open command to select an existing project file.

After creating a new project file, you are presented with the Set Project Template dialog options. You should select "None" for Runtime Support and "DOS EXE" for Project Template.

Next, you arrive at the Edit Project window, where you can add and delete names of files (source, header, library, and so on) to be controlled by the project file. After you are done, just select <Save List> to save the project file.

To compile a program controlled by a project file, simply Open the project file from the Project menu, then choose Build or Rebuild to generate the .EXE file. The Execute command from the Run menu runs the .EXE file. Any arguments your program needs can be supplied with the Program Arguments command on the Run menu. While your program is running, a user screen is active for interactions with the running program. The user screen disappears after the program terminates.

To separately compile any source code file, use the Compile File command on the Project menu. There are also facilities to help you correct syntax problems detected by the compiler and to perform interactive debugging. Consult your computer manual for more details.

KEYBOARD INPUT

If your program reads standard input (cin), then input data comes from the keyboard. You can type multiple lines of input and when the input is done, enter ^Z (control-Z) to end the input.

SUMMARY OF C++ CONSTRUCTS

Class Declaration

```
class Name
{
            friend declarations
    public:
            public members
    protected:
            protected members
    private:
            private members
};
```

The struct and union constructs have the same form as the class.

Derived-Class Declaration

```
class Name : base-class list
{
            class body
};
```

where *base-class list* is a list of one or more base-class designations separated by commas. Each base-class designation takes the form

```
                public
[ virtual ]     protected     base-class name
                private
```

Function Definition

```
valuetype fn_name ( type arg1, type arg2, ... )      (header)
{                                                    (body begin)
        declarations and statements
}                                                    (body end)

// valuetype can be void, argument list can be empty
// zero or more declarations, statements
```

Member Function Definition

```
valuetype ClassX::fn_name ( type arg1, type arg2, ... )      (header)
{
        declarations and statements
}
```

The if Statement

```
if ( expr1 )
        statement-1
else if ( expr2 )      // optional
        statement-2
. . .

          . . .
else                   // optional
        statement-i
```

Iteration Statements

```
while ( continuation condition ) body

for ( init-stat cont-cond ; incr-expr ) body      // all parts optional

do body while ( continuation condition );
```

The switch Statement

```
switch ( expression )
{      case constant-expr1 :
             statements         // zero or more
       case constant-expr2 :
             statements
       . . .
       default:                 // optional
```

```
        statements
}
```

The typedef Declaration

typedef *declaration of Newtype as if it is a variable* ;

The goto Statement

label: *statement*

. . .

goto *label* ;

Array Declarations

```
type array_name[10];              // linear array
type array_name[10][20];          // two-dimensional array
type array_name[10][20][30];      // three-dimensional array
```

The enum Declaration

```
enum name { symbol₁[ = val₁],
            symbol₂[ = val₂],
               . . .
         };
```

The Function Prototype

```
value_type fn_name(type1, type2, . . . );
void fn_name(type1, type2, . . . );              // returns no value
value_type fn_name();                            // takes no arguments
```

The Function Pointer

```
value_type (* fn_ptr) (type1, type2, . . .);
```

Overloading ++ and --

```
type ClassX::operator ++();         // prefix ++ as class member
type operator ++(type arg);         // prefix ++ as nonmember
type ClassX::operator ++(int);      // postfix ++ as class member
type operator ++(type arg, int);    // postfix ++ as nonmember
```

The overloaded operator -- has the same forms.

Class-Defined Conversion

```
ClassX::operator type();    (converts host to type)
ClassX::ClassX(type);       (converts type to ClassX)
```

Offset Pointer to Member

```
type ClassX::* opmd;          (declares opmd data opm)
type (ClassX::* opmf)(...);   (declares opmf function opm)
& ClassX::xyz                 (gets offset value of member)
obj.*opmd                     (dereferences opmd in obj)
objptr->*opmd                 (dereferences opmd in *objptr)
(obj.*opmf)(...)              (calls function in obj via opmf)
(objptr->*opmf)(...)          (calls function in *objptr via opmf)
```

Function Template

```
template <class T1, . . . >        // one or more class parameters
function prototype or definition
```

Class Template

Formal template parameters can be either class-type or normal-type parameters.

```
template <class T1, . . . >        // one or more template parameters
class declaration or definition

ClassX<...> var( args );           // template class object declaration
```

Union as Class Member

```
union
{    type    id1;
     type    id2;
};
```

Bit-Packing Class Members

```
typedef unsigned int Bit;

Bit dept : 16;    // department code, lower 16 bits
Bit  div :  8;    // division id, next 8 bits
Bit  rgn :  6;    // region designation, next 6 bits
Bit    q :  2;    // 1st, 2nd, 3rd, or 4th quarter, next 2 bits
```

C++ Keywords

asm	auto	break	case	catch	char
class	const	continue	default	delete	do
double	else	enum	extern	float	for
friend	goto	if	inline	int	long
new	operator	private	protected	public	register
return	short	signed	sizeof	static	struct
switch	template	this	throw	try	typedef
union	unsigned	virtual	void	volatile	while

SUMMARY OF SPECIAL MEMBER FUNCTIONS

```
ClassX::ClassX( args )                          // constructor
: base and member object init-list
{ other initial actions
}

ClassX::~ClassX( );                             // destructor

ClassX::ClassX( const ClassX& );                // copy constructor
ClassX::ClassX( ClassX& );

ClassX& ClassX::operator=( const ClassX& );     // assignment

ClassX::operator type ();                       // conversion to type
```

SPECIAL MEMBER	INHERITED	MAY BE virtual	RETURN TYPE	MAY BE static	GENERATED BY DEFAULT
Constructor	No	No	No	No	Yes
Copy constructor	No	No	No	No	Yes
Destructor	No	Yes	No	No	Yes
operator=	No	Yes	Yes	No	Yes
operator()	Yes	Yes	Yes	No	No
operator[]	Yes	Yes	Yes	No	No
operator->	Yes	Yes	Yes	No	No
operator new	Yes	No	void*	Must be	No
operator delete	Yes	No	void	Must be	No
Type conversion	Yes	Yes	No	No	No

Interactive Debugging with dbx

Debugging with dbx

While the C++ compiler identifies problems at the syntax level, you still need a good tool for debugging at run time. On PCs, the C++ program development environment normally supports a convenient interactive debugger. See your PC manual for more details.

A convenient UNIX utility for source-level debugging and controlled execution of programs is dbx. It can be used to debug programs written in any source language such as C++, C, f77, or Pascal, provided that the object files have been compiled to contain the appropriate symbol information for use by dbx. On some UNIX workstations, you may find dbx available inside a window-menu-oriented debugging package that supplies multiple windows and other useful features for easier debugging. The dbxtool on SUN systems is an example.

You should use dbx as a routine tool for debugging programs. It is much more efficient than inserting cerr lines in the source code.

Because dbx provides an interactive debugging environment and correlates run-time activities to statements in the program source codes, it is called a *source-level* debugger. Debugging is performed by running the target program under the control of the dbx utility. The main features of dbx are listed here.

1. *Source-level tracing:* When a part of a program is *traced,* useful information will be displayed whenever that part is executed. If you trace a function, the name of the calling function, the value of the arguments passed, and the return value will be displayed each time the traced function is called. You can also trace specific lines of code

and individual variables. In the latter case, you are notified every time the variable value changes.

2. *Placing source-level break points:* A break point in a program causes execution to suspend when that point is reached. At the break point, you can interact with **dbx** and use its full set of commands to investigate the situation before resuming execution.

3. *Single source-line stepping:* When you are examining a section of code closely, you can have execution proceed one source line at a time. (Note that one line may consist of several machine instructions.)

4. *Displaying source code:* You can ask **dbx** to display any part of the program source from any file.

5. *Examining values:* Values, declarations, and other attributes of identifiers can also be displayed.

6. *Editing source files:* If you want to correct an error, you can edit source code files (for later recompilation) from within **dbx**.

7. *Object-level debugging:* Machine instruction-level execution control and displaying of memory contents or register values are also provided.

To debug a C++ program using **dbx**, make sure each object file has been compiled with a native-mode compiler (such as the GNU **g++**) and the -g has been specified. One simple way to achieve this is to compile all source code (.C) files at once using the following command:

g++ -g *source_files*

This results in an executable a.out file suitable to run under the control of **dbx**. Then, to invoke **dbx**, simply type

dbx a.out

to debug the executable a.out file. When you see the prompt (dbx), the debugger is ready for an interactive session. When you are finished, simply type the **dbx** command

quit

to exit from **dbx**.

A typical debugging session should follow these steps:

1. Invoke **dbx** on an executable file compiled with the -g option.
2. Put in trace and/or break points.
3. Run the program under **dbx**.
4. Examine trace output and display program values at break points.
5. Install new trace and/or break points to focus in on bugs, deleting old trace and/or break points as appropriate.

6. Resume or restart execution.
7. Repeat steps 4–7 until satisfied.

Summary of dbx Commands

Command	Meaning
run	Begins execution of the program.
cont	Continues execution.
step	Single steps one line.
next	Steps to next line (skips over calls).
trace *line#*	Traces execution of the line.
trace *function*	Traces calls to the function.
trace *var*	Traces changes to the variable.
trace *expr* at *line#*	Displays *expr* when *line* is reached.
stop at *line*	Suspends execution at the line.
stop in *function*	Suspends execution when *function* is called.
status	Displays trace/stops in effect.
delete *number*	Removes trace or stop of given number.
call *function*	Calls the function.
dump *function*	Displays values related to the function.
where	Displays currently active functions.
set *var* = *expr*	Sets variable to the value of the expression.
print *expr*	Displays the value of the expression.
whatis *name*	Displays the declaration of the name.
list *line, line*	Lists source lines.
edit *function*	Edits file containing *function*.
quit	Exits dbx.

OPERATOR PRECEDENCE

$\mathbf{A}$ll C++ operators are listed here according to their relative precedence. An operator on an earlier line takes precedence over any that comes after. Operators on the same line have the same precedence. An expression involving operators of the same precedence is evaluated according to the *associativity rule* of the operators. Most operators associate left-to-right. The ones that associate right-to-left are indicated by $\longleftarrow$ in the table. Note that the unary operators +, -, and * (value-of) take precedence over the binary forms.

OPERATOR	ASSOCIATIVITY
::	
() [] -> .	
! ~ ++ -- + - * & (*type*) sizeof new delete	$\longleftarrow$
* / %	
+ -	
<< >>	
< <= > >=	
== !=	
&	
^	
|	
&&	
||	
?:	$\longleftarrow$
= += -= *= /= %= ^= |= &= <<= >>=	$\longleftarrow$
,	

IMPLICIT TYPE-CONVERSION RULES

Inheritance-Related Conversions

A derived object, reference, or pointer is implicitly converted to a corresponding *accessible* base type. An opm (offset pointer to member) is implicitly converted from an accessible base type to a derived type. User-defined conversions are also applied by the compiler. Such conversions are applied in passing arguments, initializing, branching and iteration control, and returning value from a function.

Standard Arithmetic Conversions

When the two arguments of an operator have different types, automatic type conversion is performed before the operation is carried out. The conversion rules summarized here are applied in the order given:

RULE	IF ONE OPERAND IS	CONVERT THE OTHER OPERAND TO
1.	long double	long double
2.	double	double
3.	float	float
4.	long int	long int

After these rules are carried out, *integral promotions* are applied on both operands. Integral promotions upgrade a char, a short int, an int bit field (or their signed or unsigned varieties), or an enumeration object to type int. Then, the following rules are used in the order given:

5. If one operand has type unsigned long int, convert the other operand to the same.

6. If one operand has type long int and the other unsigned int, convert the latter to long int if this type can accommodate all values of type unsigned int; if this is not the case, convert both operands to unsigned long int.

7. If one operand has type long int, convert the other to long int.

8. If one operand has type unsigned int, convert the other to unsigned int.

9. Both operands must now have type int.

STANDARD LIBRARY FUNCTIONS

Character and String Functions

Character-set-independent functions (or macros) are supplied to deal with characters. The header <ctype.h> should be used.

FUNCTION	TEST FOR
int isupper(int c)	Uppercase letter
int islower(int c)	Lowercase letter
int isalpha(int c)	Uppercase or lowercase letter
int isdigit(int c)	Decimal digit
int isalnum(int c)	isalpha(c) || isdigit(c)
int iscntrl(int c)	Control character
int isxdigit(int c)	Hexadecimal digit
int isprint(int c)	Printing character including SPACE
int isgraph(int c)	Printing character except SPACE
int isspace(int c)	SPACE, \f, \n, \r, \t, v
int ispunct(int c)	Printing character not SPACE, digit, or letter

FUNCTION	MEANING
int toupper(int c)	Converts to upper case.
int tolower(int c)	Converts to lower case.

A large set of string-manipulation functions is available. The header <string.h> (or <strings.h> on some nonstandard systems) should be used.

FUNCTION	DESCRIPTION
char *strcat(s,cs)	Concatenates a copy of cs to end of s; returns s.
char *strncat(s,cs,n)	Concatenates a copy of at most n characters of cs to end of s; returns s.
char *strcpy(s,cs)	Copies cs to s including '\0'; returns s.
char *strncpy(s,cs,n)	Copies at most n characters of cs to s; returns s; pads with '\0' if cs has less than n characters.
char *strtok(s,cs)	Finds tokens in s delimited by characters in cs.

FUNCTION	DESCRIPTION
size_t strlen(cs)	Returns length of cs (excluding '\0').
char *strcmp(cs1,cs2)	Compares cs1 and cs2; returns negative, zero, or positive for cs1 <, ==, or > cs2, respectively.
char *strncmp(cs1,cs2,n)	Compares first n characters of cs1 and cs2; returns negative, zero, or positive for cs1 <, ==, or > cs2, respectively.
char *strchr(cs,c)	Returns pointer to first occurrence of c in cs.
char *strrchr(cs,c)	Returns pointer to last occurrence of c in cs.
char *strpbrk(cs1,cs2)	Returns pointer to first char in cs1 and in cs2.
char *strstr(cs1,cs2)	Returns pointer to first occurrence of cs2 in cs1. *These four functions all return* NULL *if the search fails.*
size_t strspn(cs1,cs2)	Returns length of prefix of cs1 consisting of characters from cs2.
size_t strcspn(cs1,cs2)	Returns length of prefix of cs1 consisting of characters *not* in cs2.

Arbitrary Types as Character Arrays

It is sometimes convenient to process data of other types as a sequence of characters in consecutive memory locations. A set of library functions exists for this purpose. The header <memory.h> should be used.

```
void *memcpy(void *target, const void *source, size_t n)
```

copies n characters from source to target, which is returned.

```
void *memmove(void *target, const void *source, size_t n)
```

is the same as `memcpy` but works even if s and ct overlap.

```
int memcmp(const void *cs, const void *ct, size_t n)
```

compares the first n characters of cs with ct and returns a positive, negative, or zero value (as `strcmp`).

```
void *memchr(const void *cs, const char c, size_t n)
```

returns a pointer to the first character c in cs or NULL if c is not among the first n characters.

```
void *memset(void *s, const char c, size_t n)
```

sets each of the first n characters of s to c and returns s.

Floating-Point Calculations

To use the functions listed here, include the header file `<math.h>`. To check possible domain and range errors, you also need the header `<errno.h>`, which defines EDOM, ERANGE, and HUGE_VAL (Section 11.6.1). In the following, the variables xx, yy are of type double, and i is an int. All functions return double.

sin(xx)	Sine of xx
cos(xx)	Cosine of xx
tan(xx)	Tangent of xx
sinh(xx)	Hyperbolic sine of xx
cosh(xx)	Hyperbolic cosine of xx
tanh(xx)	Hyperbolic tangent of xx
exp(xx)	e^{xx}
log(xx)	Natural logarithm $ln(xx)$, $xx > 0$
log10(xx)	Base 10 logarithm $log_{10}(xx)$, $xx > 0$
asin(xx)	$sin^{-1}(xx)$ in range $[-\pi/2, \pi/2]$, $xx \in [-1, 1]$
acos(xx)	$cos^{-1}(xx)$ in range $[0, \pi]$, $xx \in [-1, 1]$
atan(xx)	$tan^{-1}(xx)$ in range $[-\pi/2, \pi]$
atan2(xx, yy)	$tan^{-1}(xx/yy)$ in range $[-\pi, \pi]$
sqrt(xx)	Square root of xx, $xx \geq 0$
ceil(xx)	Ceiling of xx as double
floor(xx)	Floor of xx as double
fabs(xx)	Absolute value of xx
ldexp(xx,n)	$xx \cdot 2^n$
pow(xx,yy)	xx^{yy}; if $xx = 0$ and $yy \leq 0$ or if $xx < 0$ and yy is not equal to an integer, a domain error results

In addition to the functions just listed, there are also the following functions for fractional parts and floating remainder.

```
frexp(xx, int *exp)
```

computes the fractional and exponent parts of *xx*. The fractional part (fr) is normalized ($0.5 \le fr < 1$) and returned. The power-of-2 exponent is stored in exp so that $xx = fr \cdot 2^{(*exp)}$. If *xx* is zero, both parts of the result are zero.

```
modf(xx, double *ip)
```

computes the fractional and exponent parts of *xx*. The fractional part fr has the same sign as *xx* and is not normalized. The integer part is stored in ip so that $xx = *ip + fr$.

```
fmod(xx, yy)
```

computes a remainder of *xx* by subtracting *yy* from *xx* an integral number of times. The result is less than *xx* in magnitude and has the same sign.

Error- and Signal-Handling Functions

```
#include <stdio.h>
perror(CSTR s)
```

displays the string s and an implementation-defined error message corresponding to the value of the global variable errno to stderr.

```
#include <stdlib.h>
void exit(int status)
```

causes normal termination of the program. The value status is passed to the environment.

```
void abort(void)
```

causes abnormal termination of the program as if by raise(SIGABRT).

```
int atexit(void (* fn)(void)) [nonzero]
```

registers the function fn to be invoked when the program terminates normally. Multiple calls to atexit set up a sequence of such functions executed at exit time, in the reverse order as registered.

```
#include <setjmp.h>
int setjmp(jmp_buf env)
```

sets up env for a later longjmp nonlocal control transfer.

```
#include <setjmp.h>
int longjmp(jmp_buf env, int val)
```

restores the program state saved in env and transfers control to the corresponding setjmp call, which returns val.

```
typedef void (* H_FN)(int)
H_FN signal(int sig, H_FN new_handler)
```

replaces the handler function of the given signal sig with the function new_handler. The old handler function is returned. Valid signals are SIGABRT, SIGFPE, SIGILL, SIGINT, SIGSEGV, and SIGTERM. All except SIGABRT, which causes the executing program to terminate abnormally, are also recognized by UNIX as valid signals.

```
int raise(int sig)
```

sends sig to the program itself.

String-to-Number Conversions (<stdlib.h>)

```
double atof(CSTR str)
```

converts string str to a double, which is returned.

```
int atoi(CSTR str)
```

converts string str to an int, which is returned.

```
long atol(CSTR str)
```

converts string str to a long, which is returned.

```
double strtod(CSTR str, char **rest)
```

converts the prefix of the string str to a double, ignoring any leading white space. It also stores in *rest a pointer to the rest of the string after the consumed prefix, unless rest is NULL. Overflow and underflow are detected, and ERANGE is set.

```
long strtol(CSTR str, char **rest, int base)
```

treats the prefix of str as a number of the given base and converts it to long. It is otherwise similar to strtod. If base is zero, the integer constant notations are recognized.

```
unsigned long strtoul(CSTR str, char **rest, int base)
```

is the same as strtol, except the result is unsigned long.

Date and Time

The header <time.h> defines structures, macros, and functions for manipulating date and time. The date is kept according to the Gregorian calendar (in common use). Date and time can be represented in calendar time, local time, or Daylight Saving Time.

The *broken-down* time structure struct tm includes the following members:

`int tm_sec;`	Seconds after the minute (0–59)
`int tm_min;`	Minutes after the hour (0–59)
`int tm_hour;`	Hours since midnight (0–23)
`int tm_mday;`	Day of the month (1–31)
`int tm_mon;`	Months since January (0–11)
`int tm_year;`	Years since 1900
`int tm_wday;`	Days since Sunday (0–6)
`int tm_yday;`	Days since January 1 (0–365)
`int tm_isdst;`	Daylight Saving Time flag

The value of `tm_isdst` is positive if Daylight Saving Time is in effect, zero if not, and negative if unknown. There are also `clock_t` and `time_t`, which are arithmetic types capable of representing time.

`clock_t clock(void)`

returns the processor time used by the program since the beginning of its execution or −1 if unavailable. Use `clock()/CLOCKS_PER_SEC` to convert to seconds. To measure the time spent in a program, the `clock` function should be called at the start of the program, and its return value subtracted from subsequent calls.

`time_t time(time_t *tptr)`

returns the current calendar time in an implementation-defined encoding of type `time_t` or −1 if not available. The value is also assigned to `*tptr` if `tptr` is not `NULL`.

`struct tm *localtime(const time_t *tptr)`

converts the given calendar time `*tptr` and creates a broken-down time structure representing the corresponding local time. A pointer to the structure is returned.

`double difftime(time_t t1, time_t t2)`

returns t1 − t2 in seconds.

`time_t mktime(struct tm *tptr)`

takes the (partial) local-time information contained in the given structure `*tptr` and determines the values of all members in calendar-time form (`*tptr` is modified). It also returns the calendar time as encoded by `time` (or −1). This is useful to obtain the broken-down calendar time for a future or past date.

`char *asctime(const struct tm *tptr)`

converts the broken-down time in `*tptr` into a string in the form

`Sun  Dec   23  15:35:22  1990\n\0`

```
char *ctime(const time_t *tptr)
```

is the same as asctime(localtime(tptr)).

```
struct tm*gmtime(const time_t *tptr)     [NULL]
```

converts the calendar time *tptr into Coordinated Universal Time (UTC) and returns the broken-down structure.

```
size_t strftime(char *s, size_t slen, CSTR fmt, const struct tm *tptr)
```

formats data and time given by *tptr into the string s (maximum length is slen) according to the format specified by fmt. The format is analogous to that for printf.

%a, %A	Abbreviated or full weekday name
%b, %B	Abbreviated or full month name
%c	Local date and time representation
%d	Day of month (01–31)
%H, %I	Hour (00–23) or (01–12)
%j	Day of the year (001–366)
%m	Month (01–12)
%M, %S	Minute, second (00–59)
%p	Local equivalent of A.M. or P.M.
%U, %W	Number of weeks/year (Sunday/Monday as first day of week)
%w	Day of week (0–6; Sunday is 0)
%x, %X	Local date, time representation
%Y, %y	Year with, without century
%Z	Time-zone name, if any
%%	%

Utility Functions

Functions listed here all use the header <stdlib.h>.

```
int abs(int n)
long labs(long n)
```

returns the absolute value of n.

```
div_t div(int num, int denom)
```

computes the quotient and remainder of num divided by denom and stores the results in quot and rem, int members of the structure div_t.

```
ldiv_t ldiv(long num, long denom)
```

computes the quotient and remainder of num divided by denom and stores the results in quot and rem, long members of the structure ldiv_t.

```
void rand(void)
```

returns the next random integer in a pseudorandom sequence based on a seed given by a prior call to srand. The default seed value is 1. The random integers are in the range 0–RAND_MAX.

```
void srand(unsigned int seed)
```

sets the seed value for a new random sequence to be used by subsequent calls to rand. The same seed value gives rise to the same random sequence.

```
void *bsearch(const void *key, const void *base,
              size_t n, size_t size
              int (*cmp) (const void *key, const void *datum))
```

searches an array located at base with n elements, each of size size, for an element matching the given key. The supplied comparison function cmp takes a key and an array element and produces a negative, zero, or positive int value as strcmp. The array must be already in increasing order as defined by the same comparison function.

```
void qsort(void *base, size_t n, size_t size,
           int (*cmp)(const void*, const void *))
```

sorts an array located at base with n elements, each of size size, with the supplied comparison function cmp, which takes two array entries and returns a negative, zero, or positive int as strcmp.

```
int system(CSTR cmd)
```

passes the string cmd to the operating system for execution. If cmd is NULL, then system returns zero if there is no command processor. Otherwise, the return value is implementation-dependent.

```
char *getenv(CSTR name)
```

returns the environment string associated with the given name or NULL if no such string exists.

Implementation-Defined Data Limits

The header <limits.h> contains symbolic constants for implementation-defined size limits for integer quantities. The limits must not be more restrictive than the following values:

CHAR_BIT	Bits per character	8
MB_LEN_MAX	Byte per character	1
SCHAR_MIN	signed char minimum	-127
SCHAR_MAX	signed char maximum	127

UCHAR_MAX	unsigned char maximum	255U
CHAR_MIN	0 or SCHAR_MIN	
CHAR_MAX	SCHAR_MAX or SCHAR_MAX	
SHRT_MIN	short int minimum	-32767
SHRT_MAX	short int maximum	32767
USHRT_MAX	unsigned short int maximum	65535U
INT_MIN	int minimum	-32767
INT_MAX	int maximum	32767
UINT_MAX	unsigned int maximum	65535
LONG_MIN	long int minimum	-2147483647
LONG_MAX	long int maximum	2147483647
ULONG_MAX	unsigned long int maximum	4294967295U

Constants and limits related to floating-point computations are contained in <float.h>. The minimum values are listed here (actual values are defined by each implementation):

FLT_RADIX	Radix of exponent representation	2
FLT_ROUNT	Rounding mode for addition	
FLT_DIG	Number of decimal digits for float	6
FLT_MANT_DIG	Number of base FLT_RADIX digits in mantissa for float	
FLT_EPSILON	Smallest float ϵ that $1.0 + \epsilon \neq 1.0$	1E-5
FLT_MAX	Maximum float	1E+37
FLT_MIN	Minimum normalized float	1E-37
FLT_MAX_EXP	Maximum n such that $FLT\_RADIX^n - 1$ is representable	
FLT_MIN_EXP	Minimum n such that $FLT\_RADIX^n - 1$ is a normalized float	
DBL_DIG	Number of decimal digits for float	10
DBL_MAX	Maximum double	1E+37
DBL_MIN	Minimum normalized double	1E-37
DBL_MANT_DIG	Number of base FLT_RADIX digits in mantissa for double	
DBL_EPSILON	Smallest double ϵ that $1.0 + \epsilon \neq 1.0$	1E-9

There are other similar constants. The values for FLT_ROUNDS controls how rounding is done for floating-point addition:

- 0   Round toward zero
- 1   Round to nearest
- 2   Round toward $+\infty$
- 3   Round toward $-\infty$
- -1   Indeterminable

Standard Library Functions for Input/Output

The C++ I/O stream facility (<iostream.h>) should be sufficient for most purposes. Functions listed here are in a separate I/O library shared with C (<stdio.h>). The stdio supports buffered I/O streams (FILE *) defined in the header. The symbolic constants stdin, stdout, stderr, EOF, NULL, and others are defined in the header. The error value returned by each library function is indicated in square brackets []. Normally, the C++ I/O stream objects should be used to perform I/O. The functions listed here may be needed in special situations. The #define CSTR const char * is used.

Operations on Files

FILE *fopen(CSTR filename, CSTR mode)   [NULL]

opens filename for read, write, or update as indicated by the given mode:

Mode	Meaning
"r", "rb"	Open text/binary file for reading.
"w", "wb"	Open text/binary file for writing; discard existing contents.
"a", "ab"	Open text/binary file for appending at end.
"r+", "rb+"	Open text/binary file for *update* (reading and writing).
"w+", "wb+"	Open text/binary file for update; discard existing contents.
"a+", "ab+"	Open text/binary file for update, writing at end.

```
FILE *freopen(CSTR filename, CSTR mode, FILE *stream)    [NULL]
```

opens filename for read, write, or update as fopen but reuses an existing stream, which is returned. This function can be used to redirect stdin, stdout, and stderr.

```
int fclose(FILE *stream)    [EOF]
```

closes the given stream after flushing any unfinished output, discarding unread input, and freeing allocated buffer space.

```
int fflush(FILE *stream)
```

forces all unfinished output of the given stream to be sent out.

```
int remove(CSTR filename)    [nonzero]
```

deletes the given file.

```
int rename(CSTR oldname, CSTR newname)    [nonzero]
```

changes the name of oldname to newname.

```
int setvbuf(FILE *stream, char *buf, int flag, size_t size)    [nonzero]
```

sets the buffering mode for stream using the supplied buffer buf. If buf is NULL, the buffer will be allocated when necessary. The flag specifies the buffering mode: _IOLBF (line buffering), _IONBF (no buffering), or _IOFBF (full buffering).

```
void setbuf(FILE *stream, char *buf)
```

turns off buffering on stream if buf is NULL. Otherwise, full buffering on stream is done with the supplied buffer (size at least BUFSIZ).

```
FILE *tmpfile(void)    [NULL]
```

creates a temporary file with mode "wb+" that will be automatically deleted when closed.

```
char *tmpname(char name[L_tmpnam])    [NULL]
```

tmpname(null) returns a unique heretofore unused name string as a pointer to an internal static array. The name is also copied into name if supplied.

Formatted Input

```
int scanf(FILE *stream, CSTR format, ...)    [EOF]
```

reads input according to the given format. Conversion modes for scanf are:

CONVERSION CHARACTER	POINTER TYPE	INPUT DATA
d	int *	Base 10 number
i	int *	Integer; may be octal or hexadecimal
u	unsigned int *	Unsigned base 10 number
o, x	int *	Octal or hexadecimal with or without prefix
e, f, g	float *	Float with optional sign, decimal point, and exponent
s	char *	Characters with an added terminator ´\0´
c	char *	Characters including white space (default width 1)
p	void *	Pointer value as displayed by printf("%p")
n	int *	Number of characters read so far
u	unsigned *	Unsigned decimal integer
[...]	char *	Longest nonempty input string consisting only of characters given in [ ]
[^...]	char *	Longest nonempty input string consisting only of characters *not* given in [ ]
%		No input assignment; matches a literal %

Formatted Output

```
int fprintf(FILE *stream, CSTR format, ...)     [negative]
```

outputs to stream according to the given format and returns the number of characters sent out. Conversion modes in the format are as follows:

CONVERSION CHARACTER	ARGUMENT TYPE	FORMATTED AS
d, i	int	Base 10 number
u	unsigned	Base 10 number
f	double	$[-]m.dddddd$; number of d's given by the precision
s	char *	Characters in a string until ´\0´
c	char	Single character
o	int	Unsigned octal number (no leading 0)
e, E	double	$[-]m.ddd$e$\pm xx$ or $[-]m.ddd$E$\pm xx$
g, G	double	Use %f unless exponent is < -4 or $\geq$ precision
x, X	int	Unsigned hexadecimal (no leading 0x) with a–f or A–F
p	void *	A pointer value (implementation-dependent)
n	int *	No output; number of characters output so far is *stored* into the argument
%		Displays a %; no argument needed

For printf, the possible conversion flags are as follows:

FLAG	DESCRIPTION
-	Left-adjusted in field
+	Display number always with a sign
space	Use a space if first character is not a sign
0:	Pad numbers with leading zeros
#	Alternative format: Produce leading 0, 0x, 0X for o, x, X; preserve the decimal point for e, E, f, g, G; trailing zeros not removed for g, G

Character Input/Output

int getchar()	Same as getc(stdin).
int putchar(int c)	Same as putc(c, stdout).
int getc(FILE *stream)	Same as fgetc; if implemented as a macro, it may evaluate stream more than once.
int putc(FILE *stream)	Same as fputc; if implemented as a macro, it may evaluate stream more than once.
int fgetc(FILE *stream)	Returns next character of stream as an unsigned char converted to int [EOF].
int fputc(int c, FILE *stream)	Writes c out to stream as char and returns c [EOF].
int ungetc(int c, FILE *stream)	Pushes c back onto stream for next read; only one character can be pushed back per stream; returns c [EOF].

String Input/Output

char *gets(char *s)	Reads next line of stdin into s, *replacing terminating '\n' with '\0'*; returns s [NULL].
int puts(const char *s)	Writes string s to stdout, *replacing terminating '\0' with '\n'*; returns nonnegative [EOF].
char *fgets(char *s, int n, FILE *stream)	Reads at most the next $n - 1$ characters into array s, stopping if a '\n' is encountered; the '\n' is included in the array, which is terminated by a '\0'; returns s [NULL].
int fputs(const char *s, FILE *stream)	Writes string s to stream; returns a nonnegative [EOF].

Binary Input/Output and Error Status

`size_t fread(void *ptr, size_t s size_t n, FILE *stream)`

reads at most n objects of size s into space pointed to by ptr. The number of objects read is returned, which may be less than s. Use feof and ferror to determine status.

`size_t fwrite(const void *ptr, size_t s size_t n, FILE *stream)`

outputs n objects of size s from array pointed to by ptr. The number of objects written is returned, which is less than s only if there is an error.

`int feof(FILE *stream)`

returns nonzero if the end of file indicator of stream is set.

`int ferror(FILE *stream)`

returns nonzero if the error indicator of stream is set.

`int clearerr(FILE *stream)`

clears the end of file and error indicators of stream.

Moving File Read/Write Position

`int fseek(FILE *stream, long offset, int org)`   [nonzero]

sets the file position for stream as given by offset from the origin org. For a binary file, the position is moved to offset bytes from org, which can be SEEK_SET (beginning of file), SEEK_CUR (current position), or SEEK_END (end of file). For a text file, offset must be zero or a value obtained by ftell (relative to SEEK_SET).

`void rewind(FILE *stream)`

is the same as fseek(stream, 0L, SEEK_SET); clearerr(stream).

`long ftell(FILE *stream)`   [EOF]

returns the current file position as an offset from SEEK_SET.

`int fgetpos(FILE *stream, fpos_t *ptr)`   [nonzero]

marks the current file position in ptr for later use by fsetpos.

`int fsetpos(FILE *stream, fpos_t *ptr)`   [nonzero]

moves the file position to that marked by ptr.

INTERFACING C++ AND C PROGRAMS

It is possible to call existing library or user-defined functions written in C from C++. The techniques described here allow you to access any existing C library function as well as use other existing C codes from C++ programs and vice versa.

Calling C Functions from C++ Programs

Just because C++ admits most, if not all, of the ANSI C constructs from a syntax point of view does not mean that C programs can be freely intermixed with C++ programs. On the contrary, the same exact construct can have different semantics in C and C++. For example, in C++, the function prototype

```
int fn();
```

is the same as

```
int fn(void);
```

and means that the function fn takes no arguments and returns an int. In C, however, the first declaration says nothing about the number of arguments fn takes.

However, it is sometimes desirable (or convenient) for a C++ program to call external functions written in C contained in separate files. The C-defined functions could be user-supplied routines, library functions, system calls, or existing programs in C. Such calls are possible but must be done with great care. Use this appendix as a guide.

Function Name Encoding in C++

For various reasons, function names are encoded by the compiler. The encoded names are the actual names used internally by the compiled program. In some cases, the encoding is simply a matter of adding underscores as prefixes and/or suffixes to a function name. In other cases, it can be much more complicated. This is especially true because of function overloading. Due to encoding differences, a function name abc in a C++ file will not correspond to the same name abc contained in a C file. The encoding makes it hard to call a C-defined function from a C++ program, and vice versa.

Fortunately, C++ provides *linkage directives*, which can be used to access functions written in other languages, notably C. For example, the linkage directive

```
extern "C" void abc(int);
```

declares the function abc to have C linkage and will be identified with a C-defined function abc. The linkage directive consists of the keyword extern followed by the string constant "C" and then by a usual C++ function prototype. The linkage directive tells the C++ compiler that abc is a function name encoded by the C compiler and is exempt from the usual C++ function name encoding. Also supplied is necessary type information for argument and return type so that the function can still be subjected to full C++ argument-number/type checking.

It is also possible to give a list of function prototypes in a single linkage directive:

```
extern "C"
{    char * xyz( unsigned int );
     int uvw( ... );
}
```

Note the use of the notation "..." to indicate an unknown number of arguments.

Here is a C++ program that uses a C function testfn:

```
///////   File: interface.C   ///////
// accessing C function from C++

#include <iostream.h>

// the following enables C++ argument-type checking
// before calling the C-coded function testfn

extern "C" int testfn(int, int);
```

```
int main(int argc, char *argv[])
{    cout << testfn(3,4) << endl;
}
```

The C file for this experiment is

```
/******    File: test.c    ******/
/*  a C source code file */

int testfn(a, b)
int a, b;
{    return(a+b); }
```

Compile test.c into test.o with a C compiler. Compile interface.C into interface.o with a C++ compiler. The two .o files can now be linked together and run.

Accessing library functions written in C from C++ can be useful. Instead of using the <string.h> of C++, consider accessing the C-defined strcmp library function from your C++ program. Here is a sample C++ program that does exactly that:

```
// accessing C library functions

#include <iostream.h>

// the following enables C++ argument-type checking

extern "C" int strcmp(const char *, const char *);

main(int argc, char *argv[])
{    cout <<  "strcmp("  << argv[1]  << ", "  << argv[2]
  <<  ") gives " << strcmp(argv[1], argv[2]) << '\n';
}
```

C++ and C Header Files

The C++ language has its own complement of standard library functions together with associated C++ header files. The most frequently used is the iostream.h header file for I/O.

In addition to native headers, C++ also supplies header files to access standard C library functions and system calls. For example, header files such as <stdio.h>, <string.h>, <malloc.h>, and <signal.h> exist. Although the same names are used, these header files are *not* the same as the corresponding C header files. They are written in C++ syntax with extensive use of linkage directives to give C++ programs access to the desired C library functions or system calls.

Here is a sample C++ program that uses some C I/O functions:

```
#include <stdio.h>     // gets the C++ header file stdio.h

// For this example
// there are two active lines in the above header file
// extern "C" FILE *fopen(const char *, const char *);
// extern "C" int fprintf(FILE *, const char * ...);

main(int argc, char *argv[])
{    FILE * out = fopen(argv[1], "w");
     fprintf(out, "this is a %d test\n", 15);
}
```

There are also two catch-all C++ header files:

```
#include <stdlib.h>
```

gives you access to most C standard library functions, and

```
#include <sysent.h>
```

declares most system calls. However, the naming and the contents of these header files are not standardized. For instance, the GNU C++ system (**g++**) uses <std.h> as the header for system calls. Thus, you must check what your C++ system has to offer before using such header files. There is a possibility that your #include line may pick up a C header file because there is no such C++ header. Compile-time errors usually result from such mistakes. A regular C header file will not work at all in a C++ program.

So what can you do if you want to use a C header in your C++ program to access certain C-defined functions? If your C header is written in ANSI standard C syntax, it is possible that the declaration

```
extern "C"
{
#include "header.h"
}
```

given at the beginning of your C++ file will make things work. If the header file is in traditional C (instead of ANSI C), then the best thing to do is to rewrite each and every function prototype in the header into C++ style and to enclose the entire header file inside a "C" linkage directive. In fact, this is exactly how <string.h> and other C header files are transformed to C++ headers.

Calling C++ Functions from C Programs

Although unusual, it may sometimes be useful to call a C++-defined function from C. Because of the special function name encoding used by C++, this is usually difficult to do.

But if you write a function in C++ with the intention that it be (also) called from C, then you should give the appropriate linkage directive (extern "C") to make its name encoding match that used by the C compiler. In case this C++ function is an overloaded function, only one instance of it can be declared with a linkage directive.

INDEX

CODE DISK

A 3.5-inch disk containing more than 270 files of completed examples in this book is included. Please read these instructions carefully before opening the packaging of the code disk*. The code disk contains the following files and directories:

```
README    TXT    1423
INTRO     C1     <DIR>      OVERVIEW  C2     <DIR>
KEY       C3     <DIR>      POINTER   C4     <DIR>
CLASS     C5     <DIR>      LIBFN     C6     <DIR>
INH       C7     <DIR>      OPOVER    C8     <DIR>
OOP       C9     <DIR>      TEMPL     C10    <DIR>
DESIGN    C11    <DIR>      UNIXTAR   Z      239243
```

The file UNIXTAR.Z is for C++ on UNIX systems. Other files and directories are for C++ on PCs. Refer to Chapter 12 and Appendix 1 and 2 for compiling information.

To Load the Disk onto Your Computer:

- For PC – Assume the code disk is in Drive A and your hard disk is on drive C.

    ```
    xcopy A: C:\cppcode /s
    ```

    This copies all files on the code disk to the directory C:\cppcode. If you don't need the UNIX part, just do

    ```
    erase C:\cppcode\unixtar.Z
    ```

- For UNIX – Assume your UNIX workstation has a diskette drive (drive A). Unpack the files into a new directory c++code as follows:

    ```
    mkdir c++code
    cd c++code
    mcopy A:\unixtar.Z unixtar.Z
    uncompress unixtar.Z
    tar xvf unixtar
    ```

    To save disk space, after success of the last command, you can delete the unixtar file:

    ```
    rm unixtar
    ```
